Financial Management
for
Non-specialists

Other textbooks published by Prentice Hall in accounting and finance for non-specialist diploma and degree level students include:

Financial Accounting for Non-specialists

Management Accounting for Non-specialists

Accounting and Finance for Non-specialists 2/e

Financial Management
for
Non-specialists

PETER ATRILL

PRENTICE HALL

London New York Toronto Sydney Tokyo Singapore
Madrid Mexico City Munich Paris

First edition published 1997 by
Prentice Hall Europe
Campus 400, Maylands Avenue
Hemel Hempstead
Hertfordshire, HP2 7EZ
A division of
Simon & Schuster International Group

Typeset in 10½/12pt Melior
by MHL Typesetting Ltd, Coventry

Printed and bound in Great Britain by
Redwood Books, Trowbridge, Wiltshire

Library of Congress Cataloging-in-Publication Data

Atrill, Peter.
    Financial Management for Non-specialists / Peter Atrill
        p.   cm.
    Includes bibliographical references and index.
    ISBN 0-13-376740-X
    1. Finance.   I. Title.
    HG173.A817   1997
    658.15—dc20   96-36241
                                                             CIP

British Library Cataloguing in Publication Data

A catalogue record for this book is available from
the British Library

ISBN 0-13-376740-X

---

1   2   3   4   5   01   00   99   98   97

For Simon and Helen

Contents

Preface and acknowledgements

This text provides a broad-based introduction to financial management for those who wish, or need, to acquire an understanding of the main concepts and their practical application in decision-making, but who do not require in-depth theoretical or technical detail. It is aimed primarily at non-finance students who are following a module, either full or part-time, in financial management or business finance as part of a college or university course majoring in some other subject, such as accounting, business studies, economics or engineering; however, the content, style and approach of the text is such that it is also suitable for those who are studying independently, perhaps towards no formal qualification.

Although there are several excellent texts published in financial management, they are typically several hundred pages in length and contain mathematical formulae which many readers find daunting; consequently, such texts are normally too detailed to provide a suitable introduction to the subject for non-specialists. In writing this text, I have assumed no previous knowledge of the subject (although a basic understanding of financial statements would be useful), and I have tried to write in an accessible style, avoiding technical jargon. Where technical terminology is unavoidable, I have tried to give clear explanations.

Underpinning the text's coverage is an 'open learning' approach – that is to say, it involves the reader in a manner which is traditionally not found in textbooks, simulating the delivery of topics much as a good lecturer would do. This approach distinguishes itself through a variety of integrated and end-of-chapter assessment material, including:

- Interspersed throughout each chapter are numerous '**activities**'. These are short 'quick-fire' questions of the type a lecturer might pose at students during a lecture or tutorial, and seek to serve two purposes: firstly, to give readers the opportunity to check that they have understood the preceding section; and secondly, to encourage readers to think beyond the immediate topic and make linkages to topics either previously covered or those in the next section. An answer is provided immediately following each activity, to which readers should refer only after they have deduced their own.
- Towards the end of each chapter, there is a '**self-assessment**' question. These

are much more demanding and comprehensive than an activity, in terms of both the breadth and depth of material they encompass. A solution to each of these questions is given at the end of the text. As with the activities, it is important to make a thorough attempt at each question before referring to the solution.

- At the end of each chapter there are four **'review' questions**. These are relatively short, and are intended to enable readers to assess their recollection and understanding of the main principles in each chapter, or might be used as the basis for tutorial discussion.
- At the end of each chapter (except Chapter 1) there are usually six **'examination-style' questions**. These are typically of a numerical type, and are designed to enable readers to further apply and consolidate their understanding of topics. Each question is graded as either 'basic' or 'intermediate/advanced' according to its level of difficulty. The latter questions can be quite demanding, but are capable of being successfully completed by readers who have worked conscientiously through each chapter – undertaking the activities, self-assessment questions and the basic examination-style questions. Solutions to a selection of these questions (marked with an asterisk) are given at the end of the text. Here too, a thorough attempt should be made at each question before referring to the solution.

Coverage and structure

Although the topics covered are fairly conventional, the treatment of material is designed to meet the needs of non-specialists; therefore, the emphasis is upon the application and interpretation of information for decision-making, and the underlying concepts, rather than the extraction of data and abstract theory. I have ordered the chapters and their component topics to reflect, what I consider to be, a logical sequence. For this reason, I advise readers to work through the text in the order it is presented, particularly since I have tried to ensure that earlier chapters do not refer to concepts or terms which are not covered until a later chapter. Towards the end of the text, before the solutions, there is a **glossary of terms**.

The *Lecturer's Manual* which accompanies this text includes outline answers to all the review questions, solutions to the examination-style questions not given in the text, and OHP masters.

Acknowledgements

I would like to thank the Chartered Association of Certified Accountants for their permission to use some questions from the Certified Diploma, and for allowing me to use some material which I wrote originally for inclusion in the Certified Diploma magazine. I am also grateful for the comments received from my colleague Eddie McLaney, and another anonymous reviewers, who reviewed draft chapters of the book. Finally, I would like to thank Patricia Febbrarro for her help in proof-reading the final manuscript. Any errors or defects are, of course, my responsibility alone.

Peter Atrill

CHAPTER ONE

Introduction to Financial Management

OBJECTIVES

On completion of this chapter you should be able to:

- Discuss the role of the finance function within a business.

- Identify and discuss possible objectives for a business.

- Explain why the wealth maximisation objective is considered to be the most appropriate objective to use in financial management.

- Explain the agency problem faced by owners of a business and discuss how this problem may be either prevented or minimised.

Introduction

In this chapter we consider the role of the finance function within a business. We identify the tasks of the finance function and their relation to the tasks of managers. We then go on to consider the objectives which a business may have. Modern financial management theory is based on the assumption that the primary objective of a business is to maximise the wealth of the owners (shareholders). We consider this and other possible objectives for a business and discuss reasons why the wealth maximisation objective is considered to be the most appropriate objective to use.

The role of the finance function

The finance function within a business exists to help managers to manage. In order to understand how the finance function can help in this respect, we must

Figure 1.1   The role of managers

first be clear about what managers do. One way of describing the role of managers is to classify their activities into the following categories:

- *Strategic management* This refers to their role in developing overall objectives for the business and then formulating long-term plans which match those objectives. When formulating long-term plans, possible courses of action (strategies) must be identified and evaluated. A particular course of action will then be chosen from the options available according to which has the greatest potential for achieving the objectives specified.
- *Operations management* This refers to the day-to-day management of the business. Managers must ensure that events conform to the plans which have been made and must take appropriate actions to see that this occurs.
- *Risk management* This refers to the way in which risks faced by the business are dealt with. Risk may arise from the nature of the business operations and/ or the way in which the business is financed.

As you can see from Figure 1.1, these three categories do not represent separate and distinct areas. They are interrelated and overlaps arise between each category.

The finance function is concerned with helping managers in each of the three areas identified. The key tasks undertaken by the finance function (see Figure 1.2) are as follows:

- *Financial planning* This involves developing financial projections and plans (such as cash flow statements and profit statements) which allow managers to assess the viability of proposed courses of action.
- *Investment project appraisal* This involves evaluating investment projects

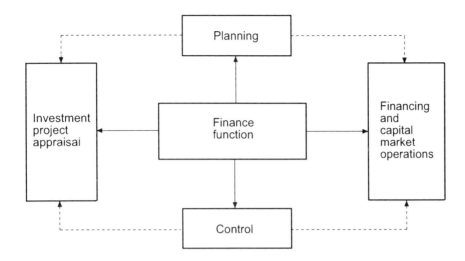

Figure 1.2   The tasks of the finance function

and assessing the relative merits of competing proposals. It also involves the assessment of risk associated with particular investment projects.

- *Financing decisions* This requires the identification of financing requirements and the evaluation of possible sources of finance. Not all financing requirements are derived from external sources; some funds may be internally generated through profits. The extent to which the business reinvests profits rather than distributing them in the form of dividend will, therefore, be an important consideration. Financing decisions also involve determining the appropriate financial structure for a business.
- *Capital market operations*   The finance function must raise funds from the capital markets and must therefore understand how they work. This involves an appreciation of how finance can be raised through the markets, how securities are priced and how the markets are likely to react to proposed investment and financing plans.
- *Financial control*   This refers to the ways in which the plans are achieved. Once plans are implemented it will be necessary for managers to ensure that things go according to plan. Control must be exercised over investment and financing decisions. This may involve such matters as the monitoring and control of investment projects and the control of stocks, debtors, creditors and liquidity.

The particular tasks of the finance function and those of management have many interrelationships. Thus, for example, financing decisions and investment project appraisal may be concerned with either strategic or operational management decisions and may also be concerned with risk management.

Structure and organisation of the text

In this text we consider each of the tasks of the finance function described above. We begin, in Chapter 2, by examining the way in which financial plans are prepared and the role of projected financial statements in helping managers to assess likely future outcomes. In Chapter 3, we go on to consider how financial statements can be analysed and interpreted. The financial techniques examined are important both for the evaluation of projected financial statements and for other areas such as financing decisions and the control of working capital, which are considered later in the text. Chapters 4 to 6 are concerned with investment decision-making. In these three chapters we look at the various methods which can be used to appraise investment proposals, the way in which investment projects are monitored, and the way in which we can deal with the problem of risk when evaluating investment proposals. Chapters 7 to 9 are concerned with various aspects of the financing decision. We consider first the various sources of finance available and the role and efficiency of capital markets. We then go on to examine the issues surrounding capital structure decisions, and then the importance of dividend policy. In Chapter 10, we look at the ways in which the managers can exert control over the working capital of the business. We look at each element of working capital (stocks, debtors, cash and creditors) and discuss the various techniques of control which are available. Finally, in Chapter 11, we look at the issue of mergers and takeovers. We consider the reasons for such activities and the ways in which merger proposals may be evaluated. We also consider the ways in which shares may be valued for merger, or other, purposes.

The essential features of financial management

Over the past four decades we have seen great changes in the discipline of financial management. In the early years of its development, financial management was viewed as an offshoot of accounting. Much of the early work was essentially descriptive and arguments were based on casual observation rather than any clear theoretical framework. However, over the years, financial management has been increasingly influenced by economic theories and the reasoning applied to particular issues has become more rigorous and analytical. Indeed, such is the influence of economic theory that modern financial management is often viewed as a branch of applied economics.

Economic theories concerning the efficient allocation of scarce resources have been taken and developed into decision-making tools for management. This development of economic theories for practical business use has usually involved taking account of both the time dimension and the risks associated with management decision-making. An investment decision, for example, must look at both the time period over which the investment extends and the degree of risk associated with the investment. This fact has led to financial management being described as the *economics of time and risk*. Certainly time and risk will be recurring themes throughout this text.

We shall also discuss, however, the importance of capital markets and the way in which shares are priced. This is another important theme of the text. Exhibit 1.1 is an extract from an article written by Professor Elroy Dimson of the London Business School. It neatly sums up the essence of modern financial management.

EXHIBIT 1.1

Finance on the back of a postage stamp

The leading textbooks in finance are nearly 1,000 pages long. Many students learn by making notes on each topic. They then summarise their notes. Here is one student's summary of his Finance course ... Time is money ... Don't put all your eggs in one basket ... You can't fool all the people all of the time.

- The idea that time is money refers to the fact that a sum of money received now is worth more than the same sum paid in the future. This gives rise to the principle that future cash flows should be discounted, in order to calculate their present value.
- You can reduce the risk of an investment if you don't put all your eggs in one basket. In other words, a diversified portfolio of investments is less risky than putting all your money in a single asset. Risks that cannot be diversified away should be accepted only if they are offset by a higher expected return.
- The idea that you can't fool all of the people all of the time refers to the efficiency of financial markets. An efficient market is one in which information is widely and cheaply available to everyone and relevant information is therefore incorporated into security prices. Because new information is reflected in prices immediately, investors should expect to receive only a normal rate of return. Possession of information about a company will not enable an investor to outperform. The only way to expect a higher expected return is to be exposed to greater risk.

These three themes of discounted cash flow, risk and diversification, and market efficiency lie at the very heart of most introductory finance courses.[1]

Each of the points raised in Exhibit 1.1 will be considered in some detail in the text.

The objectives of a business

A key idea underpinning modern financial management is that the primary objective of a business is to *maximise the wealth of its shareholders* (owners). In a market economy, the shareholders will provide funds to a business in the expectation that they will receive the maximum possible increase in wealth for the level of risk which must be faced. When evaluating competing investment opportunities, therefore, the shareholders will weigh the returns from each investment against the potential risks involved.

When we use the term *wealth* in this context we are referring to the *market value of the ordinary shares*. The market value of the shares will, in turn, reflect the future returns the shareholders will expect to receive *over time* from the shares and the level of risk involved. Note that we are not concerned with maximising shareholders' returns over the short term, but are concerned rather with providing the highest possible returns over the long term.

Wealth maximisation or profit maximisation?

Wealth maximisation is not the only financial objective which a business can pursue. Profit maximisation is often suggested as an alternative objective for a business. Profit maximisation is different from wealth maximisation in a number of important respects, as we shall see. However, before we consider these differences, we must first decide what we mean by the term *profit*.

There are different measures of profit which could be maximised, including the following:

- operating profit (i.e. net profit before interest and taxation)
- net profit before tax
- net profit after tax
- net profit available to ordinary shareholders
- net profit per ordinary share, etc.

Differences in the choice of profit measure can lead to differences in the decision reached concerning a particular opportunity.

ACTIVITY 1.1

Pointon Ltd has the following long-term capital and annual profits:

Capital invested (£1 ordinary shares)   £100,000
Net profits after tax   £15,000

It is considering the issue of 20,000 new ordinary shares and investing the amount raised in an opportunity which provides a profit after tax of £2,000. What would you advise managers to do if the objective of the business was:

1. To maximise total profits available to ordinary shareholders?
2. To maximise profit per share?

Although the total profits available to ordinary shareholders will be increased by the investment, the profit per share will be decreased. (The current rate of return per share is 15 per cent whereas the expected rate of return on the investment is 10 per cent.) An objective of maximising net profit available to shareholders would therefore lead to a decision to invest, whereas an objective of maximising net profit per ordinary share would lead to a decision to reject the opportunity.

Profit maximisation is usually seen as a short-term objective whereas wealth maximisation is a long-term objective. There can be a conflict between short-term and long-term performance. It would be quite possible, for example, to maximise short-term profits at the expense of long-term profits.

ACTIVITY 1.2

Can you think of ways in which short-term profits may be increased at the expense of long-term profits?

The managers of a business may reduce operating expenses by:

- *Cutting research and development expenditure.*
- *Cutting staff training and development.*
- *Buying cheaper quality materials.*
- *Cutting quality control mechanisms.*

These policies may all have a beneficial effect on short-term profits but may undermine the long-term competitiveness and performance of a business.

Whereas wealth maximisation takes risk into account, profit maximisation does not. As we shall discuss in some detail later, the higher the level of risk, the higher the expected return from a particular investment. This means that, logically, a profit maximisation policy should lead managers to invest in high-risk projects. Such a policy, however, may not align with the requirements of the shareholders. When considering an investment, shareholders are concerned with both *risk* and the *long-run returns* that they expect to receive. Only a wealth maximisation objective takes both of these factors into account. Managers who pursue this objective will choose investments which provide the highest returns in relation to the risks involved.

To maximise or to satisfy?

Even if we reject the use of profit and accept shareholder wealth as an appropriate financial measure, we may still question whether the *maximisation* of shareholder wealth is appropriate. This objective implies that the needs of the shareholders are paramount. The business, however, can be viewed as a coalition of various interest groups which all have a stake in the business.

ACTIVITY 1.3

Can you think who these various 'stakeholders' might be?

The following groups may be seen as stakeholders:

- *shareholders;*
- *employees;*
- *managers;*
- *suppliers;*
- *customers; and*
- *the community.*

This is not an exhaustive list. You may have thought of others.

If we accept this view of the business, the shareholders simply become one of a number of stakeholder groups whose needs have to be satisfied. It can be argued that, instead of seeking to maximise the returns to shareholders, the managers should try to provide each stakeholder group with a *satisfactory return*. (The term 'satisficing' has been used to describe this particular business objective.) Although this objective may sound appealing, there are practical problems associated with its use.

Within a market economy there are strong competitive forces at work which ensure that failure to maximise shareholder wealth will not be tolerated for long. Competition for the funds provided by shareholders and competition for managers' jobs should ensure that the interests of the shareholders prevail. If the managers of a business do not provide the expected increase in shareholder wealth, the shareholders have the power to replace the existing management team with a new team which is more responsive to shareholder needs. Alternatively, the shareholders may decide to sell their shares in the business (and reinvest in other businesses which provide better returns in relation to the risks involved). The sale of shares in the business is likely to depress the market price of the shares, which management will have to rectify in order to avoid the risk of takeover. This can only be done by pursuing policies which are consistent with the needs of shareholders.

Do the above arguments mean that the interests of shareholders are all that managers must consider and that the interests of other stakeholders are irrelevant? The answer is almost certainly 'no'. Satisfying the needs of the other stakeholder groups will often be consistent with the need to maximise share-holder wealth. A dissatisfied workforce, for example, may result in low productivity, strikes, and so forth, which will, in turn, have an adverse effect on the shareholders' investment in the business. This kind of interdependence has led to the argument that the needs of other stakeholder groups must be viewed as constraints within which shareholder wealth should be maximised.

Viewing the needs of the other stakeholders as constraints which must be satisfied is a rather neat way of reconciling the shareholder wealth maximisation objective with the interests of other stakeholders. It assumes, however, that a business should *maximise* the wealth of shareholders but only provide a *satisfactory return* to other stakeholders. Whether or not this assumption is considered valid will involve a value judgement being made. It is important to recognise, however, the implications of ignoring the needs of shareholders in a competitive market economy. It is likely that all other stakeholder groups will suffer if the share price performance of the business falls below the expectations of the shareholders.

A final argument made in support of the wealth maximisation objective is that, even if we accept the view that wealth maximisation is not necessarily appropriate, financial models based on this objective may still be useful for management decision-making. By employing such models, managers can identify the most appropriate course of action from the shareholders viewpoint and can calculate the costs borne by shareholders if a different course of action is decided upon. The managers must then account to shareholders for their decision!

Wealth maximisation and management ethics

There is always a risk that shareholder wealth maximisation may be pursued by managers in a way which it is not acceptable to many people within the community. However, wealth maximisation and ethical behaviour need not conflict. Indeed, in the long term, high ethical standards may be a necessary condition for wealth maximisation. It is interesting to note that many businesses now have an ethical code to guide managers.

Professor Harold Rose has argued:

> 'the responsibility of the finance function, in particular to seek to maximise the wealth of shareholders, does not mean that managers are being asked to act in a manner which absolves them from the considerations of morality and simple decency that they would readily acknowledge in other walks of life.'[2]

Thus, when considering a particular course of action, managers must consider the ethical dimensions. They should ask themselves whether it conforms to accepted moral standards, whether it treats people unfairly and whether it has the potential for harm.

Shareholder objectives and the agency problem

Managers are employed by the shareholders to manage the business on their behalf. Managers may, therefore, be viewed as *agents* of the shareholders (who are the *principals*). Given this agent–principal relationship, it may seem safe to assume that managers will be guided by the requirements of shareholders when making decisions. However, in practice, this does not always occur. The managers of a business may be more concerned with pursuing their own interests such as increasing their pay and 'perks' (e.g. expensive motor cars, and so on) and improving their job security and status. The managers of large businesses, where the shareholders are divorced from the day-to-day operations of the business, may be particularly well placed to put their own interests before those of the shareholders.

It can be argued that in a competitive market economy, this *agency problem*, as it is referred to, should not persist over time. The competition for the funds provided by shareholders and competition for managers' jobs referred to earlier, should ensure that the interests of the shareholders prevail. However, if competitive forces are weak, the risk of agency problems will be greater. The shareholders must be alert to such problems and should take steps to ensure that the managers operate the business in a manner which is consistent with shareholder needs.

ACTIVITY 1.4

What kind of actions might the shareholders take which ensure the managers act in accordance with their interests?

Two types of action are commonly employed in practice:

- *The shareholders may insist on monitoring closely the actions of the managers and the way in which the resources of the business are used.*
- *The shareholders may introduce incentive plans for managers which link their remuneration to the share performance of the business. In this way, the interests of managers and shareholders will become more closely aligned.*

The first option identified above can be both difficult to implement and costly. However, most competitive market economies have a framework of rules in place for ensuring that the actions of managers are monitored and controlled. In the United Kingdom, for example, company law requires that directors of a business act in the best interests of shareholders. The law also requires larger companies to have their annual accounts independently audited. The purpose of this audit is to provide credibility to the accounts prepared by the directors. In addition, both the law and the Stock Exchange places restrictions on the ability of directors to deal in the shares of the business. The purpose of these restrictions is to prevent the directors from benefiting from inside information.

In 1992, a committee set up by the Stock Exchange and the accountancy profession (known as the Cadbury Committee after the name of its chairman) produced a Code of Best Practice on Corporate Governance. This Code does not have the force of law but the directors of companies whose shares are listed on the Stock Exchange are required to state in their annual report the extent to which the Code has been implemented. This code covers such matters as the following:

- The responsibilities and composition of the board of directors.
- The role, appointment and independence of non-executive directors.
- The disclosure and determination of executive directors' pay and the period of their service contracts.
- The responsibilities for various reporting and controls procedures within the business.

The second option available to shareholders (i.e. incentive plans) can also be both difficult to implement and costly. A common form of incentive plan is to give managers *share options*. These options give managers the right, but not the obligation, to purchase shares in the business at an agreed price at some future date. If the current market value exceeds the agreed price at that due date, the managers will make a gain by taking up the options.

ACTIVITY 1.5

Can you think of any problems which may arise with this form of incentive?

One potential problem is that movements in the price of the shares of the business may be outside the control of managers. There may be movements in the market as a whole (either upwards or downwards) over which the managers have no influence but which affect the value of the shares of the business (and the remuneration which the managers receive). Another problem is that this form of incentive may encourage managers to undertake high-risk projects. As mentioned earlier, the higher the level of risk, the higher the expected returns. However, shareholders may not wish to have the risk profile of the business changed.

The agency problem will be discussed again later in the text when dealing with particular topics such as dividend policy and mergers.

Summary

In this chapter we have seen that the purpose of financial management is to help managers to manage. The tasks of the finance function within a business were identified and were related to the tasks of managers. We considered possible objectives for the business and saw why the shareholder wealth maximisation objective was considered to be superior to other objectives identified. This objective is at the root of modern financial management and we shall be referring to it throughout the text. Finally, we discussed the potential conflict of interest between shareholders and managers and how shareholders might respond to this.

References

1. E. Dimson, 'Assessing the Rate of Return', *Financial Times Mastering Management Series*, 1995, Supplement issue no. 1, p. 13.
2. H. Rose, 'Tasks of the Finance Function', *Financial Times Mastering Management Series*, 1995, Supplement issue no. 1, p. 11.

Review questions

1.1 What are the main functions of the finance department within a business?

1.2 Why is the maximisation of wealth viewed as superior to that of profit maximisation as a business objective?

1.3 Some managers, if asked what the main objective of their business is, may simply state 'To survive!'. What do you think of this as a primary objective?

1.4 Some businesses try to overcome the agency problem referred to in the chapter by using an incentive scheme which is based on the growth of profits over a period. What are the drawbacks of this type of scheme?

Further reading

You may wish to pursue some of the topics discussed in this text in greater depth. Below are some texts which you may find helpful.

Lumby, S., *Investment Appraisal and Financial Decisions*, 5th edn, Chapman & Hall, 1994.

McLaney, E.J., *Business Finance for Decision Makers*, 2nd edn, Pitman, 1994.

Samuels, J.M., Wilkes, F.M. and Brayshaw, R.E., *Management of Company Finance*, 6th edn, Chapman & Hall, 1995.

Van Horne, J., *Financial Management and Policy*, 10th edn, Prentice Hall, 1995.

CHAPTER TWO

Financial Planning and Projected Financial Statements

────────────────── OBJECTIVES ──────────────────

On completion of this chapter you should be able to:

- Prepare a simple projected cash flow statement, profit and loss account and balance sheet for a business.

- Explain the usefulness of each of the above statements for planning and decision-making purposes.

- Explain the way in which sensitivity analysis can help in evaluating projected information.

- Discuss the role of spreadsheets in the preparation of projected financial statements.

Introduction

In this chapter we will consider the nature and purpose of projected (pro forma) financial statements. We will see that projected financial statements can play an important role in the development of future plans for a business and in assessing the impact of management decisions on the performance and position of a business.

This chapter, and the following chapter, assume that you have some understanding of three major financial statements: the cash flow statement, the profit and loss account and the balance sheet. If you need to 'brush up' on the basic principles underlying these statements, you are recommended to consult Chapters 1–5 of *Financial Accounting for Non-specialists* by Peter Atrill and Eddie McLaney (Prentice Hall, 1996).

Financial planning and the role of projected financial statements

It is vitally important that businesses develop financial plans for the future. Whatever a business is trying to achieve, it is unlikely to be successful unless its managers have clear in their minds what the future direction of the business is going to be. The development of financial plans (see Figure 2.1) begins with the following key steps:

Setting the aims and objectives of the business

The aims and objectives set out what the business is basically trying to achieve. It is useful, however, to make a distinction between *aims* and *objectives*. The aims of the business are normally couched in general terms. They will often mention the high standards of products or services to which the business is committed and what the business strives to achieve for particular groups such as customers, shareholders and the community. The broad aims of the business are often set out in the form of a *mission statement*.

EXHIBIT 2.1

The mission statement of British Telecommunications plc (BT), as set out in its 1994 reports and accounts, is as follows:

> BT's mission, our central purpose, is to provide world-class telecommunications and information products and services, and to develop and exploit our networks, at home and overseas, so that we can:

- meet the requirements of our customers,
- sustain growth in the earnings of the group on behalf of our shareholders, and
- make a fitting contribution to the community in which we conduct our business.

Northern Electric plc, a regional electricity company, sets out its broad aim, in its 1994 accounts, as follows:

> Our aim is to achieve high standards of service and to operate our business in an enterprising and innovative manner, so as to create value for our shareholders, customers and employees.

The objectives of a business are usually more specific and measurable than its aims. The objectives will vary between businesses but may include the following aspects of operations and performance:

- The kind of market the business seeks to serve.
- The share of that market it wishes to achieve.
- The kind of products and/or services which should be offered.

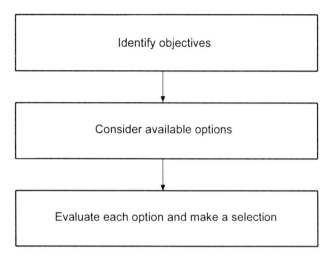

Figure 2.1   Steps in the financial planning process

■ The levels of profit and returns to shareholders which are required.
■ The levels of growth required and how this will be achieved.

Identifying the options available

In order to achieve the objectives set for the business, a number of possible options (strategies) may be available to the business. A creative search for the various strategic options available should be undertaken. This will involve collecting information, which can be extremely time consuming, particularly when the business is considering entering new markets or investing in new technology.

The type of information collected should include an *external analysis* of the competitive environment and will relate to such matters as:

- market size and growth prospects;
- level of competition within the industry;
- bargaining power; and
- cost structure of the industry.

Information should also be collected which provides an *internal analysis* of the resources and expertise of the business that are available to pursue each option. Information concerning the capabilities of the business in each of the following areas may be collected:

- marketing and distribution;
- manufacturing and production;
- finance and administration;
- research and development; and
- technical services.

Any deficiencies or gaps in these areas which could affect the ability of the business to pursue a particular option must be identified.

Evaluating the options and making a selection

When deciding on the most appropriate option(s) to choose, the managers must examine information relating to each option to see if that option fits with the objectives which have been set and to assess whether or not it is feasible to provide the resources required. The managers must also consider the effect of pursuing each option on the financial performance and position of the business. It is in the financial evaluation of the various options that projected financial statements have a valuable role to play.

The projected statements will take account of the financing and investment requirements as well as the expected revenues and costs associated with each option and will show the impact of these items on the profitability, liquidity and financial position of the business. The information contained within the projected statements will help, therefore, in deciding whether an appropriate option is acceptable. When deciding between the various strategic options available, a planning horizon of three to five years is typically employed. Projected financial statements for each year of the planning period will normally be prepared. However, when considering the preparation of these statements below, we will deal with a shorter time period for the sake of simplicity. The principles of preparation are not affected by the particular planning horizon.

Where managers are considering only one course of action, projected financial statements can still be extremely useful. The preparation of projected statements will provide a useful insight to the impact of the particular course of action on the future financial performance and position of the business. Where a business is considering a strategy to increase market share, for example, managers will need to satisfy themselves that adequate resources are available to sustain the planned growth in sales. Projected financial statements will help identify the financial constraints to growth and help managers strike an appropriate balance between sales, operating capability and finance levels.

Projected financial statements are usually prepared for internal purposes only. Managers are usually reluctant to share this information with those outside the business. Managers usually feel that the publication of projected information could damage the competitive position of the business. They may also feel that those outside the business might not fully understand the nature of projected statements and may not, therefore, appreciate that the projections may prove to be inaccurate. There may be a significant difference between projected financial outcomes and the actual final outcomes, particularly where the business operates in a fast-changing or turbulent environment. Nevertheless, there are certain occasions when managers are prepared to release projected information to those outside the business.

ACTIVITY 2.1

Can you think of any circumstances under which managers might be prepared to provide projected financial information to those outside the business?

Managers will often be prepared to provide projected financial statements when trying to raise finance for the business. Prospective lenders may require projected financial statements before considering a loan application. When making an offer of new shares to the public, projected statements are published by the company in order to attract investor interest. Projected statements may also be published if the managers feel the business is under threat. For example, a company which is the subject of a takeover bid to which the managers are opposed, may publish projected financial statements in order to give its shareholders confidence in the future of the company as a separate entity and to encourage them to retain their shares in the company.

Preparing projected financial statements

For most businesses, the most important item in the preparation of projected statements is the projection for sales. The expected level of sales for a period will be influenced by a number of factors including the degree of competition, the planned expenditure on advertising, the quality of the product, changes in consumer tastes and the general state of the economy. Only some of these factors will be under the control of the business. A reliable sales projection is essential as many other items including certain expenses, stock levels, fixed asset and financing requirements will be determined partially or completely by the level of sales for the period.

Not all expenses relating to a business will vary with the level of sales. Some expenses will vary directly and proportionately with the level of sales. Other expenses, however, may be unaffected by the level of sales for a period.

ACTIVITY 2.2

Can you name two expenses which are likely to vary directly with the level of sales and two expenses which are likely to stay constant irrespective of the level of sales?

Your answer to this activity may have identified cost of sales, materials consumed, and salesforce commission as examples of expenses which vary directly with sales output. Other expenses such as depreciation, rent, rates, insurance and salaries may stay fixed during a period irrespective of the level of sales generated. Some expenses have both a variable and a fixed element and so may vary partially with sales output. Heat and light may be an example of such an expense. A certain amount of heating and lighting costs will be incurred irrespective of the level of sales. However, if overtime is being worked due to heavy demand, this expense will increase.

The sales projection of a business may be developed in a number of ways. It may be done by simply aggregating the projections made by the salesforce or regional sales managers. These projections may rely heavily on subjective judgement and will usually attempt to take account of various aspects of the market and likely changes in market conditions. However, sales projections may also be based on certain statistical techniques or (in the case of large businesses) economic models. There are no hard and fast rules concerning the most appropriate method of projecting into the future for a business. Each business must assess the available methods in terms of reliability and accuracy for their particular situation and associated costs. The particular techniques of projecting into the future are not the subject of this chapter. Rather we are concerned with the preparation of projected financial statements and their subsequent evaluation.

Projected financial statements are prepared using the same methods and principles employed in relation to historic financial statements. The only real difference lies in the fact that the statements are prepared using *projected* information rather than *actual* information. This means that projected statements are less reliable and rely more on the use of judgement.

In order to illustrate the preparation of financial statements let us consider the following example.

Example 2.1

Designer Dresses Limited is a small company to be formed by James and William Clark to sell an exclusive range of dresses from a boutique in a fashionable suburb of London. On 1 January 19X9 they plan to invest £50,000 cash to purchase 25,000 £1 shares each in the company. Of this £30,000 is to be invested in new fittings in January. These fittings are to be depreciated over three years on the straight-line basis (their scrap value is assumed to be zero at the end of their lives). A half-year's depreciation is to be charged in the first six months. The sales and purchases projections for the company are as follows:

	January	February	March	April	May	June	Total
Sales (£000)	10.2	30.6	30.6	40.8	40.8	51.0	204.0
Purchases (£000)	20.0	30.0	25.0	25.0	30.0	30.0	160.0
Other costs (£000)*	9.0	9.0	9.0	9.0	9.0	9.0	54.0

* These include wages but exclude depreciation.

The sales will all be made by credit card. The credit card company will take one month to pay and will deduct its fee of 2 per cent of gross sales before paying amounts due to Designer Dresses. One month's credit is allowed by suppliers. Other costs shown above do not include rent and rates of £10,000 per quarter, payable on 1 January and 1 April. All other costs will be paid in cash. Closing stock at the end of June is expected to be £58,000.

You should ignore taxation. For your convenience you are advised to work to the nearest £000.

Required:

(a) Prepare a cash projection for the 6 months to 30 June 19X9.
(b) Prepare a projected profit and loss account for the same period.
(c) Prepare a projected balance sheet at 30 June 19X9.

Projected cash flow statement

A projected cash flow statement is useful because it helps to identify changes in the liquidity of a business over time. Cash has been described as the 'life blood' of a business. It is vital for a business to have sufficient liquid resources to meet its maturing obligations. Failure to maintain an adequate level of liquidity can have

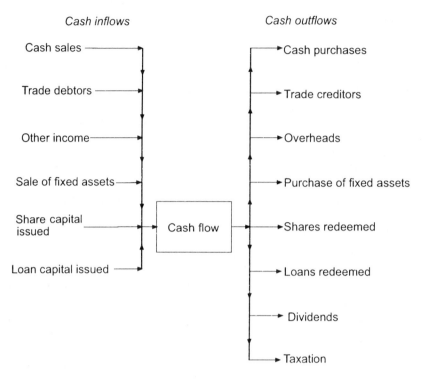

Figure 2.2   The main sources of cash inflows and outflows

disastrous consequences for the business. The projected cash flow statement helps to assess the impact of expected future events on the cash balance. It will identify periods where there are cash surpluses and cash deficits and will allow managers to plan for these occurrences. Where there is a cash surplus, managers should consider the profitable investment of the cash. Where there is a cash deficit, managers should consider the ways in which this can be financed.

You may already know from your previous studies that the cash flow statement is fairly easy to prepare. This statement simply records the cash inflows and outflows of the business. The main sources of cash inflows and outflows are set out in Figure 2.2.

Projected cash flow statements can be prepared for any period of time. When preparing the cash flow statement for the short term, it is useful to provide a monthly breakdown of the cash inflows and outflows. This helps managers to monitor closely changes in the cash position of the business. However, the longer the time period covered by the statement, the more difficult it will usually become to provide a monthly breakdown.

There is no set format for the cash flow statement when it is used for internal purposes. Management are free to decide on the form of presentation which best suits their needs. Below is set out an outline cash flow statement for Designer

Dresses for the six months to 30 June 19X9. This format is widely used and it is recommended that you use it when preparing this type of statement.

Projected cash flow statement for the six months to 30 June 19X9

	January £000	February £000	March £000	April £000	May £000	June £000
Cash inflows						
Issue of shares						
Credit sales	___	___	___	___	___	___
	___	___	___	___	___	___
Cash outflows						
Credit purchases						
Other costs						
Rent and rates						
Fittings	___	___	___	___	___	___
	___	___	___	___	___	___
Net cash flow						
Opening balance	___	___	___	___	___	___
Closing balance	___	___	___	___	___	___

You can see from this outline that each column represents a monthly period. At the top of each column the cash inflows are set out. Below these cash inflows the cash outflows are set out. The difference between the cash inflows and outflows is the net cash flow for the period. If we add this net cash flow to the opening cash balance brought forward from the previous month, we derive the cash balance at the end of the month.

When preparing a cash flow statement there are really two questions you must ask when considering each item of information presented to you. The first question is: Does the item of information concern a cash transaction (i.e. does it involve cash inflows or outflows)? If the answer to this question is 'no', then the information should be ignored for the purposes of preparing this statement. You will find that there are various items of information relating to a particular period, such as the depreciation charge, which do not involve cash movements.

If the answer to the question above is 'yes', then a second question must be asked. This question is: When did the cash transaction take place? It is important to identify the particular month in which the cash movement takes place. Often the cash movement will occur after the period in which a particular transaction has been agreed. For example, where sales and purchases are made on credit.

Problems in preparing cash flow statements usually arise because these two questions have not been properly addressed.

ACTIVITY 2.3

Fill in the outline cash flow statement for Designer Dresses Ltd for the six months to 30 June 19X9 using the information contained in Example 2.1 above.

Your answer to the above activity should be as follows:

Projected cash flow statement for the six months to 30 June 19X9

	January £000	February £000	March £000	April £000	May £000	June £000
Cash inflows						
Issue of shares	50					
Credit sales	–	10	30	30	40	40
	50	10	30	30	40	40
Cash outflows						
Credit purchases	–	20	30	25	25	30
Other costs	9	9	9	9	9	9
Rent and rates	10			10		
Fittings	30					
	49	29	39	44	34	39
Net cash flow	1	(19)	(9)	(14)	6	1
Opening balance	–	1	(18)	(27)	(41)	(35)
Closing balance	1	(18)	(27)	(41)	(35)	(34)

Notes:
1. The receipts from credit sales will arise one month after the sale has taken place. Hence, January's sales will be received in February, and so on. Similarly, trade creditors are paid one month after the goods have been purchased.
2. The closing cash balance for each month is deduced by adding to (or subtracting from) the opening balance, the cash flow for the month.

When a cash flow statement is prepared for external reporting purposes, we provide a summary of the cash flows for the year rather than a monthly breakdown of cash flows. Furthermore, a particular format for presenting the information must be adhered to. This type of cash flow statement will be considered in Chapter 3.

Projected profit and loss account

A projected profit and loss account helps provide an insight to the expected level of future profits over time. When preparing the projected profit and loss account, it is important to include all revenues which are realised within each period (whether or not the cash has been received) and all expenses (including non-cash items) which relate to those revenues. Remember that the purpose of this statement is to show the wealth generated during the period and this may bear little relation to the cash generated.

The format for the projected profit and loss account will be as follows:

Projected profit and loss account for the six months to 30 June 19X9

	£000	£000
Credit sales		
Less: Cost of sales		
Purchases		
Less: Closing stock	____	____
Gross profit		
Credit card discounts		
Rent and rates		
Other costs		
Depreciation of fittings	____	____
Net profit		____

ACTIVITY 2.4

Fill in the outline profit and loss account for Designer Dresses Ltd for the six months to 30 June 19X9 using the information contained in Example 2.1 above.

Your answer to this activity should be as follows:

Projected profit and loss account for the six months to 30 June 19X9

	£000	£000
Credit sales		204
Less: Cost of sales		
Purchases	160	
Less: Closing stock	58	102
Gross profit		102
Credit card discounts	4	
Rent and rates	20	
Other costs	54	
Depreciation of fittings	5	83
Net profit		19

Note: The credit card discount is shown as a separate expense and not deducted from the sales figure. This approach is more informative than simply netting off the amount of the discount against sales.

Projected balance sheet

The projected balance sheet reveals the end-of-period balances for assets, liabilities and capital and should normally be the last of the three statements to be prepared. The previous statements prepared provide information to be used when preparing the projected balance sheet. The projected cash flow statement reveals the end-of-period cash balance and the projected profit and loss account reveals the projected retained profit for the period for inclusion in the share capital and reserves section of the balance sheet. The depreciation charge for the period, which appears in the projected profit and loss account, must also be taken into account when preparing the projected balance sheet.

The format for the projected balance sheet will be as follows:

Projected balance sheet as at 30 June 19X9

	£000	£000	£000
Fixed assets			
Fittings at cost			
Less: Accumulated depreciation		___	
Current assets			
Stock			
Debtors		___	
Less: **Creditors: amounts due within one year**			
Trade creditors			
Bank overdraft	___	___	___
Net assets			═══
Share capital and reserves			
Share capital			
Retained profit		___	
			═══

ACTIVITY 2.5

Fill in the outline balance sheet for Designer Dresses Ltd as at 30 June 19X9 using the information contained in Example 2.1.

Your answer to this activity should be as follows:

Projected balance sheet as at 30 June 19X9

	£000	£000	£000
Fixed assets			
Fittings at cost			30
Less: Accumulated depreciation			5
			25
Current assets			
Stock		58	
Debtors (£51,000 less 2%)		50	
		108	
Less: **Creditors: amounts due within one year**			
Trade creditors	30		
Bank overdraft	34	64	44
Net assets			69
Share capital and reserves			
Share capital			50
Retained profit			19
			69

Note: The debtors figure represents June credit sales (less the credit card discount). Similarly, the creditors represents June purchases.

Evaluation of projected financial statements

Projected financial statements must be evaluated in order to ensure that sensible financial decisions are made. When evaluating such statements you must ask yourself a number of key questions. These include the following:

- How reliable are the projections which have been made?
- What underlying assumptions have been made and are they valid?
- Are the cash flows satisfactory? Can they be improved by changing policies or plans (e.g. delaying capital expenditure decisions, requiring debtors to pay more quickly, etc.)?
- Is there a need for additional financing? Is it feasible to obtain the amount required?
- Can any surplus funds be profitably reinvested?
- Is the level of projected profit satisfactory in relation to the risks involved? If

not, what could be done to improve matters?
- Are the sales and individual expense items at a satisfactory level?
- Have all relevant expenses been included?
- Is the financial position at the end of the period acceptable?
- Is the level of borrowing acceptable? Is the company too dependent on borrowing?

ACTIVITY 2.6

Evaluate the projected financial statements of Designer Dresses Ltd. Pay particular attention to the projected profitability and liquidity of the business.

The projected cash flow statement reveals that the company will have a bank overdraft throughout most of the period under review. The maximum overdraft requirement will be £41,000 in April 19X9. Although the company will be heavily dependent on bank finance in the early months, this situation should not last for too long providing the company achieves and then maintains the level of projected profit.

The company is expected to generate a profit of 9.3p for every £1 of sales. The profit of £19,000 on the original outlay of £50,000 by the owners seems high. However, the business may be of a high-risk nature and therefore the owners will be looking to make high returns. As this is a new company it may be very difficult to project into the future with any real accuracy. Thus the basis on which the projections have been made require careful investigation.

Some further points regarding profitability can be made. It is not clear from the question whether the wages included in the profit and loss account include any remuneration for James and William Clark. If no remuneration for their efforts has been included, the level of profit shown may be overstated. It may not be possible to extrapolate the projected revenues and expenses for the six-month period in order to obtain a projected profit for the year. It is likely that the business is seasonal in nature and, therefore, the following six-month period may be quite different.

ACTIVITY 2.7

Dalgleish Ltd is a wholesale supplier of stationery. In recent months the company has experienced liquidity problems. The company has an overdraft at the end of November 19X1 and the bank has been pressing for a reduction in this overdraft over the next six months. The company is owned by the Dalgleish family who are unwilling to raise finance through long-term borrowing.

The balance sheet of the business as at 30 November 19X1 is as follows:

Balance sheet as at 30 November 19X1

	£000	£000	£000
Fixed assets			
Freehold land and premises at cost		250	
Less: Accumulated depreciation		24	226
Fixtures and fittings at cost		174	
Less: Accumulated depreciation		38	136
			362
Current assets			
Stock at cost		142	
Debtors		120	
		262	
Less: **Creditors: Amounts due within one year**			
Trade creditors	145		
Bank overdraft	126		
Corporation tax	24		
Dividends	20	315	(53)
			309
Capital and reserves			
£1 ordinary shares			200
Profit and loss account			109
			309

The following projections for the six months ended 31 May 19X2 are available concerning the business:

1. Sales and purchases for the six months ended 31 May 19X2 will be as follows:

	Sales £000	Purchases £000
December	160	150
January	220	140
February	240	170
March	150	110
April	160	120
May	200	160

2. 70 per cent of sales are on credit and 30 per cent are cash sales. Credit sales are received in the following month. All purchases are on one month's credit.
3. Wages are £40,000 for each of the first three months. However, this will

increase by 10 per cent as from March 19X2. All wages are paid in the month they are incurred.

4. The gross profit percentage on goods sold is 30 per cent.
5. Administration expenses are expected to be £12,000 in each of the first four months and £14,000 in subsequent months. These figures include a monthly charge of £4,000 in respect of depreciation of fixed assets. Administration expenses are paid in the month they are incurred.
6. Selling expenses are expected to be £8,000 per month except for May 19X2 when an advertising campaign costing £12,000 will be paid for. The advertising campaign will commence at the beginning of June 19X2. Selling expenses are paid for in the month they are incurred.
7. The dividend outstanding will be paid in December 19X1.
8. The company intends to purchase, and pay for, new fixtures and fittings at the end of April 19X2 for £28,000. These will be delivered in June 19X2.

Required:

(a) Prepare a cash flow projection for Dalgleish Ltd for each of the six months to 31 May 19X2.
(b) Prepare a projected profit and loss account for the six months to 31 May 19X2.
(c) Briefly discuss ways in which the company might reduce the bank overdraft as required by the bank.

Your answer to this activity should be along the following lines:

Cash flow projection for the six months to 31 May 19X2

	December £000	January £000	February £000	March £000	April £000	May £000
Cash inflows						
Credit sales	120	112	154	168	105	112
Cash sales	48	66	72	45	48	60
	168	178	226	213	153	172
Cash outflows						
Purchases	145	150	140	170	110	120
Admin. expenses	8	8	8	8	10	10
Wages	40	40	40	44	44	44
Selling expenses	8	8	8	8	8	20
Fixtures					28	
Dividend	20					
	221	206	196	230	200	194

	December £000	January £000	February £000	March £000	April £000	May £000
Cash flow	(53)	(28)	30	(17)	(47)	(22)
Opening balance	(126)	(179)	(207)	(177)	(194)	(241)
Closing balance	(179)	(207)	(177)	(194)	(241)	(263)

Projected profit and loss account for the six months to 31 May 19X2

	£000	£000
Sales		1,130
Less: Cost of sales (balancing figure)		791
Gross profit (30% of sales)		339
Wages	252	
Selling expenses (exc. adv. campaign)	48	
Admin. expenses (inc. depr'n)	76	376
Net loss		(37)

Note: The advertising campaign relates to the next financial period and will therefore be charged to the profit and loss account of that period

In answering part (3) of the activity you may have thought of a number of possible options. The following options (or perhaps, some combination of these) might be feasible:

■ New equity finance injected by the Dalgleish family or others.
■ Reduce stock levels.
■ Delay purchase/payment of fixtures.
■ Sell fixed assets.
■ Increase proportion of cash sales.
■ Delay payment of trade creditors.

(Note: The Dalgleish family have ruled out the possibility of raising a loan.)

Each of the above options have advantages and disadvantages and these must be carefully assessed before a final decision is made.

Sensitivity analysis

Sensitivity analysis is a useful technique to employ when evaluating projected financial statements. The technique involves taking a single variable (e.g. volume of sales) and examining the effect of changes in the chosen variable on the likely performance and position of the business. By examining the changes which occur it is possible to arrive at some assessment of the sensitivity of changes on the projected outcomes. Although only one variable is examined at a time, a number of variables, considered to be important to the performance of a business, may be examined consecutively.

One approach to sensitivity analysis is to pose a series of 'What if' questions. In relation to sales, for example, the following questions, *inter alia*, might be asked:

- What if sales volume is 5 per cent higher than expected?
- What if sales volume is 10 per cent lower than expected?
- What if sales price is reduced by 4 per cent?
- What if sales price could be increased by 6 per cent?

In answering such questions, it is possible to develop a better 'feel' for the effect of projection inaccuracies on the final outcomes. However, this technique does not assign probabilities to each possible change nor does it consider the effect of more than one variable on projected outcomes at a time.

Scenario analysis

Another approach to helping managers gain a 'feel' for each option is to prepare projected financial statements according to different possible states of the world. For example, managers may wish to examine projected financial statements prepared on the basis of the following:

- An optimistic view of likely future events.
- A pessimistic view of likely future events.
- A 'most likely' view of future events.

This type of 'scenario analysis', as it is sometimes called, can help in assessing the level of risk involved. The probability of each 'state of the world' arising should also be considered. Sensitivity analysis and scenario analysis will be considered in more detail in Chapter 6.

Projections using spreadsheets

Preparing projected financial statements is facilitated by the use of spreadsheet packages. In essence, a spreadsheet package is simply a matrix of rows and columns which can be loaded into a computer and viewed on the computer screen. The intersection of a row and a column is referred to as a cell. In each cell it is possible to insert numbers, equations or descriptions. A simple model can be built using this matrix. For example, the projected cash flow statement for Dalgleish Ltd dealt with in Activity 2.7, may be prepared using the rows and columns of a spreadsheet package as follows:

	A	B	C	D	E	F	G
		Dec.	Jan.	Feb.	Mar.	Apr.	May
1		£000	£000	£000	£000	£000	£000
2							
3	**Cash inflows**						
4	Credit sales	120	112	154	168	105	112
5	Cash sales	48	66	72	45	48	60
6		168	178	226	213	153	172
7							
8	**Cash outflows**						
9	Purchases	145	150	140	170	110	120
10	Admin. expenses	8	8	8	8	10	10
11	Wages	40	40	40	44	44	44
12	Selling expenses	8	8	8	8	8	20
13	Fixtures					28	
14	Dividend	20					
15		221	206	196	230	200	194
16							
17	Cash flow	(53)	(28)	30	(17)	(47)	(22)
18	Opening balance	(126)	(179)	(207)	(177)	(194)	(241)
19	Closing balance	(179)	(207)	(177)	(194)	(241)	(263)

Cell B6 can be made equal to the sum of cells B4 and B5, Cell C6 can be made equal to the sum of C4 and C5, etc. so that all calculations are carried out by the package. The spreadsheet package is particularly useful if managers wish to carry out sensitivity analysis on the projected statements. One variable may be altered and the spreadsheet will quickly recalculate the totals to show the effect of the change.

Not only can figures be linked through formulae within a particular statement but different financial statements can also be linked. This means, for example, that the final cash balance shown in G19 can be inserted in another cell in the spreadsheet dealing with the balance sheet. Similar links can be made between many of the figures which appear in the various projected statements. This means that the statements can be produced with the minimum of entry information and no calculation at all, yet can be produced very quickly and accurately.

In practice, the spreadsheet can have all manner of refinements and user friendly features incorporated which can reduce further the amount of data entry by the preparer. It can be so designed that data can all be entered in one corner of the spreadsheet, in a data entry area, to save the preparer scrolling up and down the spreadsheet to enter it. The spreadsheet model would automatically pick up the data from where it had been entered and use it, as appropriate, to produce the projected financial statements.

SELF-ASSESSMENT QUESTION 2.1

Quardis Ltd is an importer of high-quality laser printers which can be used with a range of microcomputers. The balance sheet of Quardis Ltd as at 31 May 19X0 is as follows:

	£000	£000	£000
Fixed assets			
Freehold premises at cost		460	
Less: Accumulated depreciation		30	430
Fixtures and fittings at cost		35	
Less: Accumulated depreciation		10	25
			455
Current assets			
Stock		24	
Debtors		34	
Cash at bank		2	
		60	
Less: **Creditors: amounts due within one year**			
Trade creditors	22		
Taxation	14		
Dividends	10	46	14
			469
Less: **Creditors: amount due beyond one year**			
Loan – Highland Bank			125
			344
Capital and reserves			
£1 ordinary shares			200
Retained profit			144
			344

The following information is available for the year ended 31 May 19X1:

1. Sales are expected to be £280,000 for the year. Sixty per cent of sales are on credit and it is expected that, at the year end, three months' credit sales will be outstanding. Sales revenues accrue evenly over the year.
2. Purchases of stock during the year will be £186,000 and will accrue evenly over the year. All purchases are on credit and at the year end it is expected that two months' purchases will remain unpaid.
3. Fixtures and fittings costing £25,000 will be purchased and paid for during the year. Depreciation is charged at 10 per cent on the cost of fixtures and fittings held at the year end.
4. Depreciation is charged on freehold premises at 2 per cent on cost.
5. On 1 June 19X0, £30,000 of the loan from the Highland Bank is to be repaid.

Interest is at the rate of 13 per cent per annum and all interest accrued to 31 May 19X1 will be paid on that day.

6. Stock-in-trade at the year end is expected to be 25 per cent higher than at the beginning of the year.

7. Wages for the year will be £34,000. At the year end it is estimated that £4,000 of this total will remain unpaid.

8. Other overhead expenses for the year (excluding those mentioned above) are expected to be £21,000. At the year end it is expected that £3,000 of this total will still be unpaid.

9. A dividend of 5p per share is expected to be announced at the year end. The dividend outstanding at the beginning of the year will be paid during the year.

10. Corporation tax is payable at the rate of 35 per cent. Corporation tax outstanding at the beginning of the year will be paid during the year.

All workings should be shown to the nearest £000.

Required:

(a) Prepare a projected profit and loss account for the year ended 31 May 19X1.
(b) Prepare a projected balance sheet as at 31 May 19X1.
(c) Comment on the significant features revealed by these statements.

(Note: A cash flow statement is not required. The cash figure in the balance sheet will be a balancing figure.)

Summary

In this chapter we have examined the role and nature of projected financial statements. We have seen that these statements are used mostly for internal planning purposes. They help managers in the evaluation and selection of options concerning the future direction of the business. They can also help managers assess the impact of likely changes in the performance and position of the business. In a fast-changing environment, projected financial statements may need to be revised at frequent intervals in order to make managers aware of changing conditions.

The preparation of projected statements is based on the same principles as the preparation of historic statements. The only difference is that we employ projected data rather than 'actual' data in their preparation. Projected statements are only useful if the projections made are reliable. Hence, the starting point in any evaluation of projected statements is to examine the way in which the projected data was developed and any assumptions made. The use of scenario analysis and sensitivity analysis can be useful in developing a 'feel' for likely future outcomes.

Review questions _____

2.1 In what ways might projected financial statements help a business which is growing fast?

2.2 'The future is uncertain and so projected financial statements will almost certainly prove to be inaccurate. It is, therefore, a waste of time to prepare them.' Comment.

2.3 Why would it normally be easier to prepare projected financial statements for an existing business than for a new one?

2.4 Why is the sales forecast normally of critical importance to the preparation of projected financial statements?

Examination-style questions _____

Solutions to those questions marked with an asterisk are given at the end of the text. Questions 2.1–2.3 are at basic level. Questions 2.4–2.6 are at intermediate/advanced level.

2.1* Prolog Ltd is a small wholesaler of microcomputers. It has in recent months been selling 50 machines a month at a price of £2,000 each. These machines cost £1,600 each. A new model has just been launched and this is expected to offer greatly enhanced performance. Its selling price and cost will be the same as for the old model. From the beginning of January, sales are expected to increase at a rate of 20 machines each month until the end of June when sales will amount to 170 units per month. They are expected to continue at that level thereafter. Operating costs including depreciation of £2,000 per month, are forecast as follows:

	January	February	March	April	May	June
Operating costs (£000)	6	8	10	12	12	12

Prolog expects to receive no credit for operating costs. Additional shelving for storage will be bought, installed and paid for in April costing £12,000. Corporation tax of £25,000 is due at the end of March. Prolog anticipates that debtors will amount to two months' sales. To give their customers a good level of service Prolog plans to hold enough stock at the end of each period to fulfil anticipated demand from customers in the following month. The computer manufacturer, however, grants one month's credit to Prolog. Prolog Ltd's balance sheet appears below.

Balance sheet at 31 December 19X4

	£000	£000
Fixed assets		80
Current assets		
Stock	112	
Debtors	200	
Cash	–	
	312	
Creditors: amounts due within one year		
Trade creditors	112	
Taxation	25	
Overdraft	68	
	205	
Net current assets		107
Total assets less current liabilities		187
Capital and reserves		
Share capital -- 25p ordinary shares		10
Profit and loss account		177
		187

Required:

(a) Prepare a cash forecast for Prolog Ltd showing the cash balance or required overdraft for the six months ending 30 June 19X5.

(b) State briefly what further information a banker would require from Prolog before granting additional overdraft facilities for the anticipated expansion of sales.

2.2 Davis Travel Limited specialises in the provision of winter sports holidays but it also organises outdoor activity holidays in the summer. You are given the following information:

Abbreviated balance sheet as at 30 September 19X7

	£000
Fixed assets	560
Current assets	
Cash	30
Total assets	590

	£000
Creditors: amounts due within one year	
Trade creditors	180
Total assets less current liabilities	410
Creditors: amounts due in over one year	
Loans	110
	300
Share capital	100
Reserves	200
	300

Its sales estimates for the next six months are:

	Numbers of bookings received	Numbers of holidays taken	Promotion expenditure (£000)
October	1,000		100
November	3,000		150
December	3,000	1,000	150
January	3,000	4,000	50
February		3,000	
March		2,000	
Total	10,000	10,000	450

1. Holidays sell for £300 each. Ten per cent is payable when the holiday is booked and the remainder after two months.
2. Travel agents are paid a commission of 10 per cent of the price of the holiday one month after the booking is made.
3. The cost of a flight is £50 per holiday and a hotel £100 per holiday. Flights and hotels must be paid for in the month when the holidays are taken.
4. Other variable costs are £20 per holiday and are paid in the month of the holiday.
5. Administration costs, including depreciation of fixed assets of £42,000, amount to £402,000 for the six months. Administration costs can be spread evenly over the period.
6. Loan interest of £10,000 is payable on 31 March 19X8 and a loan repayment of £20,000 is due on that date. For your calculations you should ignore any interest on the overdraft.
7. The creditors of £180,000 at 30 September are to be paid in October.
8. A payment of £50,000 for fixed assets is to be made in March 19X8.
9. The airline and the hotel chain base their charges on Davis Travel's forecast requirements and hold capacity to meet those requirements. If Davis is unable

to fill this reserved capacity a charge of 50 per cent of those published above is made.

Required:

(a) Prepare:
    (i)   A cash forecast for the six months to 31 March 19X8.
    (ii) A profit and loss account for the six months ended on that date.
    (iii) A balance sheet at 31 March 19X8.
(b) Discuss the main financial problems confronting Davis Travel.

Ignore taxation in your calculations.

2.3 Changes Limited owns a chain of eight shops selling fashion goods. In the past the company maintained a healthy cash balance. However, this has fallen in recent months and at the end of September 19X6 it had an overdraft of £70,000. In view of this, its managing director has asked you to prepare a cash forecast for the next six months. You have collected the following data:

	Oct. £000	Nov. £000	Dec. £000	Jan. £000	Feb. £000	Mar. £000
Sales forecast	140	180	260	60	100	120
Purchases	160	180	140	50	50	50
Wages and salaries	30	30	40	30	30	32
Rent			60			
Rates						40
Other expenses	20	20	20	20	20	20
Refurbishing shops				80		

Stock at 1 October amounted to £170,000 and creditors were £70,000. The purchases in October, November and December are contractually committed and those in January, February and March, the minimum necessary to restock with spring fashions. Cost of sales is 50 per cent of sales and suppliers allow one month's credit on purchases. Taxation of £90,000 is due on 1 January. The rates payment is a charge for a whole year and other expenses include depreciation of £10,000 per month.

Required:

(a) Compute the cash balance at the end of each month, for the six months to 31 March 19X7.
(b) Compute the stock levels at the end of each month for the six months to 31 March 19X7.
(c) Prepare a profit and loss account for the six months ended 31 March 19X7.
(d) What problems might Changes Limited face in the next six months and how would you attempt to overcome them?

2.4*   Kwaysar Ltd sells television satellite dishes both to retail outlets and direct to the public. The balance sheet of the company as at 31 May 19X3 is as follows:

Balance sheet as at 31 May 19X3

	£000	£000	£000
Fixed assets			
Freehold premises at cost		350	
Less: accumulated depreciation		60	290
Fixtures and fittings at cost		80	
Less: accumulated depreciation		42	38
			328
Current assets			
Stock at cost		44	
Debtors		52	
Cash at bank		120	
		216	
Creditors: amounts due within one year			
Trade creditors	32		
Accrued overheads	12		
Dividends	48	92	124
			452
Capital and reserves			
£1 ordinary shares			200
Share premium account			80
General reserve			40
Retained profit			132
			452

In the second half of the financial year to 31 May 19X3, the company generated a net profit of £62,400 and sales of £525,000. It is believed that this level of performance will be repeated in the forthcoming six-month period providing the company does not implement any changes to its marketing strategy. The company, however, is determined to increase its market share and is considering the adoption of a new marketing strategy which has been developed by the marketing department.

The main elements of the new strategy are as follows:

1.   The selling price of each satellite dish will be reduced to £90. At present each dish is sold for £120.
2.   There will be an increase in the amount of advertising costs incurred by the company. Advertising costs will increase from £6,500 per month to £12,000 per month.

3. Retail outlets will be allowed to pay for satellite dishes three months after delivery. At present, trade debtors are allowed one month's credit. Those retail outlets who continue to pay within one month will, for future sales, be given a 2 per cent discount.

The marketing department believes that, by adopting the new strategy, sales in each of the first three months to retail outlets will rise to 1,000 units and sales to the public will rise to 300 units. Thereafter, sales each month will be 1,200 units and 400 units respectively.

Assuming the strategy is adopted, the following forecast information is available:

1. The purchase of satellite dishes will be made at the beginning of each month and will be sufficient to meet that month's sales. Each satellite dish costs £50. Trade creditors are paid one month after the month of purchase.
2. Depreciation will be charged on freehold premises at 2 per cent per annum on cost and for fixtures and fittings at 15 per cent per annum on cost.
3. Motor vans costing £80,000 will be acquired and paid for immediately. These are required to implement the new strategy and will be depreciated at 30 per cent per annum on cost.
4. Wages will be £18,000 per month and will be paid in the month in which they are incurred.
5. Advertising costs will be paid for in the month incurred.
6. Other overheads (excluding those mentioned above) will be £14,000 per month and will continue to be paid for one month after the month in which they are incurred.
7. The dividends outstanding will be paid for in July 19X3.
8. Sales direct to the public will continue to be paid for in cash. No credit will be allowed.
9. It is estimated that 50 per cent of retail sales will continue to be on one month's credit and 50 per cent will be on three months' credit.

Ignore taxation.

Required:

Assuming that the new marketing strategy is adopted:

(a) Prepare a forecast profit and loss account for the six-month period to 30 November 19X3. (A monthly breakdown of profit is not required.)
(b) Prepare a forecast cash flow statement for the six-month period to 30 November 19X3. (A monthly breakdown of cash flows is not required.)
(c) Comment on the financial results of Kwaysar Ltd for the six-month period to 30 November 19X3.

2.5 Newtake Records Ltd owns a chain of fourteen shops selling cassette tapes and compact discs. At the beginning of June 19X4 the company had an overdraft of

£35,000 and the bank has asked for this to be eliminated by the end of November 19X4. As a result, the directors of the company have recently decided to review their plans for the next six months in order to comply with this requirement.

The following forecast information was prepared for the business some months earlier:

	May £000	June £000	July £000	Aug. £000	Sept. £000	Oct. £000	Nov. £000
Expected sales	180	230	320	250	140	120	110
Purchases	135	180	142	94	75	66	57
Administration expenses	52	55	56	53	48	46	45
Selling expenses	22	24	28	26	21	19	18
Taxation payment				22			
Finance payments	5	5	5	5	5	5	5
Shop refurbishment	–	–	14	18	6	–	–

Notes:

1.   Stock held at 1 June 19X4 was £112,000. The company believes it is necessary to maintain a minimum stock level of £40,000 over the period to 30 November 19X4.
2.   Suppliers allow one month's credit. The first three months' purchases are subject to a contractual agreement which must be honoured.
3.   The gross profit margin is 40 per cent.
4.   All sales income is received in the month of sale. However, 50 per cent of customers pay with a credit card. The charge made by the credit card company to Newtake Records Ltd is 3 per cent of the sales value. These charges are in addition to the selling expenses identified above. The credit card company pays Newtake Records Ltd in the month of sale.
5.   The company has a bank loan which it is paying off in monthly instalments of £5,000 per month The interest element represents 20 per cent of each instalment.
6.   Administration expenses are paid when incurred. This item includes a charge of £15,000 each month in respect of depreciation.
7.   Selling expenses are payable in the following month.

Required:

(a) Prepare a cash flow forecast for the six months ended 30 November 19X4 which shows the cash balance at the end of each month.
(b) Compute the stock levels at the end of each month for the six months to 30 November 19X4.
(c) Prepare a profit and loss account for the six months ended 30 November 19X4. (A monthly breakdown of profit is not required.)

(d) What problems is Newtake Records Ltd likely to face in the next six months? Can you suggest how the company might deal with these problems?

2.6 International Golf Ltd operates a large warehouse selling golf equipment direct to the public by mail order and to small retail outlets. The cash position of the company has caused some concern in recent months. At the beginning of December 19X3 there was an overdraft at the bank of £56,000. The following data concerning income and expenses has been collected in respect of the forthcoming six months:

	December £000	January £000	February £000	March £000	April £000	May £000
Expected sales	120	150	170	220	250	280
Purchases	156	180	195	160	150	160
Advertising	15	18	20	25	30	30
Rent	40			40		
Rates		30				
Wages	16	16	18	18	20	20
Sundry expenses	20	24	24	26	26	26

The company also intends to purchase and pay for new motor vans in February at a cost of £24,000 and to pay taxation due on 1 March of £30,000.

Sales to the public are on a cash basis and sales to retailers are on two months' credit. Approximately 40 per cent of sales are made to the public. Debtors at the beginning of December are £110,000, 70 per cent of which are in respect of November sales.

Purchases are on one month's credit and, at the beginning of December, the trade creditors were £140,000. The purchases made in December, January and February are considered necessary to stock up for the sales demand from March onwards.

All other expenses are paid in the month in which they are incurred. Sundry expenses include a charge of £8,000 per month in respect of depreciation.

Required:

(a) Explain the benefits to a business of preparing a cash flow forecast.
(b) Identify and discuss the costs to a business associated with:
   (i) holding too much cash; and
   (ii) holding too little cash.
(c) Prepare a cash flow forecast for International Golf Ltd for the six months to 31 May 19X4 which shows the cash balance at the end of each month.
(d) State what problems International Golf Ltd is likely to face during the next six months and how these might be dealt with.

CHAPTER THREE

Financial Statement Analysis and Interpretation

OBJECTIVES

On completion of this chapter you should be able to:

- Identify the main categories of ratios which can be used for analysis purposes.

- Calculate important ratios for determining the financial performance and position of a business and explain the significance of the ratios calculated.

- Discuss the limitations of ratios as a tool of financial analysis.

- Discuss the use of ratios in helping to predict financial distress.

Introduction

In this chapter we will see how financial ratios can help in analysing and interpreting financial information. We will also consider problems which are encountered when applying this technique. Financial ratios can be used to examine various aspects of financial position and performance and are widely used for planning, control and evaluation purposes. They can be used to evaluate financial statements and can also be used in decisions concerning working capital management, financial structure and mergers. We shall come across a nunber of the ratios studied in this chapter again at different points in the text.

Financial ratios

Financial ratios provide a quick and relatively simple means of examining the financial health of a business. A ratio simply expresses one figure appearing in the financial statements with some other figure appearing in the financial statements (e.g. net profit in relation to capital employed) or perhaps some resource of the business (e.g. net profit per employee, sales per square metre of counter space, etc.).

By calculating a relatively small number of ratios, it is often possible to build up a reasonably good picture of the position and performance of a business. Thus it is not surprising that ratios are widely used by those who have an interest in businesses and business performance. Although ratios are not difficult to calculate, they can be difficult to interpret. For example, a change in the net profit per employee of a business may be due to a number of possible reasons such as:

- A change in the number of employees without a corresponding change in the level of output.
- A change in the level of output without a corresponding change in the number of employees.
- A change in the mix of goods/services being offered which in turn, changes the level of profit, and so forth.

It is important to appreciate that ratios are really only the starting point for further analysis. They help to highlight the financial strengths and weaknesses of a business but they cannot, by themselves, explain *why* certain strengths or weaknesses exist or *why* certain changes have occurred. Only a detailed investigation will reveal underlying reasons.

A major problem when comparing the financial health of different businesses is the differences which exist in the scale of operations. Thus a direct comparison of, say, the profits of each business may be misleading due to differences in size. By expressing profit in relation to some other measure (e.g. sales), the ratio derived can be used as a basis for comparison for similarly derived ratios for other similar businesses.

Ratios can be expressed in various forms (e.g. as a percentage, as a fraction, as a proportion, etc.). The way a particular ratio is presented will depend on the needs of those who will use the information. Although it is possible to calculate a large number of ratios, only a relatively few, based on key relationships, may be required by the user. Many ratios which could be calculated from the financial statements (e.g. rent payable in relation to taxation) may not be considered because there is no clear or meaningful relationship between the items.

There is no generally accepted list of ratios which can be applied to the financial statements, nor is there a standard method of calculating many ratios. Variations in both the choice of ratios and their calculation will be found in the literature and in practice. However, it is important to be consistent in the way in which ratios are calculated for comparison purposes. The ratios discussed below are those which many consider to be among the more important for decision-making purposes.

Financial ratio classification

Ratios can be grouped into certain categories, each of which reflect a particular aspect of financial performance or position. The following broad categories provide a useful basis for explaining the nature of the financial ratios to be dealt with.

1. *Profitability.* Businesses come into being with the primary purpose of creating wealth for their owners. Profitability ratios provide an insight to the degree of success attained in achieving this purpose. They express the profits made (or figures bearing on profit, such as overheads) in relation to other key figures in the financial statements or to some business resource.
2. *Efficiency.* Ratios may be used to measure the efficiency with which certain resources have been utilised within the business. These ratios are also referred to as *activity* ratios.
3. *Liquidity.* We have seen in Chapter 2 that it is vital to the survival of a business for there to be sufficient liquid resources available to meet maturing obligations. Certain ratios may be calculated which examine the relationship between liquid resources held and creditors due for payment in the near future.
4. *Gearing.* Gearing is an important issue which managers must consider when making financing decisions. The relationship between the amount financed by the owners of the business and the amount contributed by outsiders has an important effect on the degree of risk associated with a business as we will see.
5. *Investment.* Certain ratios are concerned with assessing the returns and performance of shares held in a particular business.

The need for comparison

Calculating a ratio by itself will not tell you very much about the position or performance of a business. For example, if a ratio revealed that the business was generating £100 in sales per square metre of counter space, it would not be possible to deduce from this information alone whether this level of performance was good, bad or indifferent. It is only when you compare this ratio with some 'benchmark' that the information can be interpreted and evaluated.

ACTIVITY 3.1

Can you think of any bases which could be used to compare a ratio you have calculated from the financial statements of a particular period?

In answering this activity you may have thought of the following bases:

■ *Past periods.* By comparing the ratio you have calculated with the ratio of a previous period, it is possible to detect whether there has been an improvement or deterioration in performance. Indeed, it is often useful to track particular ratios over time (say, five or ten years) in order to see whether it is possible to detect trends. However, the comparison of ratios from different time periods brings certain problems. In particular, there is always the possibility that trading *conditions may have been quite different in the periods being compared. There is the further problem that when comparing the performance of a single business over time, operating inefficiencies may not be clearly exposed. For example, the fact that net profit per employee has risen by 10 per cent over the previous period may at first sight appear to be satisfactory; however, this may not be the case if similar businesses have shown an improvement of 50 per cent for the same period. Finally, there is the problem that inflation may have distorted the figures on which the ratios are based. As we shall see later, inflation can lead to an overstatement of profit and an understatement of asset values.*

- **Planned performance.** *Ratios may be compared with the targets which management developed before the commencement of the period under review. The comparison of planned performance with actual performance may therefore be a useful way of revealing the level of achievement attained. However, the planned levels of performance must be based on realistic assumptions if they are to be useful for comparison purposes.*

- **Similar businesses.** *In a competitive environment, a business must consider its performance in relation to those of other businesses operating in the same industry. Survival may depend on the ability to achieve comparable levels of performance. Thus a very useful basis for comparing a particular ratio is the ratio achieved by similar businesses during the same period. This basis is not, however, without its problems. Competitors may have different year ends and, therefore, trading conditions may not be identical. They may also have different accounting policies, which can have a significant effect on reported profits and asset values (e.g. different methods of calculating depreciation, different methods of valuing stock, and so on). Finally, it may be difficult to get hold of the accounts of competitor businesses. Sole proprietorships and partnerships, for example, are not obliged to publish their financial statements. In the case of limited companies, there is a legal obligation to publish accounts. However, a diversified company may not provide a detailed breakdown of activities sufficient for analysts to compare with the activities of other businesses.*

The key steps in financial ratio analysis

When employing financial ratios, a sequence of three steps (see Figure 3.1) is carried out by the analyst. The first step involves identifying the key indicators and relationships which require examination. In order to carry out this step the analyst must be clear *who* the target users are and *why* they need the information. Different users of financial information are likely to have different information needs which will, in turn, determine the ratios which they find useful. For example, shareholders are likely to be interested in their returns in relation to the level of risk associated with their investment. Thus profitability, investment and gearing ratios will be of particular interest. Long-term lenders are concerned with

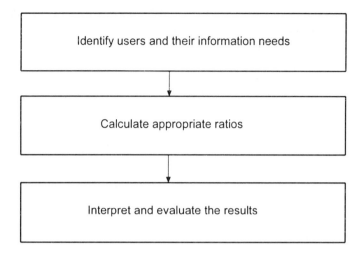

Figure 3.1   Financial ratio analysis: the key steps.

the long-term viability of the business. In order to help them to assess this, the profitability ratios and gearing ratios of the business are also likely to be of particular interest. Short-term lenders, such as suppliers, may be interested in the ability of the business to repay the amounts owing in the short term. As a result, the liquidity ratios should be of interest.

The next step in the process is to calculate ratios which are considered appropriate for the particular users and the purpose for which they require the information. The final step is interpretation and evaluation of the ratios. Interpretation involves examining the ratios in conjunction with an appropriate basis for comparison and any other information which may be relevant. The significance of the ratios calculated can then be established. Evaluation involves forming a judgement concerning the value of the information uncovered in the calculation and interpretation stage. Whilst calculation is usually straightforward, the interpretation and evaluation are more difficult and often require high levels of skill. This skill can only really be acquired through much practice.

The ratios calculated

Probably the best way to explain financial ratios is to go through an example. Example 3.1 provides a set of financial statements from which we can calculate important ratios. Note that the format of the cash flow statement is different to that used in Chapter 2. The cash flow statements in this earlier chapter were set out in a format suitable for internal management purposes and revealed a monthly breakdown of cash flows. The cash flow statement set out in Example 3.1, however, is a summary statement for the whole year and uses a format which is consistent with the accounting rules relating to the published financial reports of companies. Note that this format separates the cash flows into five categories in order to help users identify the main sources of cash flows. You may well be familiar with this format from your previous studies.

Example 3.1

The following financial statements relate to Alexis plc which owns a small chain of wholesale/retail carpet stores.

Balance sheets as at 31 March

	19X2		19X3	
	£000	£000	£000	£000
Fixed assets				
Freehold land and buildings at cost	451.2		451.2	
Less: Accumulated depreciation	70.0	381.2	75.0	376.2
Fixtures and fittings at cost	129.0		160.4	
Less: Accumulated depreciation	64.4	64.6	97.2	63.2
		445.8		439.4
Current assets				
Stock at cost	300.0		370.8	
Trade debtors	240.8		210.2	
Bank	33.5		41.0	
	574.3		622.0	
Creditors: amounts due within one year				
Trade creditors	(221.4)		(228.8)	
Dividends proposed	(40.2)		(60.0)	
Corporation tax due	(60.2)		(76.0)	
	(321.8)	252.5	(364.8)	257.2
		698.3		696.6
Creditors: amounts due beyond one year				
12% Debentures (secured)		200.0		60.0
		498.3		636.6
Capital and reserves				
£0.50 Ordinary shares		300.0		334.1
General reserve		26.5		40.0
Retained profit		171.8		262.5
		498.3		636.6

Profit and loss accounts for the year ended 31 March

	19X2		19X3	
	£000	£000	£000	£000
Sales		2,240.8		2,681.2
Less: cost of sales				
Opening stock	241.0		300.0	
Purchases	1,804.4		2,142.8	
	2,045.4		2,442.8	
Less: Closing stock	300.0	1,745.4	370.8	2,072.0
Gross profit		495.4		609.2
Wages and salaries	137.8		195.0	
Directors' salaries	48.0		80.6	
Rates	12.2		12.4	
Heat and light	8.4		13.6	
Insurance	4.6		7.0	
Interest payable	24.0		6.2	
Postage and telephone	3.4		7.4	
Audit fees	5.6		9.0	
Depreciation				
Freehold buildings	5.0		5.0	
Fixtures and fittings	27.0	276.0	32.8	369.0
Net profit before tax		219.4		240.2
Less: Corporation tax		60.2		76.0
Net profit after tax		159.2		164.2
Add: Retained profit brought forward		52.8		171.8
		212.0		336.0
Less:				
Transfer to general reserve		—		(13.5)
Dividends proposed		(40.2)		(60.0)
Retained profit carried forward		171.8		262.5

Cash flow statements for the year ended 31 March

	19X2		19X3	
	£000	£000	£000	£000
Net cash inflow from operations		231.0		251.4
Returns on investments and servicing of finance				
Interest paid	(24.0)		(6.2)	
Dividends paid	(32.0)		(40.2)	
Net cash inflow (outflow) from returns on investments and servicing of finance		(56.0)		(46.4)

Taxation	£000	£000	£000	£000
Corporation tax paid	(46.4)		(60.2)	
Tax paid		(46.4)		(60.2)
Investing activities				
Purchase of fixed assets	(121.2)		(31.4)	
Net cash inflow (outflow) from investing activities		(121.2)		(31.4)
Net cash inflow before financing		7.4		113.4
Financing activities				
Issue of ordinary shares	20.0		34.1	
Repayment of loan capital	—	20.0	(140.0)	(105.9)
Increase in cash and cash equivalents		27.4		7.5

Notes:
1. The company employed fourteen staff in 19X2 and eighteen in 19X3.
2. All sales and purchases are made on credit.
3. The market value of the shares of the company at the end of each year was £2.50 and £3.50 respectively. The issue of equity shares during the year ended 31 March 19X3 occurred at the beginning of the year.

Profitability

The following ratios may be used to evaluate the profitability of the business:

Return on owners' equity (ROE)

This ratio compares the amount of profit for the period available to the owners to the owners' stake in the business. For a limited company, the ratio (which is normally expressed in percentage terms) is as follows:

$$\text{ROE} = \frac{\text{Net profit after taxation and preference dividend (if any)}}{\text{Ordinary share capital plus reserves}} \times 100$$

The net profit after taxation and any preference dividend is used in calculating the ratio as this figure represents the amount of profit available to the owners.

In the case of Alexis plc, the ratio for the year ended 31 March 19X2 is:

$$= \frac{159.2}{498.3} \times 100$$

$$= 31.9\%.$$

ACTIVITY 3.2

Calculate the return on owners' equity (ROE) for Alexis plc for the year to 31 March 19X3.

The return on owners' equity (ROE) for the following year will be as follows:

$$ROE = \frac{164.2}{636.6} \times 100$$

$$= 25.8\%.$$

Note that in calculating the ratios above, the owners' equity as at the end of the year has been used. However, it can be argued that it is preferable to use an average figure for the year, as this would be more representative of the amount invested by owners during the period. The easiest approach to calculating the average equity investment would be to take a simple average based on the opening and closing figures for the year. However, where these figures are not available, it is acceptable to use the year-end figures.

Return on capital employed (ROCE)

This is a fundamental measure of business performance. This ratio expresses the relationship between the net profit generated by the business and the long-term capital invested in the business.

The ratio is expressed in percentage terms and is as follows:

$$ROCE = \frac{\text{Net profit before interest and taxation}}{\text{Share capital + reserves + long-term loans}} \times 100$$

Note, in this case, that the profit figure used in the ratio is the net profit *before* interest and taxation. This figure is used because the ratio attempts to measure the returns to all suppliers of long-term finance before any deductions for interest payable to lenders or payments of dividends to shareholders are made.

For the year to 31 March 19X2 the ratio for Alexis plc is:

$$ROCE = \frac{243.4}{698.3} \times 100$$

$$= 34.9\%.$$

ACTIVITY 3.3

Calculate the return on capital employed (ROCE) for the company for the year to 31 March 19X3.

For the year ended 31 March 19X3 the ROCE ratio is:

$$= \frac{246.8}{696.6} \times 100$$

$$= 35.4\%.$$

ROCE is considered by many to be a primary measure of profitability. It compares inputs (capital invested) with outputs (profit). This comparison is of vital importance in assessing the effectiveness with which funds have been deployed. Once again, an average figure for capital employed may be used where the information is available.

Net profit margin

This ratio relates the net profit for the period to the sales during that period. The ratio is expressed as follows:

$$\text{Net profit margin} = \frac{\text{Net profit before interest and taxation}}{\text{Sales}} \times 100$$

The net profit before interest and taxation is used in this ratio as it represents the profit from trading operations before any costs of servicing long-term finance are taken into account. This is often regarded as the most appropriate measure of operational performance for comparison purposes, as differences arising from the way in which a particular business is financed will not influence this measure. However, this is not the only way in which this ratio may be calculated in practice. The net profit after taxation is also used on occasions as the numerator.

For the year ended 31 March 19X2 the net profit margin ratio for Alexis plc (based on the net profit before interest and taxation) is:

$$\frac{243.4}{2,240.8} \times 100 = 10.9\%.$$

This ratio compares one output of the business (profit) to another output (sales). The ratio can vary considerably between types of business. For example, a supermarket will often operate on low profit margins in order to stimulate sales and thereby increase the total amount of profit generated. A jeweller, on the other hand, may have a high net profit margin but have a much lower level of sales volume. Factors such as the degree of competition, the type of customer, the economic climate and industry characteristics (such as the level of risk) will influence the net profit margins of a business.

┌─── **ACTIVITY 3.4** ───┐

Calculate the net profit margin for the company for the year to 31 March 19X3.

The net profit margin for the year to 31 March 19X3 will be:

$$= \frac{246.4}{2,681.2} \times 100$$

$$= 9.2\%.$$

Gross profit margin

This ratio relates the gross profit of the business to the sales generated for the same period. Gross profit represents the difference between sales and the cost of sales. The ratio is therefore a measure of profitability in buying (or producing) and selling goods before any other expenses are taken into account. As cost of sales represents a major expense for retailing and manufacturing businesses, a change in this ratio can have a significant effect on the 'bottom line' (i.e. the net profit for the year). The gross profit ratio is calculated as follows:

$$\text{Gross profit margin} = \frac{\text{Gross profit}}{\text{Sales}} \times 100$$

For the year to 31 March 19X2 the ratio for Alexis plc is as follows:

$$\text{Gross profit margin} = \frac{495.4}{2,240.8} \times 100$$

$$= 22.1\%.$$

┌─── **ACTIVITY 3.5** ───┐

Calculate the gross profit margin for the company for the year to 31 March 19X3.

The gross profit margin for the year to 31 March 19X3 is as follows:

$$= \frac{609.2}{2,681.2} \times 100$$

$$= 22.7\%.$$

The profitability ratios for the company over the two years can be set out as follows:

	19X2 (%)	19X3 (%)
Return on owners' equity	31.9	25.8
ROCE	34.9	35.4
Net profit margin	10.9	9.2
Gross profit margin	22.1	22.7

ACTIVITY 3.6

What do you deduce from a comparison of the profitability ratios over the two years?

The gross profit margin shows a slight increase in 19X3 over the previous year. This may be due to a number of reasons, such as increase in selling prices and a decrease in the cost of sales. However, the net profit margin has shown a slight decline over the period. This means that operating expenses (wages, rates, insurance, etc.) are absorbing a greater proportion of sales income in 19X3 than in the previous year.

The net profit available to equity shareholders has risen only slightly over the period, whereas the share capital and reserves of the company have increased considerably (see the financial statements). The effect of this has been to reduce the return to owners' equity. The ROCE has improved slightly in 19X3. The slight decrease in long-term capital over the period and increase in net profit before interest and tax has resulted in a better return.

Efficiency

Efficiency ratios examine the ways in which various resources of the business are managed. The following ratios consider some of the more important aspects of resource management.

Average stock turnover period

Stocks often represent a significant investment for a business. For some types of business (e.g. manufacturers), stocks may account for a substantial proportion of the total assets held. The average stock turnover period measures the average period for which stocks are being held. The ratio is calculated thus:

$$\text{Stock turnover period} = \frac{\text{Average stock held}}{\text{Cost of sales}} \times 365$$

The average stock for the period can be calculated as a simple average of the opening and closing stock levels for the year. However, in the case of a highly seasonal business, where stock levels may vary considerably over the year, a monthly average may be more appropriate.

In the case of Alexis plc the stock turnover period for the year ended 31 March 19X2 is:

$$\frac{(241 + 300)/2}{1,745.4} \times 365$$

= 57 days (to nearest day).

This means that, on average, the stock held is being 'turned over' every 57 days. A business will normally prefer a low stock turnover period to a high period, as funds tied up in stocks cannot be used for other purposes. In judging the amount of stock to carry, the business must consider such things as the likely future demand, the possibility of future shortages, the likelihood of future price rises, the amount of storage space available, the perishability of the product, and so on. The management of stocks will be considered in more detail in Chapter 10.

This ratio is sometimes expressed in terms of months rather than days. Multiplying by 12 rather than 365 will achieve this.

ACTIVITY 3.7

Calculate the average stock turnover period for Alexis plc for the year ended 31 March 19X3.

The stock turnover period for the year to 31 March 19X3 will be:

$$= \frac{(300 + 370.8)/2}{2,072} \times 365$$

= *59 days.*

Average settlement period for debtors

A business will usually be concerned with how long it takes for customers to pay the amounts owing. The speed of payment can have a significant effect on the cash flows of the business. The average settlement period calculates how long, on average, credit customers take to pay the amounts which they owe to the business. The ratio is as follows:

$$\text{Average settlement period} = \frac{\text{Trade debtors}}{\text{Credit sales}} \times 365$$

We are told that all sales made by Alexis plc are on credit and so the average settlement period for debtors for the year ended 31 March 19X2 is:

$$= \frac{240.8}{2,240.8} \times 365$$

$$= 39 \text{ days.}$$

As no figures for opening debtors are available, the year-end debtors figure only is used. This is common practice.

| ACTIVITY 3.8 |

Calculate the average settlement period for debtors for the year ended 31 March 19X3. (For the sake of consistency use the year-end debtors figure, rather than an average figure.)

The average settlement period for the year to 31 March 19X3 is:

$$\frac{210.2}{2,681.2} \times 365$$

$$= 29 \text{ days.}$$

A business will normally prefer a shorter average settlement period than a longer one as, once again, funds are being tied up which may be used for more profitable purposes. Although this ratio can be useful, it is important to remember that it produces an *average* figure for the number of days debts are outstanding. This average may be badly distorted by, for example, a few large customers who are very slow payers.

Average settlement period for creditors

This ratio measures how long, on average, the business takes to pay its trade creditors. The ratio is calculated as follows:

$$\text{Average settlement period} = \frac{\text{Trade creditors}}{\text{Credit purchases}} \times 365$$

For the year ended 31 March 19X2, the average settlement period for Alexis plc is:

$$= \frac{221.4}{1,804.4} \times 365$$

$$= 45 \text{ days.}$$

Once again, the year-end figure rather than an average figure for creditors has been employed in the calculations.

ACTIVITY 3.9

Calculate the average settlement period for creditors for Alexis plc for the year ended 31 March 19X3. (For the sake of consistency, use a year-end figure for creditors.)

The average settlement period is:

$$= \frac{228.8}{2,142.8} \times 365$$

$$= 39 \ days.$$

This ratio provides an average figure which, like the average settlement period for debtors ratio, can be distorted by the payment period for one or two large suppliers.

As trade creditors provide a free source of finance for the business, it is, perhaps, not surprising that some businesses attempt to increase their average settlement period for trade creditors. However, such a policy can be taken too far and can result in a loss of goodwill by suppliers. We will return to the issues concerning the management of trade debtors and trade creditors in Chapter 10.

Asset turnover ratio

This ratio examines how effectively the assets of the business are being employed in generating sales revenue. The ratio is calculated as follows:

$$\text{Asset turnover ratio} = \frac{\text{Sales}}{\text{Total assets employed}}$$

For the year ended 31 March 19X2 this ratio for Alexis plc is as follows:

$$= \frac{2,240.8}{(445.8 + 574.3)}$$

$$= 2.2 \ times.$$

Once again, year-end figures have been employed, although an average figure for total assets could also be used if sufficient information was available.

ACTIVITY 3.10

Calculate the asset turnover ratio for Alexis plc for the year ended 31 March 19X3. (For the sake of consistency, use a year-end figure for total assets.)

The asset turnover ratio for the year ended 31 March 19X3 will be:

$$= \frac{2,681.2}{(439.4 + 622.0)}$$

$$= 2.5 \ times$$

Generally speaking, a higher asset turnover ratio is preferred to a lower ratio. A higher ratio will normally suggest that assets are being used more productively in the generation of revenue. However, a very high ratio may suggest that the business is 'overtrading on its assets', that is, it has insufficient assets to match the level of sales achieved. When comparing this ratio between businesses, such factors as the age and condition of assets held, the valuation bases for assets and whether assets are rented or purchased outright can complicate interpretation.

A variation of this formula is to use the total assets less current liabilities (which is equivalent to long-term capital employed) in the denominator.

Sales per employee

This ratio relates sales generated to a particular business resource. It provides a measure of the productivity of the workforce. The ratio is:

$$\text{Sales per employee} = \frac{\text{Sales}}{\text{Number of employees}}$$

For the year ended 31 March 19X2 the ratio for Alexis plc is:

$$= \frac{£2,240,800}{14}$$

$$= £160,057$$

It would also be possible to calculate sales per square metre of floor space in order to help assess productivity. This ratio is often used by retail businesses.

ACTIVITY 3.11

Calculate the sales per employee for Alexis plc for the year ended 31 March 19X3.

The ratio for the year ended 31 March 19X3 is:

$$= \frac{£2,681,200}{18}$$

$$= £148,956$$

The activity ratios may be summarised as follows:

	19X2	19X3
Stock turnover period	57 days	59 days
Average settlement period for debtors	39 days	29 days
Average settlement period for creditors	45 days	39 days
Asset turnover	2.2 times	2.5 times
Sales per employee (£)	160,057	148,956

ACTIVITY 3.12

What do you deduce from a comparison of the efficiency ratios over the two years?

A comparison of the efficiency ratios between years provides a mixed picture. The average settlement period for both debtors and creditors has reduced. The reduction may have been the result of deliberate policy decisions (e.g. tighter credit control for debtors, paying creditors promptly in order to maintain goodwill or to take advantage of discounts). However, it must always be remembered that these ratios are average figures and may, therefore, be distorted by a few exceptional amounts owed to, or owed by, the company.

The stock turnover period has shown a slight decrease over the period but this may not be significant. Overall there has been an increase in the asset turnover ratio, which means that the sales have increased by a greater proportion than the assets of the company. Sales per employee, however, have declined and the reasons for this should be investigated.

The relationship between profitability and efficiency

In our earlier discussions concerning profitability ratios you will recall that return on capital employed (ROCE) is regarded as a key ratio by many businesses. The ratio is:

$$\text{ROCE} = \frac{\text{Net profit before interest and taxation}}{\text{Long-term capital employed}} \times 100$$

(i.e. share capital plus reserves plus long-term loans)

This ratio can be broken down into two elements, as shown in Figure 3.2. The first ratio is, of course the net profit margin ratio, and the second ratio is a slight variation of the asset turnover ratio which we discussed earlier (long-term capital employed is equal to total assets *less* current liabilities).

By breaking down the ROCE ratio in this manner, we highlight the fact that the overall return on funds employed within the business will be determined both by the profitability of sales and by efficiency in the use of assets.

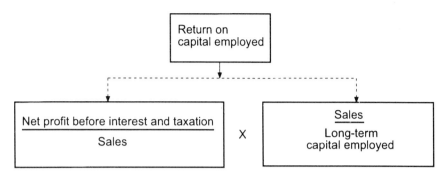

Figure 3.2 The main elements comprising the ROCE ratio.

Example 3.2

Consider the following information concerning two different businesses operating in the same industry:

	Business	
	A	B
Profit before interest and tax (£m)	20	15
Long-term capital employed (£m)	100	75
Sales (£m)	200	300

The ROCE for each business is identical (i.e. 20 per cent). However, the manner in which the return was achieved by each business was quite different. In the case of Business A, the net profit margin is 10 per cent and the asset turnover is 2 times (hence, ROCE = 10 per cent × 2 = 20 per cent). In the case of Business B, the net profit margin is 5 per cent and the asset turnover ratio is 4 times (hence, ROCE = 5 per cent × 4 = 20 per cent).

This demonstrates that a relatively low net profit margin can be compensated for by a relatively high asset turnover ratio and a relatively low asset turnover ratio can be compensated for by a relatively high net profit margin. In many areas of retail and distribution (e.g. supermarkets and delivery services), the net profit margins are quite low but the ROCE can be high, providing the assets are used productively.

Liquidity

Current ratio

This ratio compares the 'liquid' assets (i.e. cash and those assets held which will soon be turned into cash) of the business with the short-term liabilities (creditors due within one year). The ratio is calculated as follows:

$$\text{Current ratio} = \frac{\text{Current assets}}{\text{Current liabilities (creditors due within one year)}}$$

For the year ended 31 March 19X2 the current ratio of Alexis plc is:

$$\frac{574.3}{321.8}$$

$$= 1.8 \text{ times}$$

The ratio reveals that the current assets cover the current liabilities by 1.8 times. In some texts the notion of an 'ideal' current ratio (usually 2 times or 2:1) is suggested for businesses. However, this fails to take into account the fact that different types of business require different current ratios. For example, a manufacturing business will often have a relatively high current ratio because it is necessary to hold stocks of finished goods, raw materials and work-in-progress. It will also normally sell goods on credit, thereby incurring debtors. A supermarket chain, on the other hand, will have a relatively low ratio as it will hold only fast-moving stocks of finished goods and will generate mostly cash sales.

The higher the ratio, the more liquid the business is considered to be. As liquidity is of vital importance to the survival of a business, a higher current ratio is normally preferred to a lower ratio. However, if a business has a very high ratio, this may suggest that funds are being tied up in cash or other liquid assets and are not being used as productively as they might otherwise be.

ACTIVITY 3.13

Calculate the current ratio for Alexis plc for the year ended 31 March 19X3.

The current ratio for the year ended 31 March 19X3 is:

$$= \frac{622.0}{364.8}$$

$$= 1.7 \text{ times}$$

Acid-test ratio

This ratio represents a more stringent test of liquidity. It can be argued that, for many businesses, the stock in hand cannot be converted into cash quickly. (Note that in the case of Alexis plc the stock turnover period was more than fifty days in both years.) As a result, it may be better to exclude this particular asset from any measure of liquidity. The acid-test ratio is based on this idea and is calculated as follows:

$$\text{Acid-test ratio} = \frac{\text{Current assets (excluding stock)}}{\text{Current liabilities}}$$

The acid-test ratio for Alexis plc for the year ended 31 March 19X2 is:

$$= \frac{(574.3 - 300)}{321.8}$$

$$= 0.9 \text{ times}$$

We can see that the 'liquid' current assets do not quite cover the current liabilities and so the business may be experiencing some liquidity problems. In some types of business, however, where cash flows are strong, it is not unusual for the acid-test ratio to be below 1.0 without causing liquidity problems for the particular businesses.

The current and acid-test ratios for 19X2 can be expressed as 1.8:1 and 0.9:1 respectively, rather than as a number of times. This form can be found in some texts. The interpretation of the ratios, however, will not be affected by this difference in form.

ACTIVITY 3.14

Calculate the acid-test ratio for Alexis plc for the year ended 31 March 19X3.

The acid-test ratio for the year ended 31 March 19X3 is:

$$= \frac{(622.0 - 370.8)}{364.8}$$

$$= 0.7 \text{ times}$$

Both the current ratio and acid-test ratio derive the relevant figures from the balance sheet. As the balance sheet is simply a 'snapshot' of the financial position of the business at a single moment in time, care must be taken when interpreting the ratios. It is possible that the balance sheet figures are not representative of the liquidity position during the year. This may be due to exceptional factors or simply due to the fact that the business is seasonal in nature and the balance sheet figures represent the cash position at one particular point in the seasonal cycle only.

Operating cash flows to maturing obligations

This ratio compares the operating cash flows to the current liabilities of the business. It provides a further indication of the ability of the business to meet its maturing obligations. The ratio is calculated as follows:

Operating cash flows
———————————
Current liabilities

The higher this ratio, the better the liquidity of the business. This ratio has the advantage that the operating cash flows for a period usually provide a more reliable guide to the liquidity of a business than the current assets held at the balance sheet date. The ratio for the year ended 31 March 19X2 is:

$$= \frac{231.0}{321.8}$$

$$= 0.7 \text{ times}$$

This ratio indicates that the operating cash flows for the period are not sufficient to cover the current liabilities at the end of the period.

ACTIVITY 3.15

Calculate the operating cash flows to maturing obligations ratio for Alexis plc for the year ended 31 March 19X3:

The ratio is:

$$= \frac{251.4}{364.8}$$

$$= 0.7 \text{ times}$$

The liquidity ratios for the two year period may be summarised as follows:

	19X2	19X3
Current ratio	1.8	1.7
Acid-test ratio	0.9	0.7
Operating cash flows to maturing obligations	0.7	0.7

ACTIVITY 3.16

What do you deduce from a comparison of the liquidity ratios over the two years?

The table above reveals a decrease in both the current ratio and the acid-test ratio. These changes suggest a worsening liquidity position for the business. The company must monitor its liquidity carefully and be alert to any further deterioration in these ratios. The operating cash flows to maturing obligations ratio has not changed over the period. This ratio is quite low and reveals that the cash flows for the period do not cover the maturing obligations. This ratio should give some cause for concern.

Gearing

Gearing occurs when a business is financed, at least in part, by contributions from outside parties. The level of gearing (i.e. the extent to which a business is financed by outside parties) associated with a business is often an important factor in assessing risk. Where a business borrows heavily, it takes on a commitment to pay interest charges and make capital repayments. This can be a real financial burden and can increase the risk of a business becoming insolvent. Nevertheless, it is the case that most businesses are geared to some extent.

Given the risks involved, you may wonder why a business would want to take on gearing. One reason may be that the owners have insufficient funds and, therefore, the only way to finance the business adequately is to borrow from others. Another reason is that gearing can be used to increase the returns to owners. This is possible providing the returns generated from borrowed funds exceed the cost of paying interest. The issue of gearing is important and we will leave a detailed discussion of the topic until Chapter 8.

Gearing ratio

The following ratio measures the contribution of long-term lenders to the long-term capital structure of a business:

$$\text{Gearing ratio} = \frac{\text{Long-term liabilities}}{\text{Share capital} + \text{reserves} + \text{long-term liabilities}} \times 100$$

The gearing ratio for Alexis plc for the year ended 31 March 19X2 is:

$$= \frac{200}{(498.3 + 200)} \times 100 = 28.6\%$$

This ratio reveals a level of gearing which would not normally be considered to be very high.

ACTIVITY 3.17

Calculate the gearing ratio of Alexis plc for the year ended 31 March 19X3.

The gearing ratio for the following year will be:

$$= \frac{60}{(636.6 + 60)} \times 100$$

$$= 8.6\%$$

This ratio reveals a substantial fall in the level of gearing over the year.

Interest cover ratio

This ratio measures the amount of profit available to cover interest payable. The ratio may be calculated as follows:

$$\text{Interest cover ratio} = \frac{\text{Profit before interest and taxation}}{\text{Interest payable}}$$

The ratio for Alexis plc for the year ended 31 March 19X2 is:

$$= \frac{(219.0 + 24)}{24}$$

$$= 10.1 \text{ times}$$

This ratio shows that the level of profit is considerably higher than the level of interest payable. Thus a significant fall in profits could occur before profit levels failed to cover interest payable. The lower the level of profit coverage, the greater the risk to lenders that interest payments will not be met.

ACTIVITY 3.18

Calculate the interest cover ratio of Alexis plc for the year ended 31 March 19X3.

The interest cover ratio for the year ended 31 March 19X3 is:

$$= \frac{(240.2 + 6.2)}{6.2}$$

$$= 39.7 \text{ times}$$

ACTIVITY 3.19

What do you deduce from a comparison of the gearing ratios over the two years?

The ratios are:

	19X2	19X3
Gearing ratio	28.6%	8.6%
Interest cover ratio	10.1 times	39.7 times

Both the gearing ratio and interest cover ratio have improved significantly in 19X3. This is mainly due to the fact that a substantial part of the long-term loan was repaid during 19X3. This repayment has had the effect of reducing the relative contribution of long-term lenders to the financing of the company and reducing the amount of interest payable.

The gearing ratio at the end of 19X3 would normally be considered to be very low and may indicate that the business has some debt capacity (i.e. it is capable of borrowing more if required). However, the availability of adequate security and profitability must also be taken into account before the debt capacity of a business can be properly established.

Investment ratios

There are various ratios available which are designed to help investors assess the returns on their investment. Below we consider some of these ratios.

Dividend per share

The dividend per share ratio relates the dividends announced during a period to the number of shares in issue during that period. The ratio is calculated as follows:

$$\text{Dividend per share} = \frac{\text{Dividends announced during the period}}{\text{Number of shares in issue}}$$

In essence, the ratio provides an indication of the cash return which an investor receives from holding shares in a company.

Although it is a useful measure, it must always be remembered that the dividends received will usually only represent a partial measure of return to investors. Dividends are usually only a proportion of the total earnings generated by the company and available to shareholders. A company may decide to plough back some of its earnings into the business in order to achieve future growth. These ploughed-back profits also belong to the shareholders and should, in principle, increase the value of the shares held.

When assessing the total returns to investors we must take account of the cash returns received *plus* any change in the market value of the shares held.

The dividends per share for Alexis plc for the year ended 31 March 19X2 is:

$$= \frac{40.2}{600} \text{ (i.e 300 @ £0.50)}$$

$$= 6.7\text{p}$$

This ratio can be calculated for each class of share issued by a company. Alexis plc has only ordinary shares in issue and therefore only one dividend per share ratio can be calculated.

ACTIVITY 3.20

Calculate the dividend per share of Alexis plc for the year ended 31 March 19X3.

Your answer to this activity should be as follows:

$$= \frac{60.0}{668.2}$$

$$= 9.0p$$

Dividends per share can vary considerably between companies. A number of factors will influence the amount a company is prepared to issue in the form of dividends to shareholders. These factors will be considered in detail in Chapter 9. Comparing dividend per share between companies is not always useful, as there may be differences between the nominal value of shares issued. However, it is often useful to monitor the trend of dividends per share for a company over a period of time.

Dividend payout ratio

The dividend payout ratio measures the proportion of earnings which a company pays out to shareholders in the form of dividends. The ratio is calculated as follows:

$$\text{Dividend payout ratio} = \frac{\text{Dividends announced for the year}}{\text{Earnings for the year available for dividends}} \times 100$$

In the case of ordinary shares, the earnings available for dividend will normally be the net profit after taxation and after any preference dividends announced during the period. This ratio is normally expressed as a percentage.

The dividend payout ratio for Alexis plc for the year ended 31 March 19X2 is:

$$\text{Dividend payout ratio} = \frac{40.2}{159.2} \times 100$$

$$= 25.3\%$$

ACTIVITY 3.21

Calculate the dividend payout ratio of Alexis plc for the year ended 31 March 19X3.

Your answer to this activity should be as follows:

$$= \frac{60.0}{164.2} \times 100$$

$$= 36.5\%$$

Dividend yield ratio

This ratio relates the cash return from a share to its current market value. This can help investors assess the cash return on their investment in the company. The ratio is:

$$\text{Dividend yield} = \frac{\text{Dividend per share}/(1-t)}{\text{Market value per share}} \times 100$$

This ratio is also expressed as a percentage.

The numerator of this ratio requires some explanation. In the United Kingdom, investors who receive a dividend from a company also receive a tax credit. This tax credit is equal to the amount of tax that would be payable on the dividends received by a lower rate taxpayer. As this tax credit can be offset against any tax liability arising from the dividends received, this means the dividends are effectively issued net of tax to lower rate income tax payers.

Investors may wish to compare the returns from shares with the returns from other forms of investment. As these other forms of investment are often quoted on a 'gross' (i.e. pre-tax) basis, it is useful to 'gross up' the dividend in order to facilitate comparisons. This can be done by dividing the dividend per share by $(1 - t)$ where t is the lower rate of income tax.

Assuming a lower rate of income tax of 20 per cent, the dividend yield for Alexis plc for the year ended 31 March 19X2 is:

$$\text{Dividend yield} = \frac{6.7/(1-0.20)}{2.50} \times 100$$

$$= 3.4\%$$

ACTIVITY 3.22

Calculate the dividend yield for Alexis plc for the year ended 31 March 19X3.

Your answer to this activity should be as follows:

$$= \frac{9.0/(1-0.20)}{3.50} \times 100$$

$$= 3.2\%$$

Earnings per share

The earnings per share (EPS) of a company relates the earnings generated by the company during a period and available to shareholders, to the number of shares in issue. For ordinary shareholders, the amount available will be represented by the net profit after tax (less any preference dividend where applicable). The ratio for ordinary shareholders is calculated as follows:

$$\text{Earnings per share} = \frac{\text{Earnings available to ordinary shareholders}}{\text{Number of ordinary shares in issue}}$$

In the case of Alexis plc, the earnings per share for the year ended 31 March 19X2 will be as follows:

$$\text{Earnings per share} = \frac{159.2}{600}$$

$$= 26.5\text{p}$$

This ratio is regarded by many investment analysts as a fundamental measure of share performance. The trend in earnings per share over time is used to help assess the investment potential of a company's shares.

Although it is possible to make total profits rise through ordinary shareholders investing more in the company, this will not necessarily mean that the profitability *per share* will rise as a result.

ACTIVITY 3.23

Calculate the earnings per share of Alexis plc for the year ended 31 March 19X3.

The earnings per share for the year ended 31 March 19X3 will be:

$$= \frac{164.2}{668.2}$$

$$= 24.6p$$

In this case, the new issue of shares occurred at the beginning of the financial year. Where an issue is made part the way through the year, a weighted average of the shares in issue will be taken based on the date at which the new share issue took place.

It is not usually very helpful to compare the earnings per share of one company with those of another. Differences in capital structures can render any such comparison meaningless. However, like dividend per share, it can be very useful to monitor the changes which occur in this ratio for a particular company over time.

Operating cash flow per share

It can be argued that, in the short run at least, operating cash flows provide a better guide to the ability of a company to pay dividends and to undertake planned expenditures than the earnings figure. The operating cash flow per share is calculated as follows:

$$\frac{\text{Operating cash flows} - \text{preference dividends}}{\text{Number of ordinary shares in issue}}$$

The ratio for Alexis plc for the year ended 31 March 19X2 is as follows:

$$= \frac{231.0}{600.0}$$

$$= 38.5p$$

ACTIVITY 3.24

Calculate the operating cash flow (OCF) per share for Alexis plc for the year ended 31 March 19X3.

Your answer should be as follows:

$$= \frac{251.4}{668.2}$$

$$= 37.6p$$

There has been a slight decline in this ratio over the two-year period.

Note that, for both years, the operating cash flow per share is higher than the earnings per share. This is not unusual. The effect of adding back depreciation in order to derive operating cash flows will usually ensure that a higher figure is derived.

Price-earnings ratio

The price-earnings (P/E) ratio relates the market value of a share to the earnings per share. This ratio can be calculated as follows:

$$\text{Price-earnings ratio} = \frac{\text{Market value per share}}{\text{Earnings per share}}$$

The P/E ratio for Alexis plc for the year ended 31 March 19X2 will be:

$$P/E \text{ ratio} = \frac{£2.50}{26.5p}$$

$$= 9.4 \text{ times.}$$

This ratio reveals that the capital value of the share is 9.4 times higher than its current level of earnings. The ratio is, in essence, a measure of market confidence concerning the future of a company. The higher the P/E ratio, the greater the confidence in the future earning power of the company and, consequently, the more investors are prepared to pay in relation to the earnings stream of the company.

P/E ratios provide a useful guide to market confidence concerning the future and can therefore be helpful when comparing different companies. However, differences in accounting conventions between businesses can lead to different profit and earnings per share figures and this can distort comparisons.

ACTIVITY 3.25

Calculate the P/E ratio of Alexis plc for the year ended 31 March 19X3.

Your answer to this activity should be as follows:

$$= \frac{£3.50}{24.6p}$$

$$= 14.2 \text{ times}$$

The investment ratios for Alexis plc over the two-year period are as follows:

	19X2	19X3
Dividend per share	6.7p	9.0p
Dividend payout ratio	25.3%	36.5%
Dividend yield ratio	3.4%	3.2%
Earnings per share	26.5p	24.6p
Operating cash flow per share	38.5p	37.6p
P/E ratio	9.4T	14.2T

ACTIVITY 3.26

What do you deduce from the investment ratios set out above?

There has been a significant increase in the dividend per share in 19X3 as compared to the previous year. The dividend payout ratio reveals that this can be attributed, at least in part, to an increase in the proportion of earnings distributed to ordinary shareholders. However, the payout ratio for the year ended 31 March 19X3 is still fairly low. Only about a third of earnings available for dividend is being distributed.

The dividend yield has changed very little over the period and remains fairly low at less than 4.0 per cent.

Earnings per share show a slight fall in 19X3 when compared with the previous year. A slight fall also occurs in the operating cash flows per share. However, the price earnings ratio shows a significant improvement. The market is clearly much more confident about the future prospects of the business at the end of the year to 31 March 19X3.

EXHIBIT 3.1

Investment ratios can vary significantly between companies and between industries. To give you some indication of the variation which occurs, the average dividend yield ratio and P/E ratio for Stock Exchange listed businesses falling within twelve different industries are shown in Figures 3.3 and 3.4 respectively (see page 72).

SELF-ASSESSMENT QUESTION 3.1

A plc and B plc operate electrical wholesale stores in the south of England. The accounts of each company for the year ended 30 June 19X4 are as follows:

Balance sheets as at 30 June 19X4

	A plc		B plc	
	£000	£000	£000	£000
Fixed assets				
Freehold land and buildings at cost	436.0		615.0	
Less: Accumulated depreciation	76.0	360.0	105.0	510.0
Fixtures and fittings at cost	173.4		194.6	
Less: Accumulated depreciation	86.4	87.0	103.4	91.2
		447.0		601.2
Current assets				
Stock at cost	592.0		403.0	
Debtors	176.4		321.9	
Cash at bank	100.6		109.0	
	869.0		833.9	
Creditors: amounts due within one year				
Trade creditors	(271.4)		(180.7)	
Dividends	(135.0)		(95.0)	
Corporation tax	(32.0)		(34.8)	
	(438.4)	430.6	(310.5)	523.4
		877.6		1,124.6

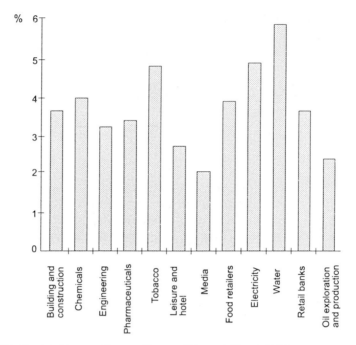

Figure 3.3   Dividend yield ratios (Source: *Financial Times*, 1 March 1996)

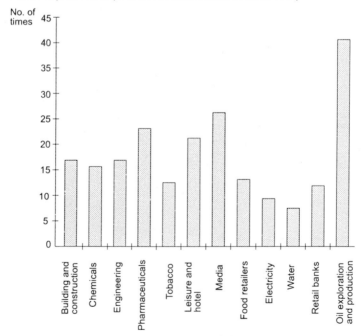

Figure 3.4   P/E ratios (Source: *Financial Times*, 1 March 1996)

Creditors: amounts due beyond one year	£000		£000
Debentures	190.0		250.0
	687.6		874.6
Capital and reserves			
£1 Ordinary shares	320.0		250.0
General reserves	355.9		289.4
Retained profit	11.7		335.2
	687.6		874.6

Trading and profit and loss accounts for the year ended 30 June 19X4

	A plc		B plc	
	£000	£000	£000	£000
Sales		1,478.1		1,790.4
Less: Cost of sales				
Opening stock	480.8		372.6	
Purchases	1,129.5		1,245.3	
	1,610.3		1,617.9	
Less: Closing stock	592.0	1,018.3	403.0	1,214.9
Gross profit		459.8		575.5
Wages and salaries	150.4		189.2	
Directors' salaries	45.4		96.2	
Rates	28.5		15.3	
Heat and light	15.8		17.2	
Insurance	18.5		26.8	
Interest payments	19.4		27.5	
Postage and telephone	12.4		15.9	
Audit fees	11.0		12.3	
Depreciation				
Freehold buildings	8.8		12.9	
Fixtures and fittings	17.7	327.9	22.8	436.1
Net profit before tax		131.9		139.4
Less: Corporation tax		32.0		34.8
Net profit after taxation		99.9		104.6
Add: Retained profit brought forward		46.8		325.6
		146.7		430.2
Dividends proposed		135.0		95.0
Retained profit carried forward		11.7		335.2

Notes:
1. All purchases and sales are on credit.
2. The market value of the shares in each company at the end of the year were £6.50 and £8.20 respectively.

> Required:
>
> (a) Calculate six different ratios which are concerned with liquidity, gearing and investment.
> (b) What can you conclude from the ratios you have calculated?

Financial ratios and the problem of overtrading

Overtrading occurs where a business is operating at a level of activity which cannot be supported by the amount of finance which has been committed. This situation usually reflects a poor level of financial control over the business. The reasons for overtrading are varied. It may occur in young expanding businesses which fail to prepare adequately for the rapid increase in demand for their goods or services. It may also occur in businesses where the managers may have miscalculated the level of expected sales demand or have failed to control escalating project costs. It may occur where the owners are unable to inject further funds into the business and are unable to persuade others to invest in the business. Whatever the reason for overtrading, the problems which it brings must be dealt with if the business is to survive over the longer term.

Overtrading results in liquidity problems such as exceeding borrowing limits, slow repayment of lenders and creditors, and so on. It can also result in suppliers withholding supplies, thereby making it difficult to meet customer needs. The managers of the business may be forced to direct all their efforts to dealing with immediate and pressing problems such as finding cash to meet interest charges due, or paying wages. Longer-term planning becomes difficult and managers may spend their time going from crisis to crisis. At the extreme, a business may collapse because it cannot meet its maturing obligations. In order to deal with the overtrading problem, a business must ensure that the finance available is commensurate with the level of operations. Thus, if a business which is overtrading is unable to raise new finance, it should cut back its level of operations in line with existing finance available. Although this may mean lost sales and lost profits in the short term, it may be necessary to ensure survival over the longer term.

ACTIVITY 3.27

If a business is overtrading, do you think the following ratios would be higher or lower than normally expected?

1. Current ratio.
2. Average stock turnover period.
3. Average settlement period for debtors.
4. Average settlement period for creditors.

Your answer should be as follows:

1. *The current ratio would be lower than normally expected. This is a measure of liquidity and lack of liquidity is an important symptom of overtrading.*
2. *The average stock turnover period would be lower than normally expected. Where a business is overtrading, the level of stocks held will be low because of the problems of financing stocks. In the short term, sales may not be badly affected by the low stock levels and therefore stocks will be turned over more quickly.*
3. *The average settlement period for debtors may be lower than normally expected. Where a business is suffering from liquidity problems it may chase debtors more vigorously so as to improve cash flows.*
4. *The average settlement period for creditors may be higher than normally expected. The business may try to delay payments to creditors because of the liquidity problems arising.*

Trend analysis

It is important to see whether there are trends occurring which can be detected from the use of ratios. Thus key ratios can be plotted on a graph to provide users with a simple visual display of changes occurring over time. The trends occurring within a company may be plotted against trends occurring within the industry as a whole for comparison purposes. An example of trend analysis is shown in Figure 3.5.

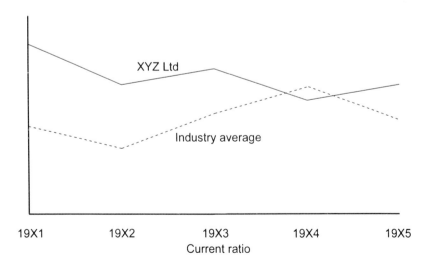

Figure 3.5 Graph plotting current ratio against time

EXHIBIT 3.2

Some companies publish certain key financial ratios as part of their annual accounts in order to help users identify important trends. These ratios may cover several years. The following ratios are included in the accounts of Marks & Spencer plc for 1994:

	1994	*1993*	*1992*	*1991*	*1990*
Gross margin (%)	35.1	34.8	33.8	33.1	32.8
Net margin (%)	13.4	12.5	11.9	11.1	11.3
Return on equity (%)	18.4	17.7	14.6	17.1	19.2
Dividend cover* (times)	2.3	2.2	1.9	2.1	2.3
Gearing ratio (%)	–	4.2	9.8	13.5	16.7

* The dividend cover ratio is, basically, the converse of the dividend payout ratio considered earlier. The ratio is the earnings available for dividend divided by the dividends announced. It measures the extent to which dividends are covered by current earnings.

The use of ratios in predicting financial distress

Financial ratios, based on current or past performance, are often used to help predict the future. However, both the choice of ratios and the interpretation of results are normally dependent on the judgement of the analyst. In recent years, however, attempts have been made to develop a more rigorous and systematic approach to the use of ratios for prediction purposes. In particular, researchers have shown an interest in the ability of ratios to predict financial distress in a business. This, of course, is an area with which all those connected with the business are likely to be concerned.

A number of methods and models employing ratios have now been developed which claim to predict future financial distress. Early research focused on the examination of ratios on an individual basis to see whether they were good or bad predictors of financial distress. The first research in this area was carried out by Beaver (1966) which compared the mean ratios of 79 businesses which failed over a ten-year period with a sample of 79 businesses which did not fail over this period.[1] (The research used a matched pair design so that each failed business was matched with a non-failed business which was similar in size and industry type.) Beaver found that certain mean ratios exhibited a marked difference between the failed and non-failed businesses for up to five years prior to failure. The results of six ratios employed by Beaver in his study are set out in Figure 3.6.

Research by Zmijewski (1983) using a sample of 72 failed and 3,573 non-failed businesses over a six-year period found that failed businesses were characterised

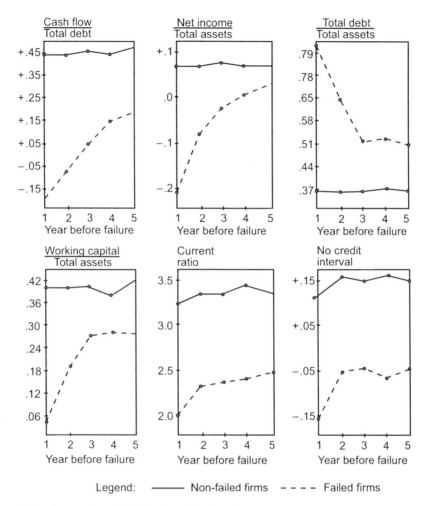

Figure 3.6 Mean ratios of failed and non-failed businesses

by lower rates of return, higher levels of gearing, lower levels of coverage for their fixed interest payments and more variable returns on shares.[2] Whilst you may not find these results very surprising, it is interesting to note that Zmijewski, like a number of other researchers in this area, did not find liquidity ratios particularly useful in identifying financial distress.

The approach adopted by Beaver and Zmijewski is referred to as univariate analysis because it looks at one ratio at a time. Although this approach can produce interesting results, there are practical problems associated with its use. Let us say, for example, that past research has identified two ratios as being good predictors in identifying financial distress. When applied to a particular business, however, it may be found that one ratio will predict financial distress, whereas the other does not. Given these conflicting signals, how should the decision-maker interpret the results?

The weaknesses of univariate analysis have led researchers to develop models which combine ratios in such a way as to produce a single index that can be interpreted more clearly. One approach to model development, much favoured by researchers, employs multiple discriminate analysis (MDA). This is, in essence, a statistical technique which can be used to draw a boundary line between those businesses which fail and those businesses which do not fail. This boundary line is referred to as the *discriminate function*. MDA is similar to regression analysis, insofar that it attempts to identify those factors which are likely to influence a particular event (such as financial failure). However, unlike regression analysis, it assumes the observations come from two different populations (e.g. failed and non-failed businesses) rather than a single population.

To illustrate this approach, let us assume we wish to test whether two ratios (say, the current ratio and the return on capital employed ratio) can help predict distress. To do this, we can calculate these ratios for a sample of failed businesses and then for a matched sample of non-failed businesses. From these two sets of data, we can produce a scatter diagram which plots each business according to these two ratios to produce a single coordinate. In Figure 3.7, we see an illustration of this approach. The businesses which have a coordinate marked with a × are the failed businesses and the businesses which have a coordinate marked with a • are the non-failed businesses. Using the observations displayed on the diagram, we then try to identify the boundary line between the failed and the non-failed businesses.

We can see that those businesses which fall to the left of the boundary line are predominantly failed companies and those which fall to the right are predominantly non-failed companies. Note that, in the diagram, there is some overlap between the two populations. The boundary line produced is unlikely, in practice, to eliminate all errors (i.e. some companies which fail may fall on the side of the boundary with non-failed companies or vice versa). However, it will *minimise* the misclassification errors.

The boundary line shown in the diagram can be expressed in the following form:

$$Z = a + b \text{ (current ratio)} + c \text{ (ROCE)}$$

where a is a constant and where b and c are weights to be attached to each ratio. A weighted average or total score (Z) is then derived. The weights given to the two ratios will depend on the slope of the boundary line and its absolute position.

Edward Altman (1968) in the United States was the first to develop a discriminant function using financial ratios, in order to predict financial distress.[3] The Z score model (as it is known) which Altman developed is based on five financial ratios and is as follows:

$$Z = 1.2a + 1.4b + 3.3c + 0.6d + 1.0e$$

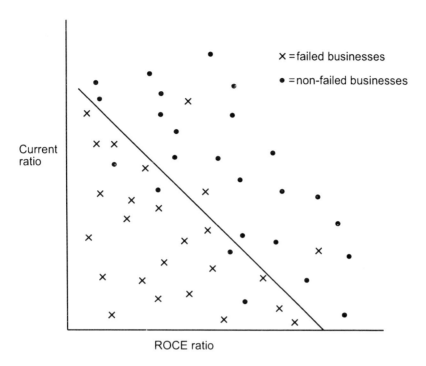

Figure 3.7 Scatter diagram showing the distribution of failed and non-failed businesses

where:

a = working capital/total assets;
b = accumulated retained profits/total assets;
c = profit before interest and taxation/total assets;
d = market value of ordinary and preference shares/total liabilities at book value; and
e = sales/total assets.

In order to develop this model, Altman carried out experiments using a paired sample of failed businesses and non-failed businesses and collected relevant data for each business for five years prior to failure. He found that the model shown above was able to predict failure for up to two years prior to bankruptcy. However, the predictive accuracy of the model became weaker the further the period from failure. The ratios used in this model were identified by Altman through a process of trial and error as there is no underlying theory of financial distress to help guide researchers select appropriate ratios. According to Altman, those companies with a Z score of less than 1.81 failed and the lower the score the greater the probability of failure. Those with a Z score greater than 2.99 did not fail. Those businesses with a Z score between 1.81 and 2.99 occupied a 'zone of ignorance' and were more difficult to classify as either being failed or non-failed businesses. However, the model, overall, was able to classify 95 per cent of the businesses correctly.

In recent years this model has been updated, and other models, using a similar approach, have been developed throughout the world. In the United Kingdom, Taffler has developed separate Z score models for different types of business.

The prediction of financial distress is not the only area where research into the predictive ability of ratios has taken place. Researchers have also developed ratio-based models which claim to assess the vulnerability of a company to takeover by another company. This is, of course, another area which is of vital importance to all those connected with the business and is considered in more detail in Chapter 11.

Limitations of ratio analysis

Although ratios offer a quick and useful method of analysing the position and performance of a business, they are not without their problems and limitations. Some of the more important limitations are now considered.

Quality of financial statements

It must always be remembered that ratios are based on financial statements and the results of ratio analysis are dependent on the quality of these underlying statements. Ratios will inherit the limitations of the financial statements on which they are based. In recent years, for example, the conventional accounts have been distorted as a result of changing price levels. Traditional accounting assumes, unfortunately, that the monetary unit will remain stable over time, even though there have been high levels of inflation during the last few decades. One effect of inflation has been that values for assets held for any length of period may bear little relation to current values. Generally speaking, the value of assets held will be understated in current terms during a period of inflation as they are recorded at their original cost (less any amount written off for depreciation). This means that comparisons, either between businesses or between periods, will be hindered. A difference in, say, an asset turnover ratio may simply be due to the fact that assets in one of the balance sheets being compared were acquired more recently (ignoring the effect of depreciation on asset values).

The value of freehold land, in particular, increased rapidly during the 1970s and 1980s, at least partly as a result of inflation. In order to present a more realistic view of the financial position, some companies began the practice of revaluing their freehold land periodically and showing the revalued amount on the balance sheet. This partial response to inflation, however, can create further problems when comparing ratios. Certain key ratios such as return on capital employed and asset turnover can be greatly changed as a result of changes in the values assigned to freehold land (or indeed other assets).

Another effect of changing prices is to distort the measurement of profit. Sales revenue for a period is often matched against costs from an earlier period. This is because there is often a time lag between acquiring a particular resource and using it in the business. For example, stocks may be acquired in one period and sold in a later period. During a period of inflation, this will mean that the costs do not reflect current prices. As a result, costs will be understated in the current profit and loss account, and this, in turn, means that profits will be overstated. One effect of this will be to distort the profitability ratios discussed above.

The restricted vision of ratios

It is important not to rely on ratios exclusively and thereby lose sight of information contained in the underlying financial statements. Some items reported in these statements can be of vital importance in assessing position and performance. For example, the total sales, capital employed and profit figures may be useful in assessing changes in absolute size which occur over time, or differences in scale between businesses. Ratios do not provide such information. In comparing one figure with another, ratios measure *relative* performance and position and, therefore, provide only part of the picture. Thus, when comparing two businesses, it will often be useful to assess the absolute size of profits, as well as the relative profitability of each business. For example, Company A may generate £1m. profit and have a ROCE of 15 per cent and Company B may generate £100,000 profit and have a ROCE of 20 per cent. Although Company B has higher level of *profitability*, as measured by ROCE, it generates lower total profits.

The basis for comparison

We saw earlier that ratios require a basis for comparison in order to be useful. Moreover, it is important that the analyst compares like with like. When comparing businesses, however, no two businesses will be identical, and the greater the differences between the businesses being compared, the greater the limitations of ratio analysis. Furthermore, when comparing businesses, differences in such matters as accounting policies, financing policies and financial year ends will add to the problems of evaluation.

Balance sheet ratios

Because the balance sheet is only a 'snapshot' of the business at a particular moment in time, any ratios based on balance sheet figures, such as the liquidity ratios above, may not be representative of the financial position of the business for the year as a whole. For example, it is common for a seasonal business to have a financial year end which coincides with a low point in business activity. Thus stocks and debtors may be low at the balance sheet date and the liquidity ratios may also be low as a result. A more representative picture of liquidity can only really be gained by taking additional measurements at other points in the year.

Summary

In this chapter, we saw that ratios can be used to analyse various aspects of the position and performance of a business. Used properly, they help to provide a quick thumbnail sketch of a business. However, they require a sound basis for comparison and will only be as useful as the quality of the underlying financial statements permit. Although they can highlight certain strengths and weaknesses concerning financial performance and position, they do not identify underlying causes. This can only be done through a more detailed investigation of business practices and records.

We have also seen that ratios are being used increasingly to predict the future. In this chapter we saw how certain ratios, when combined into a single index, can be used to predict financial distress.

References

1.   W.H. Beaver, 'Financial ratios as predictors of failure' Empirical Research in Accounting: Selected Studies', *Journal of Accounting Research*, Supplement, 1966, pp. 71–111.
2.   M.E. Zmijewski, *Predicting Corporate Bankruptcy: An empirical comparison of the extent of financial distress models*, State University of New York, 1983.
3.   E.I. Altman, 'Financial ratios, discriminant analysis and the prediction of corporate bankruptcy', *Journal of Finance*, September 1968, pp. 589–609.

Review questions

3.1   Some businesses operate on a low net profit margin (e.g. a supermarket chain). Does this mean that the return on capital employed from the business will also be low?

3.2   What potential problems arise for the external analyst from the use of balance sheet figures in the calculation of financial ratios?

3.3   Is it responsible to publish the Z scores of companies which are in financial difficulties? What are the problems of doing this?

3.4   Identify and discuss three reasons why the P/E ratio of two companies operating within the same industry may differ.

Examination-style questions _____

Solutions to those questions marked with an asterisk are given at the end of the text. Question 3.1–3.3 are at a basic level. Questions 3.4–3.6 are at an intermediate/ advanced level.

3.1 C. George (Western) Ltd has recently produced its accounts for the current year. The board of directors met to consider the accounts and, at this meeting, concern was expressed that the return on capital employed had decreased from 14 per cent last year to 12 per cent for the current year.

The following reasons were suggested as to why this reduction in ROCE had occurred:

1. Increase in the gross profit margin.
2. Reduction in sales.
3. Increase in overhead expenses.
4. Increase in amount of stock held.
5. Repayment of a loan at the year end.
6. Increase in the time taken for debtors to pay.

Required:

State, with reasons, which of the above might lead to a reduction in ROCE.

3.2* Business A and Business B are both engaged in retailing, but seem to take a different approach to this trade according to the information available. This information consists of a table of ratios, as follows:

Ratio	Business A	Business B
Return on capital employed (ROCE)	20%	17%
Return on owners equity (ROE)	30%	18%
Average settlement period for debtors	63 days	21 days
Average settlement period for creditors	50 days	45 days
Gross profit percentage	40%	15%
Net profit percentage	10%	10%
Stock turnover	52 days	25 days

Required:

(a) Explain how each ratio is calculated.
(b) Describe what this information indicates about the differences in approach between the two businesses. If one of them prides itself on personal service and one of them on competitive prices, which do you think is which and why?

3.3 Conday and Co. Ltd has been in operation for three years and produces antique reproduction furniture for the export market. The most recent set of accounts for the company is set out below:

Balance sheet as at 30 November 19X0

	£000	£000	£000
Fixed assets			
Freehold land and buildings at cost			228
Plant and machinery at cost		942	
Less: Accumulated depreciation		180	762
			990
Current assets			
Stocks		600	
Trade debtors		820	
		1,420	
Less: **Creditors: amounts falling due within one year**			
Trade creditors	665		
Taxation	95		
Bank overdraft	385	1,145	275
			1,265
Less: **Creditors amounts falling due in more than one year**			
12% debentures (note 1)			200
			1,065
Capital and reserves			
Ordinary shares of £1 each			700
Retained profits			365
			1,065

Profit and loss account for the year ended 30 November 19X0

	£000	£000
Sales		2,600
Less: Cost of sales		1,620
Gross profit		980
Less: Selling and distribution expenses (note 2)	408	
Administration expenses	174	
Finance expenses	78	660
Net profit before taxation		320
Less: Corporation tax		95
Net profit after taxation		225
Less: Proposed dividend		160
Retained profit for the year		65

Notes:
1. The debentures are secured on the freehold land and buildings.
2. Selling and distribution expenses include £170,000 in respect of bad debts.

An investor has been approached by the company to invest £200,000 by purchasing ordinary shares in the company at £6.40 each. The company wishes to use the funds to finance a programme of further expansion.

Required:

(a) Analyse the financial position and performance of the company and comment on any features you consider to be significant.
(b) State, with reasons, whether or not the investor should invest in the company on the terms outlined.

3.4* The directors of Helena Beauty Products Ltd have been presented with the following abridged accounts for the current year and the preceding year:

Profit and loss accounts for the year ended 30 September

	19X6		19X7	
	£000	£000	£000	£000
Sales		3,600		3,840
Less: Cost of sales				
Opening stock	320		400	
Purchases	2,240		2,350	
	2,560		2,750	
Less: Closing stock	400	2,160	500	2,250
Gross profit		1,440		1,590
Less: Expenses		1,360		1,500
Net profit		80		90

Balance sheets as at 30 September

	19X6		19X7	
	£000	£000	£000	£000
Fixed assets		1,900		1,860
Current assets				
Stock	400		500	
Debtors	750		960	
Bank	8		4	
	1,158		1,464	
Less: **Creditors: amounts due within one year**	390	768	450	1,014
		2,668		2,874

Capital and reserves	£000	£000
£1 Ordinary shares	1,650	1,766
Reserves	1,018	1,108
	2,668	2,874

Required:

Using six ratios, comment on the profitability and efficiency of the business as revealed by the accounts shown above.

3.5   Threads Limited manufactures nuts and bolts which are sold to industrial users. The abbreviated accounts for 19X8 and 19X7 are given below.

Profit and loss account for the year ended 30 June

	19X8		19X7	
	£000	£000	£000	£000
Sales		1,200		1,180
Cost of sales		(750)		(680)
Gross profit		450		500
Operating expenses	(208)		(200)	
Depreciation	(75)		(66)	
Interest	(8)		(−)	
		(291)		(266)
Profit before tax		159		234
Tax		(48)		(80)
Profit after tax		111		154
Dividend – proposed		(72)		(70)
Retained profit for year		39		84

Balance sheets as at 30 June

	19X8		19X7	
	£000	£000	£000	£000
Fixed assets (note 1)		687		702
Current assets				
Stocks	236		148	
Debtors	156		102	
Cash	4		32	
	396		282	

	19X8		19X7	
	£000	£000	£000	£000
Creditors: amounts due within one year				
Trade creditors	(76)		(60)	
Other creditors and accruals	(16)		(18)	
Dividend	(72)		(70)	
Tax	(48)		(80)	
Bank overdraft	(26)		–	
	(238)		(228)	
Net current assets		158		54
Creditors: amounts due beyond one year				
Bank loan (note 2)		(50)		–
		795		756
Capital and reserves				
Ordinary share capital of £1 (fully paid)		500		500
Retained profits		295		256
		795		756

Note I **Fixed assets**

	Buildings	Fixtures and fittings	Vehicles	Total
	£000	£000	£000	£000
Cost 1.7.X7	900	100	80	1,080
Purchases	–	40	20	60
Cost 30.6.X8	900	140	100	1,140
Depreciation 1.7.X7	288	50	40	378
Charge for year	36	14	25	75
Depreciation 30.6.X8	324	64	65	453
Net book value 30.6.X8	576	76	35	687

Note 2

The bank loan was taken up on 1 July 19X7 and is repayable on 1 January 19X3. It carries a fixed rate of interest of 12 per cent per annum and is secured by a fixed and floating charge on the assets of the company.

Required:

(a) Calculate the following financial statistics for *both* 19X8 and 19X7, using end of year figures where appropriate:

   (i)   return on capital employed;
   (ii)   net profit margin;
   (iii)   gross profit margin;
   (iv)   current ratio;
   (v)   liquid ratio (acid-test ratio);
   (vi)   day's debtors;
   (vii)   day's creditors; and
   (viii)   stock turnover ratio.

(b) Comment on the performance of Threads Limited from the viewpoint of a company considering supplying a substantial amount of goods to Threads Limited on usual credit terms.

(c) What action could a supplier take to lessen the risk of not being paid should Threads Limited be in financial difficulty?

3.6 Bradbury Ltd is a family-owned clothes manufacturer based in the south-west of England. For a number of years the chairman and managing director of the company was David Bradbury. During his period of office the company's sales turnover had grown steadily at a rate of 2–3 per cent each year. David Bradbury retired on 30 November 19X8 and was succeeded by his son Simon. Soon after taking office Simon decided to expand the business. Within weeks he had successfully negotiated a five-year contract with a large clothes retailer to make a range of sports and leisurewear items. The contract will result in an additional £2 million sales during each year of the contract. In order to fulfil the contract new equipment and premises were acquired by Bradbury Ltd.

    Financial information concerning the company is given below.

Profit and loss account for the year ended 30 November

	19X8 £000	19X9 £000
Turnover	9,482	11,365
Profit before interest and tax	914	1,042
Interest charges	22	81
Profit before tax	892	961
Taxation	358	385
Profit after tax	534	576
Dividend	120	120
Retained profit	414	456

Balance sheet as at 30 November

	19X8		19X9	
	£000	£000	£000	£000
Fixed assets				
Freehold premises at cost		5,240		7,360
Plant and equipment (net)		2,375		4,057
		7,615		11,417
Current assets				
Stock	2,386		3,420	
Trade debtors	2,540		4,280	
Cash	127		–	
	5,053		7,700	
Creditors: amounts due within				
one year				
Trade creditors	1,157		2,245	
Taxation	358		385	
Dividends payable	120		120	
Bank overdraft	–		2,424	
	1,635		5,174	
Net current assets		3,418		2,526
		11,033		13,943
Creditors: amounts due beyond one year				
Loans		1,220		3,674
Total net assets		9,813		10,269
Capital and reserves				
Share capital		2,000		2,000
Reserves		7,813		8,269
Net worth		9,813		10,269

Required:

(a) Calculate for each year the following ratios:
- (i) net profit margin;
- (ii) return on capital employed;
- (iii) current ratio;
- (iv) gearing ratio;
- (v) day's debtors (settlement period);
- (vi) net asset turnover.

(b) Using the above ratios, and any other ratios or information you consider relevant, comment on the results of the expansion programme.

—

CHAPTER FOUR

Capital Investment Appraisal

On completion of this chapter you should be able to:

- Explain the nature and importance of investment decision-making.

- Identify the four main investment appraisal methods used in practice.

- Use each method to reach a decision on a particular practical investment opportunity.

- Discuss the advantages and disadvantages of each of the methods.

Introduction

In this chapter we shall look at how businesses can make decisions involving investments in new plant, machinery, buildings and similar long-term assets. However, the general principles we will consider can equally well be applied to investments in the shares of companies, irrespective of whether the investment is being considered by a business or by a private individual.

The nature of investment decisions

The essential feature of investment decisions, irrespective of who is to make the decision, is the time factor. Investment involves making an outlay at one point in time of something of economic value, usually cash, which is expected to yield economic benefits to the investor at some other point in time. Typically, the outlay precedes the benefits. Also, the outlay is typically one large amount and the benefits arrive in a stream over a fairly protracted period.

Investment decisions tend to be of crucial importance to the investor because:

- *Large amounts of resources are often involved.* Many investments made by a business involve laying out a significant proportion of its total resources. If the wrong decision is made, the effects on the business could be significant, if not catastrophic.
- *It is often difficult and/or expensive to 'bail-out' of an investment once it has been undertaken.* Investments made by a business are often specific to its needs. For example, a manufacturing business may have a factory built which has been designed to accommodate the particular flow of production of that business. This may make the factory of little value to other potential users with different needs. If the business found, after having made the investment, that the product which is being produced in the factory is not selling as well as expected, the only course of action may be to close down production and sell the factory at a significant loss.

| **ACTIVITY 4.1** |

When managers are making decisions involving capital investments, what should their decisions seek to achieve?

Investment decisions must be consistent with the objectives of the business. For a private sector business, shareholder wealth maximisation (which we discussed in Chapter 1) is usually assumed to be the key objective.

Methods of investment appraisal

Given the importance of investment decisions to investors, it is essential that proper screening of investment proposals takes place. An important part of this screening process is to ensure that appropriate methods of evaluating the profitability of investment projects are employed.

Research shows that there are basically four methods used in practice by businesses in the United Kingdom (and elsewhere in the world) to evaluate investment opportunities. It is possible to find businesses which use variants of these four methods. It is also possible to find businesses, particularly smaller ones, which do not use any formal appraisal method, but rely more on the 'gut-feeling' of its managers. Most businesses, however, seem to use one, or more, of the four methods which we shall now review.

To help us to consider each of the four methods, it is probably helpful to analyse how each of them would cope with a particular investment opportunity, as set out in Example 4.1.

Example 4.1

Billingsgate Battery Company has carried out some market research which shows that it is possible to manufacture and sell a product which has recently been developed. The decision to manufacture would require an investment in a machine costing £100,000, which is payable immediately. Production and sales of the product would take place throughout the next five years, at the end of which time, the machine can be sold for £20,000.

Production and sales of the product are expected to occur as follows:

	Number of units
Next year	5,000
Second year	10,000
Third year	15,000
Fourth year	15,000
Fifth year	5,000

It is estimated that the new product can be sold for £12 a unit and that the relevant material and labour costs will total £8 a unit.

To simplify matters, we shall assume that cash from sales and payments for production costs are received and paid, respectively, at the end of each year.

Bearing in mind that each product sold will give rise to a net cash inflow of £4 (i.e. £12−£8), the cash flows (receipts and payments) over the life of the product will be as follows:

		£000
Immediately	Cost of machine	(100)
1 year's time	Net profit before depreciation (£4 × 5,000)	20
2 years' time	Net profit before depreciation (£4 × 10,000)	40
3 years' time	Net profit before depreciation (£4 × 15,000)	60
4 years' time	Net profit before depreciation (£4 × 15,000)	60
5 years' time	Net profit before depreciation (£4 × 5,000)	20
5 years' time	Disposal proceeds from the machine	20

Note that, broadly speaking, the net profit before deducting depreciation (i.e. before non-cash items) equals the net amount of cash flowing into the business.

Having set up the example, we shall now look at the techniques used to assess investment opportunities and see how each deals with this investment problem.

Accounting rate of return (ARR)

This method takes the average accounting profit which the investment will generate and expresses it as a percentage of the average investment in the project as measured in accounting profit terms. Thus:

$$ARR = \frac{\text{Average annual profit}}{\text{Average investment to earn that profit}} \times 100\%$$

We can see from the above that to calculate ARR, we need to deduce two pieces of information:

1. the annual average profit; and
2. the average investment for the particular project.

The average annual profit *before* depreciation over the five years is £40,000 (i.e. (£20,000 + £40,000 + £60,000 + £60,000 + £20,000)/5). Assuming 'straight-line' depreciation (i.e. equal amounts), the annual depreciation charge will be £16,000 (i.e. (cost £100,000 minus disposal value £20,000)/5). The average annual profit *after depreciation* is therefore £24,000 (i.e. £40,000 − £16,000).

The average investment over the five years can be calculated as follows:

$$= \frac{\text{Cost of machine} - \text{disposal value}}{2}$$

$$= \frac{£100,000 + £20,000}{2}$$

$$= £60,000$$

Thus the ARR of the investment is:

$$= \frac{£24,000}{£60,000} \times 100\%$$

$$= 40\%$$

The figure we have calculated must be compared to a minimum required rate of return to decide whether or not the investment proposal is acceptable.

ACTIVITY 4.2

Chaotic Industries is considering an investment in a fleet of ten delivery vans to take its products to customers. The vans will cost £15,000 each to buy, payable immediately. The annual running costs are expected to total £20,000 for each van (including the driver's salary). The vans are expected to operate successfully for six years, at the end of which period they will all have to be scrapped, with disposal proceeds expected to be about £3,000 per van. At present the business uses a commercial carrier for all of its deliveries. It is expected that this carrier will charge a total of £230,000 each year for the next six years to undertake the deliveries. What is the ARR of buying the vans? (Note that cost savings are as relevant a benefit from an investment as are actual net cash inflows.)

The vans will save the business £30,000 a year (i.e. 230 − (20 × 10)), before depreciation, in total.

   Thus the inflows and outflows will be:

		£000
Immediately	Cost of vans	(150)
I year's time	Net saving before depreciation	30
2 years' time	Net saving before depreciation	30
3 years' time	Net saving before depreciation	30
4 years' time	Net saving before depreciation	30
5 years' time	Net saving before depreciation	30
6 years' time	Net saving before depreciation	30
6 years' time	Disposal proceeds from the vans (£3000×10)	30

The total annual depreciation expense (assuming a 'straight line' approach) will be £20,000 (i.e. (150 − 30)/6). Thus the average annual saving, after depreciation, is £10,000 (i.e. 30 − 20).

   The average investment will be:

$$= \frac{£150,000 + £30,000}{2}$$

$$= £90,000$$

Thus the ARR of the investment is:

$$= \frac{£10,000}{£90,000} \times 100\%$$

$$= 11.1\%$$

ARR and the return on capital employed (ROCE) ratio adopt the same approach to performance measurement. We saw in Chapter 3 that ROCE is a popular means of assessing the performance of a business *as a whole*. In theory, if all investments made by Chaotic Industries (Activity 4.2) actually proved to have an ARR of 11.1 per cent, then the ROCE for that business as a whole should be 11.1 per cent. Thus where a pre-set ROCE is used as a financial objective for businesses, it would seem logical to use ARR when considering new investments.

   As mentioned above, a business using ARR would compare the returns achieved to a minimum required rate of return. This minimum rate may be determined in various ways. For example, it may reflect the rate which previous investments had achieved (as measured by ROCE), or the industry average ROCE, and so forth. Where there are competing projects which all seem capable of exceeding the minimum rate, the one with the higher or highest ARR would normally be selected.

   ARR is said to have a number of advantages as a method of investment appraisal. It was mentioned earlier that ROCE is a widely used measure of business performance and it may therefore seem sensible to employ a method of investment appraisal which is consistent with this overall approach to measuring business performance. ARR is also a measure of profitability that many believe is the correct way to evaluate investments. Finally, ARR produces a percentage return which managers understand. Percentages are often used when setting targets for a business and so managers feel comfortable with investment appraisal methods which adopt this form of measurement.

ACTIVITY 4.3

ARR suffers from a very serious defect as a means of assessing investment opportunities. What do you think this is? Take a look back at the Billingsgate Battery Company example (above). (Hint: the defect is not concerned with the ability of the decision-maker to forecast future events, though this too can be a problem.)

The problem with ARR is that it almost completely ignores the time factor. In the Billingsgate Battery Company example, exactly the same ARR would have been computed under any of the following three scenarios:

		Original £000	Option I £000	Option 2 £000
Immediately	*Cost of machine*	*(100)*	*(100)*	*(100)*
1 year's time	*Net profit before depreciation*	*20*	*10*	*160*
2 years' time	*Net profit before depreciation*	*40*	*10*	*10*
3 years' time	*Net profit before depreciation*	*60*	*10*	*10*
4 years' time	*Net profit before depreciation*	*60*	*10*	*10*
5 years' time	*Net profit before depreciation*	*20*	*160*	*10*
5 years' time	*Disposal proceeds*	*20*	*20*	*20*

Since the same total profit over the five years arises in all three of these cases, the average net profit after depreciation must be the same in each case. This means that each case will give rise to the same ARR of 40 per cent.

Given a financial objective of maximising the wealth of the owners of the business, any rational decision-maker faced with these three competing scenarios would strongly favour Option 2. This is because most of the benefits from the investment arise within 12 months of initial investment. The original scenario would rank second and Option 1 would come a poor third in the rankings. Any appraisal technique which is not capable of distinguishing between these three situations is seriously flawed. We shall look in more detail at the reason for timing being so important later in this chapter.

There are other defects associated with the ARR method. For investment appraisal purposes, it is cash flows rather than accounting profits which are important. Cash is the ultimate measure of the economic wealth generated. This is because it is cash which can be used to acquire resources and for distribution to shareholders. Accounting profit, on the other hand, is more appropriate for reporting purposes. It is a measure of productive effort for a particular reporting period such as a year or half-year.

The ARR method can also create problems when considering competing investments of different size.

ACTIVITY 4.4

Sinclair Wholesalers plc is currently considering the opening of a new outlet in Coventry. Two possible sites have been identified for the new outlet. Site A has a capacity of 30,000 sq. metres. It will require an average investment of £6m. and will produce an average profit of £600,000 per annum. Site B has a capacity of 20,000 sq. metres. It will require an average investment of £4m. and will produce an average profit of £500,000 per annum. What is the ARR of each investment opportunity? Which site would you select, and why?

The ARR of Site A is £600,000/£6m = 10 per cent. The ARR of Site B is £500,000/£4m = 12.5 per cent. Thus Site B has the highest ARR. However, in terms of the absolute profit generated, Site A is the more attractive. If the ultimate objective is to maximise the wealth of the shareholders of Sinclair Wholesalers plc, it would be better to choose Site A even though the percentage return is lower. It is the absolute size of the return rather than the relative (percentage) size which is important.

Payback period (PP)

The payback period (PP) is the length of time it takes for an initial investment to be repaid out of the net cash inflows from a project. It might be useful to consider PP in the context of the Billingsgate Battery Company example. You will recall that essentially the project's costs and benefits can be summarised as:

		£000
Immediately	Cost of machine	(100)
1 year's time	Net profit before depreciation	20
2 years' time	Net profit before depreciation	40
3 years' time	Net profit before depreciation	60
4 years' time	Net profit before depreciation	60
5 years' time	Net profit before depreciation	20
5 years' time	Disposal proceeds	20

Note that all of these figures are approximate measures of cash to be paid or received.

The payback period (PP) for this investment is nearly three years (i.e. it will be nearly three years before the £100,000 outlay is covered by the inflows). The payback period can be derived by calculating the cumulative cash flows as follows:

		Net cash flows £000	Cumulative cash flows £000
Immediately	Cost of machine	(100)	(100)
1 year's time	Net profit before depreciation	20	(80)
2 years' time	Net profit before depreciation	40	(40)
3 years' time	Net profit before depreciation	60	20
4 years' time	Net profit before depreciation	60	80
5 years' time	Net profit before depreciation	20	100
5 years' time	Disposal proceeds	20	120

We can see that the cumulative cash flows become positive in the third year. If we assume that the cash flows accrue evenly over the year, the precise payback period will be:

2 years + (40/60) = $2\frac{2}{3}$ years

A decision-maker using PP would need to have a minimum payback period in mind. For example, if Billingsgate Battery Company had a minimum payback period of three years it would accept the project. If there were two competing projects which both met the minimum payback period requirement, the decision-maker should select the project with the shorter payback period.

ACTIVITY 4.5

What is the payback period of the Chaotic Industries project from Activity 4.2?

The inflows and outflows are expected to be:

		Net cash flows £000	Cumulative net cash flows £000
Immediately	*Cost of vans*	*(150)*	*(150)*
1 year's time	*Net saving before depreciation*	*30*	*(120)*
2 years' time	*Net saving before depreciation*	*30*	*(90)*
3 years' time	*Net saving before depreciation*	*30*	*(60)*
4 years' time	*Net saving before depreciation*	*30*	*(30)*
5 years' time	*Net saving before depreciation*	*30*	*0*
6 years' time	*Net saving before depreciation*	*30*	*30*
6 years' time	*Disposal proceeds from the machine*	*30*	*60*

The payback period here is five years (i.e. it is not until the end of the fifth year that the vans will pay for themselves out of the savings which they are expected to generate).

The PP approach has certain advantages. It is quick and easy to calculate and can be easily understood by managers. Projects which can recoup their cost quickly are viewed as more attractive than those with longer payback periods. However, this method does not provide us with the whole answer to the problem.

ACTIVITY 4.6

In what respect is PP not the whole answer as a means of assessing investment opportunities? Consider the cash flows arising from three competing projects:

		Project 1	Project 2	Project 3
		£000	£000	£000
Immediately	Cost of machine	(200)	(200)	(200)
1 year's time	Net profit before depreciation	40	10	80
2 years' time	Net profit before depreciation	80	20	100
3 years' time	Net profit before depreciation	80	170	20
4 years' time	Net profit before depreciation	60	20	200
5 years' time	Net profit before depreciation	40	10	500
5 years' time	Disposal proceeds	40	10	20

(Hint: again the defect is not concerned with the ability of the decision-maker to forecast future events. This is a problem whatever approach we take.)

The PP for each project is three years and so the PP approach would make the projects equally acceptable. The PP method cannot distinguish between those projects which pay back a significant amount before the three-year payback period and those which do not. However, any decision-maker concerned with maximising shareholder wealth would prefer Project 3 to either of the other two scenarios because the cash flows come in earlier and they are greater in total. The cumulative cash flows of each project are set out in Figure 4.1.

The PP method does not measure the profitability of projects, it is simply concerned with their payback periods. We saw in the activity above that beyond the payback period, the cash flows are ignored. Whilst this neatly avoids the practical problems of forecasting cash flows over a longer period, it means that relevant information will be ignored. It is true that, by favouring projects with a short payback period the PP approach does provide us with a means of dealing with the problems of risk and uncertainty. However, this is a fairly crude

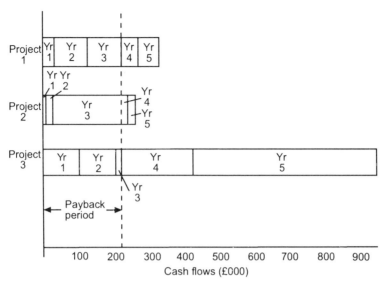

Figure 4.1 The cumulative cash flows of a project

approach to the problem. We shall see in the next chapter that there are more systematic approaches to dealing with risk.

Net present value (NPV)

What we really need to help us make sensible investment decisions is a method of appraisal which takes account of all of the costs and benefits of each investment opportunity and which also makes a logical allowance for the timing of those costs and benefits. The net present value (NPV) method provides us with this.

Consider the Billingsgate Battery Company example, the cash flows of which can be summarised as follows:

		£000
Immediately	Cost of machine	(100)
1 year's time	Net profit before depreciation	20
2 years' time	Net profit before depreciation	40
3 years' time	Net profit before depreciation	60
4 years' time	Net profit before depreciation	60
5 years' time	Net profit before depreciation	20
5 years' time	Disposal proceeds	20

Given that the principal financial objective of the business is probably to maximise shareholder wealth, it would be very easy to assess this investment if all of the cash inflows and outflows were to occur at the same time. All that we should need to do is to add up the cash inflows (total £220,000) and compare it with the outflows (£100,000). This would lead us to the conclusion that the project should go ahead, because the business would be better off by £120,000 as a result. Of course, it is not as easy as this because time is involved. The cash outflow (payment) will, if the project is undertaken, occur immediately. The inflows (receipts) will arise at a range of later times.

The time factor arises because people do not see paying out, say, £100 now in order to receive £100 in a year's time as being equivalent in value.

ACTIVITY 4.7

Why would you see £100 to be received in a year's time as unequal in value to £100 to be paid immediately? (There are basically three reasons.)

The reasons are:

1. *Interest lost.*
2. *Effects of inflation.*
3. *Risk.*

We shall now take a closer look at these three factors in turn.

Interest lost

If you are to be deprived of the use of your money for a year, you could equally well be deprived of its use by placing it on deposit in a bank or building society. In this case, at the end of the year you could have your money back and have interest as well. Thus, unless the opportunity to invest will offer similar returns, you will be incurring an *opportunity cost*. An opportunity cost occurs where one course of action (e.g. making an investment in, say, a computer) deprives you of the opportunity to derive some benefit from an alternative action (e.g. putting the money in the bank).

From this we can see that any investment opportunity must, if it is to make you more wealthy, do better than the returns which are available from the next best opportunity. Thus, if Billingsgate Battery Company sees putting the money in the bank on deposit as the alternative to investment in the machine, the returns from investing in the machine must be better than those from investing in the bank. If the bank offered better returns the business would become more wealthy by putting the money on deposit.

Risk

Buying a machine to manufacture a product which is to be sold in the market is often a risky venture. Things may not turn out as expected.

ACTIVITY 4.8

Can you suggest why things may not turn out as expected?

You may have come up with the following:

- *The machine might not work as well as expected; it might break down, leading to loss of production and to loss of sales.*
- *Sales of the product may not be as buoyant as expected.*
- *The life of the product may be shorter than expected.*
- *Labour costs may prove to be higher than was expected.*
- *The sale proceeds of the machine could prove to be less than was estimated.*

It is important to remember that the decision whether or not to invest in the machine must be taken *before* any of these things are known. It is only after the machine has been purchased that we might discover that the level of sales, which had been estimated before the event, were not going to be achieved. It is not possible to wait until we know for certain whether the market will behave as we expected before we buy the machine. We can study reports and analyses of the market. We can commission sophisticated market surveys and these may give us more confidence in the likely outcome. We can advertise strongly and try to expand sales. Ultimately, however, we have to jump off into the dark and accept the risk.

Normally, people expect to receive greater returns where they perceive risk to be a factor. Examples of this in real life are not difficult to find. One such example is the fact that a bank will tend to charge a higher rate of interest to a borrower whom the bank perceives to be more risky, than to one who can offer good security for the loan and can point to a regular source of income.

Going back to Billingsgate Battery Company's investment opportunity, it is not enough to say that we would not advise making the investment unless the returns from it are higher than those from investing in a bank deposit. Clearly we would want returns above the level of bank deposit interest rates because the logical equivalent investment opportunity to investing in the machine is not putting the money on deposit. It is making an alternative investment which seems to have a risk similar to that of the investment in the machine.

In practice, we tend to expect a higher rate of return from investment projects where the risk is perceived as being higher. How risky a particular project is, and, therefore, how large this *risk premium* should be, are matters which are difficult to handle. In practice, it is usually necessary to make some judgement on these questions.

Inflation

If you are to be deprived of £100 for a year, when you come to spend that money it will not buy as much in the way of goods and services at it would have done a year earlier. Generally, you will not be able to buy as many tins of baked beans or loaves of bread or bus tickets for a particular journey as you could have done a year earlier. Clearly the investor needs this loss of purchasing power to be compensated for if the investment is to be made. This is on top of a return which takes account of the returns that could have been gained from an alternative investment of similar risk.

To summarise these factors, we can say that the logical investor, who is seeking to increase his or her wealth, will only be prepared to make investments that will compensate for the loss of interest and purchasing power of the money invested and for the fact that the returns which are expected may not materialise (risk). This is usually assessed by seeing whether the proposed investment will yield a return which is greater than the basic rate of interest (which would include an allowance for inflation) plus a risk premium.

Let us now return to the Billingsgate Battery Company example. You will recall that the cash flows expected from this investment are:

		£000
Immediately	Cost of machine	(100)
1 year's time	Net profit before depreciation	20
2 years' time	Net profit before depreciation	40
3 years' time	Net profit before depreciation	60
4 years' time	Net profit before depreciation	60
5 years' time	Net profit before depreciation	20
5 years' time	Disposal proceeds	20

Let us assume that instead of making this investment the business could make an alternative investment with similar risk and obtain a return of 20 per cent a year.

You will recall that we have concluded that it is not sufficient just to compare the basic cash inflows and outflows listed above. It would be useful if we could express each of these cash flows in similar terms so that we could make a direct comparison between the sum of the inflows and the £100,000 investment. In fact we can do this.

ACTIVITY 4.9

We know that Billingsgate Battery Company could alternatively invest its money at a rate of 20 per cent a year. How much do you judge the present (immediate) value of the expected first-year receipt of £20,000 to be? In other words, if, instead of having to wait a year for the £20,000 and being deprived of the opportunity to invest it at 20 per cent, you could have some money now, what sum to be received now would you regard as exactly equivalent to getting £20,000, but having to wait a year for it?

We should obviously be happy to accept a lower amount if we could get it immediately than if we had to wait a year. This is because we could invest it at 20 per cent (in the alternative project). Logically, we should be prepared to accept the amount which with a year's income will grow to £20,000. If we call this amount PV (for present value) we can say:

$$PV + (PV \times 20\%) = £20,000$$

i.e. the amount plus income from investing the amount for the year equals £20,000.

We can restate this equation as:

$$PV \times (1 + 0.2) = £20,000$$

(Note that 0.2 is the same as 20 per cent, but expressed as a decimal.)
This equation can then be rearranged as:

$$PV = £20,000/(1 + 0.2)$$

$$PV = £16,667.$$

Thus rational investors who have the opportunity to invest at 20 per cent a year would not mind whether they have £16,667 now or £20,000 in a year's time. In this sense we can say that, given a 20 per cent investment opportunity, the present value of £20,000 to be received in one year's time is £16,667.

If we could derive the present value (PV) of each of the cash flows associated with the machine investment, we could easily make the direct comparison between the cost of making the investment (£100,000) and the various benefits which will derive from it in years 1 to 5. Fortunately, we can do precisely this.

We can make a more general statement about the PV of a particular cash flow. It is:

PV of the cash flow of year n = Actual cash flow of year n divided by $(1 + r)^n$

where n is the year of the cash flow (i.e. how many years into the future) and r is the opportunity investing rate expressed as a decimal (instead of as a percentage).

We have already seen how this works for the £20,000 inflow for year 1. For year 2 the calculation would be:

PV of year 2 cash flow (£40,000) = $£40,000/(1 + 0.2)^2$

$$PV = £40,000/(1.2)^2 = £40,000/1.44 = £27,778.$$

Thus the present value of the £40,000 to be received in two year's time is £27,778.

ACTIVITY 4.10

See if you can show that an investor would be indifferent to £27,778 receivable now, or £40,000 receivable in two years' time, assuming that there is a 20 per cent investment opportunity.

The reasoning is something like this:

	£
Amount available for immediate investment	27,778
Add: *interest for year 1 (20% × 27,778)*	5,556
	33,334
Add: *interest for year 2 (20% × 33,334)*	6,668
	40,002

(The extra £2 is only a rounding error.)

   Thus, because the investor can turn £27,778 into £40,000 in two years, these amounts are equivalent and we can say that £27,778 is the present value of £40,000 receivable after two years (given a 20 per cent rate of return).

Now let us calculate the present values of all of the cash flows associated with the machine project and hence the *net present value* of the project as a whole. The relevant cash flows and calculations are as follows:

Time	Cash flow £000	Calculation of PV	PV £000
Immediately (time 0)	(100)	$(100)/(1+0.2)^0$	(100.00)*
1 year's time	20	$20/(1+0.2)^1$	16.67
2 years' time	40	$40/(1+0.2)^2$	27.78
3 years' time	60	$60/(1+0.2)^3$	34.72
4 years' time	60	$60/(1+0.2)^4$	28.94
5 years' time	20	$20/(1+0.2)^5$	8.04
5 years' time	20	$20/(1+0.2)^5$	8.04
			24.19

(* Note that $(1+0.2)^0 = 1$.)

We can now say that, given the investment opportunities available to the business elsewhere, investing in the machine will make the business £24,190 better off. In other words, the gross benefits from investing in this machine are worth a total of £124,190 today and since the business can 'buy' these benefits for just £100,000, the investment should be made. Clearly at any price up to £124,190 the investment would be worth making since the wealth of the owners of the business would be increased.

Using discount tables

Deducing the present values of the various cash flows was a little laborious using the approach which we have just taken. To deduce each PV we took the relevant cash flow and multiplied it by $1/(1 + r)^n$. Fortunately, there is a quicker way. Tables exist which show values of this *discount factor* for a range of values of r and n. Such a table is appended at the end of this chapter. Take a look at it.

Look at the column for 20 per cent and the row for 1 year. We find that the factor is 0.833. Thus the PV of a cash flow of £1 receivable in one year is £0.833. So a cash flow of £20,000 receivable in one year's time is £16,667 (i.e. 0.833 × £20,000), the same result as we found doing it longhand.

ACTIVITY 4.11

What is the net present value of the Chaotic Industries project from Activity 4.2, assuming a 15% opportunity cost of finance (discount rate)?

Remember that the inflows and outflows are expected to be:

		£000
Immediately	Cost of vans	(150)
1 year's time	Net saving before depreciation	30
2 years' time	Net saving before depreciation	30
3 years' time	Net saving before depreciation	30
4 years' time	Net saving before depreciation	30
5 years' time	Net saving before depreciation	30
6 years' time	Net saving before depreciation	30
6 years' time	Disposal proceeds from the machine	30

You should use the discount table at the end of this chapter.

The calculation of the NPV of the project is as follows:

Time	Cash flows £000	Discount factor (from the table)	Present value £000
Immediately	(150)	1.000	(150.00)
1 year's time	30	0.870	26.10
2 years' time	30	0.756	22.68
3 years' time	30	0.658	19.74
4 years' time	30	0.572	17.16
5 years' time	30	0.497	14.91
6 years' time	30	0.432	12.96
6 years' time	30	0.432	12.96
		Net present value	(23.49)

ACTIVITY 4.12
How would you interpret this result?

The fact that the project has a negative NPV means that the benefits from the investment are worth less than the cost of entering into it. Any cost up to £126,510 (i.e. the present value of the benefits) would be worth paying, but not £150,000.

Figure 4.2 shows how the value of £100 diminishes as its receipt goes further into the future, assuming an opportunity cost of finance of 20 per cent per annum. The £100 to be received immediately, obviously, has a present value of £100. However, as the time before it is to be received increases, the present value diminishes significantly.

NPV is a better method of appraising investment opportunities than either ARR or PP.

NPV fully addresses each of the following:

- *The timing of the cash flows.* By discounting the various cash flows associated with each project according to when they are expected to arise, NPV takes

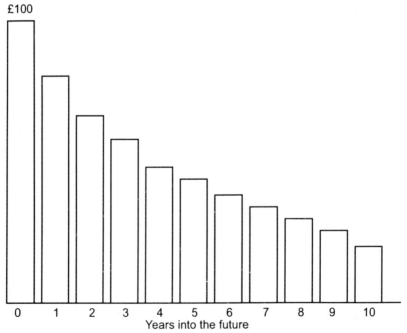

Figure 4.2 Present value of £100 receivable at various times in the future, assuming an annual financing cost of 20 per cent

account of the time value of money. The discount factor is based on the opportunity cost of finance (i.e. the return which the next best alternative opportunity would generate) and so the net benefit after financing costs have been met is identified (as the NPV). The way in which we calculate the discount rate for an investment project will be discussed in more detail in Chapter 8.

■ *The whole of the relevant cash flows.* NPV includes all of the relevant cash flows, irrespective of when they are expected to occur. It treats them differently according to their date of occurrence, but they all have, or can have, an influence on the decision.

■ *The objectives of the business.* The output of the NPV analysis has a direct bearing on the wealth of the shareholders of a business. (Positive NPVs enhance wealth, negative ones reduce it.) Since we assume that private sector businesses seek to maximise shareholder wealth, NPV is superior to the methods previously discussed.

Users of the NPV approach should adopt the following decision rules:

■ Take on all projects with positive NPVs, when they are discounted at the opportunity cost of finance.

■ Where a choice has to be made between two or more projects, select the one with the larger or largest NPV.

Internal rate of return (IRR)

This is the last of the four chief methods of investment appraisal which are found in practice. It is quite closely related to the NPV method as it also involves discounting future cash flows. The IRR is the discount rate which, when applied to the future cash flows, will make them equal the initial outlay. In essence, it represents the yield from an investment opportunity.

You will recall that when we discounted the cash flows of the Billingsgate Battery Company investment project at 20 per cent, we found that the NPV was a positive figure of £24,190.

ACTIVITY 4.13

What does the NPV of the machine project tell us about the rate of return which the investment will yield for the business?

The fact that the NPV is positive when discounting at 20 per cent implies that the rate of return which the project generates is more than 20 per cent. The fact that the NPV is a pretty large figure implies that the actual rate of return is quite a lot above 20 per cent. Increasing the size of the discount rate will reduce NPV because a higher discount rate gives lower discounted cash inflows.

We saw above that the IRR can be defined as the discount rate which equates the discounted cash inflows with the cash outflows. To put it another way, the IRR is the discount rate which will have the effect of producing an NPV of precisely zero.

It is somewhat laborious to deduce the IRR by hand, since it cannot usually be calculated directly. Thus iteration (trial and error) is the approach we will adopt. Let us try a higher rate – say, 30 per cent – and see what happens:

Time	Cash flow £000	Discount factor	PV
Immediately (time 0)	(100)	1.000	(100.00)
I year's time	20	0.769	15.38
2 years' time	40	0.592	23.68
3 years' time	60	0.455	27.30
4 years' time	60	0.350	21.00
5 years' time	20	0.269	5.38
5 years' time	20	0.269	5.38
			(1.88)

In increasing the discount rate from 20 per cent to 30 per cent, we have reduced the NPV from £52,600 (positive) to £1,880 (negative). Since the IRR is the discount

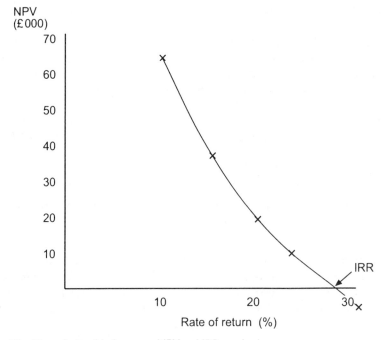

Figure 4.3   The relationship between NPV and IRR methods

rate which will give us an NPV of exactly zero, we can conclude that the IRR of Billingsgate Battery Company's machine project is very slightly under 30 per cent. Further trials could lead us to the exact rate, but there is probably not much point, given the likely inaccuracy of the cash flow estimates.

The relationship between the NPV method discussed earlier and the IRR is shown graphically in Fig. 4.3, using the information relating to the Billingsgate Battery Company. In this figure, we can see that where the discount rate is zero, the NPV will be the sum of the net cash flows. In other words, no account is taken of the time value of money. However, as the discount rate increases there is a corresponding decrease in the NPV of the project. When the NPV line touches the horizontal axis there will be a zero NPV and that will also represent the IRR.

ACTIVITY 4.14

What is the internal rate of return of the Chaotic Industries project from Activity 4.2? You should use the discount table at the end of this chapter. (Hint: remember that you already know the NPV of this project at 15 per cent).

Since we know (from a previous activity) that at a 15 per cent discount rate the NPV is a relatively large negative figure, our next trial should use a lower discount rate, say 10 per cent.

Time	Cash flows £000	Discount factor (from the table)	Present value £000
Immediately	(150)	1.000	(150.00)
1 year's time	30	0.909	27.27
2 years' time	30	0.826	24.78
3 years' time	30	0.751	22.53
4 years' time	30	0.683	20.49
5 years' time	30	0.621	18.63
6 years' time	30	0.565	16.95
6 years' time	30	0.565	16.95
		Net present value	(2.40)

We can see that NPV rose about £21,000 (£23,490 − £2,400) for a 5 per cent drop in the discount rate (i.e. about £4,200 per 1 per cent). We need to know the discount rate for a zero NPV. (This represents an increase of a further £2,400 in the NPV where the discount rate used is 10 per cent.) As a 1 per cent change in the discount rate results in a £4,200 change in NPV, the required change in the discount rate will be roughly 0.6 per cent (i.e. £2,400/£4,200). Thus the IRR is close to 9.4 per cent (i.e. 10 per cent − 0.6 per cent). However to say that the IRR is about 9 per cent is near enough for most purposes.

In answering the above activity, we were fortunate in using a discount rate of 10 per cent for our second iteration as this happened to be very close to the IRR figure. However, what if we had used 6 per cent? This discount factor will provide us with a large positive NPV as we can see below:

Time	Cash flows £000	Discount factor (from the table)	Present value £000
Immediately	(150)	1.000	(150.00)
1 year's time	30	0.943	28.29
2 years' time	30	0.890	26.70
3 years' time	30	0.840	25.20
4 years' time	30	0.792	23.76
5 years' time	30	0.747	22.41
6 years' time	30	0.705	21.15
6 years' time	30	0.705	21.15
		Net present value	18.66

We can see that the IRR will fall somewhere between 15 per cent, which gives a negative NPV, and 6 per cent, which gives a positive NPV. We could undertake further iterations in order to derive the IRR. Most businesses have computer software packages which will do this very quickly. If, however, you are required to calculate the IRR manually, further iterations can be time-consuming. Nevertheless, by *linear interpolation* we can get to the answer fairly quickly. Linear interpolation assumes a straight-line relationship between the discount rate and NPV which may be a reasonable approximation over a relatively short range. In order to understand the principles behind this method it is useful to study the diagram in Figure 4.4.

The graph in this figure plots the NPV of the investment against the discount rates. Thus Point D represents the NPV at a discount rate of 6 per cent and Point F represents the NPV at a discount rate of 15 per cent. The point at which the sloping line DF intersects the discount rate line is the IRR. We can derive this point either graphically (as shown) or by using a simple equation. As the triangles DEF and DGH are identical in shape, the relationship between the lengths of the corresponding sides will be the same. Thus:

$$\frac{GH}{DG} = \frac{EF}{DE}$$

We need to find out GH on the graph. As we know the other variables in the equation, this is fairly straightforward. Hence:

$$\frac{GH}{18,660} = \frac{(15-6)}{(18,660+240)}$$

$$GH = 8.9\% \text{ (say, 9.0\%)}$$

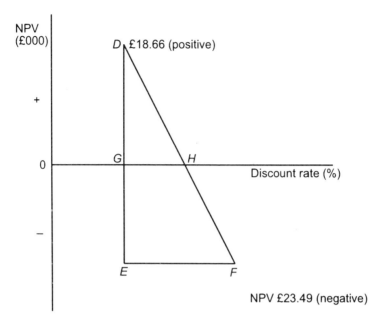

Figure 4.4 Finding the IRR of an investment by plotting the NPV against the discount rate

We can see that the figure derived through this process is slightly different to the figure for IRR calculated earlier where one of the discount rates used was very close to the actual IRR. It is less accurate because of the linearity assumption employed (which is strictly incorrect) but will provide a reasonable approximation providing the two discount rates chosen are not too far apart.

Users of the IRR approach should apply the following decision rules:

- For any project to be acceptable, it must meet a minimum IRR requirement. Logically, this minimum should be the opportunity cost of finance.
- Where there are competing projects (e.g. the business can choose one of the projects, but not all), the one with the higher or highest IRR would be selected.

IRR has certain attributes in common with NPV. All cash flows are taken into account and the timing of them is logically handled. The main disadvantage with IRR is the fact that it does not address the issue of wealth maximisation. IRR will always see a return of 25 per cent being preferable to a 20 per cent IRR (assuming an opportunity cost of finance of, say, 15 per cent). Although by accepting the project with the higher percentage return will often maximise shareholder wealth, this may not always be the case. This is because the scale of *investment* has been ignored. With a 15 per cent cost of finance, £1 million invested at 20 per cent would make you richer than £0.5 million invested at 24 per cent. IRR does not recognise this. It should be acknowledged that it is not usual for projects to be competing where there is such a large difference in scale. Even though the problem may be rare and though, typically, IRR will give the same signal as NPV, it must be better to use a method (NPV) which is always reliable, rather than use IRR.

A further problem with the IRR method is that it has difficulty handling projects with unconventional cash flows. In the examples studied so far, each project has a negative cash flow arising at the start of its life and then positive cash flows thereafter. However, in some cases, a project may have both positive and negative cash flows at future points in its life. Such a pattern of cash flows can result in the the IRR method providing more than one solution.

Example 4.2

Let us assume that a project had the following pattern of cash flows:

Time	Cash flows
	£000
Immediately	(4,000)
I year's time	9,400
2 years' time	(5,500)

The cash flows above will give a zero NPV at both 10 per cent and 25 per cent. Thus we will have two IRRs which can be confusing for decision-makers. Assume, for example, the minimum acceptable IRR is 15 per cent. Should the project be accepted or rejected?

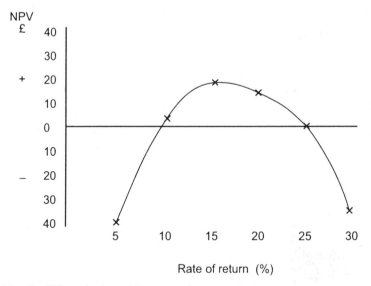

Figure 4.5   The IRR method providing more than one solution

Those who support IRR point out that it is possible to get around the problem of two (or more) solutions by discounting the future negative cash flow back to its present value and then adding the negative present value figure derived to the initial outlay. They also point out that, in real life situations, the pattern of cash flows required to bring about more than one IRR being calculated is rare and, therefore, of little practical significance. Nevertheless, it would be much simpler to use the NPV approach which does not suffer from such problems.

Figure 4.5 shows the NPV of the project for different discount rates. Once again, where the NPV line touches the horizontal axis there will be a zero NPV and that will also represent the IRR.

Some practical points

When dealing with questions relating to investment appraisal, there are a number of practical points you should bear in mind.

Relevant costs

As with all decision-making, we should only take account of *cash flows which vary according to the decision* in our analysis. Thus cash flows which will be the same, irrespective of the decision under review, should be ignored. For example, overheads which will be incurred in equal amount whether the investment is made or not should be ignored, even though the investment could not be made without the infrastructure which the overhead costs create. Similarly, *past costs* should be ignored as they are not affected by, and do not vary with, the decision.

Opportunity costs

Opportunity costs arising from benefits forgone must be taken into account. Thus, for example, when considering a decision concerning whether or not to continue to use a machine for producing a new product, the realisable value of the machine may be an important opportunity cost.

Taxation

Tax will usually be an important consideration when making an investment decision. The profits from the investment will be taxed and the capital investment may attract tax relief. This means that, in practice, unless tax is formally taken into account, the wrong decision could be made. In practice, some, if not all, of the taxation relating to the current year's profits will be paid in a later period (usually the following year). Thus the timing of the tax outflow should be taken into account when preparing the cash flows for the project.

Cash flows not profit flows

We have seen that for the NPV, IRR and PP methods, it is cash flows rather than profit flows which are relevant to the evaluation of investment projects. In a problem requiring the application of any of these methods, you may be given details of the profits for the investment period and so will be required to adjust these in order to derive the cash flows. Remember, the net profit before non-cash items (i.e. depreciation) is an approximation to the cash flows for the period and so you should work back to this figure.

When the data is expressed in profit rather than cash flow terms, an adjustment in respect of working capital may also be necessary. Some adjustment to take account of changes in the net cash investment (or disinvestment) in trade debtors, stock and creditors should be made. For example, launching a new product may give rise to an increase in working capital requiring an immediate outlay of cash. This outlay for additional working capital should be shown in your NPV calculations as part of the initial cost. However, the additional working capital may be released at the end of the life of the product. This disinvestment resulting in an inflow of cash at the end of the project should also be taken into account in your calculations at the point at which it is received.

Year end assumption

In the examples above we have assumed that cash flows arise at the end of the relevant year. This is a simplifying assumption which is normally made. The assumption is clearly unrealistic, as money will have to be paid to employees on a weekly or a monthly basis and customers will pay within a month or two of buying the product. Nevertheless, it is probably not a serious distortion. You should be clear, however, that there is nothing about any of the appraisal methods which demands that this assumption be made.

Interest payments

When using discounted cash flow techniques, interest payments which have been charged to the profit and loss account should not be taken into account in deriving the cash flows for the period (i.e. the relevant figure is net profit *before interest* and depreciation). The discount factor already takes account of the costs of financing, so to take account of interest charges in deriving cash flows for the period would be double counting.

Other factors

Investment decision-making must not be viewed as simply a mechanical exercise. The results derived from a particular investment appraisal method will be only one input into the decision-making process. There may be broader issues connected to the decision which have to be taken into account but which may be difficult or impossible to quantify. For example, a regional bus company may be considering an investment in a new bus to serve a particular route which local residents would like to see operated. Although the NPV calculations may reveal that a loss will be made on the investment, it may be that, by not investing in the new bus and not operating the route, the renewal of the company's licence to operate will be put at risk. In such a situation, the size of the expected loss, as revealed by the calculations made, must be weighed against the prospect of losing the right to operate before a final decision is made.

The reliability of the forecasts and the validity of the assumptions used in the evaluation will also have a bearing on the final decision. We shall see in the next chapter that various techniques may be applied to the information concerning the proposed investment in order to take account of risk and to assess sensitivity to any inaccuracies in the figures used.

ACTIVITY 4.15

The directors of Manuff (Steel) Ltd have decided to close one of its factories. There has been a reduction in the demand for the products made at the factory in recent years and the directors of the company are not optimistic about the long-term prospects for these products. The factory is situated in the north of England where unemployment is high.

The factory is leased and there are four years of the lease remaining. The directors are uncertain as to whether the factory should be closed immediately or at the end of the period of the lease. Another company has offered to sublease the premises from Manuff (Steel) Ltd at a rental of £40,000 per annum for the remainder of the lease period.

The machinery and equipment at the factory cost £1,500,000 and have a written down value of £400,000. In the event of immediate closure, the machinery and equipment could be sold for £220,000. The working capital at the factory is £420,000 and could be liquidated for that amount immediately if required. Alternatively, the working capital can be liquidated in full at the end of the lease period. Immediate closure would result in redundancy payments to employees of £180,000.

If the factory continues in operation until the end of the lease period, the following operating profits (losses) are expected:

	Year I	Year 2	Year 3	Year 4
	£000	£000	£000	£000
Operating profit (loss)	160	(40)	30	20

The above figures include a charge of £90,000 per year for depreciation of machinery and equipment. The residual value of the machinery and equipment at the end of the lease period is estimated at £40,000.

Redundancy payments are expected to be £150,000 at the end of the lease period if the factory continues in operation. The company has a cost of capital of 12 per cent. Ignore taxation.

Required:

(a) Calculate the incremental cash flows arising from a decision to continue operations until the end of the lease period rather than to close immediately.

(b) Calculate the net present value of continuing operations until the end of the lease period rather than closing immediately.

(c) What other factors might the directors of the company take into account before making a final decision on the timing of the factory closure?

(d) State, with reasons, whether or not the company should continue to operate the factory until the end of the lease period.

Your answer to this activity should be as follows:

(a)   *Incremental cash flows*

		Years			
	0	1	2	3	4
	£000	£000	£000	£000	£000
Operating cash flows (note 1)		250	50	120	110
Sale of machinery (note 2)	(220)				40
Redundancy costs (note 3)	180				(150)
Sublease rentals (note 4)		(40)	(40)	(40)	(40)
Working capital invested (note 5)	(420)				420
	(460)	210	10	80	380

(b)

Discount rate 12%	1.00	0.89	0.80	0.71	0.64
Present value	(460)	186.9	8.0	56.8	243.2
Net present value	34.9				

Notes

1. *The operating cash flows are calculated by adding back the depreciation charge for the year to the operating profit for the year. In the case of an operating loss, the depreciation charge is deducted.*

2. *In the event of closure, machinery could be sold immediately. Thus an opportunity cost of £220,000 is incurred if operations continue.*

3. *By continuing operations, there will be a saving in immediate redundancy costs*

of £180,000. However, redundancy costs of £150,000 will be paid in four years' time.
4. By continuing operations, the opportunity to sublease the factory will be forgone.
5. Immediate closure would mean that working capital could be liquidated. By continuing operations, this opportunity is forgone. However, working capital can be liquidated in four years' time.

(c) Other factors which may influence the decision include:

■ The overall strategy of the company. The company may need to set the decision within a broader context. It may be necessary to manufacture the products made at the factory because they are an integral part of the company's product range. The company may wish to avoid redundancies in an area of high unemployment for as long as possible.

■ Flexibility. A decision to close the factory is probably irreversible. If the factory continues, however, there may be a chance that the prospects for the factory will brighten in the future.

■ Creditworthiness of sublessee. The company should investigate the creditworthiness of the sublessee. Failure to receive the expected sublease payments would make the closure option far less attractive.

■ Accuracy of forecasts. The forecasts made by the company should be examined carefully. Inaccuracies in the forecasts or any underlying assumptions may change the expected outcomes.

(d) The NPV of the decision to continue operations rather than close immediately is positive. Hence, shareholders would be better off if the directors took this course of action. The factory should, therefore, continue in operation rather than close down. This decision is likely to be welcomed by employees, as unemployment is high in the area.

SELF-ASSESSMENT QUESTION 4.1

Beacon Chemicals plc is considering the erection of a new plant to produce a chemical named X14. The new plant's capital cost is estimated at £100,000 and if its construction is approved now, the plant can be erected and commence production by the end of 19X6. £50,000 has already been spent on research and development work. Estimates of revenues and costs arising from the operation of the new plant appear below:

	19X7	19X8	19X9	19X0	19X1
Sales price (£ per unit)	100	120	120	100	80
Sales volume (units)	800	1,000	1,200	1,000	800
Variable costs (£ per unit)	50	50	40	30	40
Fixed costs (£000s)	30	30	30	30	30

If the new plant is erected, sales of some existing products will be lost and this will result in a loss of contribution of £15,000 per year over its life.

The accountant has informed you that the fixed costs include depreciation of £20,000 per annum on new plant. They also include an allocation of £10,000 for fixed overheads. A separate study has indicated that if the new plant was built, additional overheads, excluding depreciation, arising from its construction would be £8,000 per year. The plant would require additional working capital of £30,000. For the purposes of your initial calculations ignore taxation.

Required:

(a) Deduce the relevant annual cash flows associated with building and operating the plant.
(b) Deduce the payback period.
(c) Calculate the net present value using a discount rate of 8 per cent.

(Hint: You should deal with the investment in working capital by treating it as a cash outflow at the start of the project and an inflow at the end.)

Summary

In this chapter we considered how managers might approach the problem of assessing investment opportunities. We saw that there are basically four methods which are used to any significant extent in practice: accounting rate of return; payback period; net present value; and internal rate of return. The first two of these are very seriously flawed by their failure to take full account of the time dimension of investments. Assuming that the objective of making investment is to maximise the wealth of shareholders, the NPV method is, theoretically, far the most superior of the four methods in that it rationally and fully takes account of all relevant information. Since IRR is similar to NPV, it tends to give similar signals to those provided by NPV. However, IRR does suffer from a fundamental theoretical flaw which can lead to it giving misleading signals on some occasions.

Review questions

4.1 Why is the net present value method of investment appraisal considered to be theoretically superior to other methods of investment appraisal found in the literature?

4.2 The payback method has been criticised for not taking into account the time value of money. Could this limitation be overcome? If so, would this method then be preferable to the NPV method?

4.3 Research indicates that the IRR method is a more popular method of investment appraisal than the NPV method. Why might this be?

4.4 Why are cash flows rather than profit flows used in the IRR, NPV and PP methods of investment appraisal?

Examination-style questions ─────────────────────────────

Solutions to those questions marked with an asterisk are given at the end of the text. Questions 4.1–4.3 are at basic level. Questions 4.4–4.6 are at intermediate/ advanced level.

4.1* The directors of Mylo Ltd are currently considering two mutually exclusive investment projects. Both projects are concerned with the purchase of new plant. The following data is available for each project:

	Project	
	I	*2*
	£	£
Cost (immediate outlay)	100,000	60,000
Expected annual net profit (loss):		
Year I	29,000	18,000
2	(1,000)	(2,000)
3	2,000	4,000
Estimated residual value	7,000	6,000

The company has an estimated cost of capital of 10 per cent and employs the straight-line method of depreciation for all fixed assets when calculating net profit. Neither project would increase the working capital of the company. The company has sufficient funds to meet all capital expenditure requirements.

Required:

(a) Calculate for each project:
   (i) the net present value;
   (ii) the approximate internal rate of return; and
   (iii) the payback period.
(b) State which, if any, of the two investment projects the directors of Mylo Ltd should accept, and why.
(c) State, in general terms, which method of investment appraisal you consider to be most appropriate for evaluating investment projects and why.

4.2 C. George (Controls) Ltd manufactures a thermostat that can be used in a range of kitchen appliances. The manufacturing process is, at present, semi-

automated. The equipment used cost £540,000 and has a written-down value of
£300,000. Demand for the product has been fairly stable and output has been
maintained at 50,000 units per annum in recent years.

The following data, based on the current level of output, has been prepared in
respect of the product:

	Per unit	
	£	£
Selling price		12.40
Less:		
Labour	3.30	
Materials	3.65	
Overheads: Variable	1.58	
Fixed	1.60	
		10.13
Profit		2.27

Although the existing equipment is expected to last for a further four years
before it is sold for an estimated £40,000, the company has recently been
considering purchasing new equipment which would completely automate much
of the production process. The new equipment would cost £670,000 and would
have an expected life of four years, at the end of which it would be sold for an
estimated £70,000. If the new equipment is purchased, the old equipment could be
sold for £150,000 immediately.

The assistant to the company accountant has prepared a report to help assess
the viability of the proposed change which includes the following data:

	Per unit	
	£	£
Selling price		12.40
Less:		
Labour	1.20	
Materials	3.20	
Overheads: Variable	1.40	
Fixed	3.30	
		9.10
Profit		3.30

Depreciation charges will increase by £85,000 per annum as a result of
purchasing the new machinery; however, other fixed costs are not expected to
change.

In the report the assistant wrote:

The figures shown above which relate to the proposed change are based on the
current level of output and take account of a depreciation charge of £150,000 per

annum in respect of the new equipment. The effect of purchasing the new equipment will be to increase the net profit to sales ratio from 18.3% to 26.6%. In addition, the purchase of the new equipment will enable us to reduce our stock level immediately by £130,000.

In view of these facts I recommend purchase of the new equipment.

The company has a cost of capital of 12 per cent. Ignore taxation.

Required:

(a) Prepare a statement of the incremental cash flows arising from the purchase of the new equipment.
(b) Calculate the net present value of the proposed purchase of new equipment.
(c) State, with reasons, whether the company should purchase the new equipment.
(d) Explain why cash flow forecasts are used rather than profit forecasts to assess the viability of proposed capital expenditure projects.

4.3 Lansdown Engineers Limited is considering replacing its existing heating system. A firm of heating engineers has recommended two schemes each of which will give a similar heating performance. Details of these and of the cost of the existing system appear below:

	Year	Existing system £000	System A £000	System B £000
Capital cost	0		70	150
Annual running cost	1–10	145	140	120
Scrap value	10	10	14	30

The existing heating system at present has a book value of £50,000 and a scrap value of £5,000. To keep the existing system working an overhaul costing £20,000 would be required immediately. For your calculations you should ignore inflation and taxation. The company has a 12 per cent cost of capital.

Required:

(a) Calculate the net present cost of each of the two new schemes. You should consider each in isolation and ignore the existing system.
(b) Calculate the incremental cash flows of scheme B over the existing system.
(c) Calculate the internal rate of return on the cash flow calculated in section (b).
(d) On the basis of your calculations give briefly your recommendations with reasons.

4.4 Chesterfield Wanderers is a professional football club which has enjoyed considerable success in both national and European competitions in recent years. As a result, the club has accumulated £1 million to spend on the further development of the club. The board of directors is currently considering two mutually exclusive options for spending the funds available.

The first option is to acquire another player. The team manager has expressed a keen interest in acquiring Basil ('Bazza') Ramsey, a central defender, who currently plays for a rival club. The rival club has agreed to release the player immediately for £1 million if required. A decision to acquire 'Bazza' Ramsey would mean that the existing central defender, Vinnie Smith, could be sold to another club. Chesterfield Wanderers has recently received an offer of £220,000 for this player. This offer is still open but will only be accepted if 'Bazza' Ramsey joins Chesterfield Wanderers. If this does not happen, Vinnie Smith will be expected to stay on with the club until the end of his playing career in five years' time. During this period, Vinnie will receive an annual salary of £40,000 each year and a loyalty bonus of £20,000 at the end of his five-year period with the club.

Assuming 'Bazza' Ramsey is acquired, the team manager estimates that gate receipts will increase by £250,000 in the first year and £130,000 in each of the four following years. There will also be an increase in advertising and sponsorship revenues of £120,000 for each of the next five years if the player is acquired. At the end of five years, the player can be sold to a club in a lower division and Chesterfield Wanderers will expect to receive £100,000 as a transfer fee. During his period at the club, 'Bazza' will receive an annual salary of £80,000 and a loyalty bonus of £40,000 after five years.

The second option is for the club to improve its ground facilities. The West Stand of the football ground could be converted into an all-seater area and 'Executive Boxes' could be built for companies wishing to offer corporate hospitality to business clients. These improvements would also cost £1 million and would take one year to complete. During this period, the West Stand would be closed resulting in a reduction of gate receipts of £180,000. However, gate receipts for each of the following four years would be £440,000 higher than current receipts. In five years' time, the football club has plans to sell the existing ground and to move to a new stadium nearby. Payment for the improvements will be made when the work has been completed at the end of the first year.

Whichever option is chosen, the board of directors has decided to take on additional ground staff. The additional wage bill is expected to be £35,000 per annum over the next five years. The club has a cost of capital of 10 per cent. Ignore taxation.

Required:

(a) Calculate the incremental cash flows arising from each of the options available to the club.

(b) Calculate the net present value of each of the options.

(c) On the basis of the calculations made in (b) above, which of the two options would you choose and why?

(d) Discuss the validity of using the net present value method in making investment decisions for a professional football club.

4.5* Newton Electronics Ltd has incurred expenditure of £5 million over the past three years researching and developing a miniature hearing aid. The hearing aid is now fully developed and the directors of the company are considering which of three mutually exclusive options should be taken to exploit the potential of the new product. The options are as follows:

1. The company could manufacture the hearing aid itself. This would be a new departure for the company which has so far concentrated on research and development projects only. However, the company has manufacturing space available which it currently rents to another business for £100,000 per annum. The company would have to purchase plant and equipment costing £9 million and invest £3 million in working capital immediately for production to begin.

   A market research report, for which the company paid £50,000, indicates that the new product has an expected life of five years. Sales of the product during this period are predicted as follows:

   Predicted sales for the year ended 30 November

	19X3	19X4	19X5	19X6	19X7
Number of units (000s)	800	1,400	1,800	1,200	500

   The selling price per unit will be £30 in the first year but will fall to £22 in the following three years. In the final year of the product's life, the selling price will fall to £20. Variable production costs are predicted to be £14 per unit and fixed production costs (including depreciation) will be £2.4 million per annum. Marketing costs will be £2 million per annum.

   The company intends to depreciate the plant and equipment using the straight-line method and based on an estimated residual value at the end of the five years of £1 million. The company has a cost of capital of 10 per cent.

2. Newton Electronics Ltd could agree to another company manufacturing and marketing the product under licence. A multinational company, Faraday Electricals plc, has offered to undertake the manufacture and marketing of the product and, in return, will make a royalty payment to Newton Electronics Ltd of £5 per unit. It has been estimated that the annual number of sales of the hearing aid will be 10 per cent higher if the multinational company, rather than Newton Electronics Ltd, manufactures and markets the product.

3. Newton Electronics Ltd could sell the patent rights to Faraday Electricals plc for £24 million, payable in two equal instalments. The first instalment would be payable immediately and the second instalment would be payable at the end of two years. This option would give Faraday Electricals the exclusive right to manufacture and market the new product.

Ignore taxation,

Required:

(a) Calculate the net present value of each of the options available to Newton Electronics Ltd.
(b) Identify and discuss any other factors which Newton Electronics Ltd should consider before arriving at a decision.
(c) What do you consider to be the most suitable option, and why.

4.6   Haverhill Engineers Limited, manufactures components for the car industry. It is considering automating its line for producing crankshaft bearings. The automated equipment will cost £700,000. It will replace equipment with a scrap value of £50,000 and a book written-down value of £180,000.

At present the line has a capacity of 1.25 million units per annum but typically it has only been run at 80 per cent of capacity because of the lack of demand for its output. The new line has a capacity of 1.4 million units per annum. Its life is expected to be 5 years and its scrap value at that time £100,000.

The accountant has prepared the following cost estimates based on output of 1,000,000 units per annum:

	Old line (per unit)	New line (per unit)
	P	P
Materials	40	36
Labour	22	10
Variable overheads	14	14
Fixed overheads	44	20
	120	80
Selling price	150	150
Profit per unit	30	70

Fixed overheads include depreciation on the old machine of £40,000 per annum and £120,000 for the new machine. It is considered that for the company overall, fixed overheads are unlikely to change.

The introduction of the new machine will enable stocks to be reduced by £160,000. The company uses 10 per cent as its cost of capital. You should ignore taxation.

Required:

(a) Prepare a statement of the incremental cash flows arising from the project.
(b) Calculate the project's net present value.
(c) Calculate the project's approximate internal rate of return.
(d) Explain the terms net present value and internal rate of return. State which method you consider to be preferable, giving reasons for your choice.

Appendix: present value table

Present value of 1, i.e. $(1 + r)^{-n}$

where r = discount rate
n = number of periods until payment

Discount rates (r)

Periods (n)	1%	2%	3%	4%	5%	6%	7%	8%	9%	10%	
1	0.990	0.980	0.971	0.962	0.952	0.943	0.935	0.926	0.917	0.909	1
2	0.980	0.961	0.943	0.925	0.907	0.890	0.873	0.857	0.842	0.826	2
3	0.971	0.942	0.915	0.889	0.864	0.840	0.816	0.794	0.772	0.751	3
4	0.961	0.924	0.888	0.855	0.823	0.792	0.763	0.735	0.708	0.683	4
5	0.951	0.906	0.863	0.822	0.784	0.747	0.713	0.681	0.650	0.621	5
6	0.942	0.888	0.837	0.790	0.746	0.705	0.666	0.630	0.596	0.564	6
7	0.933	0.871	0.813	0.760	0.711	0.665	0.623	0.583	0.547	0.513	7
8	0.923	0.853	0.789	0.731	0.677	0.627	0.582	0.540	0.502	0.467	8
9	0.914	0.837	0.766	0.703	0.645	0.592	0.544	0.500	0.460	0.424	9
10	0.905	0.820	0.744	0.676	0.614	0.558	0.508	0.463	0.422	0.386	10
11	0.896	0.804	0.722	0.650	0.585	0.527	0.475	0.429	0.388	0.350	11
12	0.887	0.788	0.701	0.625	0.557	0.497	0.444	0.397	0.356	0.319	12
13	0.879	0.773	0.681	0.601	0.530	0.469	0.415	0.368	0.326	0.290	13
14	0.870	0.758	0.661	0.577	0.505	0.442	0.388	0.340	0.299	0.263	14
15	0.861	0.743	0.642	0.555	0.481	0.417	0.362	0.315	0.275	0.239	15

	11%	12%	13%	14%	15%	16%	17%	18%	19%	20%	
1	0.901	0.893	0.885	0.877	0.870	0.862	0.855	0.847	0.840	0.833	1
2	0.812	0.797	0.783	0.769	0.756	0.743	0.731	0.718	0.706	0.694	2
3	0.731	0.712	0.693	0.675	0.658	0.641	0.624	0.609	0.593	0.579	3
4	0.659	0.636	0.613	0.592	0.572	0.552	0.534	0.516	0.499	0.482	4
5	0.593	0.567	0.543	0.519	0.497	0.476	0.456	0.437	0.419	0.402	5
6	0.535	0.507	0.480	0.456	0.432	0.410	0.390	0.370	0.352	0.335	6
7	0.482	0.452	0.425	0.400	0.376	0.354	0.333	0.314	0.296	0.279	7
8	0.434	0.404	0.376	0.351	0.327	0.305	0.285	0.266	0.249	0.233	8
9	0.391	0.361	0.333	0.308	0.284	0.263	0.243	0.225	0.209	0.194	9
10	0.352	0.322	0.295	0.270	0.247	0.227	0.208	0.191	0.176	0.162	10
11	0.317	0.287	0.261	0.237	0.215	0.195	0.178	0.162	0.148	0.135	11
12	0.286	0.257	0.231	0.208	0.187	0.168	0.152	0.137	0.124	0.112	12
13	0.258	0.229	0.204	0.182	0.163	0.145	0.130	0.116	0.104	0.093	13
14	0.232	0.205	0.181	0.160	0.141	0.125	0.111	0.099	0.088	0.078	14
15	0.209	0.183	0.160	0.140	0.123	0.108	0.095	0.084	0.074	0.065	15

CHAPTER FIVE

Capital Investment Appraisal – Further Issues

OBJECTIVES

On completion of this chapter you should be able to:

- Discuss the use of investment appraisal methods in practice.

- Discuss the issues raised when a business invests in advanced manufacturing technology (AMT).

- Outline the methods used to review and control capital investment projects.

- Explain the modifications to the simple NPV decision rule which we must undertake where there is capital rationing, or when comparing competing projects which have unequal lives.

- Discuss the effect of inflation on the appraisal of projects and how inflation may be dealt with.

- Explain shareholder value analysis (SVA) and its relationship to the discounted cash flow principles discussed in the previous chapter.

Introduction

In this chapter we explore a number of issues relating to investment appraisal. We begin by considering some research evidence relating to the use of the appraisal techniques in practice. We will see that, although NPV may be theoretically superior to other techniques, it is not the most popular method of investment appraisal. We then go on to consider the appraisal of investments in advanced manufacturing technology (AMT) and the particular issues this can raise.

Once a decision has been made to implement a capital investment proposal, there must be proper review and control procedures in place. In this chapter, we discuss the ways in which managers can oversee capital investment projects and how control may be exercised throughout the life of the project. We also consider the impact of inflation on project appraisal and the way in which inflation may be dealt with.

The simple NPV decision rules which we considered in the previous chapter were: (1) that we should accept all projects with a positive NPV, as this would lead to the maximisation of shareholder wealth; and (2) that, where there are competing projects, the project with the higher (or highest) NPV should be selected. In practice, things are not always very straightforward and there are certain circumstances which call for a modification to these simple decision rules. In this chapter, we consider three such circumstances.

Finally, we consider how the discounted cash flow approach to investment appraisal can form the basis for a new way of setting financial goals and for managing a business enterprise. A number of progressive companies, particularly those in the United States, employ a technique known as 'shareholder value analysis' (SVA) which uses the discounted cash flow principle discussed in the previous chapter as a basis for strategic management decisions.

Investment decision-making in practice

As a footnote to our examination of investment appraisal techniques, it is interesting to consider the practical significance of these techniques. In recent years, there have been a number of studies concerning the use of investment appraisal techniques by businesses. These studies are illuminating as they reveal a clear gulf between the theory and practice of investment appraisal. For example, a study of 278 UK manufacturing companies in 1993 revealed insights into the use of the different investment appraisal methods dealt with earlier, as shown in Table 5.1.[1] This table shows that payback is the most popular method of appraisal, and that where discounted cash flow methods are used, the IRR method

Table 5.1   The use of different investment appraisal methods by UK manufacturing companies

	Used either often or always %
Payback (unadjusted)	63
Payback (using discounted cash flows)	42
ARR	41
IRR	57
NPV	43

Source: Adapted from Drury et al. (1993).

is more popular than the NPV method. These research findings are consistent with earlier studies undertaken on this topic.

ACTIVITY 5.1

How do you explain the popularity of the payback method given the theoretical limitations discussed in the previous chapter?

A number of possible reasons may explain this finding:

■ *PP is easy to understand and use.*
■ *It can avoid the problems of forecasting far into the future.*
■ *It gives emphasis to the early cash flows when there is greater certainty concerning their accuracy.*
■ *It emphasises the importance of liquidity. Where a business has liquidity problems, a short payback period for a project is likely to appear attractive.*

The use of discounted cash flows rather than unadjusted cash flows in the payback calculation overcomes one of the weaknesses of this method (i.e. that it ignores the time value of money). However, other serious problems with this method (which were discussed in the previous chapter) still remain.

The importance of payback may suggest a lack of sophistication among managers concerning investment appraisal. This criticism is most often made against managers of smaller businesses. In fact, the survey found that smaller businesses were much less likely to use discounted cash flow methods than larger businesses. This finding is also consistent with earlier research in this area.

The table indicates, however, that many businesses use more than one method to appraise investments. Indeed, the survey found that only 14 per cent of businesses surveyed used the payback method without combining it with another method. It is, therefore, possible that payback is used by some businesses as an initial screening device and that projects which pass successfully through this stage are then subject to more sophisticated discounted cash flow analysis. Table 5.1 may suggest that most businesses use one of the two discounted cash flow methods.

The possible reasons why IRR is more popular than NPV have been dealt with in a review question at the end of the previous chapter. You will recall that the expression of outcomes in percentage terms rather than absolute terms appears to be more acceptable to managers. This may be due to the fact that they are used to using percentage figures as targets (e.g. return on capital employed). It is probably worth mentioning again that although NPV is theoretically superior to IRR, both methods will produce the same result in most cases.

Investment appraisal and advanced manufacturing technology (AMT)

In recent years, we have seen new forms of manufacturing, often using computer technology, being introduced into businesses. The impetus for the use of advanced manufacturing technology (AMT) has been an increasingly competitive environment, which has, in turn, led to a need to produce high-quality products at relatively low unit cost. The use of high technology can lead to real cost savings by:

- Reducing the level of stock requirements as new systems of stock planning control are often implemented in tandem with the new technology (this point will be dealt with in Chapter 10).
- Reducing the factory space requirements, as new technology is often more compact than older methods of production.
- Reducing labour costs as less staff is required.
- Reducing the amount of wastage and inspection times required through the production of higher-quality products.
- Increasing flexibility of production through the ability to switch easily between products.

In addition, AMT can often increase the production capacity of the business and allow greater flexibility in production runs.

However, investment in AMT can be costly and may result in a pattern of future cash flows which reveals increases over time and which extend over a significant period (see Figure 5.1).

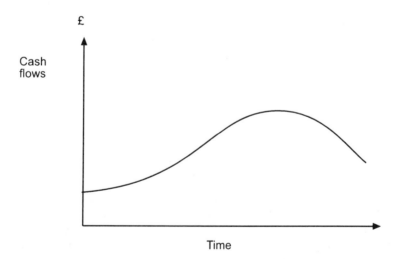

Figure 5.1   Possible pattern of cash flows for AMT investment

---

ACTIVITY 5.2

What are the implications of this cash flow pattern for businesses which use the following methods:

1. the payback method; and
2. the NPV method of investment appraisal?

We saw in the previous chapter that the PP method has an inherent problem, namely, that it places emphasis on the short term and ignores relevant information beyond the payback period. Where the cash flow pattern cited above exists for AMT projects, the use of the payback period (PP) can result in a bias against these projects. Given the widespread use of PP, as mentioned above, this can be a significant problem.

The NPV approach will take account of cash flows over the whole period and then adjust these flows to take account of the time value of money. It should, therefore, continue to provide the most appropriate means of evaluating proposals.

EXHIBIT 5.1

In practice, a business which uses the PP method may acknowledge the long-term nature of AMT investment through the use of a longer payback period. The ACCA survey mentioned earlier, compared the AMT and non-AMT payback periods and found the following:

	%
The same payback period used	74
Longer payback period for AMT projects:	
1 year longer	15
2 years longer	3
3 years longer	1
4 years longer	1
Shorter payback for AMT projects	6

The results reveal that only a minority of businesses extend the payback period. Moreover, some businesses adopt a shorter payback period. This latter practice may be due to the fact that AMT projects are viewed as being more risky and, therefore, a shorter payback period is required.

Although, in principle, the NPV method should not produce any bias, there is evidence to suggest that some businesses use discount rates which are too high. Where this occurs, there will be a bias against projects, such as AMT projects, which have strong cash flows in the later years, as these cash flows will be discounted too heavily.

Whilst there is no difference in principle between the evaluation of AMT investments and other forms of investment, it is often the case that AMT will lead to some benefits which are difficult to quantify and which will not fit easily into investment appraisal calculations. As a result, the calculations produced may ignore these benefits and so understate the profitability of AMT projects.

ACTIVITY 5.3

What benefits might AMT bring which are difficult to quantify?

Possible benefits may include:

- *Improved quality of products, leading to increased sales.*
- *Fewer staff, leading to fewer 'people problems' and, as a consequence, lower costs.*
- *An ability to produce goods more in line with customer specifications, leading to increased sales.*
- *An ability to maintain market share and survive in a competitive environment.*

You may have thought of others.

In view of these possible benefits, it becomes even more important for managers to give consideration to any 'other factors' before making a final decision. This is of course particularly important when the NPV calculation reveals a negative figure. Where a negative net cash flow is indicated for an AMT project, the unquantifiable benefits must be identified and weighed against the NPV calculations.

Management of the investment project

So far, we have been concerned with the process of carrying out the necessary calculations which will enable managers to select between already identified investment opportunities. This topic is given a great deal of emphasis in the literature on investment appraisal. Whilst the evaluation of projects is undoubtedly important, we must bear in mind, however, that it is only part of the process of investment decision-making. There are other important aspects to which managers must also give consideration.

It is possible to see the investment process as a sequence of five key stages (see Figure 5.2). Each of these stages must be given proper consideration by managers. The five stages are outlined below:

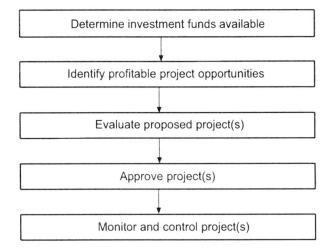

Figure 5.2   Managing the investment decision

Decide on the amount of funds available for investment

The amount available for investment may be determined by the external market for funds or may be determined by internal management. In practice, it seems that it is often the latter which has the greatest influence on the amount available for investment. Whichever factor determines the upper limit on available capital for a period, it may be that the funds available will not be sufficient to finance the profitable investment opportunities available. When this occurs some form of 'capital rationing' has to be undertaken. This means that managers are faced with the task of deciding on the most profitable use of the investment funds available. This problem requires some modification to the NPV decision rule; we discussed this topic in the previous chapter and it is one to which we will return in a subsequent section.

Identify profitable opportunities

A vitally important part of the investment process is the search for profitable investment opportunities. The business should carry out methodical routines for identifying feasible projects. This may be done through a research and development section or by some other means. One way or another, however, the business must look for good investment opportunities. Failure to do so will inevitably lead to the business losing its competitive position regarding product development, production methods or market penetration. To help identify good investment opportunities, some businesses provide financial incentives to staff who have good ideas. The search process will, however, usually involve looking outside the business to identify changes in technology, customer demand, market conditions, and so on. Information will need to be gathered and this may take some time, particularly for unusual or non-routine investment opportunities.

Evaluate project

In order for management to agree to the investment of funds in a project there must be a proper screening of each proposal put forward. For projects of any size, this will involve providing answers to a number of key questions including the following:

- What is the nature and purpose of the project?
- Does the project align with the overall objectives of the business?
- How much finance is required?
- What other resources (e.g. expertise, factory space, and so forth) is required for successful completion of the project?
- How long will the project last and what are the key stages of the project?
- What is the expected pattern of cash flows?
- What are the main problems associated with the project and how can they be overcome?
- What is the NPV/IRR of the project? How does this compare with other opportunities available?
- Has risk and inflation been taken into account in the appraisal process and, if so, what are the results?

It is important to appreciate that the ability and commitment of those responsible for proposing and managing the project will be vitally important to the success of the investment. Hence, when evaluating a new project, those proposing the project will be judged along with the project. In some cases, top management may decide not to support a project, which appears profitable on paper, if they lack confidence in the ability of key managers to see the project through successfully to completion.

Approve project

Once the managers responsible for investment decision-making are satisfied that the project should be undertaken, formal approval can be given. However, a decision on a project may be postponed if top management believe they need more information from those proposing the project or that revisions are required to the proposal. In some cases, the project proposal may be rejected if it is considered unprofitable or likely to fail. Before rejecting a proposal, however, the implications of not pursuing the project for such areas as market share, staff morale and existing business operations must be carefully considered.

Monitor and control the project

Making a decision to invest in the necessary plant to go into production of a new product does not automatically cause the investment to be made and production to go smoothly ahead. Managers will need actively to manage the project through to completion. This, in turn, will require further information gathering.

Management should receive progress reports at regular intervals concerning the project. These reports should provide information relating to the actual cash flows for each stage of the project, which can then be compared with the forecast figures provided when the proposal was submitted for approval. The reasons for any significant variations should be ascertained and corrective action taken where possible. Any changes in the expected completion date of the project or expected variations in future cash flows from budget should be reported immediately. In extreme cases, managers may abandon the project if circumstances appear to have changed dramatically for the worse.

Project management techniques (e.g. critical path analysis) should be employed wherever possible and their effectiveness reported to top management.

An important part of the control process is a *post-completion audit* of the project. This is essentially a review of the project performance in order to see whether it lived up to expectations and whether any lessons can be learned from the way in which the investment process was carried out. In addition to an evaluation of financial costs and benefits, non-financial measures of performance such as the ability to meet deadline dates and levels of quality achieved should also be reported on.

The fact that a post-completion audit is an integral part of the management of the project should also encourage those who submit projects to use realistic estimates. Where overoptimistic estimates are used in order to secure project approval, the managers responsible will find themselves accountable at the post-completion audit stage.

ACTIVITY 5.4

Can you think of any drawbacks with the use of post-completion audits?

One problem that has been suggested is that a post-completion audit may inhibit managers from proposing and supporting projects which carry a high level of risk. If things go wrong they could be blamed. This may result in only low-risk projects being submitted for consideration. Another problem is that managers may feel threatened by the post-audit investigations and so will not co-operate fully with the audit team.

However, manager behaviour is likely to be influenced by the way in which the post-completion audit is conducted. If it is seen by managers as simply a device to apportion blame, then the problems mentioned above may well occur. However, if it is used as a constructive tool where the main objective is to learn from past experience, and the high-risk nature of particular projects are taken into account, the problems mentioned should not arise.

Post-completion audits, however, can be difficult and time-consuming, and so the likely benefits must be weighed against the costs involved. A business may feel, therefore, that only projects above a certain size should be subject to a post-completion audit.

Investment decisions when funds are limited

We have made it clear above that projects which reveal a positive NPV should be undertaken if the company wishes to maximise shareholder wealth. However, what if there are insufficient funds available to undertake all the projects with a positive NPV? In practice, it may be that either the market will not be prepared to provide the necessary funds or top management has decided to impose a limit on the amount of funds to be allocated to investment projects. Where, for any reason, finance is rationed, the basic NPV rules mentioned in the previous chapter require modification. In order to illustrate the modifications required, let us consider Example 5.1.

Example 5.1

Unicorn Engineering Ltd is currently considering three possible investment projects: X, Y and Z. The expected pattern of cash flows for each project is as follows:

	Project cash flows		
	X	Y	Z
	£m.	£m.	£m.
Initial outlay	(8)	(9)	(11)
1 year's time	5	5	4
2 years' time	2	3	4
3 years' time	3	3	5
4 years' time	4	5	6.5

The company has a cost of finance of 12 per cent and the investment budget for the year is restricted to £12m. Each project is divisible (i.e. it is possible to undertake part of a project if required).

Which investment project(s) should the company undertake?

If we discount the cash flows, using the cost of finance as the appropriate discount rate, we obtain the following NPVs:

Project X			Project Y			Project Z		
Cash £m.	12% discount rate	PV £m.	Cash £m.	12% discount rate	PV £m.	Cash £m.	12% discount rate	PV £m.
(8)	1.00	(8.0)	(9)	1.00	(9.0)	(11)	1.00	(11.0)
5	0.89	4.5	5	0.89	4.5	4	0.89	3.6
2	0.80	1.6	3	0.80	2.4	4	0.80	3.2
3	0.71	2.1	3	0.71	2.1	5	0.71	3.6
4	0.64	2.6	5	0.64	3.2	6.5	0.64	4.2
Net present value		2.8			3.2			3.6

Given the calculations above, you may feel that the best approach to the problem of limited finance in the current year would be to rank the projects according to their NPV. Hence, Project Z would be ranked first, Project Y would be ranked second and Project X would be ranked last. As finance is limited to £12m. in the current year, this approach would lead to the acceptance of Project Z (£11m.) and part of Project Y (£1m.). The total NPV from the £12m. invested would, therefore, be £3.6 + 1/9 (£3.2) = £4.0. However, this solution would not represent the most efficient use of the limited finance available.

The best approach, when projects are divisible, is to maximise the *present value per £ of scarce finance*. By dividing the present values of the future cash inflows by the outlay for each project, we obtain a figure which represents the present value per £ of scarce finance. This figure is known as the *profitability index*.

Using the information in the example above, the following figures would be obtained for the profitability index for each project:

Project X	Project Y	Project Z
$= \dfrac{10.8^*}{8.0}$	$\dfrac{12.2}{9.0}$	$\dfrac{14.6}{11.0}$
$= 1.35$	1.36	1.33

Note: * The numerators represent the future cash flows *before* deducting the investment outlays.

The profitability index will be greater than 1 where the NPV from the project is positive.

ACTIVITY 5.5

What do you think the profitability index calculated above indicates? What would be the NPV of the £12m. invested, assuming the profitability index approach is used?

The above calculations indicate that Project Y should be ranked first, Project X should be ranked second and Project Z should be ranked third. To maximise the use of the limited funds available (£12m.) we should, therefore, undertake Project Y (£9m.) and part of Project X (£3m.).

The total NPV of the £12m. invested would be £3.2 + 3/8 (£2.8) = £4.3. This figure is higher than the total NPV obtained where projects were ranked according to their absolute NPVs.

In some cases, there may be a requirement for investment finance covering more than one period and limits may be placed on the funding of projects in each of the periods. In such circumstances, there will be more than one constraint to consider. A mathematical technique known as *linear programming* can be used to maximise the NPV, given that not all projects with a positive NPV can be undertaken. This technique adopts the same approach (i.e. it maximises the NPV per £ of scarce finance) as that illustrated above. Software programmes are available to undertake the analysis required for multiperiod capital rationing problems.

It was mentioned above that the profitability index approach is only suitable where projects are divisible. Where this is not the case, we must look at the problem of limited funds in a different way.

ACTIVITY 5.6

What solution would you recommend for Unicorn Engineering Ltd if the projects were not divisible (i.e. it was not possible to undertake part of a project) and the finance available was:

1. £12m;
2. £18m;
3. £20m?

---

*If the projects are not divisible, we must look at the **total NPV** for each project (or combination of projects) and select that project (or combination) which will give the highest NPV for the finance available. If the capital available was £12m., we would recommend only Project Z as this would provide the highest NPV (£3.6m.) for the funds available for investment. If the capital available was £18m., we would recommend Projects X and Y as this would provide the highest NPV (£6.0m.). If the capital available was £20m. we would recommend Projects Y and Z as this would provide the highest NPV (£6.8m.)*

In some cases, the business may be faced with a situation where certain investment projects are competing for funds and so a decision must be made between them.

ACTIVITY 5.7

What solution would you recommend if all three projects were divisible but the business could select *either* Project X *or* Project Z but not both (i.e. they were mutually exclusive)? Assume the capital available is £12m.

In this case, it is useful to compare the combinations which are possible within the £12m. budget limit, to see which provides the highest NPV. There are really only two combinations:

1. *Project Y plus part of Project X; or*
2. *Project Y plus part of Project Z.*

The outcomes from each combination are shown below:

	Combination			
	1		2	
	Outlay £m.	NPV £m.	Outlay £m.	NPV £m.
Project Y	9	3.2	9	3.2
Project X (3/8 of total)	3	1.1		
Project Z (3/11 of total)			3	1.0
	12	4.3	12	4.2

We can see that the first combination would be the preferred one as it has a slightly higher NPV.

ACTIVITY 5.8

Assume the budget limit was £18m. rather than £12m. What would now be your recommended combination?

Your answer should be as follows:

	Combination			
	1		2	
	Outlay £m.	NPV £m.	Outlay £m.	NPV £m.
Project Y	9	3.2	9	3.2
Project X (whole)	8	2.8		
Project Z (9/11)			9	2.9
	17	6.0	18	6.1

In this case, we can see that we would recommend the second combination as this would give a slightly higher NPV.

Comparing projects with unequal lives

In the previous section, we considered a situation where it may be necessary to modify the simple NPV decision rules in order to make optimal investment decisions. In this section, we will consider a further situation where some modification to these rules is required.

On occasions, a business may find itself in a position where it has to decide between two (or more) competing projects which have different life spans. When this situation arises, there is a possibility that accepting the project with the shorter life will offer the business the opportunity to invest in a new project, which generates a positive NPV, sooner than if the project with the longer life was accepted. Where this is the case, we should take this fact into account in our analysis so that direct comparisons between the profitability of each project can be made. The problem with the simple form of NPV analysis is that future investment opportunities that may be available as a result of accepting a project with a shorter rather than a longer life, are not considered.

To illustrate how direct comparisons between two (or more) competing projects with unequal lives can be made, under the circumstances described above, let us consider Example 5.2.

Example 5.2

Khan Engineering Ltd has the opportunity to invest in two competing machines. Details of each machine are as follows:

	Machine A £000	Machine B £000
Initial outlay	(100)	(140)
Cash flows		
1 year's time	50	60
2 years' time	70	80
3 years' time	–	30

The company has a cost of capital of 10 per cent.

In which of the two machines, if either, should the company invest?

There are basically two ways of tackling this problem. The first way is to assume that the machines form part of a repeat chain of replacement and to compare the machines over a common period of time. If we assume that investment in Machine A can be repeated every two years and that investment in Machine B can be repeated every three years, the *shortest common period of time* over which the machines can be compared is six years (i.e. 2 × 3).

The first step in this process of comparison is to calculate the NPV for each project over their expected lives. Thus the NPV for each project will be as follows:

	Machine A		
	Cash flows	Discount rate	Present value
	£000	10%	£000
Initial outlay	(100)	1.00	(100.0)
1 year's time	50	0.91	45.5
2 years' time	70	0.83	58.1
Net present value			3.6

	Machine B		
	Cash flows	Discount rate	Present value
	£000	10%	£000
Initial outlay	(140)	1.00	(140.0)
1 year's time	60	0.91	54.6
2 years' time	80	0.83	66.4
3 years' time	32	0.75	24.0
Net present value			5.0

The next step is to calculate the NPV arising for each machine, over a six-year period, using the reinvestment assumption discussed above. That is, investment in Machine A will be repeated three times and investment in Machine B will be repeated twice during the six-year period.

This means that, for Machine A, the NPV over the six-year period will be equal to the NPV above (i.e. £3.6) plus equivalent amounts two years and four years later. The calculation will be:

$$\text{NPV} = £3.6 + \frac{3.6}{(1 + 0.1)^2} + \frac{3.6}{(1 + 0.1)^4}$$

$$= £9.1$$

These calculations can be shown in the form of a diagram as in Figure 5.3.

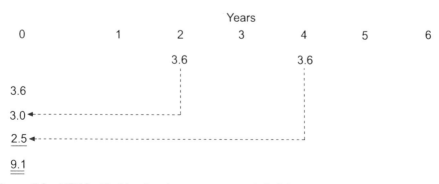

Figure 5.3 NPV for Machine A, using a common period of time

ACTIVITY 5.9

What is the NPV for Machine B over the six-year period? What would you advise the company to do?

In the case of Machine B, the NPV over the six-year period will be equal to the NPV above plus the equivalent amount three years later. The calculation will be:

$$NPV = 5.0 + \frac{5.0}{(1 + 0.1)^3}$$

$$= 8.8$$

The calculations set out above suggest that Machine A is the better buy as it will have the higher NPV over the six-year period.

You can imagine that, when investment projects have a longer life span than those in the example above, the calculations required using this method can be time-consuming. Fortunately, there is another method which can be used which avoids the need for laborious calculations. This approach uses the annuity concept to solve the problem. An annuity is simply an investment which pays a constant sum each year over a period of time. Thus fixed payments made in respect of a loan or mortgage or a fixed amount of income received from an investment bond would be examples of annuities.

Let us assume that you were given a choice of purchasing a new car either by paying £6,000 immediately or by paying three annual instalments of £2,410 commencing at the end of year one. Assuming interest rates of 10 per cent, the present value of the annuity payments would be:

	Cash outflows	Discount rate	Present value
	£	10%	£
I year's time	2,410	0.91	2,193
2 years' time	2,410	0.83	2,000
3 years' time	2,410	0.75	1,807
			6,000

As the present value of the immediate payment is £6,000, the above calculations mean that you will be indifferent as to the form of payment as they are equal in present value terms.

In the car loan example above, we saw that a cash sum paid today was the equivalent of making three annuity payments over a three-year period. The second approach to solving the problem of competing projects which have unequal lives, is based on the annuity principle. Put simply, the *equivalent annual annuity approach*, as it is referred to, converts the NPV of a project into an annual annuity stream over its expected life. This conversion is carried out for each competing project and the one which provides the higher (or highest) annual annuity is the most profitable project.

In order to establish the annual annuity equivalent of the NPV of a project, we apply the formula:

$$\frac{i}{1 - (1 + i)^{-n}}$$

where:

i = interest rate
n = number of years

Thus, using the information from the car loan example above, the annual value of an annuity which lasts for three years, which has a present value of £6,000 and where the discount rate is 10 per cent, is:

$$= £6,000 \times \frac{0.1}{1 - (1.1)^{-3}}$$

$$= £6,000 \times 0.402$$

$$= £2,412$$

(The small difference between this figure and the one used in the example earlier is due to rounding.)

There are tables which make life easier by providing the annual equivalent factors for a range of possible discount rates. An example of such a table is given at the end of this chapter.

ACTIVITY 5.10

Use the table provided to calculate the equivalent annual annuity for each machine referred to in Example 5.2 above. Which machine is the better buy?

The equivalent annual annuity for Machine A is:

3.6 × 0.5762 = 2.07

The equivalent annual annuity for Machine B is:

5.0 × 0.4021 = 2.01

This shows, once again, that Machine A is the better buy as it provides the higher annuity value.

SELF-ASSESSMENT QUESTION 5.1

Choi Ltd is considering the purchase of a new photocopier which could lead to considerable cost savings. There are two machines on the market that are suitable for the business. The two machines have the following outlays and expected cost savings:

	Lo-tek £	Hi-tek £
Initial outlay	10,000	15,000
Cost savings		
1 year's time	4,000	5,000
2 years' time	5,000	6,000
3 years' time	5,000	6,000
4 years' time		5,000

The company has a cost of finance of 12 per cent.

Required:

(a) evaluate each machine using:
    (i) the shortest common period of time approach; and
    (ii) the equivalent annual annuity approach.
(b) Which machine would you recommend and why?

The NPV approach and the ability to delay

In recent years we have witnessed some criticism of the NPV approach. This criticism is based on the view that conventional theory does not recognise the fact that, in practice, it is often possible to delay making an investment decision. This ability to delay, so it is argued, can have a profound effect on the final investment decision.

ACTIVITY 5.11

What are the possible benefits of delaying an investment decision?

By delaying a decision it may be possible to acquire more information concerning the likely outcome of the investment proposal. If a business decides not to delay, the investment decision, once made, may be irreversible. This may lead to losses if conditions prove unfavourable.

It is argued, therefore, that if managers do not exercise their option to delay, there may be an opportunity cost in the form of the benefits lost from later information. It has been claimed that this opportunity cost can often be large and that failure to take this into account can lead to grossly incorrect investment decisions. One way of dealing with this criticism is to modify the NPV decision rule so that the present value of the future cash flows must exceed the initial outlay *plus* any expected benefits from delaying the decision in order to obtain additional information.

The problem of inflation

Inflation is a problem with which modern businesses have to cope. Although the rate of inflation within an economy may change over time, there has been a persistent tendency for the general price level to rise in most economies. It is important to recognise this phenomenon when evaluating investment projects, as inflation will have an effect on both the cash flows and the discount rate over the life of the project.

During a period of inflation, the physical monetary amount required to acquire resources will rise over time and the business may seek to pass on any increase to customers in the form of higher prices. Inflation will also have an effect on the cost of financing the business, as investors seek to protect their investment from a decline in purchasing power by demanding higher returns. As a result of these changes, the cash flows and discount rates relating to the investment project will be affected.

In order to deal with the problem of inflation in the appraisal of investment projects, two possible approaches can be used:

Either

1. Include inflation in the calculations by adjusting annual cash flows by the expected rate of inflation, and by using a discount rate which is also adjusted for inflation. This will mean estimating the actual monetary cash flows expected from the project and using a market rate of interest which will take inflation into account.

Or

2. Exclude inflation from the calculations by adjusting cash flows accordingly and by using a 'real' discount rate which does not include any element to account for inflation.

Both methods, properly applied, will give the same result.

If all cash flows are expected to increase in line with the general rate of inflation, it would be possible to use current prices in your calculations, as these would represent the real cash flows from the project. However, it is unlikely that the relationship between the various items which go to make up the net cash flows of the business will remain constant over time. In practice, inflation is likely to affect the various items in different ways.

ACTIVITY 5.12

Can you explain why this might be the case?

Material costs may increase at a different rate than labour costs due to relative changes in demand. Certain costs may be fixed over time (e.g. lease payments) and may therefore be unaffected by inflation over the period of the project. In a highly competitive environment, a business may be unable to pass on all of the increase in costs to customers and so will have to absorb some of the increase by reducing profits. Thus cash inflows over time may not fully reflect the rise in the prices of the various inputs.

The differential impact of inflation means that separate adjustment for each of the monetary cash flows will be necessary. To compute the real cash flows from a project, it will be necessary to calculate the monetary cash flows relating to each item and then deflate these amounts by the *general* rate of inflation. This adjustment will provide us with the *current general purchasing power* of the cash flows. This measure of general purchasing power is of more relevance to investors than if the cash flows were deflated by a specific rate of inflation relevant to each type of cash flow. Similarly, the real discount rate will be deduced by deflating the market rate of interest by the *general* rate of inflation.

It is important to appreciate that the two approaches outlined are alternatives which cannot be mixed. Unfortunately, research evidence suggests that, in practice, this can often happen.

EXHIBIT 5.2

The ACCA survey, mentioned earlier, found that a large number of companies deal with inflation in an incorrect way. A sample of 195 companies revealed that 61 used a 'real' discount rate (i.e. a rate excluding inflation) and 134 used a nominal discount rate. The following combinations were found concerning the treatment of cash flows and discount rates:

	Discount rates	
	Real	Nominal
Adjustment to cash flows:		
By expected inflation rate	22	39*
No adjustment (i.e. current prices)	25	85
In real terms	14*	10
	61	134

Note * Indicates the correct treatment.

These results suggest a lack of understanding among many managers concerning the correct treatment of inflation. The application of incorrect methods of dealing with inflation will have a distorting effect on the NPV/IRR calculations which can lead to incorrect decisions being made. For example, discounting the expected cash flows which have been adjusted to take account of inflation using a real discount rate (i.e. which eliminates the inflation effect) will lead to an overstatement of NPV. This can, in turn, lead to the acceptance of a project which should have been rejected.

Extending the NPV concept: shareholder value analysis (SVA)

In recent years, there has been increasing recognition that NPV analysis can play an important role in setting overall financial goals for the business as a whole and for strategic decision-making. Shareholder value analysis (SVA) is a technique which is based on the idea that the primary role of the directors is to maximise the wealth of the shareholders. This, of course, is not a new idea and its role in financial management was discussed in Chapter 1. You will also find that it is a stated objective of many companies. It can be argued, however, that traditional measures of performance such as earnings per share, growth in profits and return on equity do not really capture the essence of this objective. These measures can be criticised for their emphasis on the short-term performance of the businesses. In practice, it is possible to take decisions which will lead to an improvement in these traditional measures over the short term but which will adversely affect the long-term wealth of shareholders (e.g. by cutting back on staff training, research expenditure, and so on).

We know from our earlier study of NPV that, when evaluating an investment project, shareholder wealth will be maximised by maximising the net present value of the cash flows generated from the project. As a corollary to this point, it is possible to argue that the business as a whole is simply a portfolio of investment projects, and so in order to maximise the wealth of shareholders, the same principles should apply.

When adopting the SVA perspective, strategic decisions will be evaluated according to their ability to maximise value, or wealth, for shareholders. In order to find out whether a certain strategy adopted by management increases or decreases shareholder value, we must first identify a suitable measure of shareholder value. We have seen that the net present value of a project represents the value of that particular project. Given that the business can be viewed as a portfolio of projects, the value of the business can be viewed as the net present value of the cash flows generated by the business as a whole.

ACTIVITY 5.13

If the net present value of future cash flows generated by the business represents the value of the business as a whole, how can we derive that part of the value of the business which is available to shareholders?

A business will normally be financed by a combination of loan capital and equity capital. Thus holders of loan capital will also have a claim on the total value of the business. That part of the total business value which is available to equity shareholders can therefore be derived by deducting from the total value of the business (total NPV) the market value of any loans outstanding. Hence:

Shareholder value = Total business value − Market value of outstanding loans

---

Supporters of SVA believe this measure should replace the traditional accounting measures of value creation such as earnings per share and return on equity. Thus, only if shareholder value (as defined above) increases can we say that there has been an increase in shareholder wealth. SVA takes a long-term view and is not concerned with reported annual profit numbers. Rather, it is concerned with measuring and managing cash flows over time. These cash flows are not affected by accounting policies and have the advantage that they take account of both risk and the time value of money.

Two US management consultants have summed up the position as follows:

The stock market sends a clear message that earnings per share is not the most important measure. Nor is growth for growth's sake. What matters is long-term cash generation. That's what drives long-term stock (share) performance, and that's how we should manage.[2]

ACTIVITY 5.14

What are the practical problems, do you think, of adopting SVA?

Two practical problems spring to mind:

1. *Forecasting future cash flows lies at the heart of this approach. In practice, forecasting can be a difficult task and simplifying assumptions will usually have to be made.*
2. *SVA requires more comprehensive information than the traditional measures discussed earlier.*

SVA uses the discounted future 'free' cash flows of the business as the basis for deriving shareholder value. These 'free' cash flows can be defined as:

Net profit after tax + depreciation + (−) changes in working capital

− the investment in fixed assets.

Any increase in the investment in working capital will be deducted from the net profit after tax and any decrease in working capital will be added. These free cash flows reflect the wealth generated from business operations and which are available to suppliers of capital.

How can managers maximise shareholder value?

Now that we have an idea how shareholder value can be measured, we can turn to the issue of how managers should manage their business in order to ensure value maximisation. Managing for shareholder value requires managers to identify the 'key value drivers' of the business. These value drivers are the things which determine the cash generating ability of the business. According to one commentator,[3] there are seven value drivers as shown in Figure 5.4.

To maximise the cash flows of the business, targets for each value driver should be established and managers assigned responsibility for achievement of the targets set. Each of the value drivers can be broken down, in turn, into their various elements for control purposes. Thus one of the value drivers identified above was the investment in working capital. This item may be broken down to show the various elements of working capital (stock, debtors, creditors, cash) and

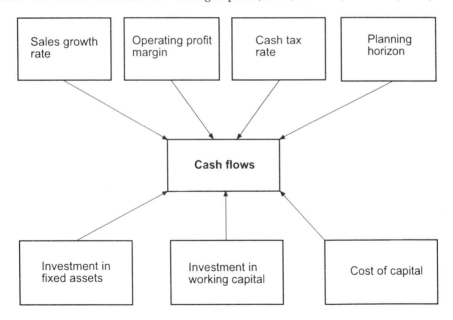

Figure 5.4   Factors influencing cash-generating ability of a business

the factors which influence each of those elements. These factors should then be the subject of close monitoring and control.

In the case of stocks, for example, management may find that the investment in stocks is largely influenced by the number of stock lines and the quantity of each line held. Where a business has very high investments in stock, this may be due to the particular performance measure which has driven the company. For example, an objective of sales maximisation may result in the business carrying too much stock (in order to avoid stock-outs) and carrying too many lines of stock (in order to maintain customer goodwill). This may lead, in turn, to very high investment in stocks, high carrying costs and costly write-offs of obsolete and slow-moving stocks. By changing the performance measure to cash flow generation, the business may decide to reduce stock levels and to concentrate on a few high-profit stock lines. As a result, it may be able to generate cash savings through lower investment in stocks, lower stock carrying costs, lower production costs through rationalisation of production capacity, and so forth.

SVA and strategic decisions

SVA is seen as an important tool for making strategic decisions as well as improving the efficiency of operating units. When considering possible future strategies the impact of each strategy on shareholder value should be considered. This means that we should attempt to measure the incremental change in shareholder value arising from each strategy. This change will be the difference between the present value of future cash flows after implementation of the strategy as compared with those before. The business should also accept only those strategies which will result in a positive change to the cash flows of the business.

ACTIVITY 5.15

Can you think of the kind of strategies which a business might wish to evaluate using SVA?

Examples of strategies which may be evaluated using SVA include:

- *acquisition and divestment decisions;*
- *new products and markets;*
- *new technology; and*
- *customer care.*

Implementing SVA

Implementing SVA may well require radical changes to the way in which a business operates. In order to implement these changes, the senior managers of the business must show a clear commitment to the SVA philosophy and objectives. They can do this by making it known that SVA must be employed when making important strategic decisions. If shareholder value is accepted as the primary measure of financial performance for a business, there must be changes to the financial incentives offered to managers. The incentives offered must be linked to improvements in shareholder value rather than traditional measures of performance. Unless this is done the impact of SVA will be undermined.

There must also be changes to the management reporting systems so that changes in shareholder value can be identified. Movements in the key value drivers and in the expected future cash flows from the business must be carefully monitored. Staff are also likely to require training in the SVA approach and the ways in which the value drivers need to be controlled. For some staff, this may require a radical change of outlook. The introduction of SVA may lead to measures which were previously considered relevant becoming irrelevant or even counterproductive to the achievement of increased shareholder value.

Summary

In this chapter we have looked at various issues relating to investment appraisal. We began by looking at evidence concerning the use of appraisal techniques in practice. We saw that there was a clear gap between the theory of investment appraisal and what is being practised. Despite its theoretical limitations, the payback method is the most widely used evaluation technique. However, the research evidence suggests that the discounted cash flow methods are slowly gaining in popularity over time.

An important element of this chapter concerned the procedures for managing the investment process. We saw that investment appraisal techniques are only one aspect of the investment process and that other aspects, such as the search for suitable projects and the monitoring and control of projects, are of vital importance to successful investment decisions.

The chapter also considered the effect of placing limits on the funds available for investment. We saw that where not all projects which yielded a positive NPV could be financed, it was necessary to modify the NPV decision rule in order to maximise the NPV generated by the funds available. The general principle adopted is to maximise the NPV per £ of scarce funds available. Other modifications to the NPV rule were also considered.

Finally, we dealt with an extension to the NPV concept which has, in recent years, captured the imagination of many managers and commentators in the

United States. Shareholder value analysis (SVA) uses discounted future cash flows as a basis for measuring the performance of the business as a whole and for deciding between different strategic choices. It replaces traditional forms of performance measurement which emphasise the short term and offers a new approach to managing the business.

References

1. C. Drury, S. Braund, P. Osborne and M. Tayles, 'A survey of management accounting practices in UK manufacturing companies', ACCA Research Report No. 32, 1993.
2. D. L. Wenner and R. LeBer, *Managing for Shareholder Value – from Top to Bottom*, Finance for Corporate Growth Series, *Harvard Business Review* paperback, 1991, pp. 33–9.
3. A. Rappaport, *Creating Shareholder Value*, The Free Press, 1986.

Review questions

5.1 It was suggested in the chapter that the payback method may be used by businesses as an initial screening device. If projects pass this first test of viability, they will then be assessed using more sophisticated appraisal methods. What problems may arise if this two-stage approach to investment appraisal is employed?

5.2 Much of the literature on investment appraisal is concerned with the techniques required to evaluate projects. What other factors are important to the investment process?

5.3 We saw in the chapter that a large number of businesses fail to take inflation into account correctly. Does this really matter, in practice, given that, in recent years, the level of inflation has been quite low? What would be the effect on NPV calculations (i.e. to overstate or understate) of (a) discounting nominal cash flows at real discount rates, and (b) discounting real cash flows at nominal discount rates?

5.4 'Investment projects are difficult to control because each one is unique and so past experience cannot be used to help determine what the future cash flows should be.' To what extent do you agree with this statement? What controls might a business impose in order to manage an investment project?

Examination-style questions —————————————————

Solutions to the questions marked with an asterisk are given at the end of the text.

5.1* Bowers Holdings plc has recently acquired a controlling interest in Shaldon Engineering plc which produces high-quality machine tools for the European market. Following this acquisition, the internal audit department of Bowers Holdings plc examined the financial management systems of the newly acquired company and produced a report which was critical of its investment appraisal procedures. The report summary stated: 'Overall, investment appraisal procedures in Shaldon Engineering plc are very weak. Evaluation of capital projects is not undertaken in a systematic manner and post-decision controls relating to capital projects are virtually non-existent.'

Required:

Prepare a report for the directors of Shaldon Engineering plc stating what you consider to be the primary characteristics of a system for evaluating, monitoring and controlling capital expenditure projects.

5.2 Not all businesses undertake post-completion audits. Research evidence in the United Kingdom suggests that post-completion audits are more likely to be carried out by the following types of business:

(a) businesses which are large in size;
(b) businesses which are engaged in manufacturing; and
(c) businesses which have a parent company outside the United Kingdom.

Can you suggest possible reasons for these findings?

5.3 Investment projects can go awry because those connected with, or affected by, the project create problems which were not anticipated or properly taken into account. Can you think of the kind of problems, relating to people employed within the business, which might cause a project to achieve results below expectations?

5.4* Lee Caterers Ltd is about to make an investment in new kitchen equipment. It is considering whether to replace the existing kitchen equipment with cook/freeze or cook/chill technology. The following cash flows are expected from each form of technology:

	Cook/chill £000	Cook/freeze £000
Initial outlay	(200)	(390)
Year		
1	85	88
2	94	102
3	86	110
4	62	110
5	–	110
6	–	90
7	–	85
8	–	60

The company would expect to replace the new equipment purchased with similar equipment at the end of its life. The cost of finance for the business is 10 per cent.

Required:

Which type of equipment should the company invest in? Use both approaches considered in the chapter to support your conclusions.

5.5 D'Arcy (Builders) Ltd is considering three possible investment projects – A, B and C. The expected pattern of cash flows for each project is:

	Project cash flows		
	A £000	B £000	C £000
Initial outlay	(17)	(20)	(24)
1 year's time	11	12	9
2 years' time	5	7	9
3 years' time	7	7	11
4 years' time	6	6	13

The company has a cost of finance of 10 per cent and the capital expenditure budget for next year is £25m.

Required:

Which investment project(s) should the company undertake assuming:

(a) each project is divisible; and
(b) each project is indivisible?

5.6 What issues and problems will arise in implementing a system of SVA within a business? What are the possible drawbacks of using SVA as the primary financial objective of a business?

Appendix: Annuity table

Annual equivalent factor $A_{N,i}^{-1}$

	i	0.04	0.06	0.08	0.10	0.12	0.14	0.16	0.18	0.20
N	1	1.0400	1.0600	1.0800	1.1000	1.1200	1.1400	1.1600	1.1800	1.2000
	2	0.5302	0.5454	0.5608	0.5762	0.5917	0.6073	0.6230	0.6387	0.6545
	3	0.3603	0.3741	0.3880	0.4021	0.4163	0.4307	0.4453	0.4599	0.4747
	4	0.2755	0.2886	0.3019	0.3155	0.3292	0.3432	0.3574	0.3717	0.3863
	5	0.2246	0.2374	0.2505	0.2638	0.2774	0.2913	0.3054	0.3198	0.3344
	6	0.1908	0.2034	0.2163	0.2296	0.2432	0.2572	0.2714	0.2859	0.3007
	7	0.1666	0.1791	0.1921	0.2054	0.2191	0.2332	0.2476	0.2624	0.2774
	8	0.1485	0.1610	0.1740	0.1874	0.2013	0.2156	0.2302	0.2452	0.2606
	9	0.1345	0.1470	0.1601	0.1736	0.1877	0.2022	0.2171	0.2324	0.2481
	10	0.1233	0.1359	0.1490	0.1627	0.1770	0.1917	0.2069	0.2225	0.2385
	11	0.1141	0.1268	0.1401	0.1540	0.1684	0.1834	0.1989	0.2148	0.2311
	12	0.1066	0.1193	0.1327	0.1468	0.1614	0.1767	0.1924	0.2086	0.2253
	13	0.1001	0.1130	0.1265	0.1408	0.1557	0.1712	0.1872	0.2037	0.2206
	14	0.0947	0.1076	0.1213	0.1357	0.1509	0.1666	0.1829	0.1997	0.2169
	15	0.0899	0.1030	0.1168	0.1315	0.1468	0.1628	0.1794	0.1964	0.2139

CHAPTER SIX

Risk, Return and Capital Investment Appraisal

OBJECTIVES

On completion of this chapter you should be able to:

■ Discuss the nature of risk and explain why it is important in the context of investment decisions.

■ Identify the different risk preferences which individuals may have and explain why most individuals are risk averse.

■ Discuss the traditional approaches to the measurement of risk and identify their limitations.

■ Explain how investment in a diversified portfolio of projects can help reduce the level of risk for a business.

Introduction

We have seen in previous chapters that financial decision-making involves making estimates about the future. However, producing reliable estimates can be difficult. It can be particularly difficult where the environment is fast changing or where new products are being developed. The issue of risk – the likelihood that what is estimated to occur will not actually occur – is, therefore, an important part of financial decision-making.

In this chapter we consider the problem of risk in the context of investment decision-making. We will see that methods proposed for dealing with risk vary greatly in their level of sophistication. We begin by looking at traditional methods of dealing with risk which view each investment project in isolation. We then go on to examine a more sophisticated approach to managing risk which takes account of the interrelationships between investment projects within a portfolio of projects undertaken by a business.

Risk and investment decisions

Risk arises where the future is unclear and where a range of possible future outcomes exist. As the future is uncertain, there is a chance (or risk) that estimates made concerning the future will not occur. Risk is particularly important in the context of investment decisions. This is because of the relatively long time scales involved (there is more time for things to go wrong between the decision being made and the end of the project) and because of the size of the investment. If things do go wrong, the impact can be both significant and lasting. Sometimes, a distinction is made in the literature between *risk* and *uncertainty*. However, this distinction is not particularly useful for our purposes and, in this chapter, the two words are used interchangeably.

In the sections which follow, we examine various methods which can be used to help managers deal with the problem of risk. This examination will focus on the more useful and systematic approaches to dealing with risk which have been proposed. In practice, crude methods of dealing with risk are sometimes used, such as shortening the required payback period and employing conservative cash flows. However, these methods rely on arbitrary assumptions and have little to commend them. They have, therefore, been excluded from our examination.

Sensitivity analysis

A popular way of assessing the level of risk associated with a project is to carry out *sensitivity analysis*. This involves an examination of the key input values affecting the project in order to see how changes in each input might influence the profitability of the project. Assuming that the result of the investment appraisal, using the best estimates, is positive, each input value will be examined to see by how much the estimated figure could differ from the best estimate before the project becomes unprofitable for that reason alone.

Suppose, for example, we carried out NPV calculations for the purchase of a new machine which is to be used to produce a particular product, and the analysis came up with a positive value of £15,000. If we then decide to carry out a sensitivity analysis on this investment proposal, we would consider each of the input values in turn (i.e. cost of the machine, sales volume and price of the goods produced, manufacturing costs, life of the machine, discount rate, and so forth – see Figure 6.1). We would seek to find the most adverse value which each of these inputs could have before the NPV figure becomes zero. The difference between the adverse value calculated and the estimated value represents the 'margin of safety' for that particular input. A computer spreadsheet model of the project can be extremely valuable for this exercise. It then becomes a very simple matter to calculate the degree of change required for the various inputs.

As a result of carrying out a sensitivity analysis, the managers are able to get a better 'feel' for the investment project. They will be able to see the margin of safety

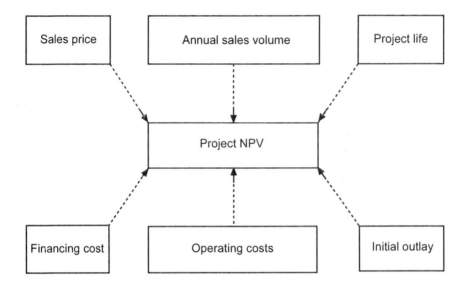

Figure 6.1 Factors affecting the sensitivity of NPV calculations for a new machine

for each input and will be able to identify any highly sensitive inputs. In some cases, the managers may decide to seek more information concerning sensitive inputs before proceeding. If, for example, the price of the product to be made on the machine was extremely sensitive to change, the managers may decide to undertake more market research in order to satisfy themselves that customers will be prepared to pay the price which has been used in the NPV calculations.

The following activity is concerned with measuring the sensitivity of particular inputs. It was mentioned earlier that, in practice, sensitivity calculations are usually carried out using a computer spreadsheet as the calculations can often be complex or laborious. However, this particular activity can be undertaken without recourse to a spreadsheet.

ACTIVITY 6.1

David Russell (Property Developers) Ltd intends to bid at an auction, to be held today, for a manor house which has fallen into disrepair. The auctioneer who will be conducting the auction believes that the manor house will be sold for about £450,000. The company wishes to renovate the property and to divide it into luxury flats to be sold for £150,000 each. The renovation will be in two stages and will cover a two-year period. Stage 1 will cover the first year of the project. It will cost £500,000 and the six flats completed during this stage are expected to be sold for a total of £900,000 at the end of the first year. Stage 2 will cover the second year of the project. It will cost £300,000 and the three remaining flats are expected to be sold at the end of the second year for a total of £450,000.

The cost of renovation is the subject of an agreed figure with local builders. However, there is some uncertainty over the remaining input values. The company has an estimated cost of capital of 12 per cent.

Required:

(a) What is the NPV of the proposed project?
(b) Assuming none of the other inputs deviate from the best estimates provided:
    (i) What auction price would have to be paid for the manor house to cause the project to have a zero NPV?
    (ii) What cost of capital would cause the project to have a zero NPV?
    (iii) What is the sale price of each of the flats which would cause the project to have a zero NPV? (Each flat must be sold for the same price.)
(c) Is the level of risk associated with the project high or low? Discuss your findings.

The NPV of the proposed project is as follows:

	Cash flows £	Discount factor 12%	Present value £
Year 1 (£900,000 – £500,000)	400,000	0.893	357,200
Year 2 (£450,000 – £300,000)	150,000	0.797	119,550
Less initial outlay			(450,000)
Net present value			26,750

In order to obtain a zero NPV, the auction price for the manor house would have to be £26,750 higher than the current estimate (i.e. a total price of £476,750). This is about 6 per cent above the current estimated price.

As there is a positive NPV, the cost of capital which would cause the project to have a zero NPV must be higher than 12 per cent. Let us try 20 per cent.

	Cash flows £	Discount factor 12%	Present value £
Year 1 (£900,000 – £500,000)	400,000	0.833	333,200
Year 2 (£450,000 – £300,000)	150,000	0.694	104,100
Less initial outlay			(450,000)
Net present value			(12,700)

The cost of capital lies somewhere between 12 per cent and 20 per cent. By linear interpolation we obtain:

$$IRR = 12\% + \frac{(20 - 12)26{,}750}{26{,}750 + 12{,}700}$$

$$= 17.4\%$$

This calculation is, of course, the same as that used when calculating the IRR of the project. (i.e. 17.4% is the IRR of the project.)

In order to obtain a zero NPV, the sale price of each flat must be reduced so that the NPV is reduced by £26,750. In year 1, six flats are sold (and in year 2, three flats are sold). The discount factor for year 1 is 0.897 and for year 2 it is 0.797. We can derive the fall in value per flat (Y), in order to obtain a zero NPV, by using the equation:

$$(6Y \times 0.897) + (3Y \times 0.797) = £26{,}750$$

$$Y = £3{,}441$$

The sale price of each flat necessary to obtain a zero NPV is therefore £150,000 − £3,441 = £146,559. This represents a fall in the estimated price of 2.3 per cent.

The calculations above indicate that the auction price would have to be about 6 per cent above the estimated price before a zero NPV is obtained. The margin of safety, therefore, is not very high for this variable. The calculations also reveal that the price of the luxury flats would only have to fall by 2.3 per cent from the estimated price before a zero NPV is obtained. Hence, the margin of safety for this variable is even smaller. However, the cost of capital is less sensitive to changes and there would have to be an increase from 12 per cent to 17.4 per cent before the project produced a zero NPV.

It seems from the calculations that the sale price of the flats is the most sensitive of the factors. A careful re-examination of the market value of the flats therefore seems appropriate before a final decision is made.

In your previous studies of accounting, you may have studied breakeven analysis. Sensitivity analysis is, in essence, a form of breakeven analysis. The point at which the NPV is zero is the point at which the project breaks even. The margin of safety for a particular variable associated with the project is interpreted in the same way as the margin of safety is interpreted in breakeven analysis.

Although sensitivity analysis can help managers gain a better understanding of the nature and degree of risk associated with a project, it has certain drawbacks which limit its usefulness.

ACTIVITY 6.2

Can you think of any drawbacks to the sensitivity analysis approach to measuring risk?

Sensitivity analysis has two major drawbacks which you may have identified. These are:

1. *It does not give managers clear decision rules concerning acceptance or rejection of the project. There is no single figure outcome which will indicate whether the project is worth undertaking. This means that managers must rely on their own judgement when assessing the information gained from the sensitivity analysis exercise.*
2. *It is a static form of analysis. Only one input is considered at a time while the rest are held constant. In practice, however, it is likely that more than one input value will differ from the best estimates provided.*

Scenario analysis

A slightly different approach, which overcomes the problem of dealing with a single variable at a time, is *scenario analysis*. This approach changes a number of variables simultaneously so as to provide a particular scenario for managers to consider. A popular form of scenario analysis is to provide three different combinations of variables which set out:

1. a pessimistic view of the project;
2. a most likely view of the project; and
3. an optimistic view of the project.

The approach is open to criticism because it does not indicate the likelihood of each scenario occurring nor does it identify the other possible scenarios which might occur. Nevertheless, the portrayal of optimistic and pessimistic scenarios may be useful in providing managers with some feel for the 'downside' and 'upside' risk associated with a project.

Risk preferences of investors

Identifying the level of risk associated with a project is not, of itself, enough. The attitude of investors towards risk should also be determined. Unless we know how investors are likely to react to the presence of risk in investment opportunities we cannot really make an informed decision. It is important, therefore, to consider what the attitude of investors is likely to be towards risk.

In theory, investors may display three possible attitudes towards risk which are as follows:

1. *Risk seeking* Some investors enjoy a gamble. Given two projects with the same expected return, but with different levels of risk, the risk-seeking investor would choose the project with the higher level of risk.

2. *Risk neutral*   Some investors are indifferent to risk. Thus, given two projects
    with the same expected return, but with different levels of risk, the risk
    neutral investor would have no preference. Both projects provide the same
    expected return and the fact that one project has a higher level of risk would
    not be an issue.
3. *Risk aversion*   Some investors are averse to risk. Given two projects with the
    same expected return, but with different levels of risk, a risk averse investor
    would choose the project which has a lower level of risk. Being risk averse,
    however, does *not* mean that an investor will not be prepared to take on risky
    investments. It means, rather, that investors will require compensation in the
    form of higher returns from projects which have higher levels of risk.

Whilst some investors may be risk seekers and some investors may be indifferent
to risk, the evidence suggests that the vast majority of investors are risk averse.
An explanation for why this is the case can be found in *utility theory*. To describe
this theory, let us assume you could measure the satisfaction, or utility, you
receive from money in the form of '*utils of satisfaction*' and let us also assume that
you are penniless! If a rich benefactor gave you £1,000, this may give you a great
deal of satisfaction as it would allow you to buy many things you have yearned
for. Let us say it provides you with twenty utils of satisfaction. If the benefactor
gave you a further £1,000, this may also give you a great deal of satisfaction, but
not as much as the first £1,000 as your essential needs have now been met. Let us
say it provides you with ten utils of satisfaction. If the benefactor then gave you a
further £1,000, the additional satisfaction received from this additional sum may
reduce to, say, six utils and so on. (The term *diminishing marginal utility of wealth*
is often used to describe the situation where the additional satisfaction declines
with each additional amount received.)

The level of satisfaction received from wealth at different levels of wealth can be
expressed in the form of a *utility function*. For a risk averse individual, the utility
function, when shown graphically, would take the shape of a downward-sloping
curve as shown in Figure 6.2. We can see clearly from this graph that each
increment in wealth provides a diminishing level of satisfaction for the individual.
We can also see that the increase in satisfaction from gaining additional wealth is
not the same as the decrease in satisfaction from losing the same amount of wealth.

An individual with wealth of, say, £2,000 would receive satisfaction from this
amount of thirty utils. If, however, the wealth of the individual fell by £1,000 for
some reason, the loss of satisfaction would be greater than the satisfaction gained
from receiving an additional £1,000. We can see the loss of satisfaction from a fall
in wealth of £1,000 would be ten utils, whereas the gain in satisfaction from
receiving an additional £1,000 would only be six utils. As the satisfaction, or
happiness, lost from a fall in wealth is greater than the satisfaction, or happiness,
gained from acquiring an equivalent amount of wealth, the individual will be
averse to risk and will only be prepared to undertake risk in exchange for the
prospect of higher returns.

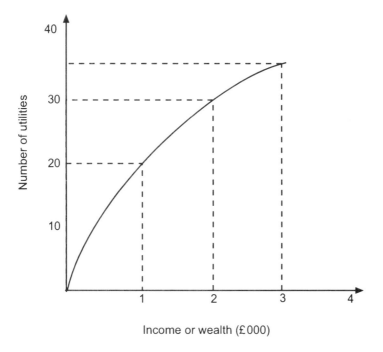

Figure 6.2 Utility function for a risk averse individual

The particular shape of the utility curve will vary between individuals. Some individuals are likely to be more risk averse than others. The more risk averse an individual is, the more concave the shape of the curve will become. However, this general concave curve shape will apply to all risk averse individuals.

For an individual who is indifferent to risk, the marginal satisfaction, or utility, of wealth will not diminish as described above. Instead, the marginal utility of wealth will remain constant. This means the individual's utility function will look quite different to that of a risk averse individual.

ACTIVITY 6.3

Try to draw a graph which plots the utility of wealth against wealth for an individual who is indifferent to risk. Explain the shape of the graph line.

An individual who is indifferent to risk would have a utility function which can be plotted in the form of a straight line, as shown in Figure 6.3. The satisfaction, or happiness, lost from a fall in wealth will be equal to the satisfaction, or happiness, gained from acquiring an equivalent amount of wealth.

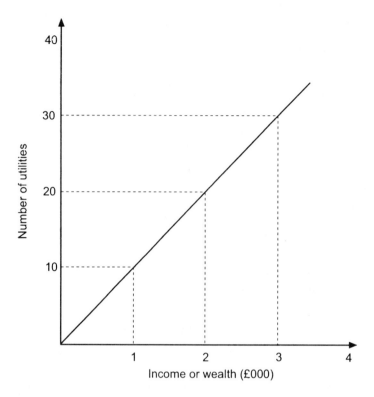

Figure 6.3   Utility function for a risk neutral individual

For a risk-seeking individual, the marginal satisfaction or utility of wealth will increase rather than decrease or remain constant. This means that the shape of a risk-seeking individual's utility function, when displayed in the form of a graph, will be quite different to the two described above.

ACTIVITY 6.4

Draw a graph plotting the utility of wealth against wealth for an individual who is risk-seeking and explain the shape of the graph line.

The graph for a risk-seeking individual will be as shown in Figure 6.4. We can see from the graph that the curve is upward sloping. The satisfaction, or happiness, gained from an increase in wealth would be greater than the satisfaction, or happiness, lost from a decrease in wealth of an equivalent amount. This means the individual will be prepared to take on risks in order to obtain additional wealth.

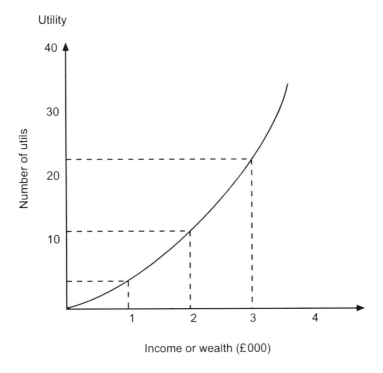

Figure 6.4 Utility function for a risk-seeking individual

Although utility theory helps us to understand why investors are risk averse, it would not be possible to identify the utility functions of individual investors and then combine these in some way so as to provide a guide for management decisions. The practical value of this theory is therefore limited. In the real world, managers may make decisions based on their own attitudes towards risk rather than those of investors, or make assumptions about the risk preferences of investors.

Risk-adjusted discount rate

We have seen from the section above that there is a relationship between risk and the rate of return required by investors. The reaction of a risk averse individual will be to require a higher rate of return for risky projects. The higher the level of risk associated with a project, the higher the required rate of return. The *risk-adjusted discount rate* is based on this simple relationship between risk and return. Thus, when evaluating investment projects, managers will increase the NPV discount rate in the face of increased risk. In other words, a *risk premium* will be required for risky projects. The higher the level of risk, the higher the risk premium which will be required.

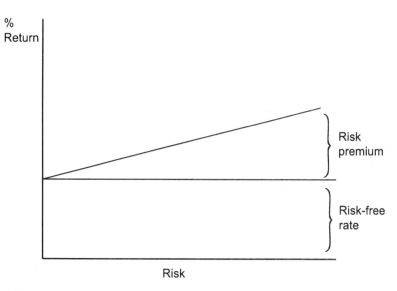

Figure 6.5 The relationship between risk and return

The risk premium is usually added to a 'risk-free' rate of return in order to derive the total return required. The 'risk-free' rate is normally taken to be equivalent to the rate of return from long-term government loan stock. In practice, a business may divide projects up into risk categories (e.g. low, medium and high risk) and then assign a risk premium to each risk category. The cash flows from a particular project will then be discounted using a rate based on the risk-free rate plus the appropriate risk premium. This relationship between risk and return is illustrated in Figure 6.5.

The use of a risk-adjusted discount rate provides managers with a single-figure outcome which can be used when making a decision either to accept or reject a project. Moreover, managers are likely to have an intuitive grasp of the relationship between risk and return and may well feel comfortable with this technique. However, there are practical difficulties with implementing this approach.

ACTIVITY 6.5

Can you think what the practical problems with this approach might be?

Subjective judgement is required when assigning an investment project to a particular risk category and then in assigning a risk premium to each category. The choices made will reflect the personal views of the managers responsible and this may differ from the views of the shareholders they represent. The choices made can, nevertheless, make the difference between accepting or rejecting a particular project. (We will see in Chapter 8, however, that there is a more sophisticated approach to deriving a risk premium which does not rely on subjective judgement.)

Another problem which you may not have thought of is that the use of a risk-adjusted discount rate is based on the assumption that risk increases with time (i.e. the further into the future the cash flows are due to be received, the more risky they will be). This may, however, not always be the case. Risk is usually determined by the type of project that is being undertaken. Certain products or services are more risky than others for reasons which may not be time-related.

Expected values and risk assessment

A further method of assessing risk is through the use of *statistical probabilities*. It may be possible to identify a range of possible outcomes and to assign a probability of occurrence to each one of the outcomes in the range. Using this information, we can derive an *expected NPV*. This figure represents a weighted average of the possible outcomes where the probabilities are used as weights. To illustrate this method, let us consider Example 6.1.

Example 6.1

Patel Properties Ltd has the opportunity to acquire a lease on a block of flats which has only two years remaining before it expires. The cost of the lease would be £100,000. The occupancy rate of the block of flats is currently around 70 per cent and the flats are let almost exclusively to naval personnel. There is a large naval base located nearby and there is little other demand for the flats. The occupancy rate of the flats will change in the remaining two years of the lease depending on the outcome of a defence review. The navy is currently considering three options for the naval base. These are as follows:

- *Option 1* Increase the size of the base by closing down a naval base in another region and transferring the naval personnel to the base located near to the flats.
- *Option 2* Close down the naval base near to the flats and only leave a skeleton staff there for maintenance purposes. The personnel at the naval base would be moved to a base in another region.
- *Option 3* Leave the naval base open but reduce staffing levels by 20 per cent.

The directors of Patel Properties Ltd have estimated the following net cash flows for each of the two years under each option and the probability of their occurrence:

	£	Probability
Option 1	80,000	0.6
Option 2	12,000	0.1
Option 3	40,000	0.3
		1.0

The company has a cost of capital of 10%

Note: The sum of the probabilities above is 1.0 (i.e. it is certain that one of the possible options will arise).

Required:

Should the company purchase the lease on the block of flats?

To calculate the expected NPV of the proposed investment, we must first calculate the weighted average of the expected outcomes for each year where the probabilities are used as weights. Thus the expected annual net cash flows will be as follows:

	Cash flows £	Probability	Expected cash flows £
Option 1	80,000	0.6	48,000
Option 2	12,000	0.1	1,200
Option 3	40,000	0.3	12,000
Expected cash flows in each year			61,200

Having derived the expected annual cash flows, we can now discount these using a rate of 10 per cent to reflect the cost of capital, as follows:

Year	Expected cash flows £	Discount rate 10%	Expected present value £
1	61,200	0.909	55,631
2	61,200	0.826	50,551
			106,182
Less: Initial investment			100,000
Expected net present value			6,182

We can see that the expected net present value is positive. Hence, the wealth of shareholders will be expected to increase by purchasing the lease.

The expected NPV approach has the advantage of producing a single figure outcome and of having a clear decision rule to apply (i.e. if the expected NPV is positive we should invest, if it is negative we should not).

However, the expected value approach produces an average figure which may not be capable of actually occurring. This point was illustrated in the example above where the expected value does not correspond to any of the stated options. It is sometimes argued that this problem may not be significant where the business is engaged in several similar projects as it will be lost in the averaging process. However, where investment projects are unique 'one-off' events, this argument will not apply. Also, where the project is large in relation to other projects undertaken, the averaging argument loses its force.

Using an average figure can also obscure the underlying risk associated with the project. This point is illustrated in Activity 6.6.

ACTIVITY 6.6

Ukon Ltd is considering two competing projects. Details of each project are as follows:

- Project A has a 0.8 probability of producing a negative NPV of £500,000, a 0.1 probability of producing a positive NPV of £1.0m. and a 0.1 probability of producing a positive NPV of £5.5m.
- Project B has a 0.2 probability of producing a positive NPV of £125,000, a 0.3 probability of producing a positive NPV of £250,000 and a 0.5 probability of producing a positive NPV of £300,000.

What is the expected net present value (ENPV) of each project? Which project do you consider to be the more risky?

The expected NPV of Project A is:

Probability	NPV	Expected value
	£	£
0.8	(500,000)	(400,000)
0.1	1,000,000	100,000
0.1	5,500,000	550,000
ENPV		250,000

The expected NPV of Project B is:

Probability	NPV	Expected value
	£	£
0.2	125,000	25,000
0.3	250,000	75,000
0.5	300,000	150,000
ENPV		250,000

> *We can see from the information provided that Project A has a high probability of making a loss, whereas Project B is not expected to make a loss under any of the possible outcomes. Thus Project A appears to be a more risky venture than Project B. (We shall see in a later section how measuring the distribution of possible outcomes can provide a useful indicator of risk.)*

Where the expected value approach is being used, it is probably a good idea to reveal the different possible outcomes and the probability attached to each outcome for managers. By so doing, they will be able to gain an insight into the 'downside risk' attached to the project. The information relating to each outcome can be presented in the form of a diagram if required. The construction of such a diagram is illustrated in Example 6.2.

Example 6.2

Zeta Computing Services Ltd has recently produced some computer software for a client organisation. The material has a life of two years and will then become obsolete. The cost of producing the material was £10,000. The client organisation has agreed to pay a licence fee of £8,000 per annum for the material if it is used in only one of its two divisions and £12,000 per annum if it is used in both of its divisions. The client may use the material for either one or two years in either division.

Zeta Training Services believes there is a 0.6 chance that the licence fee received in any one year will be £8,000 and a 0.4 chance that it will be £12,000.

There are four possible outcomes attached to this project, as follows:

- *Outcome 1* Year 1 cash flow £8,000 (p = 0.6) and Year 2 cash flow £8,000 (p = 0.6). The probability of both years having cash flows of £8,000 will be (0.6 × 0.6) = 0.36.
- *Outcome 2* Year 1 cash flow £12,000 (p = 0.4) and Year 2 cash flow £12,000 (p = 0.4). The probability of both years having cash flows of £12,000 will be (0.4 × 0.4) = 0.16.
- *Outcome 3* Year 1 cash flow £12,000 (p = 0.4) and Year 2 cash flow £8,000 (p = 0.6). The probability of this sequence of cash flows occurring will be (0.4 × 0.6) = 0.24.
- *Outcome 4* Year 1 cash flow £8,000 (p = 0.6) and Year 2 cash flow £12,000 (p = 0.4). The probability of this sequence of cash flows occurring will be (0.6 × 0.4) = 0.24.

This information can be displayed in the form of a diagram as shown in Figure 6.6.

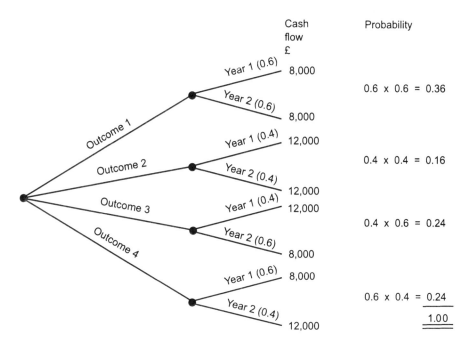

Figure 6.6 Diagram showing different possible project outcomes

SELF-ASSESSMENT QUESTION 6.1

Kernow Cleaning Services Ltd provides street-cleaning services for local councils in the far south-west of England. The work is currently labour intensive and few machines are employed. However, the company has recently been considering the purchase of a fleet of street-cleaning vehicles at a total cost of £540,000. The vehicles have a life of four years and are likely to result in a considerable saving of labour costs. Estimates of the likely labour savings and their probability of occurrence are as follows:

	Estimated savings £	Probability of occurrence
Year 1	80,000	0.3
	160,000	0.5
	200,000	0.2
Year 2	140,000	0.4
	220,000	0.4
	250,000	0.2

Year 3	140,000	0.4
	200,000	0.3
	230,000	0.3
Year 4	100,000	0.3
	170,000	0.6
	200,000	0.1

Estimates for each year are independent of other years. The company has a cost of capital of 10 per cent.

The company has never assigned probabilities to possible outcomes in evaluating previous investment decisions but has relied instead on sensitivity analysis. One of the directors has expressed concern about this new approach and believes that sensitivity analysis would be a more useful approach to dealing with risk and uncertainty.

Required:

(a) Calculate the expected net present value (ENPV) of the street-cleaning machines.

(b) Calculate the net present value (NPV) of the worst possible outcome and the probability of its occurrence.

(c) State, with reasons, whether or not the company should purchase the street-cleaning machines.

Risk and the standard deviation

In the problems discussed so far, the number of possible outcomes relating to a particular project have been fairly small. Only two or three possible outcomes have been employed to illustrate particular principles. In reality, however, there may be a large number of outcomes which could occur. Indeed, a project may have thousands of possible outcomes, each with their own probability of occurrence. Although it would not be a practical idea, let us suppose that there are a large number of outcomes for a particular project and we have assigned probabilities to each possible outcome. This would mean that we could plot a probability distribution which could be displayed in the form of a continuous curve, such as the one shown in Figure 6.7.

The particular shape of the curve will vary between projects. Variations in the shape of the curve can occur even where projects have identical expected values. To illustrate this point, the probability distribution for two separate projects which have the same expected value, is shown in Figure 6.8. We can see, however, that Project A has a range of possible values which is much more tightly distributed around the expected value than Project B.

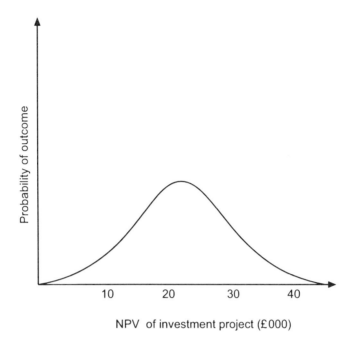

NPV of investment project (£000)

Figure 6.7   Probability distribution of outcomes of a single investment project

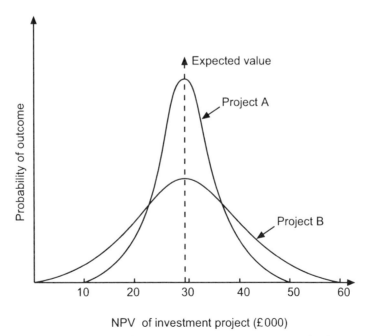

NPV of investment project (£000)

Figure 6.8   Probability distribution of two projects with the same expected value

This difference in the shape of the two probability distributions can provide us with a useful indicator of risk. We can see from the graph that the tighter the distribution of possible future values, the greater the chance that the actual value will be close to the expected value. In other words, *the tighter the probability distribution, the lower the risk associated with the investment project.* The graph in Figure 6.8 shows that the possible outcomes for Project A are much less spread out than those of Project B. Hence, Project A will be considered a less risky venture than Project B.

The variability of possible future values associated with a project can be measured using a statistical measure called the *standard deviation.* This is a measure of spread which is based on deviations from the mean, or expected value. In order to demonstrate how the standard deviation can be calculated, let us consider Example 6.3.

Example 6.3

Telematix plc is considering two mutually exclusive projects – Cable and Satellite. The possible NPVs for each project and their associated probabilities are as follows:

Cable		Satellite	
NPV	Probability of	NPV	Probability of
£m.	occurrence	£m.	occurrence
10	0.1	15	0.6
20	0.5	20	0.2
25	0.4	40	0.2

When calculating the standard deviation, the first step is to calculate the expected NPV for each project. In the case of the Cable project, the expected NPV is as follows:

NPV	Probability	Expected
	of occurrence	NPV
£m.		£m.
10	0.1	1.0
20	0.5	10.0
25	0.4	10.0
		21.0

The next step is to calculate the deviations around the expected NPV by deducting the expected NPV from each possible outcome. For the Cable project, the following set of deviations will be obtained:

Possible NPV £m.	Expected NPV £m.	Deviations £m.
10	21	−11
20	21	−1
25	21	4

You can see that two of the deviations are negative and one is positive. To prevent the positive and negative deviations from cancelling each other out, we can eliminate the negative signs by squaring the deviations. The sum of the squared deviations is referred to as the *variance*. The variance for the Cable project will be:

Deviations	Squared deviations
−11	121
−1	1
4	16
Variance	138

The problem with the variance is that it provides a unit of measurement which is the square of the NPV deviations. In this case, the variance is 138 (£m.).^{2} To make interpretation easier, it is probably a good idea to take the square root of the variance.

The final step in calculating the standard deviation is to find the square root of the variance. Hence the standard deviation is:

$$\text{Standard deviation} = \sqrt{\text{Variance}}$$

For the Cable project, the standard deviation is:

$$= \sqrt{138}$$

$$= £11.74\text{m.}$$

The higher the standard deviation for a particular investment project, the greater the variability of possible outcomes.

ACTIVITY 6.7

Calculate the standard deviation for the Satellite project. Which project has the higher level of risk?

In order to answer this activity, you need to go through the steps outlined above, as follows:

Step 1   Calculate the ENPV:

NPV	Probability of occurrence	Expected NPV
£m.	£m.	£m.
15	0.6	9.0
20	0.2	4.0
40	0.2	8.0
		21.0

Step 2   Calculate the deviations around the expected NPV:

Possible NPV	Expected NPV	Deviations
£m.	£m.	£m.
15	21	−6
20	21	−1
40	21	19

Step 3   Calculate the variance (Sum the squared deviations):

Deviations	Squared deviations
−6	36
−1	1
19	361
Variance	398

Step 4   Find the square root of the variance:

Standard deviation $= \sqrt{398}$

$= £19.95m$

Based on this measure, the Satellite project has the higher level of risk.

The standard deviation and the normal distribution

If the distribution of possible outcomes has a symmetrical bell-shape when plotted on a graph, it is referred to as a *normal distribution*. In Figure 6.9 we can see an example of a normal distribution. Note that this kind of distribution has a single peak and that there is an equal tapering off from the peak to each tail. In practice, distributions of data often display this pattern. Where a normal distribution

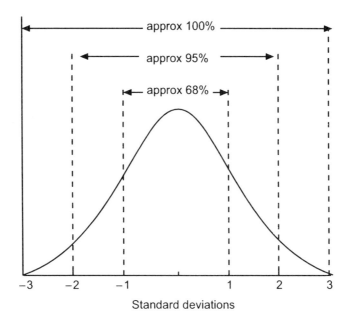

Figure 6.9 The normal distribution and standard deviations

occurs, it is possible to identify the extent to which possible outcomes will deviate from the mean or expected values. The following rules will apply:

■ Approximately 68 per cent of possible outcomes will fall within one standard deviation from the mean or expected value.

■ Approximately 95 per cent of possible outcomes will fall within two standard deviations from the mean or expected value.

■ Approximately 100 per cent of possible outcomes will fall within three standard deviations from the mean or expected value.

Even when the possible outcomes do not form a precise symmetrical bell-shape, or normal distribution, these rules can still be reasonably accurate. We will see later how these rules may be useful in interpreting the level of risk associated with a project.

The mean–standard deviation rule

If we know the expected returns of investment opportunities and their standard deviation, we have both a measure of return and a measure of risk which can be used for management decision-making. If we assume that investors are risk averse, we know they will be seeking the highest level of return for a given level of risk (or the lowest level of risk for a given level of return). The following decision rules can, therefore, be applied where the possible outcomes for investment projects are normally distributed:

Where there are two competing projects, X and Y, Project X should be chosen when either:

- *the expected return of Project X is equal to, or greater than, that of Project Y and the standard deviation of Project X is lower than that of Project Y; or*
- *the expected return of Project X is greater than that of Project Y and the standard deviation of Project X is equal to, or lower than, that of Project Y.*

These decision rules do not cover all possibilities. For example, the rules cannot help us discriminate between two projects where one has both a higher expected return and a higher standard deviation. Nevertheless, they provide some help for decision-makers.

ACTIVITY 6.8

Refer back to Example 6.3 above. Which project would you choose and why? (Assume the possible outcomes are normally distributed.)

We can see from our earlier calculations that the Cable and Satellite projects have an identical expected NPV. However, the Cable project has a much lower standard deviation, indicating less variability of possible outcomes. Applying the decision rules mentioned above, this means that the Cable project should be selected; or to put it another way, a risk averse investor would prefer the Cable project as it provides the same expected return for a lower level of risk.

The standard deviation and the coefficient of variation

Using the standard deviation as a measure of risk can be a problem if the distribution of possible outcomes is skewed (i.e. the distribution has a long tail in one direction) and so does not follow a normal distribution. In Figure 6.10, the pattern of possible outcomes and the expected values of two different projects with skewed distributions are set out.

Each project has the same expected value and each has the same standard deviation. However, would a risk averse investor regard both projects as equally attractive? The answer is probably 'no', as Project Y has a much greater 'downside risk' than Project X, as indicated by the long tail on the left-hand side of the distribution.

Figure 6.10 illustrates why the standard deviation is more suited to where the distribution of outcomes follows a more symmetrical pattern. However, even then

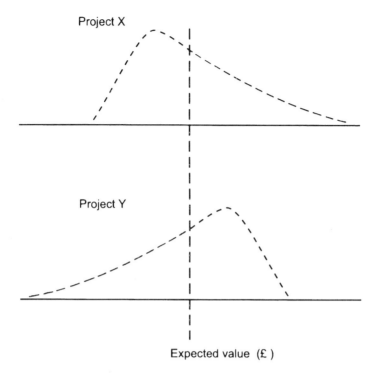

Figure 6.10 Pattern of outcomes of two different investment projects with skewed distributions

the standard deviation may be misleading as a relative measure of risk. Once again, it is the problem of 'downside' risk which may not be properly taken into account. Let us consider Example 6.4.

Example 6.4

Cameo Rolls Ltd is considering making an investment in new baking equipment. The company has a choice between investing in the Beaton range of equipment, which is traditional, and which has an expected NPV of £12m. and a standard deviation of £6m., or the Floyd range which is ultra modern and which has an expected NPV of £20m. and a standard deviation of £8m. In both cases, the distribution of possible outcomes is normal.

Required:

Which is the riskier investment?

You may feel that the answer to the above question is the Floyd range as this option has the higher standard deviation, and therefore greater variability of possible outcomes. We discussed earlier, however, the properties of the standard deviation where the outcomes are normally distributed. We saw that approximately 95 per cent of possible outcomes fall within two standard deviations of the expected outcomes and approximately 100 per cent of possible outcomes fall within three standard deviations of the expected outcomes. If we use these rules to interpret the information contained in the example, we can see that the Beaton range has a greater possibility of generating a negative NPV than the Floyd range. In other words, the Beaton range has greater 'downside' risk than the Floyd range.

To deal with this problem, it is sometimes suggested that we should calculate the level of risk in relation to the expected level of return for each investment. The *coefficient of variation* is a measure which divides the standard deviation by the expected returns from the investment. Thus:

$$\text{Coefficient of variation} = \frac{\text{standard deviation}}{\text{expected NPV}}$$

This statistic can provide us with a measure of risk per £ of investment return.

ACTIVITY 6.9

Calculate the coefficient of variation for each of the above investment projects.

The coefficient of variation for each investment opportunity is:

$$\text{Beaton range} = \frac{£6m.}{£12m.}$$

$$= 0.50$$

$$\text{Floyd range} = \frac{£8m.}{£20m.}$$

$$= 0.40$$

The Floyd range has a lower coefficient of variation than the Beaton range. Based on this measure, therefore, the Floyd range can be regarded as relatively less risky than the Beaton range. As the Floyd range also has a higher expected return than the Beaton range, the Floyd range appears to be the more attractive investment opportunity. The coefficient of variation, however, also has its drawbacks and does not always distinguish satisfactorily between competing projects.

Measuring probabilities

As you might expect, assigning probabilities to possible outcomes can be a problem. There may be many possible outcomes arising from a particular investment project and to identify each outcome and then assign a probability to it may prove to be an impossible task. When assigning probabilities to possible outcomes, either an objective or a subjective approach may be used. *Objective probabilities* are based on information gathered from past experience. Thus, for example, the transport manager of a company operating a fleet of motor vans may be able to provide information concerning the possible life of a newly purchased motor van based on the record of similar vans acquired in the past. From the information available, probabilities may be developed for different possible life spans. However, past experience may not always be a reliable guide to the future, particularly during a period of rapid change. In the case of the motor vans mentioned above, for example, changes in design and technology or changes in the purpose for which the motor vans are being used may undermine the validity of using past data. *Subjective probabilities* are based on opinion and will be used where past data is either inappropriate or unavailable. However, opinions including those of independent experts, can contain bias which will affect the reliability of the judgements made.

Despite these problems, we should not dismiss the use of probabilities. Assigning probabilities can help make explicit some of the risks associated with a project and should help decision-makers appreciate the uncertainties which have to be faced.

Portfolio effects and risk reduction

So far, our consideration of risk has looked at the problem from the viewpoint of an investment project being undertaken in isolation. However, in practice, a business will normally invest in a range, or *portfolio*, of investment projects rather than a single project. This approach to investment provides a potentially useful way of reducing risk. The problem with investing all available funds in a single project is, of course, that an unfavourable outcome could have disastrous consequences for the business. By investing in a spread of projects, an adverse outcome from a single project is less likely to have severe repercussions. The saying 'don't put all your eggs in one basket' neatly sums up the best advice concerning investment policy.

Investing in a spread of projects is referred to as *diversification*, and by holding a diversified portfolio of investment projects, the total risk associated with the business can be reduced. Indeed, in theory, it is possible to combine two risky investment projects so as to create a portfolio of projects which is riskless. To illustrate this point let us consider Example 6.5.

Example 6.5

Frank N. Stein plc has the opportunity to invest in two investment projects in Transylvania. The possible outcomes from each project will depend on whether the ruling party of the country win or lose the next election. (For the sake of simplicity, we will assume the ruling party will either win or lose outright and there is no possibility of another outcome, such as a hung parliament.) The expected NPV from each project under each outcome is as follows:

	Project	
	1	2
	NPV	NPV
	£m.	£m.
Ruling party win	(20)	30
Ruling party lose	40	(30)

By investing in *both* projects, the total NPV for the company under each outcome will be as follows:

	Project		
	1	2	
	NPV	NPV	Total returns
	£m.	£m.	£m.
Ruling party win	(20)	30	10
Ruling party lose	40	(30)	10

We can see that, whatever the outcome of the election, the total NPV for the company will be the same (i.e. £10m.). Although the possible returns from each project vary according to the results of the election, they are inversely related and so the total returns will be stabilised. As risk can be diversified away in this manner, the relationship between the returns from individual investment projects is an important issue for managers.

The coefficient of correlation

We can see that a business may eliminate the variability in total returns by investing in projects whose returns are inversely related. Ideally, a business should invest in a spread of investment projects such that when certain projects generate low (or negative) returns, other projects are generating high returns, and vice versa. It is possible to measure the degree to which the returns from individual projects are related by using the *coefficient of correlation*. This coefficient is an abstract measure which ranges between +1 and −1.

When the coefficient for two projects, X and Y, is positive, it means that

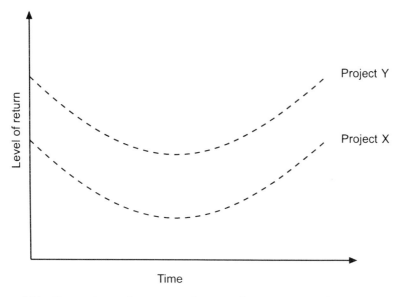

Figure 6.11   Two projects whose returns have a perfect positive correlation

increases in the returns from Project X will be accompanied by increases in returns from Project Y. The higher the positive measure, the stronger the relationship between the returns of the two projects. A coefficient of $+1$ indicates a perfect positive correlation and this means that the returns are moving together in perfect step. In Figure 6.11, we see a graph showing the returns for two investment projects which have a perfect positive correlation.

If the coefficient of correlation is negative, increases in the returns from Project X will be accompanied by decreases in the returns from Project Y. A coefficient of -1 indicates a perfect negative correlation between two projects. In other words, the projects' returns will move together in perfect step, but *in opposite directions*.

ACTIVITY 6.10

Suppose the returns from Project Y had a perfect negative correlation with those of Project X. Draw a graph depicting the relationship between the two projects.

The graph for two investment projects whose returns are perfectly negatively correlated is shown in Figure 6.12.

If the coefficient of correlation is 0, this means that the returns from Project X and Project Y move independently of one another and so there is no relationship between them.

In order to eliminate risk completely, a company should invest in projects whose

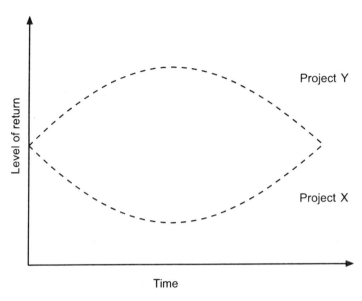

Figure 6.12   Two projects whose returns have a perfect negative correlation

returns are perfectly negatively correlated. When this is achieved, the variability in returns between projects will cancel each other out and so risk is completely diversified away. Unfortunately, it is rarely possible to follow such an investment policy. In the real world, projects whose returns are perfectly negatively correlated are extremely difficult to find. Nevertheless, risk can still be diversified away, to some extent, by investing in projects whose returns do not have a perfect positive correlation. Providing the correlation between projects is less than + 1, some offsetting will occur. The further the coefficient of correlation moves away from + 1 and towards −1 on the scale, the greater this offsetting effect will be.

ACTIVITY 6.11

Can you think of any problems associated with project diversification? Should the managers of a business seek project diversification as their primary objective?

One potential problem is that a spread of projects can create greater project management problems. Managers will have to deal with a variety of different projects with different technical and resource issues to resolve. The greater the number of projects the greater the management problems are likely to be. The answer to the second part of the question is 'no'. Even if two projects could be found whose returns had a perfect negative correlation this does not necessarily mean that they should be pursued. The expected returns from the projects must also be considered when making any investment decision.

Diversifiable and non-diversifiable risk

The benefits of risk diversification can be obtained by increasing the number of projects within the investment portfolio. As each investment project is added to the portfolio, the variability of total returns will diminish, providing that the projects are not perfectly correlated. However, there are limits to the benefits of diversification due to the nature of the risks faced. The total risk relating to a particular project can be divided into two elements: *diversifiable risk* and *non-diversifiable risk*. (As the names suggest, it is only the former type of risk which can be eliminated through diversification.) These elements are defined as follows:

1. *Diversifiable risk* is that part of the total risk which is specific to the project, such as changes in key personnel, legal regulations, the degree of competition, and so on. By spreading available funds between investment projects, it is possible to offset adverse outcomes occurring in one project against beneficial outcomes in another. (Diversifiable risk is also referred to as unique risk, company risk or systematic risk.)
2. *Non-diversifiable risk* is that part of the total risk which is common to all projects and which, therefore, cannot be diversified away. This element of risk arises from general market conditions and will be affected by such factors as the rate of inflation, the general level of interest rates, exchange rate movements and the rate of growth within the economy. (Non-diversifiable risk is also referred to as market risk or unsystematic risk.)

In Figure 6.13, we can see the relationship between the level of portfolio risk and

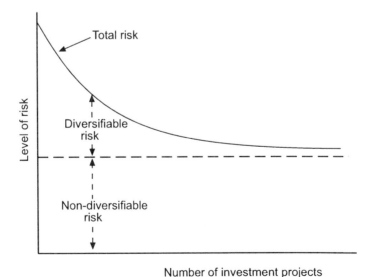

Figure 6.13 Reducing risk through diversification

the size of the portfolio. We can see that, as the number of projects increases, the diversifiable element of total risk is reduced. This does not mean, necessarily, that a business should invest in a large number of projects. Many of the benefits from diversification can often be reaped from investing in a relatively small number of projects. Again in Figure 6.13, we can see the additional benefits from each investment project diminish quite sharply. This suggests that a business with a large portfolio of projects may gain very little from further diversification.

Non-diversifiable risk is based on general economic conditions and therefore all businesses will be affected. However, certain types of business are more sensitive to changes in economic conditions than others. For example, during a recession, some types of businesses will be badly affected, whereas other types of businesses will be only slightly affected.

ACTIVITY 6.12

Can you give two examples of:

1.   a type of business which is likely to be badly affected by an economic recession; and
2.   a type of business which is likely to be only slightly affected by an economic recession?

The types of business which are likely to be badly hit by recession will include those selling expensive or luxury goods and services such as:

- *hotels and restaurants;*
- *travel companies;*
- *house builders and construction;*
- *airlines; and*
- *jewellers.*

The types of business which are likely to be only mildly affected by recession will include those selling essential goods and services such as:

- *gas and electricity suppliers;*
- *water suppliers;*
- *basic food retailers and producers;*
- *undertakers.*

The former group of businesses will usually have a cyclical pattern of profits. Thus, during a period of economic growth, these businesses may make large profits and during periods of recession may make large losses. The latter group of businesses will tend to have a fairly stable pattern of profits over the economic cycle.

The distinction between diversifiable and non-diversifiable risk is an important issue which we will return to when we discuss the cost of capital in the following chapter.

E X H I B I T 6 . I

In Chapter Five we discussed the findings of a survey of UK manufacturing companies published in 1993 concerning investment appraisal techniques. This survey also examined the extent to which different risk measures were used by companies. The survey found that, in general, sophisticated methods of risk analysis, such as portfolio analysis, were either never or rarely employed. However, there was evidence that less sophisticated techniques were being used. The following table shows the percentage of companies which often or always used unsophisticated measures of risk:

		Organisations	
Technique	All	Smaller	Larger
	(%)	(%)	(%)
Sensitivity analysis	51	30	82
Adjusting payback period	37	42	33
Conservative cash flows	32	24	43
Adjusting discount rate	18	9	31

Source: Drury et al. (1993), p. 45.[1]

The table shows that sensitivity analysis is the most popular way of dealing with risk and that there is a wide difference between the use of different methods between larger and smaller companies. The fact that the percentage totals are greater than 100 per cent indicates that some companies are using more than one method.

Summary

In this chapter, we considered the problem of risk. We examined various ways in which risk may be dealt with in investment decision-making. We began by reviewing the traditional methods which included sensitivity analysis, the risk-adjusted discount rate and the use of expected values. However, identifying the level of risk associated with a project is not, of itself, enough. The attitude of investors towards risk is also an important factor. We saw that both theory and evidence supports the view that investors tend to be risk averse. This means that investors will only be prepared to take on higher levels of risk if there is an expectation of higher returns. We examined the use of the standard deviation as a measure of risk and the decision rules which can be applied for risk averse investors where the expected returns and standard deviation of the possible outcomes are known.

The traditional approaches to dealing with risk assume that investment projects are undertaken in isolation. However, a business of any size will normally have a portfolio of projects. We saw that by having a spread of investment projects, the total risk associated with the business can be reduced. It is possible to reduce the variability of returns by investing in projects whose returns do not have a perfect positive correlation. However, there are limits to the benefits which can be reaped from diversification. An element of total risk is common to all projects and cannot be diversified away.

Reference

1. C. Drury *et al.*, 'A survey of management accounting practices in UK manufacturing companies', ACCA Research Report, No. 32, 1993.

Review questions _____

6.1 What is risk and why is it an important issue for investment decision making?

6.2 Evaluate the strengths and weaknesses of the expected net present value approach to dealing with risk in investment appraisal decisions.

6.3 What practical problems arise when using the risk adjusted discount rate to deal with the problem of risk?

6.4 What problems arise with the use of the standard deviation as a measure of project risk?

Examination-style questions _____

Solutions to those questions marked with an asterisk are given at the end of the text. Questions 6.1–6.3 are at basic level. Questions 6.4–6.6 are at intermediate/ advanced level.

6.1* Davies Ltd, a toy manufacturer, has recently developed a new electronic toy. The development costs incurred were £220,000. In order to ascertain potential demand for the new toy the company commissioned a specialist firm to undertake market research. The cost of this research, which is due for payment in August 19X9, is £30,000. The market research findings were presented to the chairman of Davies Ltd in June 19X9. These findings suggested that the new product had an expected life of four years. On the basis of the estimates of demand resulting from the market research the following forecast profit and loss accounts have been prepared.

Forecast profit and loss accounts for the year ended 30 June

	19X0 £000	19X1 £000	19X2 £000	19X3 £000
Sales	500	640	480	320
Cost of goods sold	(200)	(256)	(192)	(128)
Gross profit	300	384	288	192
Variable overheads	(100)	(128)	(96)	(64)
Fixed overheads	(50)	(50)	(50)	(50)
Depreciation	(130)	(130)	(130)	(130)
Net profit (loss)	20	76	12	(52)

In order to commence production on the new toy a machine costing £550,000 will have to be purchased at the end of June 19X9. The salvage value of this machine at the end of four years is estimated to be £30,000. Additional working capital of £40,000 will also be required at the end of June 19X9.

Fixed overheads of £40,000 per annum have been charged as a result of a reallocation of existing overheads. The remaining £10,000 p.a. represents additional fixed overheads resulting from the decision to undertake production of the new toy.

The chairman of Davies Ltd called a meeting of the product development team soon after receiving the forecast profit figures. At this meeting he said:

> 'I am sorry to say that the forecast profit figures for the new product are very disappointing. In three out of the four years of the product's life the net profit margin is less than 5 per cent. However, the cost of capital to finance the new product is 10 per cent. The projected profit margins are particularly disappointing given that the development costs, market research costs and new equipment costs total £800,000. It does not seem, therefore, that the product is financially viable.'

Required:

(a) Prepare calculations which will help the chairman to assess further the profitability of the new toy.
(b) State, with reasons, whether you would recommend that the new product be produced.
(c) Outline three methods of dealing with risk and uncertainty in project appraisal.

6.2 Simonson Engineers plc is considering the building of a new plant in Indonesia to produce products for the Southeast Asian market. To date, £450,000 has been invested in market research and site surveys. The cost of building the plant will be £9m. and it will be in operation and paid for in one year's time.

Estimates of the likely cash flows from the plant and their probability of occurrence are set out below:

	Estimated cash flows £m.	Probability of occurrence
Year 2	2.0	0.2
	3.5	0.6
	4.0	0.2
Year 3	2.5	0.3
	3.0	0.4
	5.0	0.3
Year 4	3.0	0.2
	4.0	0.7
	5.0	0.1
Year 5	2.5	0.2
	3.0	0.5
	6.0	0.3

Estimates for each year are independent of each other. The cost of capital for the company is 10 per cent.

Required:

(a) Calculate the expected net present value of the proposed plant.
(b) Calculate the net present value of the worst possible outcome and the probability of its occurrence.
(c) Should the company invest in the new plant? Why?

6.3   Pro Com Ltd is a distributor of computer software packages in accounting and finance. It is currently considering the acquisition of two competing software packages which have been developed by separate software houses and which are designed to help in the management of cash flows. The following information concerning each package is available:

CashMate		CashPak	
Possible IRRs (%)	Probability of occurring	Possible IRRs (%)	Probability of occurring
14	0.5	10	0.5
15	0.2	20	0.3
20	0.3	25	0.2

Required:

Which package would you advise the company to acquire? State any relevant assumptions regarding risk.

6.4* Helena Chocolate Products Ltd is considering the introduction of a new chocolate bar into their range of chocolate products. The new chocolate bar will require the purchase of a new piece of equipment costing £30,000 which will have no other use and no residual value on completion of the project. Financial data relating to the new product is as follows:

	Per bar (£)
Selling price	0.60
Variable costs	0.22

Fixed costs of £20,000 per annum will be apportioned to the new product. These costs represent a 'fair share' of the total fixed costs of the company. The costs are unlikely to change as a result of any decision to introduce new products into the existing range. Other developments currently being finalised will mean that the new product will have a life of only three years and the level of expected demand for the new product is uncertain. The Marketing Department has produced the following levels of demand and the probability of each for all three years of the product's life.

Year 1		Year 2		Year 3	
Sales (units)	Probability	Sales (units)	Probability	Sales (units)	Probability
100,000	0.2	140,000	0.3	180,000	0.5
120,000	0.4	150,000	0.3	160,000	0.3
125,000	0.3	160,000	0.2	120,000	0.1
130,000	0.1	200,000	0.2	100,000	0.1

A rival business has offered to buy the right to produce and sell the new chocolate bar for £100,000. The cost of finance is 10 per cent and interest charges on the money borrowed to finance the project is expected to be £3,000.

Required:

(a) Compute the expected net present value of the product.
(b) Advise the directors on the appropriate course of action to take. Give reasons.

6.5 Devonia (Laboratories) Ltd has recently carried out successful clinical trials on a new type of skin cream which has been developed to reduce the effects of ageing. Research and development costs incurred by the company in relation to the new product amount to £160,000. In order to gauge the market potential of the new product an independent firm of market research consultants were hired at a cost of £15,000. The market research report submitted by the consultants indicates that the skin cream is likely to have a product life of four years and could be sold to retail chemists and large department stores at a price of £20 per 100 ml container. For each of the four years of the new product's life sales demand has been estimated as follows:

Number of 100 ml containers sold	Probability of occurrence
11,000	0.3
14,000	0.6
16,000	0.1

If the company decides to launch the new product it is possible for production to begin at once. The necessary equipment to produce the product is already owned by the company and originally cost £150,000. At the end of the new product's life it is estimated that the equipment could be sold for £35,000. If the company decides against launching the new product the equipment will be sold immediately for £85,000 as it will be of no further use to the company.

The new skin cream will require two hours' labour for each 100 ml container produced. The cost of labour for the new product is £4.00 per hour. Additional workers will have to be recruited to produce the new product. At the end of the product's life the workers are unlikely to be offered further work with the company and redundancy costs of £10,000 are expected. The cost of the ingredients for each 100 ml container is £6.00. Additional overheads arising from production of the product is expected to be £15,000 p.a.

The new skin cream has attracted the interest of the company's competitors. If the company decides not to produce and sell the skin cream it can sell the patent rights to a major competitor immediately for £125,000.

Devonia (Laboratories) Ltd has a cost of capital of 12%. Ignore taxation.

Required:

(a) Calculate the expected net present value (ENPV) of the new product.
(b) State, with reasons, whether or not Devonia (Laboratories) Ltd should launch the new product.
(c) Discuss the strengths and weaknesses of the expected net present value approach for making investment decisions.

6.6 Nimby plc is considering two mutually exclusive projects – Delphi and Oracle. The possible NPVs for each project and their associated probabilities are as follows:

Delphi		Oracle	
NPV £m.	Probability of occurrence	NPV £m.	Probability of occurrence
20	0.2	30	0.5
40	0.6	40	0.3
60	0.2	65	0.2

Required:

(a) Calculate the expected net present value and the standard deviation associated with each project.
(b) Which project would you select and why? State any assumptions you have made in coming to your conclusions.
(c) Discuss the limitations of the standard deviation as a measure of project risk.

CHAPTER SEVEN

Sources of Finance and Financial Markets

——————————— OBJECTIVES ———————————

On completion of this chapter you should be able to:

- Identify the main forms of finance available to a business and explain the advantages and disadvantages of each form.

- Discuss the ways in which share capital may be issued.

- Explain the role of venture capital organisations in financing businesses.

- Explain the role and efficiency of the Stock Exchange.

Introduction

In this chapter we examine various aspects of financing the business. We begin by considering the various external and internal sources of finance available to a business. We then go on to consider various aspects of the capital markets including the role of venture capital and the role and efficiency of the Stock Exchange.

Sources of external finance

In order to examine the various sources of finance available to a business it is useful to distinguish between *external* sources and *internal* (i.e. arising from internal management decisions) sources of finance. When considering the various external sources of finance it is helpful to distinguish between *long-term* and *short-term* sources. For the purposes of this chapter, long-term sources of finance are defined as sources of finance which are not due for repayment within one year

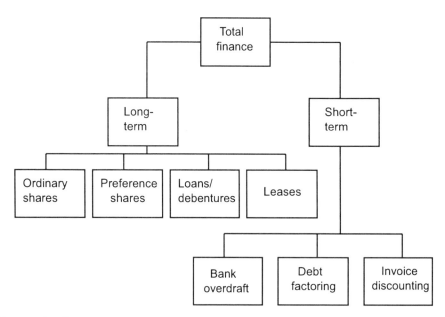

Figure 7.1   The major external sources of finance

whereas short-term sources of finance are repayable within one year. Figure 7.1 summarises the main sources of external finance available for a company.

The sections below consider the sources of external finance under each of these headings, dealing first with long-term sources and then short-term sources. Following these sections, we go on to consider the main sources of internal finance.

Long-term sources

Ordinary shares

Ordinary shares form the backbone of the financial structure of a company. Ordinary share capital represents the risk capital of a company. There is no fixed rate of dividend and ordinary shareholders will only receive a dividend if profits available for distribution still remain after other investors (preference shareholders and lenders) have received their interest or dividend payments. If the company is wound up, the ordinary shareholders will only receive any proceeds from asset disposals after lenders and creditors and, often, after preference shareholders have received their entitlements. Because of the high risks associated with this form of investment, ordinary shareholders will normally require a higher rate of return from the company.

Although ordinary shareholders have limited loss liability, based on the amount which they have agreed to invest, the potential returns from their investment are unlimited. Ordinary shareholders will also have control over the company. They are given voting rights and have the power both to elect the directors and to remove them from office.

From the company perspective, ordinary shares can be a valuable form of financing as, at times, it is useful to be able to avoid paying a dividend. In the case of a new expanding company, or a company in difficulties, the requirement to make a cash payment to investors can be a real burden. The drain on liquid resources may inhibit growth or recovery. Where the company is financed by ordinary shares, these problems need not occur. However, the costs of financing ordinary shares may be high over the longer term for the reasons mentioned earlier. Moreover, the company does not obtain any tax relief on dividends paid to shareholders, whereas interest on borrowings is tax deductible.

Preference shares

Preference shares offer investors a lower level of risk than ordinary shares. Providing there are sufficient profits available, preference shares will normally be given a fixed rate of dividend each year and preference dividends will be paid before ordinary dividends are paid. Where the company is wound up, preference shareholders may be given priority over the claims of ordinary shareholders. (The documents of incorporation will determine the precise rights of preference shareholders in this respect.) Because of the lower level of risk associated with this form of investment, investors will be offered a lower level of return than that offered for ordinary shares. Preference shareholders are not usually given voting rights, although these may be granted where the preference dividend is in arrears.

There are various types of preference shares which may be issued by a company. *Cumulative* preference shares give investors the right to receive arrears of dividends which have arisen as a result of the company having insufficient profits in previous periods. The unpaid dividends will accumulate and will be paid when the company has generated sufficient profits. *Non-cumulative* preference shares do not give investors the right to receive arrears of dividends. Thus, if a company is not in a position to pay the preference dividend due for a particular period, the preference shareholder loses the right to receive the dividend. *Participating* preference shares give investors the right to a further share in the profits available for dividend after they have been paid the fixed rate due on the preference shares and in conjunction with or after ordinary shareholders have been awarded a dividend. *Redeemable* preference shares allow the company to buy back the shares from shareholders at some agreed future date. Redeemable preference shares are seen as a lower-risk investment than non-redeemable shares and so carry a lower dividend. (A company can also issue redeemable ordinary shares.)

┌─────────────────────── **ACTIVITY 7.1** ───────────────────────┐

Would you expect the market price of ordinary shares or preference shares to be the more volatile? Why?

└──┘

The dividends of preference shares tend to be fairly stable over time and there is usually an upper limit on the returns which can be received. As a result, the share price, which reflects the expected future returns from the share, will normally be less volatile than for ordinary shares.

Preference shares are no longer an important source of new finance for most companies. An important reason why this particular form of fixed return capital has declined in popularity is that dividends paid to preference shareholders are not allowable against taxable profits whereas interest on loan capital is an allowable expense.

Share issues

A company may issue shares in a number of different ways. These may involve direct appeals by the company to investors or may involve the use of financial intermediaries. The following are the most common methods of share issue.

Rights issues

The company may offer existing shareholders the right to acquire new shares in the company in exchange for cash. The new shares will be allocated to shareholders in proportion to their existing shareholdings. In order to make the issue appear attractive to shareholders, the new shares are often offered at a price significantly below the current market value of the shares. Rights issues are now the most common form of share issue. For companies, it is a relatively cheap and straight-forward way of issuing shares. Issue expenses are quite low and issue procedures are simpler than for other forms of share issue. The fact that those offered new shares already have an investment in the company, which presumably suits their risk/return requirements, is likely to increase the chances of a successful issue.

The law now requires shares which are to be issued *for cash* to be offered first to existing shareholders. (This is known as 'pre-emptive rights'.) The advantage of this requirement is that control of the company by existing shareholders will not be diluted providing they take up the rights offer. However, it can be argued that the rights given to existing shareholders will prevent greater competition for new shares in the company. This may, in turn, increase the costs of raising finance for the company as other forms of share issue may raise the required amount of finance more cheaply.

A rights offer allows existing shareholders to acquire shares in the company at a price below the current market price. This means that entitlement to participate in a rights offer has a cash value. Existing shareholders who do not wish to take up the rights offer can sell their rights to other investors. Calculating the cash value of the rights entitlement is quite straightforward. Example 7.1 illustrates how this is done.

Example 7.1

Shaw Holdings plc has 20 million ordinary shares of 50p in issue. These shares are currently valued on the Stock Exchange at £1.60 per share. The directors of Shaw Holdings believe the company requires additional long-term capital and have decided to make a one-for-four issue (i.e. one new share for every four shares held) at £1.30 per share.

The first step in the valuation process is to calculate the price of a share following the rights issue. This is known as the *ex-rights price* and is simply a weighted average of the price of shares before the issue of rights and the price of the rights shares. In this example we have a one-for-four rights issue. The theoretical ex-rights price is, therefore, calculated as follows:

	£
Price of four shares before the rights issue (4 × £1.60)	6.40
Price of taking up one rights share	1.30
	7.70

$$\text{Theoretical ex-rights price} = \frac{7.70}{5}$$

$$= 1.54$$

As the price of each share, in theory, should be £1.54 following the rights issue and the price of a rights share is £1.30, the value of the rights offer will be the difference between the two, as follows:

£1.54 – £1.30 = £0.24 **per new share**

Market forces will usually ensure the actual price of rights shares and the theoretical price will be fairly close.

ACTIVITY 7.2

An investor with 2,000 shares in Shaw Holdings plc has contacted you for investment advice. She is undecided whether to take up the rights issue, sell the rights or allow the rights offer to lapse.

   Calculate the effect on the net wealth of the investor of each of the options being considered.

If the investor takes up the rights issue she will be in the following position:

	£
Value of holding after rights issue ((2000 + 500) × £1.54)	3,850
Less: cost of buying the rights shares (500 × £1.30)	650
	3,200

If the investor sells the rights she will be in the following position:

	£
Value of holding after rights issue (2,000 × £1.54)	3,080
Sale of rights (500 × £0.24)	120
	3,200

If the investor lets the rights offer lapse, she will be in the following position:

	£
Value of holding after rights issue (2,000 × £1.54)	3,080

As we can see, the first two options should leave her in the same position concerning net wealth. However, she will be worse off if she allows the rights offer to lapse than under the other two options. In practice, the company may sell the rights offer on behalf of the investor and pass on the proceeds in order to ensure that she is not worse off as a result of the issue. However, the company is under no legal obligation to do so.

When considering a rights issue, the directors of a company must first consider the amount of funds which it needs to raise. This will depend on the future plans and commitments of the company. The directors must then decide on the issue price of the rights shares. Generally speaking, this decision is not of critical importance. In the example above, the company made a one-for-four issue with the price of the rights shares set at £1.30. However, it could have raised the same amount by making a one-for-two issue and setting the rights price at £0.65p, or a one-for-one issue and setting the price at £0.325, etc. The issue price which is finally decided upon, will not affect the value of the underlying assets of the company or the proportion of the underlying assets and earnings of the company to which the shareholder is entitled. The directors of the company must, however, ensure that the issue price is not above the current market price of the shares in order for the issue to be successful.

Bonus issues

A *bonus issue* should not be confused with a rights issue of shares. A bonus, or scrip, issue also involves the issue of new shares to existing shareholders in proportion to their existing shareholdings. However, shareholders do not have to pay for the new shares issued. The bonus issue is effected by transferring a sum from the reserves to the paid-up share capital of the business and then issuing shares, equivalent in value to the amount transferred, to existing shareholders. As the reserves are already owned by the shareholders they do not have to pay for the shares issued. In effect, a bonus issue will simply convert reserves into paid-up capital. In order to understand this conversion process, and its effect on the financial position of the company, let us consider the following example.

Example 7.2

Wickham plc has the following abbreviated balance sheet as at 31 March 19X7.

	£m.
Net assets	20
Financed by	
Share capital (£1 Ordinary shares)	10
Reserves	10
	20

The directors decide to convert £5m. of the reserves to paid-up capital. As a result, it was decided that a one-for-two bonus issue should be made. Following the bonus issue, the balance sheet of Wickham plc will be as follows:

	£m.
Net assets	20
Financed by	
Share capital (£1 Ordinary shares)	15
Reserves	5
	20

We can see that the share capital of the company has increased and there has been a corresponding decrease in the reserves of the company. The net assets of the company remain unchanged by the bonus issue.

Although each shareholder will own more shares following the bonus issue, the proportion held of the total number of shares in issue will remain unchanged and so the stake in the business and the net assets of the business will remain unchanged. Thus bonus issues do not, of themselves, result in an increase in shareholder wealth. They will simply switch part of the owners' claim from reserves to share capital.

┌───┐
│   **ACTIVITY 7.3**   │
│   │
│ Assume that the market price per share in Wickham plc before the bonus issue │
│ was £2.10. What will be the market price per share following the share issue? │
└───┘

The company has made a one-for-two issue. A holder of two shares would therefore be
in the following position before the bonus issue:

2 shares held at £2.10 market price   £4.20

As the wealth of the shareholder has not increased as a result of the issue, the total
value of the shareholding will remain the same. This means that, as the shareholder
holds one more share following the issue, the market value per share will now be:

$$\frac{£4.20}{3}$$

$$= £1.40$$

You may wonder from the calculations above, why bonus issues are made by companies, particularly as the effect of a bonus issue may be to reduce the reserves available for dividend payments. Well, a number of reasons have been put forward to explain this type of share issue:

- *Share price*   The share price of a company may be very high and, as a result, may become more difficult to trade on the Stock Exchange. It seems that shares which trade within a certain price range generate more interest and activity in the market. By increasing the number of shares in issue, the market value of each share will be reduced which may have the effect of making the shares more marketable.
- *Lender confidence*   The effect of making a transfer from distributable reserves to paid-up share capital will be to increase the permanent capital base of the business. This move may increase confidence among lenders. In effect, a bonus issue will decrease the risk of the company reducing its equity capital through dividend distributions and prevent it leaving lenders in an exposed position.
- *Market signals*   The directors may use a bonus issue as an opportunity to signal to investors their confidence in the future prospects of the business. The issue may be accompanied by the announcement of good news concerning the company (e.g. securing a large contract or achieving an increase in profits). Under these circumstances, the share price of the company may rise in the expectation that earnings/dividends per share will be maintained. Shareholders would, therefore, be better off following the issue. However, it is the *information content* of the bonus issue, rather than the issue itself, which will create this increase in wealth.
- *Dividends*   A bonus issue of shares can be provided to shareholders as an

alternative to a cash dividend. This is known as a 'bonus dividend' or 'scrip dividend'. Those shareholders who decide to receive bonus shares rather than cash will increase their stake in the total value of the business and will, therefore, increase their wealth. The reasons why investors may prefer to receive a bonus issue of shares to a cash dividend are discussed in Chapter 9.

Offer for sale

This type of issue can involve a public limited company selling a new issue of shares to a financial institution known as an issuing house. However, shares which are already in issue may also be sold to an issuing house. In this case, existing shareholders agree to sell their shares to the issuing house. The issuing house will, in turn, sell the shares purchased from either the company or its shareholders to the public. The issuing house will publish a prospectus which sets out details of the company and the type of shares to be sold and investors will be invited to apply for shares. The advantage of this type of issue from the company viewpoint, is that the sale proceeds of the shares are certain. The issuing house will take on the risk of selling the shares to investors. This type of issue is often used when a company seeks a listing on the Stock Exchange and wishes to raise a large amount of funds.

Public issue

This form of issue involves the company making a direct invitation to the public to purchase shares in the company. Typically, this is done through a newspaper advertisement. The shares may once again be a new issue or shares already in issue. An issuing house may be asked by the company to help administer the issue of the shares to the public and to offer advice concerning an appropriate selling price. However, the company rather than the issuing house will take on the risk of selling the shares. An offer for sale and a public issue will both result in a widening of share ownership in the company.

When making an issue of shares, the company or the issuing house will usually set a price for the shares. However, establishing a share price may not be an easy task, particularly where the market is volatile or where the company has unique characteristics. If the share price is set too high, the issue will be undersubscribed and the company (or issuing house) will not receive the amount expected. If the share price is set too low, the issue will be oversubscribed and the company (or issuing house) will receive less than could have been achieved. Factors such as the sustainable cash flows and profits of the business, the level of risk, market conditions and information relating to similar listed companies should be considered when deciding upon an appropriate price.

One way of dealing with the problem is to make a *tender* issue of shares. This involves the investors determining the price at which the shares are issued.

Although the company (or issuing house) may publish a reserve price to help guide investors, it will be up to the individual investor to determine the number of shares to be purchased and the price the investor wishes to pay. Once the offers from investors have been received a price at which all the shares can be sold will be established (known as the *striking price*). Investors which have made offers at, or above, the striking price will be issued shares at the striking price and offers received below the striking price will be rejected. Although this form of issue is adopted occasionally, it is not popular with investors and is not, therefore, in widespread use.

Placing

This method does not involve an invitation to the public to subscribe to shares. Instead the shares are 'placed' with selected investors, such as large financial institutions. This can be a quick and relatively cheap form of raising funds as savings can be made in advertising and legal costs. However, it can result in the ownership of the company being concentrated in a few hands. Usually, smaller companies seeking relatively small amounts of cash will employ this form of issue.

Loans and debentures

Many companies rely on loan capital in order to finance operations. Lenders will enter into a contract with the company in which the rate of interest, dates of interest payments and capital repayments, and security for the loan are clearly stated. In the event that the interest payments or capital repayments in respect of the loan are not made on the due dates, the lender will usually have the right, under the terms of the contract, to seize the assets on which the loan is secured and sell them in order to repay the amount outstanding. Security for a loan may take the form of a fixed charge on particular assets of the company (freehold land and premises is often favoured by lenders) or a floating charge on the whole of the company's assets. A floating charge will 'crystallise' and fix on particular assets (e.g. stocks and debtors) in the event that the company defaults on its obligations.

ACTIVITY 7.4

What do you think is the advantage for the company of having a floating charge rather than a fixed charge on its assets?

A floating charge on assets will allow the managers of the company greater flexibility in their day-to-day operations than a fixed charge. Assets can be traded without reference to the lenders.

It is possible for a company to issue loan capital which is *subordinated* (i.e. ranked below) to other loan capital already in issue. This means that, in the event the company is wound up, the subordinated lenders will only be repaid after the other lenders, which have a higher-ranked claim, have been repaid. This increases the risks associated with the loan and, therefore, the level of return required by investors.

However, investors will normally view loans as being less risky than preference shares or ordinary shares. Lenders have priority over any claims from shareholders and will usually have security for their loans. As a result, of the lower level of risk associated with this form of investment, investors are usually prepared to accept a lower rate of return.

ACTIVITY 7.5

William Lucas Ltd has approached a financial institution for a long-term loan. What do you think would be the main factors the financial institution will take into account when considering the loan application?

The main factors would be:

- *The period of the loan and the nature of the security which is offered.*
- *The nature of the business.*
- *The purpose for which the loan will be used and the quality of the case to support the loan application.*
- *Security for the loan.*
- *The financial position of the business.*
- *The integrity and quality of the management of the business.*
- *The financial track record of the business.*

One form of long-term loan associated with limited companies is the *debenture*. This is simply a loan which is evidenced by a trust deed. The debenture loan is frequently divided into units (rather like share capital) and investors are invited to purchase the number of units they require. The debenture loan may be redeemable or irredeemable. Debentures of public limited companies are often traded on the Stock Exchange and their listed value will fluctuate according to the fortunes of the company, movements in interest rates, and so on.

Another form of long-term loan finance is the *eurobond*. Eurobonds are issued by listed companies (and other large organisations) in various countries and the finance is raised on an international basis. A distinguishing feature of eurobonds is that they are issued in a currency which is different from the currency of the country in which the company raising the funds is based. Thus, for example, a UK company may issue a eurobond which is denominated in US$. (It is quite common for eurobonds to be issued in US$, although they may also be issued in other major currencies.) They are bearer bonds and interest is normally paid (without deduction of tax) on an annual basis.

Eurobonds are part of an emerging international capital market and they are not subject to regulations imposed by authorities in particular countries. This may explain, in part, the fact that the cost of servicing eurobonds is usually lower than the cost of similar domestic bonds. There is a market for eurobonds which has been created by a number of financial institutions throughout the world. The issue of eurobonds is usually made by placing them with large banks and other financial institutions who may either retain them as an investment or sell them to their clients.

ACTIVITY 7.6

Why might a company prefer to issue eurobonds in preference to more conventional forms of loan capital?

Companies are often attracted to eurobonds because of the size of the international capital market. Access to a large number of international investors is likely to increase the chances of a successful issue. In addition, the lack of regulation in the eurobond market means that national restrictions regarding loan issues may be overcome. The fact that eurobonds are often less costly to service than equivalent domestic bonds is also likely to be an important consideration.

Interest rates

Interest rates on loan finance may be either floating or fixed. A floating rate means that the rate of return payable to lenders will rise and fall with market rates of interest. (However, it is possible for a floating rate bond to be issued which sets a maximum rate of interest and/or a minimum rate of interest payable.) The market value of the lenders' investment in the business is likely to remain fairly stable over time. The converse will normally be true for fixed interest loans and debentures. The interest payments will remain unchanged with rises and falls in market rates of interest, but the value of the loan investment will fall when interest rates rise and will rise when interest rates fall.

A company may issue redeemable loan capital which offers a rate of interest below the market rate. Such loans are issued at a discount to their redeemable value and are referred to as *deep discount bonds*. Thus a company may issue loan capital at, say, £80 for every £100 of nominal value. In some cases, the loan capital may have a zero rate of interest. These are referred to as *zero coupon bonds*. Although lenders will receive little or no interest during the period of the loan, they will receive a gain when the loan is finally redeemed. The redemption yield, as it is referred to, is often quite high and, when calculated on an annual basis, may compare favourably with returns from other forms of loan capital with the same level of risk. Deep discount bonds may have particular appeal to companies with short-term cash flow problems. They receive an immediate injection of cash and there are no significant cash outflows associated with the loan until the maturity date. Deep discount bonds may appeal to investors who do not have short-term cash flow problems as a large part of the return is received on maturity of the loan. However, deep discount bonds can often be traded on the stock market if required.

Convertible loans and debentures

This form of loan or debenture gives the investor the right to convert the loan into ordinary shares at a given future date and at a specified price. The investor remains a lender to the company and will receive interest on the amount of the loan until such time as the conversion takes place. The investor is not obliged to convert the loan or debenture to ordinary shares. This will only be done if the market price of the shares at the conversion date exceeds the agreed conversion price.

An investor may find this form of investment a useful 'hedge' against risk (i.e. it can reduce the level of risk). This may be particularly useful when investment in a new company is being considered. Initially, the investment is in the form of a loan and regular interest payments will be made. If the company is successful the investor can then decide to convert the investment into ordinary shares.

The company may also find this form of financing useful. If the company is successful the loan becomes self-liquidating as investors will exercise their option to convert and there will be no redemption costs. The company may also be able to offer a lower rate of interest to investors because investors expect future benefits arising from conversion. However, there will be dilution of control and also possibly of earnings for existing shareholders if holders of convertible loans exercise their option to convert. Dilution of earnings available to shareholders will not automatically occur as a result of the conversion of loan capital to share capital. There will be a saving in interest charges which will have an offsetting effect.

Warrants

Holders of warrants have the right, but not the obligation, to acquire ordinary shares in a company at a price and future date which is specified. In the case of both convertible loan capital and warrants, the specified price at which shares may be acquired is usually higher than the market price prevailing at the time of issue. The warrant will usually state the number of shares the holder may purchase and the time limit within which the option to buy shares can be exercised. Occasionally, perpetual warrants are issued which have no set time limits. Warrants do not confer voting rights or entitle the holders to make any claims on the assets of the company.

Share warrants are often provided as a 'sweetener' to accompany the issue of loan capital or debentures. The issue of warrants in this way may enable the company to offer lower rates of interest on the loan or to negotiate less restrictive loan conditions. The issue of warrants enables the lenders to benefit from future company success providing the option to purchase is exercised. However, an investor will only exercise this option if the market price exceeds the option price within the time limit specified. Share warrants may be *detachable*, which means that they can be sold separately from the loan capital.

Issuing warrants to lenders may be particularly useful for companies which are considered to be relatively risky. Lenders in such companies may feel that a new project offers them opportunities for loss but no real opportunity to participate in any 'upside' gains from the risks undertaken. By issuing share warrants, lenders are given the opportunity to participate in future gains which may make them more prepared to support risky projects.

Warrants have a gearing element which make them a speculative form of investment. Let us assume that a share had a current market price of £2.50 and that an investor was able to exercise an option to purchase a single share in the company at £2.00, and that the option could be exercised immediately. The value of the warrant, in theory, would be £0.50 (i.e. £2.50 − £2.00). Let us further assume that the price of the share rose by 10 per cent to £2.75 before the warrant option was exercised. The value of the warrant would now rise to £0.75 (i.e. £2.75 − £2.00), which represents a 50 per cent increase in value. This gearing effect can, of course, operate in the opposite direction as well.

ACTIVITY 7.7

What will be the difference in status within a company between holders of convertible loan capital and holders of loans with share warrants attached if both groups decide to exercise their right to convert?

The main difference will be that when holders of convertible loan capital exercise their option to convert, they become shareholders and are no longer lenders of the company. However, when lenders with warrants exercise their option to convert, they become both shareholders and lenders of the company.

Mortgages

A mortgage is a form of loan which is secured on freehold property. Financial institutions such as banks, insurance companies and pension funds are often prepared to lend to businesses on this basis. The mortgage may be over a long period and provides a business with an opportunity to acquire an asset which, until the early 1990s, tended to increase in value faster than the rate of inflation. In addition to the capital gain from holding the freehold property, businesses have also benefited from a decline in the real value of the capital sum owing because of inflation. However, lenders usually compensate for this fall in value, as mentioned earlier, by increasing the rate of interest payable.

Loan covenants

When drawing up a loan agreement the lender may impose certain obligations and restrictions in order to protect the investment in the business. Loan covenants (as they are referred to) often form part of a loan agreement and may deal with such matters as:

- *Accounts* The lender may require access to the financial accounts of the business on a regular basis.
- *Other loans* The lender may require the business to ask permission before taking on further loans.
- *Dividend payments* The lender may require dividends to be limited during the period of the loan.
- *Liquidity* The lender may require the business to maintain a certain level of liquidity during the period of the loan.

Any breach of these restrictive covenants can have serious consequences for the business. The lender may require immediate repayment of the loan in the event of a serious breach.

ACTIVITY 7.8

Both preference shares and loan capital require the company to provide a particular rate of return to investors. What are the factors which may be taken into account by a company when deciding between these two sources of finance?

The main factors are as follows:

- *Preference shares have a higher rate of return than loan capital. From the investors' point of view, preference shares are more risky. The amount invested cannot be secured and the return is paid after the returns paid to lenders.*
- *A company has a legal obligation to pay interest and make capital repayments on loans at the agreed dates. A company will usually make every effort to meet its obligations as failure to do so can have serious consequences, as mentioned earlier. Failure to pay a preference dividend, on the other hand, is less important. There is no legal obligation to pay a preference dividend if profits are not available for distribution. Although failure to pay a preference dividend may prove an*

embarrassment for the company, the preference shareholders will normally have no redress against the company if there are insufficient profits to pay the dividend due.

■ *It was mentioned above that the UK taxation system permits interest on loans to be deducted from profits for taxation purposes, whereas preference dividends cannot. Because of the tax relief which loan interest attracts, the cost of servicing loan capital is usually much less for a company than the cost of servicing preference shares.*

■ *The issue of loan capital may result in the management of a company having to accept some restrictions on their freedom of action. We have seen earlier that loan agreements often contain covenants which can be onerous. However, this is not normally the case with preference share issues.*

A further point which has not been dealt with so far is that preference shares issued form part of the permanent capital base of the company. If they are redeemed at some future date, the law requires that they are replaced, either by a new issue of shares or by a transfer from reserves, in order to ensure that the capital base of the company stays intact. However, loan capital is not viewed, in law, as part of the permanent capital base of the company and, therefore, there is no requirement to replace any loan capital which has been redeemed by the company.

EXHIBIT 7.1

Figure 7.2 plots the issues of capital made by UK-listed companies in recent years. The chart reveals that loan capital and ordinary shares are the main sources of long-term external finance. Preference shares are a much less important source of new finance.

Finance leases and sale and lease back arrangements

Instead of buying an asset direct from a supplier, a business may decide to arrange for a financial institution, such as a bank, to buy the asset and then agree to lease the asset from the institution. A finance lease is, in essence, a form of lending. Although legal ownership of the asset remains with the financial institution (the lessor), a finance lease agreement transfers virtually all the rewards and risks which are associated with the item being leased to the business (the lessee). The lease agreement covers a significant part of the life of the item being leased and, often, cannot be cancelled. A finance lease can be contrasted to an operating lease where the rewards and risks of ownership stay with the owner and where the lease is short-term in nature.

In recent years, some important benefits associated with finance leasing have

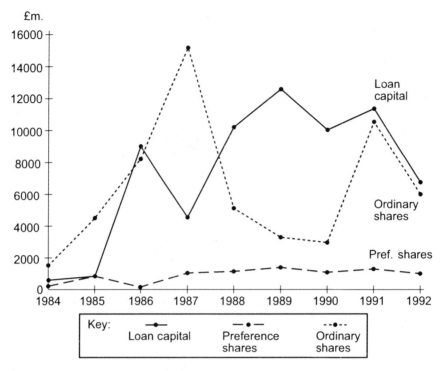

Figure 7.2 Capital issues of UK listed companies, 1984–92 (Source: Annual Abstract of Statistics, 1996)

disappeared. Changes in the tax laws no longer make it such a tax-efficient form of financing and changes in accounting disclosure requirements make it no longer possible to conceal this form of 'borrowing' from investors. Nevertheless, the popularity of finance leases has continued to increase. Other reasons must, therefore, exist for businesses to adopt this form of financing. These reasons are said to include the following:

- *Ease of borrowing*   Leasing may be obtained more easily than other forms of long-term finance. Lenders normally require some form of security and a profitable track record before making advances to a business. However, a lessor may be prepared to lease assets to a new business without a track record and to use the leased assets as security for the amounts owing.
- *Cost*   Leasing agreements may be offered at reasonable cost. As the asset leased is used as security, standard lease arrangements can be applied and detailed credit checking of lessees may be unnecessary. This can reduce administration costs for the lessor and, thereby, help in providing competitive lease rentals.
- *Flexibility*   Leasing can help provide flexibility where there are rapid changes

in technology. If an option to cancel can be incorporated into the lease, the business may be able to exercise this option and invest in new technology as it becomes available. This will help the business avoid the risk of obsolescence.

■ *Cash flows* Leasing, rather than purchasing an asset outright, means that large cash outflows can be avoided. The leasing option allows cash outflows to be smoothed out over the asset's life. In some cases, it is possible to arrange for low lease payments to be made in the early years of the asset's life, when cash inflows may be low, and for these to increase over time.

A *sale and lease back* arrangement involves a business selling freehold property to a financial institution in order to raise finance. However, the sale is accompanied by an agreement to lease the freehold property back to the business to allow it to continue to operate from the premises. The rent payable under the lease arrangement is allowable against profits for taxation purposes. There are usually rent reviews at regular intervals throughout the period of the lease and the amounts payable in future years may be difficult to predict. At the end of the lease agreement, the business must either try to renew the lease or find alternative premises. Although the sale of the premises will result in an immediate injection of cash for the business, it will lose benefits from any future capital appreciation on the property. Where a capital gain arises on the sale of the premises to the financial institution, a liability for taxation may also arise.

Short-term sources

A short-term source is one which is available for a short time period. Although there is no agreed definition of what 'short-term' means, we will define it as being up to one year. The chief sources of short-term borrowing are as follows:

Bank overdraft

This represents a very flexible form of borrowing. The size of the overdraft can (subject to bank approval) be increased or decreased according to the financing requirements of the business. It is relatively inexpensive to arrange and interest rates are often very competitive. The rate of interest charged on an overdraft will vary, however, according to how creditworthy the customer is perceived by the bank. It is also fairly easy to arrange – sometimes an overdraft can be agreed by a telephone call to the bank. In view of these advantages, it is not surprising that this is an extremely popular form of short-term finance.

Banks prefer to grant overdrafts which are self-liquidating (i.e. the funds applied will result in cash inflows which will extinguish the overdraft balance). The banks may ask for forecast cash flow statements from the business to see when the overdraft will be repaid and how much finance is required. The bank may also require some form of security on amounts advanced. One potential drawback with this form of finance is that it is repayable on demand. This may pose problems for a business which is illiquid. However, many businesses operate using an overdraft and this form of borrowing, although in theory regarded as short-term, can often become a permanent source of finance.

Debt factoring

This is a form of service which is offered by a financial institution (a factor). Many of the large factors are subsidiaries of commercial banks. Debt factoring involves the factor taking over the sales ledger of a company. In addition to operating normal credit control procedures, a factor may offer to undertake credit investigations and to provide protection for approved credit sales. The factor is usually prepared to make an advance to the company of up to 80–85 per cent of approved trade debtors. The charge made for the factoring service is based on total turnover and is often around 2–3 per cent of turnover. Any advances made to the company by the factor will attract a rate of interest similar to the rate charged on bank overdrafts.

A company may find a factoring arrangement very convenient. It can result in savings in credit management and can create more certain cash flows. It can also release the time of key personnel for more profitable ends. This may be extremely important for smaller companies which rely on the talent and skills of a few key individuals. However, there is a possibility that some will see a factoring arrangement as an indication the company is experiencing financial difficulties. This may have an adverse effect on confidence in the company. For this reason, some businesses try to conceal the factoring arrangement by collecting outstanding debts themselves.

When considering a factoring agreement, the costs and likely benefits arising must be identified and carefully weighed. Example 7.3 illustrates how this may be done.

Example 7.3

Mayo Computers Ltd has an annual turnover of £20 million before taking into account bad debts of £0.1 million. All sales made by the company are on credit and, at present, credit terms are negotiable by the customer. On average, the settlement period for trade debtors is 60 days. The company is currently reviewing its credit policies to see whether more efficient and profitable methods could be employed.

The company is considering whether it should factor its trade debts. The accounts department has recently approached a factoring company which has agreed to provide an advance equivalent to 80 per cent of trade debtors (where the trade debtors figure is based on an average settlement period of 40 days) at an interest rate of 12 per cent. The factoring company will undertake collection of the trade debts and will charge a fee of 2 per cent of sales turnover for this service. The factoring service is also expected to eliminate bad debts and will lead to credit administration savings of £90,000. The settlement period for trade debtors will be reduced to an average of 40 days, which is equivalent to that of its major competitors.

The company currently has an overdraft of £4.8 million at an interest rate of 14 per cent per annum. The bank has written recently to the company stating that it would like to see a reduction in the overdraft of the company.

In order to evaluate the factoring arrangement, it is useful to begin by considering the cost of the existing arrangements, as follows:

	£000
Bad debts written off each year	100
Interest cost of average debtors outstanding ((£20m. × 60/365) x 14%)	460
Total cost	560

The cost of the factoring arrangement can now be compared with the above:

	£000
Factoring fee (£20m. × 2%)	400
Interest on factor loan (assuming 80% advance and reduction in average credit period) ((£16m. × 40/365) × 12%)	210
Interest on overdraft (remaining 20% of debtors financed in this way) ((£4m. × 40/365) × 14%)	61
	671
Less: Savings in credit administration	90
Cost of factoring	581

The above calculations show that the net additional cost of factoring for the business would be £21,000 (i.e. £581,000 − £560,000).

Invoice discounting

This involves a business approaching a factor or other financial institution for a loan based on a proportion of the face value of credit sales outstanding. If the institution agrees, the amount advanced is usually 75–80 per cent of the value of the approved sales invoices outstanding. The business must agree to repay the advance within a relatively short period – perhaps 60 or 90 days. The responsibility for collection of the trade debts outstanding remains with the business and repayment of the advance is not dependent on the trade debt being collected. Invoice discounting will not result in such a close relationship developing between the client and the financial institution as factoring. Invoice discounting may be a one-off arrangement whereas debt factoring usually involves a longer-term arrangement between the customer and the financial institution.

Nowadays, invoice discounting is a much more important source of funds to companies than factoring. In 1994, £15.8bn was advanced against invoices through invoice discounting compared to £7.8bn advanced against invoices for factoring. There are various reasons why invoice discounting is a more attractive source of raising finance. First, it is a confidential form of financing which the client's customers will know nothing about. Second, the service charge for invoice discounting is only about 0.2–0.3 per cent of turnover compared to 2.0–3.0 per cent of turnover for factoring. Finally, many companies are unwilling to relinquish control over their sales ledger. Customers are an important resource of the business and many companies wish to retain control over all aspects of their relationship with their customers.

Long-term versus short-term borrowing

Having decided that some form of borrowing is required to finance the business, the managers must then decide whether long-term borrowing or short-term borrowing is more appropriate. There is a number of issues which should be taken into account when deciding between long-term and short-term borrowing. These include the following:

- *Matching* The business may attempt to match the type of borrowing with the nature of the assets held. Thus assets which form part of the permanent operating base of the business, including fixed assets and a certain level of current assets, will be financed by long-term borrowing. Assets held for a short period, such as current assets held to meet seasonal increases in demand, will be financed by short-term borrowing (see Figure 7.3). A business may wish to match the asset life exactly with the period of the related loan. However, this may not be possible because of the difficulty of predicting the life of many assets.

ACTIVITY 7.9

Some companies may take up a less conservative financing position than shown in Figure 7.3 and others may take up a more conservative financing position. How would the diagram differ under each of these options?

A less conservative position would mean relying on short-term finance to help fund part of the permanent capital base. A more conservative position would mean relying on long-term finance to help finance the fluctuating assets of the business.

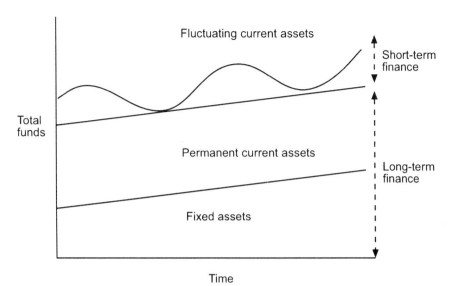

Figure 7.3 Short- and long-term financing arrangements

- *Flexibility* Short-term borrowing may be useful in order to postpone a commitment to taking on a long-term loan. This may be seen as desirable if interest rates are high and it is forecast that they will fall in the future. Short-term borrowing does not usually incur penalties if there is early repayment of the amount outstanding whereas some form of financial penalty may have to be paid if long-term debt is repaid early.
- *Refunding risk* Short-term borrowing has to be renewed more frequently than long-term borrowing. This may create problems for the business if it is already in financial difficulties or if there is a shortage of funds available for lending.
- *Interest rates* Interest payable on long-term debt is often higher than for short-term debt. (This is because lenders require a higher return where their funds are locked up for a long period.) This fact may make short-term borrowing a more attractive source of finance for a business. However, there may be other costs associated with borrowing (e.g. arrangement fees) to be taken into account. The more frequently borrowings must be renewed, the higher these costs will be.

Sources of internal finance

In addition to external sources of finance there are certain internal sources of finance which a business may use to generate funds for particular activities. These sources usually have the advantage that they are flexible. They may also be obtained quickly – particularly working capital sources – and may not require the permission of other parties. The main sources of internal funds are described below and summarised in Figure 7.4.

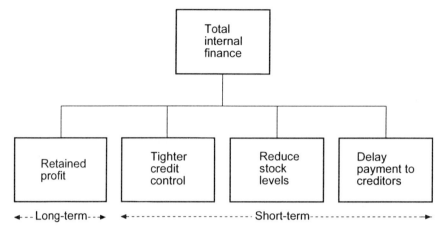

Figure 7.4 Major internal sources of finance

Retained profit

Retained profit is the main source of long-term finance for most companies. By retaining profits within the company rather than distributing them to shareholders in the form of dividends, the funds of the company are increased. It is tempting to think that retained profits are a 'cost free' source of funds for a company. However, this is not the case. If profits are reinvested rather than distributed to shareholders this means that the shareholders cannot reinvest the profits made in other forms of investment. They will therefore expect a rate of return from the profits reinvested which is equivalent to what they would receive if the funds had been invested in another opportunity with the same level of risk.

The reinvestment of profit rather than the issue of new ordinary shares can be a useful way of raising equity capital. There are no issue costs associated with retaining profits and the amount raised is certain. When issuing new shares, the issue costs may be substantial and there may be uncertainty over the success of the issue. Retaining profits will have no effect on the control of the company by existing shareholders. However, where new shares are issued to outside investors there will be some dilution of control suffered by existing shareholders.

The retention of profits is something which is determined by the directors of the company. They may find it easier simply to retain profits rather than ask investors to subscribe to a new share issue. Retained profits are already held by the company and so the company does not have to wait to receive the funds. Moreover, there is often less scrutiny when profits are being retained for reinvestment purposes than when new shares are being issued. Investors and their advisers will examine closely the reasons for any new share issue.

Some shareholders may prefer profits to be retained by the company rather than distributed in the form of dividends. By ploughing back profits, it may be expected that the company will expand and share values will increase as a result. In the United Kingdom, not all capital gains are liable for taxation. (For the fiscal year 1996/97, an individual who has capital gains of no more than £6,300 will not be taxed on those gains.) A further advantage of capital gains over dividends is that the shareholder has a choice as to when the gain is realised. Research indicates that investors are often attracted to particular companies according to the dividend/retention policies which they adopt. This point will be considered in more detail in Chapter 9.

Tighter credit control

By exerting tighter control over trade debtors it may be possible for a business to reduce the proportion of assets held in this form and to release funds for other purposes. It is important, however, to weigh the benefits of tighter credit control against the likely costs in the form of lost customer goodwill and lost sales. To remain competitive, a business must take account of the needs of its customers and the credit policies adopted by rival companies within the industry.

ACTIVITY 7.10

H. Rusli Ltd produces a single product which is used in a variety of electronic products. Details of the product are as follows:

	per unit	
	£	£
Selling price		20
Less: Variable costs	14	
Fixed costs	4	18
Net profit		2

Sales are £10m. per annum and are all on credit. The average credit period taken by customers is 45 days although the terms of credit require payment within 30 days. Bad debts are currently £100,000 per annum. Debtors are financed by a bank overdraft costing 15 per cent per annum.

The credit control department believes it can eliminate bad debts and can reduce the average credit period to 30 days if new credit control procedures are implemented. These will cost £50,000 per annum and are likely to result in a reduction in sales volume of 5 per cent per annum. Should the company implement the new credit control procedures? (Hint: In order to answer this activity it is useful to compare the current cost of trade credit with the costs under the proposed approach.)

The current cost of trade credit is:

	£
Bad debts	100,000
Overdraft ((£10m. × 45/365) × 15%)	184,931
	284,931

The cost of trade credit under the new policy will be:

	£
Overdraft ((£10m. × 30/365) × 15%)	123,288
Cost of control procedures	50,000
Net cost of lost sales ((£10m./£20 × 5%)(20−14*))	150,000
	323,288

Note: * The cost of lost sales will be the difference between the contribution per unit (i.e. the difference between the selling price and the variable costs).

The above figures reveal that the business will be worse off if the new policies were adopted.

Reducing stock levels

This is an internal source of funds which may prove attractive to a business. If a business has a proportion of its assets in the form of stock there is an opportunity cost as the funds tied up cannot be used for more profitable opportunities. (This is also true, of course, for investment in trade debtors.) By liquidating stocks, funds become available for other purposes. However, a business must ensure there are sufficient stocks available to meet likely future sales demand. Failure to do so will result in lost customer goodwill and lost sales.

The nature and condition of the stock held will determine whether it is possible to exploit this form of finance. A business may be overstocked as a result of poor buying decisions in the past. This may mean that a significant proportion of stocks held are slow-moving or obsolete and cannot, therefore, be liquidated easily.

Delaying payment to creditors

By delaying payment to creditors, funds are retained within the business for other purposes. This may be a cheap form of finance for a business. However, as we shall see in Chapter 10, which deals with working capital management, there may be significant costs associated with this form of financing.

Helsim Ltd is a wholesaler and distributor of electrical components. The most recent financial statements of the company revealed the following:

Profit and loss account for the year ended 31 May 19X9

	£m.	£m.
Sales		14.2
Opening stock	3.2	
Purchases	8.4	
	11.6	
Closing stock	3.8	7.8
Gross profit		6.4
Administration expenses	3.0	
Selling and distribution expenses	2.1	
Finance charges	0.8	5.9
Net profit before taxation		0.5
Corporation tax		0.2
Net profit after taxation		0.3

Balance sheet as at 31 May 19X9

	£m.	£m.	£m.
Fixed assets			
Land and buildings			3.8
Equipment			0.9
Motor vehicles			0.5
			5.2
Current assets			
Stock		3.8	
Trade debtors		3.6	
Cash at bank		0.1	
		7.5	
Less: **Creditors: amounts due within one year**			
Trade creditors	1.8		
Bank overdraft	3.6	5.4	2.1
			7.3
Creditors: amounts due beyond one year			
Debentures (secured on freehold land)			3.5
			3.8

	£m.
Capital and reserves	
Ordinary £1 shares	2.0
Profit and loss account	1.8
	3.8

Notes:
1. Land and buildings are shown at their current market value. Equipment and motor vehicles are shown at their written-down values.
2. No dividends have been paid to ordinary shareholders for the past three years.

In recent months trade creditors have been pressing for payment. The managing director has, therefore, decided to reduce the level of trade creditors to an average of 40 days outstanding. In order to achieve this he has decided to approach the bank with a view to increasing the overdraft to finance the necessary payments. The company is currently paying 12 per cent interest on the overdraft.

Required:

(a) Comment on the liquidity position of the company.
(b) Calculate the amount of finance required in order to reduce trade creditors, as shown on the balance sheet, to an average of 40 days outstanding.
(c) State, with reasons, how you consider the bank would react to the proposal to grant an additional overdraft facility.
(d) Evaluate four sources of finance (internal or external, but excluding a bank overdraft) which may be used to finance the reduction in trade creditors, and state, with reasons, which of these you consider the most appropriate.

Venture capital and long-term financing

Venture capital is long-term capital provided by certain institutions to help businesses exploit profitable opportunities. The businesses of interest to the venture capitalist will have higher levels of risk than would normally be acceptable to traditional providers of finance such as the major clearing banks. Venture capital providers may be interested in a variety of businesses including:

- business start-ups;
- acquisitions of existing businesses by a group of managers;
- providing additional capital to young, expanding businesses; and
- the buyout of one of the owners from an existing business.

The risks associated with the business can vary, in practice, but are often due to the nature of the products or the fact that it is a new business which either lacks a trading record or has new management. Although the risks are higher, the businesses also have potentially higher levels of return – hence their attraction to the venture capitalist. The type of businesses helped by venture capitalists are normally small or medium-sized rather than large companies listed on the Stock Exchange.

The venture capitalist will often make a substantial investment in the business and this may take the form of ordinary shares, preference shares or loan capital. In order to keep an eye on the sum invested, the venture capitalist will usually require a representative on the board of directors as a condition of the investment. The venture capitalist may not be looking for a quick return and may well be prepared to invest in a business for five years or more. The return may take the form of a capital gain on the realisation of the investment. When examining prospective investment opportunities, the venture capitalist will be concerned with such matters as the quality of management, the personal stake in the business made by the owners, the quality and nature of the product and the plans made to exploit the business opportunities, as well as financial matters.

The role and efficiency of the Stock Exchange

Earlier we considered the various forms of long-term capital which are available to a company. In this section, we examine the role which the Stock Exchange plays in the provision of finance for companies and the extent to which securities (i.e. shares or other financial claims) are efficiently priced by the Stock Exchange.

The role of the Stock Exchange

The Stock Exchange acts as an important *primary* and *secondary* market in capital for companies. As a primary market, the function of the Stock Exchange is to enable companies to raise new capital. As a secondary market, its function is to enable investors to transfer their securities (i.e. shares and loan capital) with ease. Thus it provides a 'second-hand' market where shares and loan capital already in issue may be bought and sold.

In order to issue shares or loan capital through the Stock Exchange, a company must be listed. This means that it must meet fairly stringent Stock Exchange requirements concerning size, profit history, disclosure, and so forth. Some share issues on the Stock Exchange arise from the initial listing of the company (e.g. issues made by utilities as part of the government privatisation programme over recent years); other share issues are undertaken by companies which are already listed on the Stock Exchange and which are seeking additional finance from investors.

The secondary market role of the Stock Exchange means that shares and other financial claims are easily transferable. This can bring real benefits to a company as investors may be more prepared to invest if they know their investment can be easily liquidated whenever required. It is important to recognise, however, that investors are not obliged to use the Stock Exchange as the means of transferring shares in a listed company. Nevertheless, it is usually the most convenient way of buying or selling shares. Prices of shares and other financial claims are usually determined by the market in an efficient manner (a point to which we will return later) and this should also give investors greater confidence to purchase shares. The company may benefit from this greater investor confidence by finding it easier to raise long-term finance and by obtaining this finance at a lower cost as investors will view their investment as being less risky.

A Stock Exchange listing can, however, have certain disadvantages for a company. The Stock Exchange imposes strict rules on listed companies and requires additional levels of financial disclosure to that already imposed by law and by the accounting profession (e.g. half-yearly financial reports must be published). The activities of listed companies are closely monitored by financial analysts, financial journalists and other companies and such scrutiny may not be welcome, particularly if the company is dealing with sensitive issues or experiencing operational problems. It is often suggested that listed companies are under pressure to perform well over the short term. This pressure may detract from undertaking projects which will only yield benefits in the longer term. If the market becomes disenchanted with the company and the price of its shares falls, this may make it vulnerable to a takeover bid from another company.

The efficiency of the Stock Exchange

It was mentioned above that the Stock Exchange helps to ensure that security prices are efficiently priced. The term 'efficiency' in this context does not relate to the way in which the Stock Exchange is administered but rather it relates to the fact that prices quoted for securities take account of all relevant information available. In other words, the prices quoted represent the best estimate of the 'true worth' of the securities. The term 'efficiency' does not imply, however, that investors have perfect knowledge concerning a company and its future prospects and that this knowledge is reflected in the share price. Information may come to light concerning the company which investors did not previously know about and which may indicate that the current share price is higher or lower than its 'true worth'. However in an efficient market, the new information will be quickly absorbed by investors and this will lead to an appropriate share price adjustment.

The term 'efficiency' in relation to the Stock Exchange is not synonymous with the economists' concept of perfect markets, which you may have come across in your previous studies. The definition of an efficient capital market does not rest on a set of restrictive assumptions regarding the operation of the market (e.g. that investors act in a rational way, that relevant information is freely available, and so on). In reality, such assumptions will not hold. The term 'efficient market' is a narrower concept which simply describes the situation where relevant information is *quickly* and *accurately* reflected in security prices.

In order to understand why the Stock Exchange is likely to be efficient, it is important to bear in mind that securities listed on the Stock Exchange are scrutinised by many individuals, including skilled analysts, who are constantly seeking to make gains from identifying securities which are inefficiently priced. If, for example, a share can be identified as being below its 'true worth', investors would exploit this information by buying shares in that company. When this is done on a large scale, the effect will be to drive up the price of the share, thereby eliminating any inefficiency within the market. Thus, as a result of the efforts to make gains from inefficiently priced securities, investors will, paradoxically, promote the efficiency of the market.

Three levels of efficiency (see Figure 7.5) have been identified concerning the operation of stock markets, as follows:

1. *The weak form of efficiency* The weak form means that current share prices fully reflect the information contained in past share prices. It is not, therefore, possible to make gains from simply studying past price movements. Movements in share prices are independent of past share price movements and follow a random path. This means that any attempt to study past prices in order to detect a pattern of price movements will fail. Investors and analysts who draw up charts of share price changes in order to predict future price movements will not profit from this exercise.
2. *The semi-strong form of efficiency* The semi-strong form means that share prices fully reflect all publicly available information such as published accounts, company announcements, newspaper reports, and so on. This means that investors who study publicly available information in an attempt to make above-average returns on a consistent basis will be disappointed.
3. *The strong form of efficiency* The strong form means that share prices fully reflect all available information whether or not it is publicly available. This means that even those who have 'inside' information concerning a company

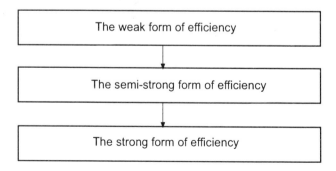

Figure 7.5 The three levels of market efficiency

will not be able to make above average returns on a consistent basis from using this information.

The three forms of efficiency described above can be viewed as a progression where each greater level of efficiency incorporates the previous level(s). Thus, if a stock market is efficient in the semi-strong form it will also be efficient in the weak form. Similarly, if a stock market is efficient in the strong form, it will also be efficient in the semi-strong and weak forms.

ACTIVITY 7.11

Can you explain why the relationship between the various forms of market efficiency explained above should be the case?

If a stock market is efficient in the semi-strong form it will reflect all publicly available information. This will include past share prices. Thus the semi-strong form will incorporate the weak form. If the stock market is efficient in the strong form, it will reflect all available information; which includes publicly available information.

The implications of stock market efficiency for managers

The efficiency of stock markets has a number of important implications for managers of companies. The most important of these are as follows:

Timing new issues

If the stock market is inefficient, there would be a risk that the price of a security would fall below its 'true worth'. As a result, the timing of new issues would become a critical management decision. Making an issue when existing securities are trading at below their real worth could be very costly for the business. However, if the market is efficient then, by definition, the price quoted for shares will faithfully reflect the available information. This implies that the timing of issues will not be critical as there is no optimal point in time for making a new issue. Even if the market is very depressed and share prices are very low, it cannot be assumed that things will improve. The share prices prevailing at the low point will still reflect the market's estimate of the future returns from the shares.

ACTIVITY 7.12

Why might a financial manager who accepts that the market is efficient in the semi-strong form, nevertheless, be justified in delaying the issue of new securities until what s/he believes will be a more appropriate time?

The justification for delaying a new issue under the circumstance described would be that the manager believes the market has got it wrong. This situation could arise if the market has inadequate information with which to price securities correctly. The manager may have access to inside information which, when made available to the market, will lead to an upward adjustment in share prices.

Security issues

We saw earlier that companies may issue mixed forms of securities. Convertible loan capital, for example, has a loan element and an equity element. It is not possible, however, to fool an efficient stock market by the issue of such securities and, thereby, obtain a 'cheap' form of finance. For a market to be efficient, it must be sophisticated enough to react quickly and accurately to relevant information. Thus the hybrid nature of convertible loan capital would be recognised and priced accordingly.

ACTIVITY 7.13

Convertible loan capital will usually be issued with rates of interest which are lower than conventional loan capital. Is this evidence that the market has been misled and is, therefore, inefficient?

If the market is prepared to accept a lower rate of interest for convertible loan capital than for more conventional forms of loan capital, this need not imply the market has been misled and that it is, therefore, inefficient. Indeed, it may well mean that the market is efficient and has taken account of all relevant information. Investors may be prepared to accept a lower rate of interest in return for the likely future benefits arising from the conversion rights.

Where a company makes a bonus issue of shares, the market will recognise that this does nothing to enhance the value of the company and so the market capitalisation of the company (i.e. the total value placed on the shares of the company) should remain unchanged. However, as there will be more shares in circulation following the bonus issue, the price per share will fall.

ACTIVITY 7.14

Sometimes, the announcement of a bonus issue to investors is followed by an increase in the total market capitalisation of the company. Does this mean that investors believe, incorrectly, that they are better off as a result of the issue and therefore the market is inefficient?

> *An increase in market capitalisation following a bonus issue need not imply the market is inefficient. A bonus issue may be accompanied by good news concerning the company or may be used to signal confidence in the future prospects of the company by the directors. When this occurs, the market will be reacting to the 'information content' of the bonus issue rather than the issue itself.*

Market prices

If the stock market accurately absorbs information concerning companies, the prices quoted for shares and other securities will represent the best estimates available of their 'true worth'. This means that investors should not spend time trying to find undervalued shares in order to make gains. Unless they have access to information which the market does not have, they will not be able to 'beat the market' on a consistent basis. This means that the best strategy for an investor is to buy a portfolio of securities and hold on to them rather than to switch between securities in order to acquire 'cheap' securities. This latter strategy will only result in time being spent and transaction costs being incurred to no avail. Similarly, managers should not try to identify undervalued shares in other companies with the intention of identifying possible takeover targets. Whilst there may be a number of valid and compelling reasons for taking over another company, the argument that shares of the target company are undervalued by the stock market is not one of them.

Accounting policies

From time to time, a company may decide to change particular accounting policies (e.g. a change from the straight-line method to the reducing-balance method of depreciation). Such a change in policy may have the effect of increasing reported profits for the period. However, if the market is efficient it will 'see through' any increases in reported profits which do not arise from improvements in the underlying economic condition of the company. As a result, the price of shares will remain unchanged. Thus deliberate attempts by managers to improve the profits of the company by switching accounting policies will not fool the market.

Rate of return

A major implication of market efficiency for managers is that the rate of return required from investments in the company will be determined by the market. The market will correctly assess the degree of risk associated with a particular investment and will impose an appropriate rate of return. Moreover, this rate of return will apply to whichever company undertakes that investment. Managers will not be able to influence the required rate of return by adopting particular financing strategies. This means, for example, that the issue of certain types of security, or combinations of securities, will not reduce the rate of return required by the market.

Evidence on stock market efficiency

Before considering the findings on stock market efficiency it is worth noting that, within each of the three levels discussed above, there are varying degrees of efficiency. In other words, efficiency within each level should be viewed as a continuum ranging from total efficiency to total inefficiency. Thus Keane argues that a stock market may be totally efficient in the weak form, near-totally efficient in the semi-strong form and totally inefficient in the strong form.[1] He also believes that, for practical purposes, market efficiency will hold if there is near-total efficiency at the weak and semi-strong levels.

Research to test the weak form has involved checking whether security price movements follow a random pattern: that is, researchers were interested to see whether or not successive price changes were independent of each other.

ACTIVITY 7.15

If share prices follow a random pattern, doesn't this mean that the market is acting in an irrational (and inefficient) manner?

No. New information concerning a company is likely to arise at random intervals and so share price adjustments to the new information will arise at those random intervals. The randomness of share price movements is, therefore, to be expected if markets are efficient.

Tests of the weak form have also involved the examination of trading rules (i.e. rules which identify the level at which to buy or sell shares) which are based on the identification of trend-like patterns to see whether superior returns can be made.

Research to test the semi-strong form of efficiency has taken various paths. For example, there have been tests which measure stock market reaction to earnings announcements. These tests are carried out to see whether the market reacts to new information in an appropriate manner. Other tests have checked to see whether the market is 'fooled' by accounting policy changes or bonus issues of shares.

Research to test the strong form of efficiency is more difficult to undertake given that Stock Exchange regulations throughout the world normally prohibit insider trading. Such regulations are designed to ensure that the Stock Exchange is a 'fair game' and that certain individuals, who have access to relevant information which the market does not have, do not use this information to their advantage. However, some tests of the strong form have been carried out. Research in the United States, for example, has used information published by the Securities and Exchange Commission (a regulatory body) which lists certain types of legal insider trading deals. The research sought to establish whether insiders were able to make superior returns from their trading.

The research evidence to date has provided confirmation of the efficiency of the world's stock markets in the weak form. In other words, security price movements do follow a random pattern and the adoption of trading rules will not lead to superior returns (after transaction costs have been taken into account). Similarly, the research evidence supports the semi-strong form of efficiency by demonstrating that new information is quickly and accurately absorbed by the market. However, recent evidence has shown that the degree of efficiency at the semi-strong level may not be quite as high as first thought. Certain anomalies have been found, such as the 'Monday effect' which reveals that, following the weekend, security prices tend to open at a lower price than when the markets closed for the weekend.

ACTIVITY 7.16

Why is the 'Monday effect' a sign that the market is inefficient in the semi-strong form?

The 'Monday effect' suggests that investors who sell on Friday, and then repurchase the same type and quantity of securities on Monday, will be able to make superior gains to those investors who simply hold on to their securities. This suggests some inefficiency in the pricing of securities.

The research evidence concerning the strong form suggests that insiders can 'beat the market'. The fact that access to information which the market does not have can lead to superior gains being made does not seem very surprising. However, it must be remembered that there are significant risks for those who engage in illegal insider trading.

Summary

In this chapter we have examined the chief sources of long-term and short-term finance available to businesses. We have seen that there are various factors to be taken into account when deciding which source of finance is appropriate to a particular business or a particular set of circumstances. We also considered the main forms of share issue and the advantages and disadvantages of each.

We examined the role of venture capital and the role and efficiency of the stock market. We saw that stock markets have a primary role in raising finance for companies and a secondary role in ensuring that investors can buy and sell securities with ease. We identified the three main forms of stock market efficiency and the implications of market efficiency for the financial management of a business.

Reference

1. S. Keane, *Stock Market Efficiency: Theory, evidence, implications*, Philip Allan, 1983.

Review questions

7.1 What are the benefits of issuing share warrants for a company?

7.2 Why might a public company which has a Stock Exchange listing revert to being an unlisted company?

7.3 Distinguish between an offer for sale and a public issue of shares.

7.4 Distinguish between invoice discounting and factoring.

Examination-style questions

Solutions to those questions marked with an asterisk are given at the end of the text. Questions 7.1–7.3 are at basic level. Questions 7.4–7.6 are at intermediate/advanced level.

7.1 H. Brown (Portsmouth) Ltd produces a range of central heating systems for sale to builders' merchants. As a result of increasing demand for its products, the directors have decided to expand production. The cost of acquiring new plant and machinery and the increase in working capital requirements is planned to be financed by a mixture of long-term and short-term debt.

Required:

(a) Discuss the major factors which should be take into account when deciding on the appropriate mix of long-term and short-term debt necessary to finance the expansion programme.

(b) Discuss the major factors which a lender should take into account when deciding whether to grant a long-term loan to the company.

(c) Identify three conditions that might be included in a long-term loan agreement and state the purpose of each.

7.2 Venture capital may represent an important source of finance for a business.

Required:

(a) What is meant by the term 'venture capital'? What are the distinguishing features of this form of finance?

(b) What types of business venture may be of interest to a venture capitalist seeking to make an investment?

(c) When considering a possible investment in a business, discuss the main factors a venture capitalist would take into account?

7.3* Answer all three questions below:

(a) Discuss the main factors which should be taken into account when choosing between long-term debt and equity finance.

(b) Explain the term 'convertible loan stock'. Discuss the advantages and disadvantages of this form of finance from the viewpoint of both the company and investors.

(c) Explain the term 'debt factoring'. Discuss the advantages and disadvantages of this form of finance.

7.4 Brocmar plc has 10 million ordinary £0.50 shares in issue. The market price of the shares is £1.80. The board of the company wishes to finance a major project at a cost of £2.88 million. Forecasts suggest that the implementation of the project will add £0.4 million to after-tax earnings available to ordinary shareholders in the coming year. After-tax earnings for the year just completed were £2 million, but this figure is expected to decline to £1.80 million in the coming year if the project proposed is not undertaken. A rights issue at a 20 per cent discount on the existing market price is proposed. Issue expenses can be ignored.

Required:

(a) To assist the board in coming to a final decision you are required to present information in the following format:

Project not undertaken
  (i) Earnings per share for the coming year.
Project undertaken and financed by a rights issue
  (ii) Rights issue price per share.
  (iii) Number of shares to be issued.
  (iv) Earnings per share for the coming year.
  (v) The theoretical ex-rights price per share.

All workings should be separately shown.

(b) What information other than that provided in the question is needed before the board can make the investment decision?

7.5 Comment on each of the following statements:

(a) 'As the stock market is depressed at this point in time, it would be better for our company to wait before issuing new shares to the public.'

(b) 'The market cannot be efficient in the semi-strong form. If it was efficient, analysts would not waste their time reading financial reports and other information in order to identify "cheap" shares.'

7.6*   On 5 April 19X4 Forward plc's shares were listed on the Stock Exchange at 100p. There were 25 million 25p shares in issue.

On 6 April 19X4 Forward announced to the press that it had unexpectedly discovered a new deposit of minerals. The deposit was estimated to have a net present value of £8 million.

On 3 May 19X4 the company announced that it was intending to raise £4 million to finance development of the deposit by means of a rights issue which was to be priced at 80p. There were no other events which influenced Forward's share price during the period covered.

Required:

(a) Calculate the market capitalisation of the company after the announcement of the mineral deposit.
(b) How many shares will be issued to raise the £4 million?
(c) Calculate the market capitalisation of the company after the rights issue.
(d) At what price are the rights likely to be traded?
(e) Why do companies issue rights at a discount? Does this represent a 'give away' by the existing shareholders?
(f) Why do listed companies normally make rights issues for new equity capital rather than public issues?

—

CHAPTER EIGHT

The Cost of Capital and the Capital Structure Decision

---------- **OBJECTIVES** ----------

On completion of this chapter you should be able to:

■ Calculate the cost of capital for a business and explain its relevance to investment decision-making.

■ Calculate the degree of financial gearing for a business and explain its significance.

■ Evaluate different capital structure options available to a business.

■ Identify and discuss the main issues in the capital structure debate.

Introduction

When appraising investment opportunities, the cost of capital has an important role to play. We saw in Chapter 4 that the cost of capital is used as the appropriate discount rate for NPV calculations. In this chapter, we examine the way in which the cost of capital may be computed. Following this examination, we turn our attention to the factors which should be taken into account when making capital structure decisions and, in particular, the impact of gearing on the risks and returns to ordinary shareholders. We touched on this area in Chapter 3 and now examine it in more detail. Finally, we examine the debate concerning whether or not an optimal capital structure exists for a business.

The cost of capital

As investment projects are normally financed from long-term capital, the discount rate which should be applied to new investment projects should reflect the expected returns required by the providers of these various forms of capital. From the viewpoint of the business, these expected returns by investors will represent the *cost of capital* which it employs. This cost is an *opportunity cost* as it represents the return which investors would expect to earn from investments with a similar level of risk.

The calculation of the cost of capital figure is an important part of investment appraisal and should be undertaken with care.

ACTIVITY 8.1

What are the possible implications for investment decision-making of failing to calculate correctly the cost of capital for a business?

If a business calculates its cost of capital incorrectly, it is likely to apply the wrong discount rate to investment projects. If the cost of capital figure which has been calculated is too low, this may lead to the acceptance of unprofitable projects. If, on the other hand, the cost of capital figure is too high, this may result in the rejection of profitable projects.

In the previous chapter, we saw that the main forms of external long-term capital for businesses include:

- ordinary shares;
- preference shares; and
- loan capital.

In addition, an important form of internal long-term capital is retained profit.

In the sections which follow we examine the ways in which the cost of each element may be deduced. We will see that there is a clear relationship between the cost of a particular element of capital and its value. For reasons which will soon become clear, we first consider how each element of capital is valued and then go on to deduce its cost to the business.

Ordinary shares

There are two major approaches to determining the cost of ordinary shares to a business: the dividend-based approach and the risk/return-based approach. We will consider each approach.

Dividend-based approach

The value of an ordinary share can be defined in terms of the future dividends which investors receive by holding the share. The value will be the present value of the expected future dividends from the particular share. In mathematical terms, the value of an ordinary share (P_O) will be expressed as follows:

$$P_O = \frac{D_1}{(1 + K_O)^1} + \frac{D_2}{(1 + K_O)^2} + \frac{D_3}{(1 + K_O)^3} + \dots \frac{D_n}{(1 + K_O)^n} + \dots$$

where:

P_O = the current market value of the share;

D_t = the expected future dividend at time t;

K_O = the cost of ordinary shares to the business (i.e. the required return for investors).

Given the above equation, we can see that the cost of ordinary shares will be the discount rate which, when applied to the stream of expected future dividends, will produce a present value which is equal to the current market value of the share. Thus the required rate of return for ordinary share investors (i.e. the cost of ordinary shares to the business) is similar to the internal rate of return (IRR) which is used in evaluating investment projects.

To deduce the required rate of return for investors we can use the same trial and error approach as that used to deduce the internal rate of return for investment projects. In practice, however, this trial and error approach is rarely used, as simplifying assumptions are normally employed concerning the pattern of dividends which make the calculations easier. The need for simplifying assumptions arises because of the problems associated with predicting the future dividend stream from an ordinary share.

Often, one of two simplifying assumptions concerning the pattern of future dividends will be employed. The first assumption is that dividends will remain constant over time. Where dividends are expected to remain constant for an infinite period, the above equation can be reduced to:

$$P_O = \frac{D_O}{K_O}$$

This equation can be re-arranged to provide an equation for deducing the cost of ordinary shares to the business. Hence:

$$K_O = \frac{D_O}{P_O}$$

ACTIVITY 8.2

Kowloon Investments plc has ordinary shares in issue which have a current market value of £2.20. The annual dividend to be paid by the business in future years is expected to be 40p. What is the cost of the ordinary shares to the business?

The cost of the ordinary shares will be:

$$K_O = \frac{0.40}{2.20}$$

$$= 18.2\%$$

The second simplifying assumption which can be employed is that dividends will grow at a constant rate over time. Where dividends are expected to have a constant growth rate, the first equation shown above can be reduced to:

$$P_O = \frac{D_1}{K_O - g}$$

where g is the expected annual growth rate. (The model assumes K_O is greater than g.)

This equation can also be rearranged to provide an equation for deducing the cost of ordinary share capital. Hence:

$$K_O = \frac{D_1}{P_O} + g$$

ACTIVITY 8.3

Avalon plc has ordinary shares in issue which have a current market price of £1.50. The dividend expected for next year is 20p per share and future dividends are expected to grow at a constant rate of 3 per cent per annum. What is the cost of the ordinary shares to the business?

Your answer should be as follows:

$$K_O = \frac{0.20}{1.50} + 0.03$$

$$= 16.3\%$$

Risk/return approach

An alternative approach to deducing the returns required by ordinary shareholders is to use the *capital asset pricing model (CAPM)*. This approach builds on the ideas which we discussed in Chapter 6. In that chapter, we saw how the total risk associated with investment projects can be reduced by holding a portfolio of projects. We also saw that total risk is made up of two elements: *diversifiable risk* and *non-diversifiable risk*. Diversifiable risk is that part of the total risk which is specific to the project and which can be eliminated by spreading available funds between investment projects. Non-diversifiable risk is that part of the total risk which is common to all projects and which, therefore, cannot be diversified away. This element of risk arises from general market conditions.

The portfolio approach to risk reduction described above can also be used by investors. The total risk associated with holding shares is also made up of diversifiable and non-diversifiable risk. By holding a portfolio of shares an investor can eliminate diversifiable risk (i.e risk which is specific to the share) and this would leave only non-diversifiable risk (which is common to all shares).

We saw in Chapter 6 that risk averse investors will only be prepared to take on increased risk if there is the prospect of increased returns. However, as diversifiable risk can be eliminated through holding a diversified portfolio, there is no reason why investors should receive additional returns for taking on this form of risk. It is, therefore, only the non-diversifiable risk element of total risk for which investors should expect additional returns. The non-diversifiable risk element for a particular share can be measured using *beta*. This is a measure of the non-diversifiable risk of the share in relation to the market as a whole, or, to put it another way, it is the degree to which a share fluctuates with movements in the market as a whole.

Using the above ideas, the required rate of return for investors for a particular share can be calculated as follows:

$$K_O = K_{RF} + b(K_m - K_{RF})$$

where:

K_O	= the required return for investors for a particular share;
K_{RF}	= the risk-free rate on short-term government securities;
b	= beta of the particular share;
K_m	= the expected returns to the market for the next period; and
$(K_m - K_{RF})$	= the expected market average risk premium for the next period.

The above equation reveals that the required return for a particular share is made up of two elements: the risk-free return plus a risk premium. We can see the risk premium is equal to the expected risk premium for the market as a whole multiplied by the beta of the particular share. This adjustment to the market risk is undertaken to derive the relative risk associated with the particular share. (As stated earlier, beta measures the non-diversifiable risk of a particular share in relation to the market as a whole.)

This relationship between risk and return as set out in the above equation is shown graphically in Figure 8.1. A share which moves in perfect step with the market will have a beta measure of 1.0. A share which is only half as volatile as the market will have a beta of 0.5 and a share which is twice as volatile as the market will have a beta of 2.0. The evidence suggests that most shares have a beta which is fairly close to the market measure of 1.0. Betas are normally measured

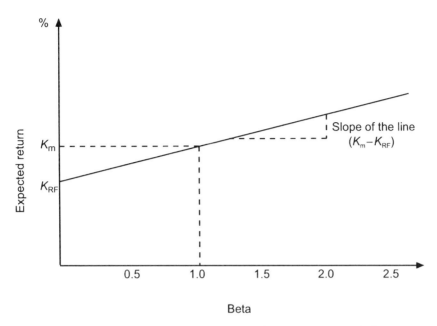

Figure 8.1 Relationship between the expected level of return and the level of risk as measured by beta

using regression analysis on past data. The returns from a particular share for a period (i.e dividends plus any increase in share value) are regressed against the returns from the market as a whole (as represented by some Stock Exchange index). However, calculation is not always necessary as measures of beta for the shares of listed companies are available from various information agencies such as the London Business School Risk Measurement Service and Bloomberg.

EXHIBIT 8.1

A selection of betas for Stock Exchange listed companies are provided for illustration purposes in Figure 8.2.

ACTIVITY 8.4

Lansbury plc has recently obtained a measure of its beta from a business information agency. The beta obtained is 1.2. The expected returns to the market for the next period is 10 per cent and the risk-free rate on government securities is 3 per cent. What is the cost of ordinary shares to the business?

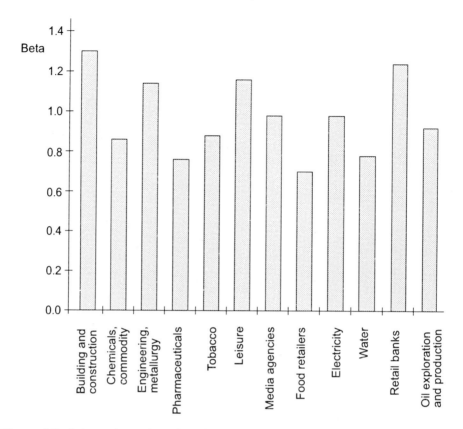

Figure 8.2 Industry betas for selected industries (Source: London Business School Risk Measurement Services)

Using the above formula we have:

$$K_O = 3\% + 1.2(10\% - 3\%)$$

$$= 11.4\%$$

The CAPM approach is not a perfect solution to the problem of deducing the cost of equity. We can see from the equation above that three important measures are required: the risk-free rate of return, the expected returns to the market as a whole, and the measure of beta. Each of these measures have practical problems surrounding them. In addition, the CAPM approach has been criticised for assuming that non-diversifiable risk can be adequately reflected in a single measure of risk. Nevertheless, this approach does attempt to deal with the problem of risk in a systematic manner which means that decision-makers do not have to rely on judgement alone.

Retained profit

We saw in Chapter 7 that retained profits cannot be regarded as a 'cost free' source of finance. If profits are reinvested by the business, the shareholders will expect to receive returns on these funds which are equivalent to the returns expected from investments in opportunities with similar levels of risk. The ordinary shareholders' interest in the business is made up of ordinary share capital plus any retained profits and the expected returns from each will be identical. Hence, when we calculate the cost of ordinary share capital we are also calculating the cost of any retained profits.

Loan capital

Loan capital may be irredeemable (i.e. the business is not expected to repay the principal sum and interest will be paid indefinitely). Where the rate of interest on the loan is fixed, the equation used to derive the value of irredeemable loan capital is similar to the equation used to derive the value of ordinary shares where the dividends remain constant over time. The equation for the value of irredeemable loan capital is:

$$P_d = \frac{I}{K_d}$$

where:

P_d = the current market value of the loan capital.
K_d = the cost of loan capital to the business;
I = the annual rate of interest on the loan capital; and

This equation can be rearranged to provide an equation for deducing the cost of loan capital. Hence:

$$K_d = \frac{I}{P_d}$$

Interest payments on loan capital are an allowable expense for taxation purposes and so the net cash flows incurred in servicing the loan capital will be the rate of interest payable *less* the tax charge which can be offset. For investment appraisal purposes we take the after-tax net cash flows resulting from a project, and so, when calculating the appropriate discount rate, we should be consistent and use the after-tax rates for the cost of capital. The after-tax cost of loan capital will be:

$$K_d = \frac{I(1 - t)}{P_d}$$

where t is the rate of corporation tax payable.

ACTIVITY 8.5

Tan and Company plc has irredeemable loan capital outstanding on which it pays an annual rate of interest of 10 per cent. The current market value of the loan capital is £88 per £100 nominal value and the corporation tax rate is 20 per cent. What is the cost of the loan capital to the business?

Using the above formula, the cost of loan capital will be:

$$K_d = \frac{10(1 - 0.20)}{88}$$

$$= 9.1\%$$

Note that the rate of interest payable on the nominal value of the loan capital does not represent the relevant cost for investment appraisal purposes. Rather, we are concerned with the *opportunity cost* of the loan capital. This represents the return that can be earned by investing in an opportunity which has the same level of risk. The *current market rate* of interest of the preference shares, as calculated above, will provide us with a measure of the relevant opportunity cost.

Where the loan capital is redeemable, deriving the cost of capital figure is a little more complex. However, the principles and calculations required to derive the relevant figure have already been covered in Chapter 3 when we discussed the internal rate of return (IRR). An investor who purchases redeemable loan capital will pay an initial outlay and then expect to receive annual interest payments plus a repayment of capital at the end of the loan period. The required rate of return for the investor will be the discount rate which, when applied to the future cash flows will produce a present value which is equal to the current market value of the investment. The rate of return the investor expects to receive over the period of his/her investment can be computed in the same way as we computed the IRR for other forms of investment opportunity.

Example 8.1

Lim Associates plc issues £20m. loan capital at par on which it pays an annual rate of interest of 10 per cent on the nominal value. The issue price of the loan capital is £88 per £100 nominal value and the rate of corporation tax is 20 per cent. The loan capital is due to be redeemed in four years' time at £110 per £100 nominal value. What is the cost of the loan capital to the business?

The cash flows for this issue of loan capital will be as follows:

Year		Cash flows £m.
0	£20m. × (88/100)	17.6
1–3	−£2m. × (1 − 0.8)	(1.6)
4	((−£20m. × (110/100)) + (−£2m. × (1 −0.8)))	(23.6)

In order to derive the cost of loan capital to the business we can use the trial and error approach used in calculating the IRR.

ACTIVITY 8.6

Calculate the cost of loan capital for the Lim Associates plc.

Let us begin by using a discount rate of 10 per cent:

Year	Cash flows £m.	Discount rate 10%	Net cash flows £m.
0	17.6	1.00	17.6
1	(1.6)	0.91	(1.5)
2	(1.6)	0.83	(1.3)
3	(1.6)	0.75	(1.2)
4	(23.6)	0.68	(16.0)
			(2.4)

This discount rate is too low as the discounted future cash flows exceed the issue price of the loan capital. Let us try 15 per cent:

Year	Cash flows £m.	Discount rate 15%	Net cash flows £m.
0	17.6	1.00	17.6
1	(1.6)	0.87	(1.4)
2	(1.6)	0.76	(1.2)
3	(1.6)	0.66	(1.1)
4	(23.6)	0.57	(13.5)
			0.4

This discount rate is a little too high as the discounted cash flows are less than the issue price of the loan capital. By linear interpolation we can derive a more precise figure if required:

$$K_d = 10\% + ((-2.4)/(-2.4) - (+0.4) \times (15 - 10\%))$$

$$= 14.3\%$$

Preference shares

Preference shares may be either redeemable or irredeemable. They are similar to loan capital insofar as the holders receive an agreed rate of return each year (which is expressed in terms of the nominal value of the shares). However, preference shares differ from loan capital in that the annual dividends paid to preference shareholders do not represent a tax-deductible expense for the business. Thus the full cost of the annual dividend payments must be borne by the business. Where the rate of dividend on the preference shares is fixed (i.e. there is no right to participate in additional profits), the equation used to derive the value of irredeemable preference shares is again similar to the equation used to derive the value of ordinary shares where the dividends remain constant over time. The equation for irredeemable preference shares is:

$$P_p = \frac{D_p}{K_p}$$

where:

P_p = the current market price of the preference shares.
K_p = the cost of preference shares to the business;
D_p = the annual dividend payments; and

This equation can be rearranged to provide an equation for deducing the cost of irredeemable preference shares. Hence:

$$K_p = \frac{D_p}{P_p}$$

ACTIVITY 8.7

Febbrarro plc has 12% preference shares in issue with a nominal value of £1. The shares have a current market price of £0.90 (excluding dividends). What is the cost of the preference shares?

The cost of the preference shares will be:

$$K_p = \frac{12}{90}$$

$$= 13.3\%$$

In the case of redeemable preference shares, the cost of capital can be deduced using the IRR approach which we used above in determining the cost of redeemable loan capital.

ACTIVITY 8.8

L.C. Conday plc has £50m. 10% £1 preference shares in issue. The current market price is £0.92 and the shares are due to be redeemed in three years' time at par. What is the cost of the preference shares?

Let us begin by using a discount rate of 11 per cent:

Year	Cash flows £m.	Discount rate 11%	Net cash flows £m.
0	46.0	1.00	46.0
1	(5.0)	0.90	(4.5)
2	(5.0)	0.81	(4.0)
3	(55.0)	0.73	(40.1)
			(2.6)

This discount rate is too low as the discounted future cash flows exceed the issue price of the loan capital. Let us try 13 per cent:

Year	Cash flows £m.	Discount rate 13%	Net cash flows £m.
0	46.0	1.00	46.0
1	(5.0)	0.89	(4.4)
2	(5.0)	0.78	(3.9)
3	(55.0)	0.69	(38.0)
			(0.3)

We can see that the cost of preference shares is approximately 13 per cent.

The weighted average cost of capital (WACC)

It is often claimed that managers of a business have a target capital structure in mind when making financing decisions. Although the relative proportions of equity and loans may vary over the short term, these proportions, it is argued, remain fairly stable when viewed over the medium to longer term. The existence of a fairly stable capital structure is consistent with the view that managers believe that a particular financing mix will minimise the cost of capital of the business; or, to put it another way, a particular financing mix provides an optimal capital structure for the business. (Whether or not there is such a thing as an optimal capital structure will be discussed later in the chapter.) However, a target capital structure is unlikely to be 'set in stone'. It may change from time to time in response to changes in the tax rates, interest rates, etc., which affect the cost of particular elements of the capital structure.

The existence of a stable capital structure has important implications for the evaluation of investment projects. It has already been argued that the required rates of return from investors (i.e. the costs of capital to the business) should provide the basis for determining an appropriate discount rate for investment projects. If we accept that a business will maintain a fairly stable capital structure over the period of the project, then the *average* cost of capital can provide an appropriate discount rate. The average cost of capital can be calculated by taking the cost of the individual elements and then weighting each element in proportion to the *target* capital structure (by market value) of the business. Example 8.2 illustrates how the weighted average cost of capital (WACC) is calculated.

Example 8.2

Danton plc has 10 million ordinary shares in issue with a current market value of £2.00 per share. The expected dividend for next year is 16p per share and this is expected to grow each year at a constant rate of 4 per cent. The business also has £20m. of irredeemable loan capital in issue with a nominal rate of interest of 10 per cent and which is quoted at £80 per £100 nominal value. Assume a rate of corporation tax of 20 per cent and that the current capital structure reflects the target capital structure of the company.

Required:

What is the weighted average cost of capital of the company?

The cost of ordinary shares in Danton plc will be calculated as follows:

$$K_O = \frac{D_1}{P_O} + g$$

$$= \frac{16}{200} + 4$$

$$= 12\%$$

(Note: Although we have used the dividend valuation model to calculate the cost of equity in this case, it would be equally valid to have used the CAPM model. Both can be used in deducing WACC.)

The cost of loan capital will be calculated as follows:

$$K_d = \frac{I(1-t)}{P_d}$$

$$= \frac{10(1-0.8)}{80}$$

$$= 10\%$$

The WACC will be:

	(a) Market value £m.	(b) Proportion	(c) Cost %	(d) Contribution to WACC (b × c)
Ordinary shares* (10m. × £2)	20	0.56	12	6.7
Loan capital (£20m. × 0.8)	16	0.44	10	4.4
			WACC	11.1%

(Note: * The market value of the capital rather than the nominal value has been used in the above calculations. This is because we are concerned with the opportunity cost of capital invested as explained earlier.)

Specific or average cost of capital?

It is often the case that an investment project will be financed by raising the necessary funds from a particular source. As a result, it is sometimes argued that the cost of capital for the investment project should be based on the particular type of capital which is being used to finance it. However, this argument is incorrect and could lead to illogical decisions being made. Assume a business is considering an investment in two new machines which are identical in every respect and that each machine has an estimated IRR of 12 per cent. Let us further assume that the first machine will be financed using loan capital with a cost of 10 per cent. However, as debt capacity of the business will then be used up, the second machine will be financed by ordinary share capital at a cost of 14 per cent. If the specific cost of capital is used to evaluate investment decisions, the business would be in the peculiar position of accepting the investment in the first machine, because the IRR exceeds the cost of capital, and rejecting the second (identical) machine because the IRR is lower than the cost of capital! By using the WACC, we avoid this kind of problem. Each machine will be evaluated according to the average cost of capital, which should result in consistent decisions being made.

Limitations of the WACC approach

The WACC approach has been criticised for not taking proper account of risk in investment decisions. In practice, different investment opportunities are likely to have different levels of risk and so it can be argued that the cost of capital for each project should be adjusted accordingly. You may recall from Chapter 6, that investors will require higher returns to compensate for higher levels of risk. This means that the WACC is really only suitable where an investment project is expected to have the same level of risk as existing investments, or the proposed project is fairly small and is, therefore, not expected to have a significant effect on overall risk of the business.

It was mentioned earlier that the WACC approach assumes that the capital structure of the business remains stable over the period of the investment project. However, if this is not the case, the validity of the WACC approach is undermined. Changes in capital structure can result in changes in the proportions of the individual capital elements and, possibly, changes in the costs of these elements.

Financial gearing

We have already seen that the presence of fixed charge capital in the long-term capital structure of a business is referred to as 'gearing' (or to be more precise 'financial gearing'). The term 'gearing' is used to convey the point that fixed charge capital can accentuate the changes on profit before interest and tax (PBIT) and on the returns to ordinary shareholders. The effect is similar to the effect of two intermeshing cog wheels of unequal size (see Figure 8.3). The movement in the larger cog wheel (profit before interest and taxation) causes a more than proportionate movement in the smaller cog wheel (returns to ordinary shareholders). The effect of financial gearing is demonstrated in Example 8.3.

Example 8.3

Alpha plc and Gamma plc are similar businesses and have generated identical profits before interest and tax (PBIT) for 19X4 of £80m. The long-term capital structure of each business is as follows:

	Alpha plc £m.	Gamma plc £m.
£1 Ordinary shares	200	340
12% Preference shares	100	50
10% Loan stock	100	10
	400	400

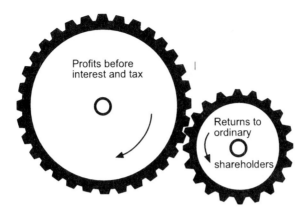

Figure 8.3 The effect of financial gearing

Although both businesses have the same total long-term capital, we can see that the level of financial gearing differs significantly between the two businesses.

A widely used measure of gearing, which we came across in Chapter 3, is as follows:

$$\text{Financial gearing ratio} = \frac{\text{Fixed charge capital}}{\text{Total long-term capital}} \times 100\%$$

For Alpha plc and Gamma plc the ratios are 50 per cent and 15 per cent respectively, indicating that Alpha has a relatively high level of financial gearing (i.e a high proportion of fixed charge capital in relation to its total long-term capital) and Gamma has a relatively low level of financial gearing.

Let us now consider the effect of financial gearing on the returns to shareholders. The earnings per share for the ordinary share investors of each business for 19X4 can be calculated as follows:

	Alpha plc £m.	Gamma plc £m.
PBIT	80.0	80.0
Less: Loan interest	10.0	1.0
Profit before taxation	70.0	79.0
Less: Corporation tax (say, 30%)	21.0	23.7
Profit after taxation	49.0	55.3
Less: Preference dividend	12.0	6.0
Profit available to ordinary shareholders	37.0	49.3
Earnings per share (EPS)	18.5p	14.5p

In this example, we can see that ordinary share investors in Alpha plc earn higher returns in 19X4 than ordinary share investors in Gamma plc due to the additional gearing or leverage effect from the use of a higher level of fixed charge capital. This is possible provided the additional profits generated from the use of fixed charge capital exceed the additional fixed payments incurred. However, the financial gearing effect can operate in both directions. If profits before interest and tax for the following year are £40m., the earnings per share for ordinary share investors in each business for 19X5 would be as follows:

	Alpha plc £m.	Gamma plc £m.
PBIT	40.0	40.0
Less: Loan interest	10.0	1.0
Profit before taxation	30.0	39.0
Less: Corporation tax (say 30%)	9.0	11.7
Profit after taxation	21.0	27.3
Less: Preference dividend	12.0	6.0
Profit available to ordinary shareholders	9.0	21.3
Earnings per share (EPS)	4.5p	6.3p

In this case, we can see that the returns to ordinary shareholders of Alpha plc are lower than those of Gamma plc. We can also see from the example that the decrease in earnings per share is much greater for ordinary shareholders in the higher-geared business than in the lower-geared business.

The degree of financial gearing

The effect of financial gearing is that any increase in the profit before interest and tax for a financially geared business will result in a more than proportionate increase in earnings per share (EPS) and any decrease in profit before interest and tax (PBIT) will result in a more than proportionate decrease in earnings per share. The higher the level of financial gearing, the more sensitive changes in earnings per share become to changes in profit before interest and tax for any given level. The *degree of financial gearing* provides a measure of the financial gearing effect and can be calculated as follows:

$$\text{Degree of financial gearing} = \frac{\%\ \text{change in EPS}}{\%\ \text{change in PBIT}}$$

For Alpha plc, the degree of financial gearing, based on the changes between 19X4 and 19X5, will be:

$$= \frac{-75.7\%}{-50\%}$$

$$= 1.5$$

ACTIVITY 8.9

What is the degree of financial gearing for Gamma plc?

For Gamma plc, the degree of financial gearing will be:

$$= \frac{-56.6\%}{-50\%}$$

$$= 1.1$$

In both cases, the figure derived is greater than 1, which indicates the presence of financial gearing. The higher the figure derived, the greater the sensitivity of earnings per share to changes in profit before interest and taxation. This measure of financial gearing indicates that, in the case of Alpha plc, a 1.0 per cent change in profit before interest and taxation from the base level of £80m. will result in a 1.5 per cent change in EPS, whereas for Gamma plc, a 1.0 per cent change in profit before interest and taxation from the base level of £80m. will only result in a 1.1 per cent change in EPS.

Another way of arriving at the degree of financial gearing for a particular level of profit before interest and taxation is as follows:

$$\text{Degree of financial gearing} = \frac{\text{PBIT}}{\text{PBIT} - I - (P \times 100/100 - t)}$$

where:

I = interest charges;
P = preference dividend; and
t = tax rate.

(Note that the preference dividend is 'grossed up' to a pre-tax amount by multiplying the dividend by $100/(100-t)$. This is done to ensure consistency with the other variables in the equation.)

The above equation has the advantage that a single measure of PBIT is all that is required to derive the degree of financial gearing. For Alpha plc, the measure will be calculated as follows for 19X4:

$$\text{Degree of financial gearing} = \frac{80}{80 - 10 - (12 \times 100/100 - 30)}$$

$$= \frac{80}{52.9}$$

$$= 1.5$$

This equation will yield the same results as the earlier equation shown above.

ACTIVITY 8.10

Use the above equation to derive the degree of financial gearing for Gamma plc for 19X4.

Your answer should be as follows:

$$\text{Degree of financial gearing} = \frac{80}{80 - 1 - (6 \times 100/100 - 30)}$$

$$= \frac{80}{70.4}$$

$$= 1.1$$

It is important to appreciate that the degree of financial gearing for a business will vary with the level of profits before interest and tax. For example, where profits before interest and tax barely cover the fixed capital charges, even small changes in the former figure can have a significant impact on earnings per share. However, as profits before interest and taxation increase in relation to fixed capital charges, earnings per share will become less sensitive to changes.

ACTIVITY 8.11

Calculate the degree of financial gearing for Alpha plc and Gamma plc for 19X5.

For Alpha plc, the degree of financial gearing in 19X5 (when profits before interest and taxation are much lower) will be:

$$= \frac{40}{40 - 10 - (12 \times 100/100 - 30)}$$

$$= 3.1$$

For Gamma plc, the degree of financial gearing in 19X5 will be:

$$= \frac{40}{40 - 1 - (6 \times 100/100 - 30)}$$

$$= 1.3$$

We can see that earnings per share for both companies are now more sensitive to changes in the level of profits before interest and tax than in the previous year when profits were higher. However, returns to ordinary shareholders in Alpha plc, which has a higher level of financial gearing, have become much more sensitive to change than Gamma plc.

Gearing and the evaluation of capital structure decisions

When evaluating capital structure decisions, the likely impact of gearing on the expected risks and returns for ordinary shareholders must be taken into account. The use of projected financial statements and gearing ratios, which were examined in earlier chapters, can help the managers of a business to assess the effect of different capital structure options on the risk/return profile of ordinary shareholders. Example 8.4 illustrates the way in which capital structure options may be evaluated.

Example 8.4

The following is a shortened version of the accounts of Woodhall Engineers plc, a company which is not listed on a Stock Exchange.

Profit and loss account year ended 31 December 19X4

	19X4 £m.	19X3 £m.
Turnover	50	47
Operating costs	47	41
Operating profit	3	6
Interest payable	2	2
Profit on ordinary activities before tax	1	4
Taxation on profit on ordinary activities	–	–
Profit on ordinary activities after tax	1	4
Dividends (net)	1	1
Profit retained for the financial year	–	3

Balance sheet at 31 December 19X4

	19X4 £m.	19X3 £m.
Fixed assets (*less* depreciation)	20	21
Current assets		
Stocks	18	10
Debtors	17	16
Cash at bank	1	3
	36	29
Creditors: amounts due within one year		
Short-term debt	(11)	(5)
Trade creditors	(10)	(10)
	(21)	(15)
Total assets (*less* current liabilities)	35	35
Less: Long-term loans (secured)	(15)	(15)
	20	20
Capital and reserves		
Called up share capital 25p		
Ordinary shares	16	16
Profit and loss account	4	4
	20	20

The company is making plans to expand its factory. New plant will cost £8m. and an expansion in output will increase working capital by £4m. Over the fifteen years' life of the project, incremental profits arising from the expansion will be £2m. per year before interest and tax. In addition, 19X5 profits before tax from its existing activities are expected to return to 19X3 levels.

Two alternative methods of financing the expansion have been discussed by Woodhall's directors. The first is the issue of £12m. 15 per cent debt repayable in year 2000. The second is a rights issue of 40 million 25p ordinary shares which will give the company 30p per share after expenses. (The company has substantial tax losses to be offset, so we can ignore taxation in our calculations.) The 19X5 dividend per share is expected to be the same as that for 19X4.

Required:

Which financing option should be chosen?

A useful starting point in tackling this problem is to prepare a forecast profit and loss account for the year ended 31 December 19X5 under each option. These will be as follows:

Forecast profit and loss account for the year ended 31 December 19X5

	Debt issue £m.	Equity issue £m.
Profit before interest and taxation (6.0 + 2.0)	8.0	8.0
Loan interest	3.8	2.0
Profit before tax	4.2	6.0
Taxation	—	—
Profit after tax	4.2	6.0
Dividends (net)	1.0	1.6
Retained profit for the year	3.2	4.4

The impact of each financing option on the overall capital structure of the business should also be considered. The revised capital structure under each option will be:

	Debt issue £m.	Equity issue £m.
Capital and reserves		
Share capital 25p Ordinary shares	16.0	26.0
Share premium account*	—	2.0
Retained profit	7.2	8.4
	23.2	36.4

Note: * This represents the amount received from the issue of shares which is above the nominal value of the shares. The amount is calculated as follows:

40m. shares × (30p − 25p) = £2m.

	Debt issue	Equity issues
Number of shares in issue (25p shares)	64m.	104m.

To help us further, gearing ratios and profitability ratios may be calculated under each option.

ACTIVITY 8.12

Using the forecast figures which have been calculated, compute the interest cover ratio, gearing ratio, return on owners' equity ratio and earnings per share, assuming:

1. The company issues debt.
2. The company issues ordinary shares.

These ratios are as follows:

	Debt issue	Equity issue
Interest cover ratio		

$$\frac{\text{Profit before interest and tax}}{\text{Interest payable}} = \frac{8}{3.8} \qquad \frac{8}{2.0}$$

$$= 2.1 \text{ times} \qquad 4.0 \text{ times}$$

Gearing ratio

$$\frac{\text{Long-term liabilities}}{\text{Share capital + reserves + long-term liabilities}} = \frac{£27m}{£23.2m + £27m} \qquad \frac{£15m}{£36.4m + £15m}$$

$$= 53.8\% \qquad 29.2\%$$

Return on owners' equity

$$\frac{\text{Earnings available to ordinary shareholders}}{\text{Ordinary shares + reserves}} = \frac{4.2 \times 100\%}{23.2} \qquad \frac{6.0 \times 100\%}{36.4}$$

$$= 18.1\% \qquad 16.5\%$$

Earnings per share

$$\frac{\text{Earnings available to ordinary shareholders}}{\text{No. of ordinary shares}} = \frac{£4.2m}{64m} \qquad \frac{£6.0m}{104m}$$

$$= 6.6p. \qquad 5.8p.$$

The information which we now have available can help assess the implications of each financing option.

ACTIVITY 8.13

What would your views of the proposed financing options be in each of the following circumstances?

1. If you were a banker and you were approached for a loan.
2. If you were an ordinary share investor in Woodhall and you were asked to subscribe to a rights issue.

A banker may be unenthusiastic about lending the company funds. The gearing ratio of 53.8 per cent is rather high and would leave the bank in an exposed position. The existing loan is already secured on assets held by the company and it is not clear whether the company is in a position to offer an attractive form of security for the new loan. The interest cover ratio of 2.1 is also rather low. If the company is unable to achieve the expected returns from the new project, or if it is unable to restore profits from the remainder of its operations to 19X3 levels, this ratio would be even lower.

Ordinary share investors may need some convincing that it would be worthwhile to make further investments in the company. The return for ordinary shareholders in 19X3 was 20 per cent and earnings per share 6.3p. Both ratios are predicted to be lower in 19X5 under the equity option. In making a decision, investors should discover whether the new investment is of a similar level of risk to their existing investment and whether the returns from the investment compare with those available from other opportunities with similar levels of risk.

ACTIVITY 8.14

Brunel Instruments Ltd produces precision measurement devices for the oil industry. The balance sheet of the company as at 30 November 19X2 is as follows:

Balance sheet as at 30 November 19X2

	£m.	£m.	£m.
Fixed assets			
Plant and machinery at cost		36.4	
Less: Accumulated depreciation		12.2	24.2
Motor vehicles at cost		1.2	
Less: Accumulated depreciation		0.6	0.6
			24.8
Current assets			
Stocks and work in progress		18.5	
Trade debtors		21.4	
Bank		1.9	
		41.8	
Less: **Creditors: amounts due within one year**			
Trade creditors	12.7		
Proposed dividend	2.4		
Taxation	4.1	19.2	22.6
			47.4

	£m.	£m.	£m.
Less: **Creditors: amounts due beyond one year**			
10% Debentures			15.0
			32.4
Capital and reserves			
£0.50 Ordinary shares			10.0
General reserve			4.6
Profit and loss account			17.8
			32.4

A profit and loss account for the year to 30 November 19X2 is as follows:

Abridged profit and loss account for the year ended 30 November 19X2

	£m.
Sales turnover	115.4
Profit before interest and taxation	17.9
Interest payable	1.5
Profit before taxation	16.4
Corporation tax	4.1
Profit after taxation	12.3
Dividend	3.6
Retained profit for the year	8.7

The company wishes to expand its production facilities in order to cope with an increase in demand for its products. Although plant and equipment costing £18m. is required, it is expected that annual profit before interest and taxation will increase by £5m.

The directors of the company are considering the following three possible methods of financing the expansion programme:

1. The issue of nine million 50p ordinary shares at a premium of £1.50 per share.
2. The issue of 12 million 12% £1 preference shares at par and £6 million 10% debentures at par.
3. The issue of six million ordinary shares at a premium of £1.50 per share and £6 million 10% debentures at par.

The directors wish to increase the dividend per share by 12p next year whichever financing scheme is adopted.

Assume a rate of corporation tax of 25 per cent.

Required:

(a) For each of the financing schemes under consideration:

> (i)   prepare a projected profit and loss account for the year ended 30 November 19X3;
> (ii) calculate the projected earnings per share for the year ended 30 November 19X3; and
> (iii) calculate the projected level of financial gearing as at 30 November 19X3.
> **(b)** Briefly assess each of the financing schemes under consideration from the viewpoint of an existing shareholder.

Your answer should be as follows:

(a) (i)

Projected profit and loss accounts under each financing scheme:

	(1) £m.	(2) £m.	(3) £m.
Profit before interest and tax	22.9	22.9	22.9
Interest charges	1.5	2.1	2.1
	21.4	20.8	20.8
Tax payable	5.4	5.2	5.2
Profit after tax	16.0	15.6	15.6
Preference dividend payable	—	1.4	—
Available to ordinary shareholders	16.0	14.2	15.6
Ordinary dividend	8.7	6.0	7.8
Retained profit	7.3	8.2	7.8

(a) (ii)

Earnings per share under each financing scheme

$$= \quad \frac{16.0}{(20+9)} \qquad \frac{14.2}{20} \qquad \frac{15.6}{(20+6)}$$

$$= \quad £0.55 \qquad £0.71 \qquad £0.60$$

(a) (iii)

Gearing ratio

$$\text{Scheme } (1) = \frac{15}{(47.4 + 7.3 + 18)} \times 100$$

$$= 20.6\%$$

$$\text{Scheme } (2) = \frac{33}{(47.4 + 8.2 + 18)} \times 100$$

$$= 44.8\%$$

$$Scheme\ (3) = \frac{21}{(47.4 + 7.8 + 18)} \times 100$$

$$= 28.7\%$$

Scheme (2) provides the highest EPS and also produces the highest gearing ratio. Thus the highest level of return to ordinary shareholders brings the highest level of risk. However, the interest cover ratio under this scheme is high (10.9 times) and, providing profits achieve expected levels, the additional gearing should not be an undue burden on the company. Scheme (1) brings the lowest return to ordinary shareholders and also produces the lowest level of gearing. The EPS of £0.55 under this scheme is also lower than the current level of EPS of £0.62. Scheme (3) provides a 'middle way' in terms of EPS and gearing, although the EPS achieved is still lower than the current level.

Managers may want to know whether a planned level of gearing is likely to be acceptable to investors. To find out, they should look at the levels of gearing of businesses operating within the same industry. If the business adopts a much higher level of gearing than similar businesses, there may be problems in raising long-term funds. The managers could also discuss the proposed level of gearing with prospective investors such as banks and financial institutions to see whether they regard the proposed level of gearing as being acceptable.

EXHIBIT 8.2

Figure 8.4 illustrates the differences in gearing ratios (i.e. loan capital to loan capital plus equity) which exist between European countries. We can see that UK businesses have fairly low levels of gearing compared to many European countries. The differences between the various countries may be due to various factors such as differences in taxation systems, differences in financial 'culture', and so forth.

Constructing a PBIT–EPS indifference chart

The returns to shareholders at different levels of profit before interest and taxation (PBIT) under different financing schemes can be presented in the form of a chart if required. In order to provide an illustration of such a chart we can use the information contained in our answer to Example 8.4 above. The chart (which is referred to as a PBIT–EPS indifference chart) is set out in Figure 8.5. We can see that the vertical axis of the chart plots the earnings per share and the horizontal axis plots the profit before interest and taxation. To show the returns to shareholders at different levels of profit, we need two coordinates for each financing scheme. The first of these will be the profit before interest and taxation necessary

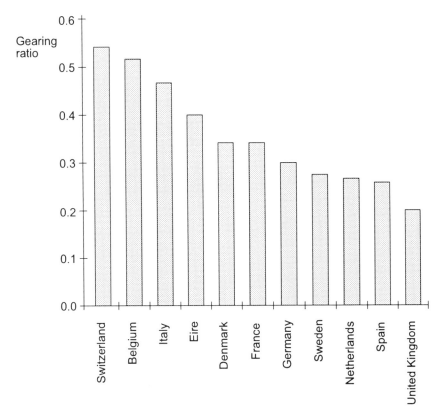

Figure 8.4   The ranking of European countries by the gearing ratios of their businesses (Source: J. Tucker, 'Capital structure: an economic perspective on Europe', in J. Pointon (ed.) *Issues in Business Taxation*, Avebury, 1994)

to cover the finance charges. For the debt issue, the relevant amount is £3.8m. and for the ordinary share issue, the amount is £2.0m. (see profit and loss accounts above). These points will be plotted on the vertical axis. The second coordinate for each financing scheme will be the earnings per share at the expected profit before interest and taxation. (However, an arbitrarily determined level of profit before interest and taxation could also be used.) For the debt issue, the EPS at the expected profit before interest and taxation is 6.6p and for the ordinary share issue, the EPS is 5.8p (see earlier calculations). By joining the two coordinates relevant to each financing scheme, we have a straight line which reveals the earnings per share at different levels of profit before interest and taxation.

We can see from the chart that, at lower levels of profit before interest and taxation, the ordinary share issue provides better returns to shareholders. However, the debt issue line has a steeper slope and returns to ordinary share-holders rise more quickly. We can see that beyond a profit before interest and

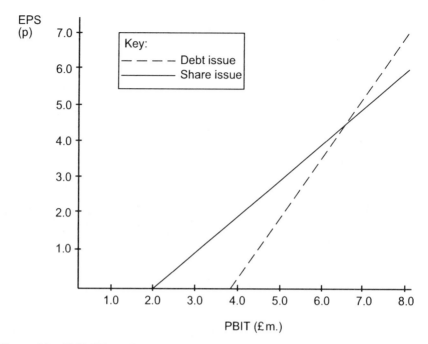

Figure 8.5   PBIT–EPS indifference chart for two financing options

taxation of £6.7m., ordinary shareholders begin to reap the benefits of gearing and their returns become higher under this alternative. The profit before interest and taxation of £6.7m. is referred to as the *indifference point* (i.e. the point at which the two financing schemes provide the same level of return to ordinary shareholders). The distance between this indifference point and the expected level of profit before interest and taxation provides us with a 'margin of safety'. The chart reveals that there is a reasonable 'margin of safety' for the debt alternative: there would have to be a fall in profits before interest and taxation of about 16 per cent before the ordinary share alternative becomes more attractive. Thus, providing the managers were confident that the expected levels of profit could be maintained at the expected level, the debt alternative would be attractive.

A business may consider issuing preference shares to finance a particular project. As preference dividends are paid out of profits *after taxation* this means that, when calculating the first coordinate for the chart, the profits *before* interest and taxation must be sufficient to cover both the dividends and the relevant corporation tax payments. In other words we must 'gross up' the preference dividend by the relevant corporation tax rate to derive the profits before interest and tax figure. In Activity 8.14 above we were told that, under one of the financing methods, 12 million 12% £1 preference shares would be issued at par as part of the total finance required. We calculated earlier that the dividends payable on these shares are £1.4m. (to one decimal point). The profit before interest and taxation required to cover these dividend payments would be £1.4m. × 100/75 = £1.9m. (Based on a tax rate of 25%.)

ACTIVITY 8.15

Refer to Activity 8.14 above. Construct a PBIT–EPS indifference chart which plots the three financing options for Brunel Instruments Ltd.

Your answer to this activity should be as shown in Figure 8.6.

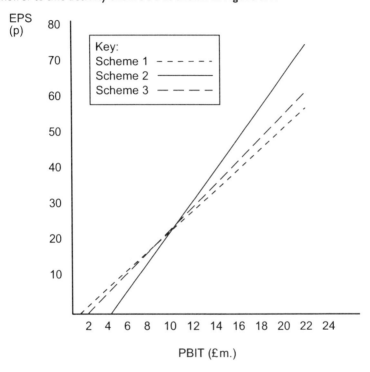

Figure 8.6 PBIT–EPS indifference chart for three financing options

---

The indifference point between two financing options above can also be derived by using a simple mathematical equation, as follows:

$$\frac{(X - I_1)(1 - t)}{E_1} = \frac{(X - I_2)(1 - t)}{E_2}$$

where:

X = the profit before interest and taxation at which the two financing options provide the same return to ordinary shareholders;

I = the annual interest charges or 'grossed up' preference dividend under each financing option; and

E = the number of ordinary shares in issue.

ACTIVITY 8.16

Refer to the Woodhall Engineering example used earlier in Example 8.4. Calculate the indifference point between the two financing options using the equation above.

Your answer should be as follows:

$$\frac{(X - 3.8)}{64} = \frac{(X - 2.0)}{104}$$

$$104 (X - 3.8) = 64(X - 2.0)$$

$$104X - 395.2 = 64X - 128$$

$$40X = 267.2$$

$$X = 6.7 (m.)$$

Note: Taxation can be ignored in this particular case.

SELF-ASSESSMENT QUESTION 8.1

Hargreaves Ltd is a medium-sized textile company supplying items of children's wear to large retail chain stores in the United Kingdom. The company has been operating for many years and is controlled by the Hargreaves family. The accounts of the company for the year ended 31 May 19X0 are as follows:

Balance sheet as at 31 May 19X0

	£m.	£m.	£m.
Fixed assets			
Freehold land and building at cost			20.1
Plant and machinery at cost		13.2	
Less: Accumulated depreciation		4.6	8.6
			28.7
Current assets			
Stock at cost		14.2	
Debtors		8.1	
Cash		1.0	
		23.3	

Less: **Creditors: amounts due within**			
one year	£m.	£m.	£m.
Trade creditors	5.7		
Proposed dividend	1.0		
Taxation	3.3	10.0	13.3
			42.0

Less: **Creditors: amounts due beyond**		
one year		
Loans (12%)		10.0
		32.0

Capital and reserves	
Ordinary shares 25p	4.0
Retained profit	28.0
	32.0

Extracts from the profit and loss account for the year ended 31 May 19X0

	£m.
Turnover	78.4
Profit before interest and taxation	10.5
Interest payable	1.2
Profit before taxation	9.3
Taxation	3.3
Profit after taxation	6.0
Dividends	1.0
Retained profit for the year	5.0

The company has recently secured a large contract to supply a new range of children's wear for one of its major customers. Although new equipment costing £8m. will have to be purchased it is estimated that the profit before interest and taxation will increase by £3.0m. as a result of taking the contract.

Industrial Finance Ltd has offered to finance the expansion in any one of the following ways:

1. the purchase of four million ordinary shares at a premium of £1.75 per share;
2. the purchase of £4 million 10% £1 preference shares at par and £4 million 12½% debentures;
3. the purchase of two million ordinary shares at a premium of £1.75 per share and £4 million 12½% debentures.

The company expects to maintain dividend per share at its current level for the foreseeable future. The rate of corporation tax is 35%.

Required:

(a) Prepare a profit and loss account for Hargreaves Ltd for the year ended 31 May 19X1 for each of the three financing schemes.
(b) Calculate the earnings per share for the year ended 31 May 19X1 and the level of gearing at that date under each financing scheme.
(c) Calculate the level of profit before interest and taxation at which the earnings per share under schemes (1) and (3) are equal.
(d) Briefly assess each of the financing schemes available to Hargreaves Ltd from the viewpoint of an existing shareholder.

Factors affecting the level of gearing

In practice, the level of gearing adopted by a business is likely to be influenced by various factors. Some of the more important are:

- *The attitude of the owners to risk* If owners are risk averse, they will prefer less risk to more risk for a particular expected rate of return. We saw in Chapter 6 that investors will only be prepared to take on more risk if there is the opportunity for higher rates of return.
- *The attitude of management to risk* Although managers are employed to operate the business on behalf of the owners and should serve the owners' best interests, they may object to high levels of gearing if they feel that this places their job security and remuneration at risk. However, managers may be more prepared to take on greater risk if they feel that there is the opportunity for greater rewards as a result.
- *The attitude of lenders towards the company* Lenders will be concerned with the ability of the company to repay the amount borrowed and to pay interest at the due dates. Their attitude towards the company will therefore be influenced by such matters as the profitability of the business, the existing level of borrowing, security for the loan, and so on.
- *The availability of equity funds* If the stock market is depressed it may be difficult to raise equity funds, and so a company wishing to raise finance may be forced to borrow the amount required.

Levels of gearing do vary significantly between industries. Generally speaking, levels of gearing will be higher in industries where profits are stable (which lenders are likely to prefer). Thus higher levels of gearing are likely to occur in utilities such as electricity, gas and water companies, which are less affected by economic recession, changes in consumer tastes, and so forth, than most businesses.

The capital structure debate

There is some debate in the finance literature over whether or not the capital structure decision is really important. The key issue is whether or not the mix of long-term funds employed can have an effect on the overall cost of capital of the company. If a particular mix of funds can produce a lower cost of capital, then the way in which the business is financed is important as it can affect the value of the company. (In broad terms, the value of a business can be defined as the net present value of its future cash flows. By lowering the cost of capital, which is used as the discount rate, the value of the business will be increased.)

The issue as to whether or not it really matters how the business is financed has been the subject of intense debate between two schools of thought: the traditional school and the modernist school. According to the traditional view, the capital structure decision is very important. The traditionalists point out that the cost of loan capital is cheaper than the cost of equity capital (see Chapter 7). This difference in the relative cost of finance suggests that, by increasing the level of borrowing (or gearing), the overall cost of capital of the business can be reduced. However, there are drawbacks to taking on additional borrowing. As the level of borrowing increases, equity shareholders will require higher levels of return on their investments to compensate for the higher levels of financial risk which they will have to bear. Existing lenders will also require higher levels of return.

The traditionalists argue, however, that at fairly low levels of borrowing, the benefits of raising finance through the use of loan capital will outweigh any costs which arise. This is because equity shareholders and lenders will not view low levels of borrowing as having a significant effect on the level of risk which they have to bear and so will not require a higher level of return in compensation. As the level of borrowing increases, however, things will start to change. Equity shareholders and existing lenders will become increasingly concerned with the higher interest charges that must be met and the risks that these will pose to their own claims on the income and assets of the business. As a result, they will seek compensation for this higher level of risk in the form of higher expected returns.

The situation just described is set out in Figure 8.7. We can see that where there are small increases in borrowing, equity shareholders and existing lenders do not require greatly increased returns. However, at significantly higher levels of borrowing, the risks involved take on greater importance for investors and this is reflected in the sharp rise in the returns required from each group. Note that the overall cost of capital (which is a weighted average of the cost of equity and loan capital) declines when small increases in the level of borrowing occur. However, at significantly increased levels of borrowing, the increase in required returns from equity shareholders and lenders will result in a sharp rise in the overall cost of capital.

An important implication of the above analysis is that managers of the business should try to establish that mix of loan/equity finance which will minimise the overall cost of capital. At this point, the business will be said to achieve an

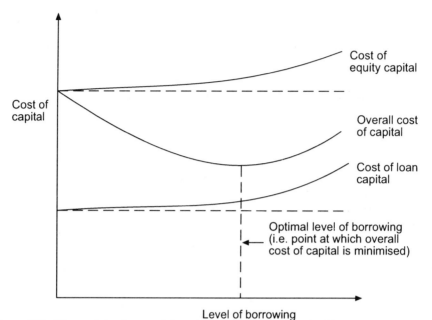

Figure 8.7   The traditional view of the relationship between levels of borrowing and expected returns

optimal capital structure. By minimising the overall cost of capital in this way, the value of the business will be maximised. This relationship between the financing of the business and its value is illustrated in Figure 8.8.

We can see that the graph of the value of the business displays an inverse

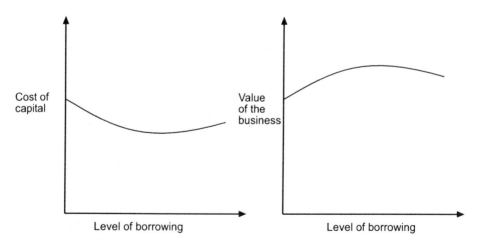

Figure 8.8   Relationship between financing of the business and its value: the traditional view

pattern to the graph of the overall cost of capital. This relationship, of course, suggests that the financing decision is critically important. Failure to identify and achieve the right financing mix could have serious adverse consequences for shareholder wealth.

Modigliani and Miller (MM), who represent the modernist school, challenged the traditional view by arguing that the required returns to equity shareholders and to lenders would not follow the pattern as set out above. They argued that the increase in returns required for equity shareholders as compensation for increased financial risk, will rise in constant proportion to the increase in the level of borrowing over the *whole range of borrowing*. This pattern contrasts with the traditional view, of course, which displays an uneven change in the required rate of return over the range of borrowing.

The MM analysis also assumes that the returns required from borrowers would remain constant as the level of borrowing increases. This latter point may appear strange at first sight. However, if lenders have good security for the loans made to the business, they are unlikely to feel at risk from additional borrowing and will not, therefore, seek additional returns. This is providing, of course, that the business does not exceed its borrowing capacity.

The MM position is set out in Figure 8.9 below. As you can see, the overall cost of capital remains constant at varying levels of borrowing. This is because the benefits obtained from raising finance through borrowing, which is cheaper than equity, is exactly offset by the increase in required returns from equity shareholders.

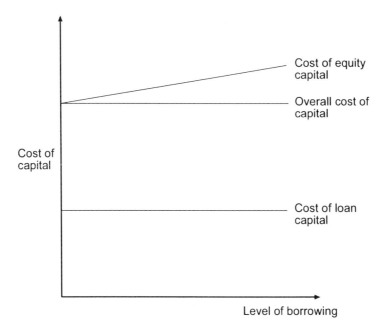

Figure 8.9   The MM view of the relationship between levels of borrowing and expected returns

An important implication of this is that the financing decision is not really important. Figure 8.9 shows that as the overall cost of capital remains constant, a business does not have an optimal capital structure as suggested by the traditionalists. This means that one particular capital structure is no better or worse than any other and so managers should not spend time on evaluating different forms of financing the business. Instead, they should concentrate their efforts on evaluating and managing the investments of the business.

ACTIVITY 8.17

In Figure 8.8 above we saw the traditional view of the relationship between the financing of a business and its value. How would the MM view of this relationship be shown on a graph do you think?

The relationship between financing and the value of the business, as viewed by MM, is set out in Figure 8.10.

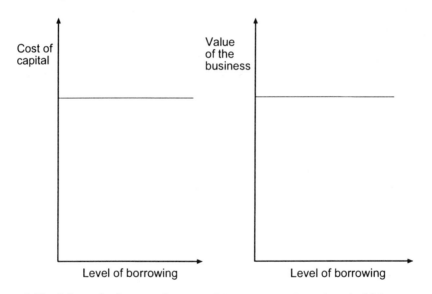

Figure 8.10 Relationship between financing of the business and its value: the MM view

---

Although the views of MM were first published in the late 1950s, they are sometimes described as modernists because they base their position on economic theory (unlike the traditional school). They argue that the value of a business is determined by the future income from its investments, and the risk associated with those investments, and not by the way in which this income is divided between the different providers of finance. In other words, it is not possible to increase the value of a business (i.e. lower the overall cost of capital) simply by borrowing as the traditionalists suggest. MM point out that borrowing is not something which only businesses are able to undertake. Borrowing can also be undertaken by individual investors. As business borrowing can be replicated by individual investors, there is no reason why it should create additional value for the investor. A simple example may help to illustrate the MM position.

Example 8.5

Two companies – X plc and Y plc – are identical except for the fact that X plc is financed entirely by equity shares and Y plc is 50 per cent financed by loans. The earnings before interest for each business for the year is £2m. The equity shareholders of X plc require a return of 12 per cent and the equity shareholders of Y plc require a return of 14 per cent. Y plc pays 10 per cent interest per annum on the £10m. loans outstanding.

	X plc £m.	Y plc £m.
Earnings before interest	2.0	2.0
Interest payable	–	1.0
Available to equity	2.0	1.0

The market value of the equity of each business will be equivalent to the earnings capitalised at the required rate of return. Thus the market value of each business is as follows:

	X plc £m.	Y plc £m.
Market value of equity shares:		
(£2,000/0.12)	16.7	
(£2,000/0.14)		14.3
Market value of loan capital		10.0
The market value of each business	16.7	24.3

MM argue that differences in the way in which each business is financed cannot result in a higher value for Y plc as shown above. This is because an investor who owns 10 per cent of the shares in Y plc would be able to obtain the same level of income from investing in X plc, for the same level of risk as the investment in Y plc and for a lower net investment. The investor, by borrowing an amount equivalent to 10 per cent of the loans of Y plc (i.e. an amount proportionate to the ownership interest in Y plc), and selling the shares held in Y plc in order to finance the purchase of a 10 per cent equity stake in X plc, would be in the following position:

Net return

	£000
Return from 10% equity investment in X plc	200
Less: Interest on borrowing (£1,000 @ 10%)	100
Net return	100
Net investment in X plc	
Purchase of shares 10% £16,667	1,670
Less: amount borrowed	1,000
	670

The investor with a 10 per cent stake in the equity of Y plc is, currently, in the following position:

	£000
Return from 10% investment in Y plc	100
Net investment in Y plc (10% £14.3m.)	1,430

As we can see, the investor would be better off by taking on personal borrowing in order to acquire a 10 per cent share of the equity of the ungeared company, X plc, than by continuing to invest in the geared company, Y plc. The effect of a number of investors switching investments in this way would be to reduce the value of the shares in Y plc (thereby increasing the returns to equity in Y plc), and to increase the value of shares in X plc (thereby reducing the returns to equity in X plc). This switching from Y plc to X plc (which is referred to as *arbitrage transactions*) would continue until the returns from each investment were the same, and so no further gains could be made from such transactions. At this point, the value of each business would be identical.

The MM analysis, whilst extremely rigorous and logical, is based on a number of restrictive assumptions. These include:

- *Perfect capital markets*   This means that there are no share transactions costs and that investors and companies can borrow unlimited amounts at the same rates of interest. Although these assumptions are unrealistic, they may not have a significant effect on the arguments made. Where the prospect of arbitrage gains are substantial, share transaction costs are unlikely to be an important issue. It is only at the margin that these costs will take on significance. Similarly, the borrowing assumption may only take on significance at the margin. Moreover, where the investor is a large institution, such as a pension fund, it may be possible to borrow at similar rates to those offered to the company.
- *No bankruptcy costs*   This means that if a business was liquidated, there would be no legal and administrative fees involved and assets could be sold for a sum equivalent to the market value of the shares held. This assumption will

not hold true in the real world. However, it is only at high levels of gearing that this is likely to be an issue.

■ *Risk*   Companies exist which have identical business risk but which have different levels of borrowing. Although this is unlikely to be true, it does not effect the validity of MM's arguments.

■ *No taxation*   A world without corporate or personal income taxes is clearly an unrealistic assumption. However, the real issue is whether or not this undermines the validity of MM's arguments. We will, therefore, consider the effect of introducing taxes on the MM position.

MM were subject to considerable criticism for not dealing with the problem of taxation in their analysis. This led them to revise their position so as to include taxation. They acknowledged in their revised analysis that the tax relief from interest payments on loans provides a real benefit to equity shareholders. As the level of borrowing increases, the more tax relief the business receives and so the smaller the tax liability of the business will become. The benefits of this tax relief will more than offset the increase in the required returns from equity shareholders, and so the overall cost of capital (after tax) will be lowered as the level of borrowing increases. In Figure 8.11 below, we can see the MM position after taxation has been introduced.

Thus the MM position moves closer to the traditional position insofar as it

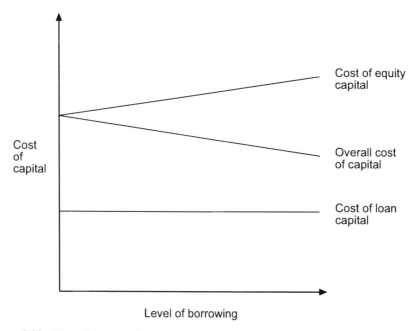

Figure 8.11   The MM view of the relationship between levels of borrowing and expected returns (including tax effects)

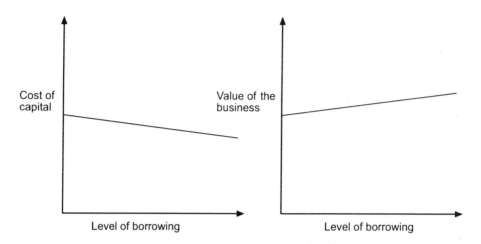

Figure 8.12   Relationship between financing of the business and its value: the MM view (including tax effect)

recognises that there is a relationship between the value of the business and the way in which it is financed. This relationship between financing of the business and its value, after taking into account the tax effects, is set out in Figure 8.12.

ACTIVITY 8.18

What do you think are the implications of the above analysis for managers who are trying to decide on an appropriate capital structure?

This revised analysis implies that a business should borrow to capacity as this will lower the after-tax cost of capital and thereby increase the value of the business.

However, in the real world, few businesses follow such a policy. When borrowing reaches very high levels, lenders are likely to feel that their security is threatened and equity investors will feel that the bankruptcy risks have increased. Thus both groups are likely to seek higher returns, which will, in turn, increase the overall cost of capital. (A business would have to attract *risk-seeking* investors in order to prevent a rise in its cost of capital.)

Summary

In this chapter, we saw how the cost of capital for individual elements of long-term capital can be deduced and how these individual costs can be combined to form a weighted average cost of capital (WACC) for investment decision-making. Following the examination of the cost of capital, we turned our attention to the issue of financial gearing and how gearing can be used to magnify the returns to ordinary shareholders. We considered gearing in the context of the capital structure decision and we saw how various techniques such as projected financial statements, financial ratios and PBIT–EPS indifference charts can be useful for evaluation purposes. Finally we considered the capital structure debate. We examined the arguments of the two main schools of thought on this issue and the limitations of each set of arguments.

Further reading

F. Modigliani and M.H. Miller, 'The cost of capital, corporate finance and the theory of investment', *American Economic Review*, 1958. Reprinted in S.H. Archer and C.A. D'Ambrosio (eds), *The Theory of Business Finance: A Book of Readings*, 3rd edn, Collier-Macmillan, 1983.

Review questions

8.1 How might a business find out whether a particular planned level of gearing would be acceptable to investors?

8.2 What factors might a prospective lender take into account when deciding whether or not to make a long-term loan to a particular business?

8.3 Should the specific cost of raising finance for a particular project be used as the appropriate discount rate for investment appraisal purposes?

8.4 What are the main implications for the financial manager who accepts the arguments of:

(a) the traditional school of thought; and
(b) the MM school of thought,

concerning capital structure?

Examination-style questions

Solutions to those questions marked with an asterisk are given at the end of the text. Questions 8.1–8.3 are at basic level. Questions 8.4–8.6 are at intermediate/advanced level.

8.1 Kipling plc is a food manufacturer which has the following long-term capital structure:

	£
£1 Ordinary shares (fully paid)	2,500,000
Share premium account	1,000,000
8% Preference shares	1,200,000
10% Debentures (secured)	1,000,000
	5,700,000

The directors of the business wish to raise further long-term finance by the issue of either preference shares or debentures. Although this will have the effect of raising the level of gearing of the company, the directors believe it will reduce the company's overall cost of capital.

Required:

Discuss the arguments for and against the view that the company's overall cost of capital can be reduced in this way. State your assumptions.

8.2* Celtor plc is a property development company operating in the London area. The company has the following capital structure as at 30 November 19X3:

	£000
£1 Ordinary shares	10,000
Retained profit	20,000
9% Debentures	12,000
	42,000

The equity shares have a current market value of £3.90 and the current level of dividend is 20p per share. The dividend has been growing at a compound rate of 4 per cent per annum in recent years. The debentures of the company are irredeemable and have a current market value of £80 per £100 nominal. Interest due on the debentures at the year end has recently been paid.

The company has obtained planning permission to build a new office block in a redevelopment area. The company wishes to raise the whole of the finance necessary for the project by the issue of more irredeemable 9 per cent debentures at £80 per £100 nominal. This is in line with a target capital structure set by the company where the amount of debt capital will increase to 70 per cent of equity within the next two years. The rate of corporation tax is 25 per cent.

Required:

(a) Explain what is meant by the term 'cost of capital'. Why is it important for a company to calculate its cost of capital correctly?

(b) Calculate the weighted average cost of capital of Celtor plc which should be used for future investment decisions.

8.3* Telford Engineers plc, a medium-sized Midlands manufacturer of automobile components, has decided to modernise its factory by introducing a number of robots. These will cost £20m. and will reduce operating costs by £6m. per year for their estimated useful life of ten years. To finance this scheme the company can take either of the following options:

1. Raise £20m. by the issue of 20 million ordinary shares at 100p.
2. Raise £20m. debt at 14 per cent interest per year, capital repayments of £3m. per year commencing at the end of 19X9.

Extracts from Telford Engineers' accounts appear below:

Summary of balance sheet at 31 December

	19X3	19X4	19X5	19X6 (estimated)
	£m.	£m.	£m.	£m.
Fixed assets	48	51	65	64
Current assets	55	67	57	55
Less: Amounts due within one year				
Creditors	(20)	(27)	(25)	(18)
Overdraft	(5)	–	(6)	(8)
	78	91	91	93
Share capital and reserves	48	61	61	63
Loans	30	30	30	30
	78	91	91	93
Number of issued 25p shares	80m.	80m.	80m.	80m.
Share price	150p	200p	100p	145p

Summary of profit and loss accounts for years ended 31 December

	19X3	19X4	19X5	19X6 (estimated)
	£m.	£m.	£m.	£m.
Sales	152	170	110	145
Profit before interest and taxation	28	40	7	15
Interest payable	4	3	4	5
Profit before taxation	24	37	3	10
Taxation	12	16	0	4

	£m.	£m.	£m.	£m.
Profit after taxation	12	21	3	6
Dividends	6	8	3	4
Retained	6	13	0	2

For your answer you should assume that the corporate tax rate for 19X7 is 40 per cent, that sales and operating profit will be unchanged except for the £6m. cost-saving arising from the introduction of the robots and that Telford Engineers will pay the same dividend per share in 19X7 as in 19X6.

Required:

(a) Prepare for each scheme, Telford Engineers' profit and loss account for the year ended 31 December 19X7 and a statement of its share capital, reserves and loans on that date.
(b) Calculate Telford's earnings per share for 19X7 for both schemes.
(c) Calculate the level of earnings (profit) before interest and tax at which the earnings per share for each scheme is equal.
(d) Which scheme would you advise the company to adopt? You should give your reasons and state what additional information you would require.

8.4   Trexon plc is a major oil and gas exploration company which has most of its operations in the Middle East and Southeast Asia. Recently, the company acquired rights to explore for oil and gas in the Gulf of Mexico. Trexon plc proposes to finance the new operations from the issue of equity shares. At present, the company is financed by a combination of equity capital and loan capital. The equity shares have a nominal value of £0.50 and a current market value of £2.60. The current level of dividend is £0.16 per share and this has been growing at a compound rate of 6 per cent per annum in recent years. The loan capital issued by the company is irredeemable and has a current market value of £94 per £100 nominal. Interest on the loan capital is at the rate of 12 per cent and interest due at the year end has recently been paid. At present, the company expects 60 per cent of its finance to come from equity capital and the rest from loan capital. In the future, however, the company will aim to finance 70 per cent of its operations from equity capital.

When the proposal to finance the new operations via the rights issue of shares was announced at the annual general meeting of the company objections were raised by two shareholders present, as follows:

Shareholder A argued:

'I fail to understand why the company has decided to issue shares to finance the new operation. Surely it would be better to reinvest profit, as this is, in effect, a free source of finance to the company.'

Shareholder B argued:

> 'I also fail to understand why the company has decided to issue shares to finance the new operation. However, I do not agree with the suggestion made by Shareholder A. I do not believe that shareholder funds should be used at all to finance the new operation. Instead, the company should issue more loan capital, as it is cheap relative to equity capital and would, therefore, reduce the overall cost of capital of the company.'

Corporation tax is at the rate of 35%.

Required:

(a) Calculate the weighted average cost of capital of Trexon plc which should be used in future investment decisions.
(b) Comment on the remarks made by:
    (i)   Shareholder A; and
    (ii) Shareholder B.

8.5 Ashcroft plc, a family-controlled company, is considering raising additional funds to modernise its factory. The scheme is expected to cost £2.34 million and will increase annual profits before interest and tax from 1 January 19X4 by £0.6 million. A summarised balance sheet and profit and loss account are shown below. Currently the share price is 200p.

Two schemes have been suggested. First, 1.3 million shares could be issued at 180p (net of issue costs). Secondly, a consortia of six city institutions have offered to buy debentures from the company totalling £2.34m. Interest would be at the rate of 13 per cent per annum and capital repayments of equal annual instalments of £234,000 starting on 1 January 19X5 would be required.

Balance sheet as at 31 December 19X3

	£m.	£m.
Fixed assets (net)		1.4
Current assets		
Stock	2.4	
Debtors	2.2	
	4.6	
Creditors: amounts due within one year		
Creditors	2.7	
Corporation tax	0.6	
Proposed final dividend	0.2	
	3.5	
Net current assets		1.1
Total assets *less* current liabilities		2.5

	£m.	£m.
Capital and reserves		
Called up share capital, 25p ordinary shares		1.0
Profit and loss account		1.5
		2.5

Profit and loss account year ended 31 December 19X3

	£m.
Turnover	11.2
Profit on ordinary activities before tax	1.2
Taxation on profit on ordinary activities	0.6
Profit on ordinary activities after tax	0.6
Dividends (net)	0.3
Retained profit for the financial year	0.3

Assume corporation tax is charged at the rate of 50 per cent.

Required:

(a) Compute the earnings per share for 19X4 under the debt and the equity alternatives.
(b) Compute the level of profits before debenture interest and tax at which the earnings per share under the two schemes will be equal.
(c) Discuss the considerations the directors should take into account before deciding upon debt or equity finance.

8.6   Hatleigh plc is a medium-sized engineering company based in South Wales. The accounts of the company for the year ended 30 April 19X2 are as follows:

Balance sheet as at 30 April 19X2

	£000	£000	£000
Fixed assets			
Freehold premises at valuation			3,885
Plant and machinery at cost less depreciation			2,520
Motor vehicles at cost less depreciation			1,470
			7,875
Current assets			
Stock: Raw materials		824	
Work in progress		2,120	
Finished goods		5,436	
Debtors		8,578	
		16,958	

	£000	£000	£000
Less: **Creditors due within one year**			
Trade creditors	2,521		
Bank overdraft	4,776		
Corporation tax	402		
Dividends	600	8,299	
			8,659
			16,534
Less: **Creditors due beyond one year**			
10% Debentures 19X7–8 (secured on freehold premises)			3,500
			13,034
Capital and reserves			
Share capital (25p shares)			8,000
Retained profit			5,034
			13,034

Profit and loss account for the year ended 30 April 19X2

	£000
Sales	34,246
Cost of sales	24,540
Gross profit	9,706
Expenses	7,564
Operating profit	2,142
Interest	994
Profit before taxation	1,148
Corporation tax (35%)	402
Net profit after taxation	746
Dividends proposed	600
Retained profit for the year	146

The company made a one-for-four rights issue of ordinary shares during the year. Sales for the forthcoming year are forecast to be the same as for the year to 30 April 19X2. The gross profit margin is likely to stay the same as in previous years but expenses (excluding interest payments) are likely to fall by 10 per cent as a result of economies.

The bank has been concerned that the company has persistently exceeded the agreed overdraft limits and, as a result, the company has now been asked to reduce its overdraft to £3m. over the next three months. The company has agreed to do this and has calculated that interest on the bank overdraft for the forthcoming year will be £440,000 (after taking account of the required reduction in the overdraft). In order to achieve the reduction in overdraft, the chairman of the company is considering either the issue of more ordinary shares for cash to existing shareholders at a discount of 20 per cent, or the issue of more 10% debentures redeemable 19X7–X8 at the end of July 19X2. It is believed that the share price will be £1.50 and the 10% debentures will be quoted at 82 at the end of July 19X2. The bank overdraft is expected to remain at the amount shown in the balance sheet until that date. Any issue costs relating to new shares or debentures should be ignored.

Required:

(a) Calculate:
   (i)   the total number of shares, and
   (ii) the total par value of debentures
   which will have to be issued in order to raise the funds necessary to reduce the overdraft to the level required by the bank.
(b) Calculate the expected earnings per share for the year to 30 April 19X3 assuming:
   (i)   the issue of shares, and
   (ii) the issue of debentures
   are carried out to reduce the overdraft to the level required by the bank.
(c) Critically evaluate the proposal of the chairman to raise the necessary funds by the issue of:
   (i)   shares; and
   (ii) debentures.
(d) Identify and discuss two other methods of raising the necessary finance (internal or external but excluding a bank overdraft) which may prove appropriate to this company.

—

Dividend Policy

On completion of this chapter you should be able to:

- Describe the nature of dividends and the way in which they are paid.

- Explain why dividends should have no effect on shareholder wealth in a world of perfect and efficient markets.

- Discuss the factors which influence dividend policy in practice.

- Discuss the alternatives to cash dividends which may be used.

Introduction

The issue of dividend policy has aroused much controversy over the years. At the centre of this controversy is whether or not the pattern of dividends adopted by a company has any effect on shareholder wealth. In this chapter, we examine the arguments which have been raised. Although the importance of dividend policy to shareholders remains a moot point, there is evidence to suggest that managers *perceive* the dividend decision to be important. In this chapter, we consider the attitudes of managers towards dividends and we examine the factors which are likely to influence dividend policy in practice. We shall also consider the alternatives to a cash dividend which might be used.

The payment of dividends

It is a good idea to begin our examination of dividends and dividend policy by describing briefly what dividends are and how they are paid. Dividends represent a return by a company to its shareholders. This return is normally paid in cash, although it would be possible for it to be paid with assets other than cash. In your previous studies, you may have discovered that there are legal limits on the amount which can be distributed in the form of dividend payments to shareholders.

ACTIVITY 9.1

Why does the law impose limits on the amount of cash which can be distributed as dividends?

If there were no legal limits, it would be possible for shareholders to withdraw their investment from the company and so leave the lenders and creditors in an exposed financial position. The law tries to protect lenders and creditors by preventing excessive withdrawals of equity capital. One way in which this can be done is through placing restrictions on dividend payments.

The law states that dividends can only be paid to shareholders of private limited companies out of *realised* profits. In essence, the maximum amount available for distribution will be the accumulated trading profits (less any losses) *plus* any profits on the disposal of fixed assets. Any surpluses arising from the revaluation of fixed assets will represent an unrealised profit which cannot be distributed. However, shareholders of public companies can be paid out of the net accumulated profits whether the profits are realised or unrealised.

ACTIVITY 9.2

Bio-tech Ltd started trading in 19X5 and made a trading profit of £200,000 in this year. In 19X6, the company made a trading loss of £150,000 but made a profit on the sale of freehold buildings of £30,000. Other fixed assets were revalued during the year leading to an increase in the revaluation reserve of £60,000.

Assuming that no dividend was paid in 19X5, what is the maximum dividend that could be paid by Bio-tech Ltd in 19X6?

Bio-tech Ltd is a private limited company, hence, the maximum dividend is calculated as follows:

	£
Trading profit 19X5	*200,000*
Profit on sale of fixed asset 19X6	*30,000*
	230,000
Less: *Trading loss 19X6*	*150,000*
Maximum amount available for distribution	*80,000*

It should be noted that companies rarely distribute the maximum amount available for distribution. Indeed, the dividend paid by a company is normally much lower than the operating profits for the year in which the dividend is declared. In other words, the operating profits usually 'cover' the dividend payment by a comfortable margin.

Dividends can also take the form of bonus shares. Instead of receiving cash, the shareholders may receive additional shares in the company. We will consider this particular form of dividend (often referred to as a scrip dividend) later in the chapter.

Dividends are often paid twice yearly by large listed companies. The first dividend is paid after the interim (half-yearly) results have been announced. The second and final dividend is paid after the year end. The final dividend will be paid after the annual financial reports have been published, and after the shareholders have agreed, at the annual general meeting, to the dividend payment proposed by the directors.

As shares are bought and sold continuously by investors, it is important to establish which investors have the right to receive the dividends declared. To do this, a *record date* is set by the company. Investors whose names appear in the share register on the record date will receive the dividends payable. When the share prices quoted on the Stock Exchange include accrued dividends payable, they are said to be quoted 'cum dividend'. However, on a specified day before the record date, the quoted share prices will exclude the accrued dividend and so will become 'ex dividend'. Assuming no other factors affect the share price, the 'ex dividend' price should be lower than the 'cum dividend' price by the amount of the dividend payable. This is because a new shareholder would not qualify for the dividend and so the share price can be expected to fall by the amount of the dividend.

EXHIBIT 9.1

Most listed companies produce a financial calendar which they include in their published financial reports and which sets out the key dates for investors. The financial calendar for National Power plc for 1995 and 1996 was set out in its financial report for 1995 as follows:

Financial year ending March	1995	1996
Announcement of interim results	–*	November 1995
Interim dividend payable	–*	January 1996
Announcement of full year results	–*	May 1996
Ex-dividend date	19 June 1995	June 1996
Report and accounts published	June 1995	June 1996
Final dividend record date	6 July 1995	July 1996
Annual General meeting	25 July 1995	July 1996
Final dividend payable	27 July 1995	July 1996

Note: *The relevant dates had already passed when the calendar was published.

Dividend policies in practice

It was mentioned above that companies rarely distribute all of the profits available to shareholders in the form of dividend. Usually the dividends are lower than the current operating profits of the business. In Figure 9.1, we can see the average dividend coverage ratios for listed companies within a range of industries. From this diagram, we can see that the average dividend cover ratio for the various industries selected falls within a broad range of 1.0 to 3.0 times. Some businesses adopt a target dividend cover ratio and state the target ratio in its reports to shareholders.

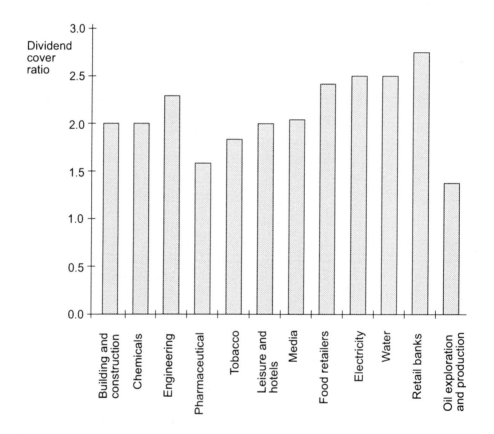

Figure 9.1   Dividend coverage ratios for various industries (Source: *Financial Times*, 1 March 1996)

EXHIBIT 9.2

The 1995 Annual Review of Powergen plc, a power-generating business, reported a dividend cover of 3.3 times for that year and stated: 'We expect to reduce dividend cover, in the absence of unforeseen circumstances, to 2.5 to 2.7 times over the coming years.'

Similarly, National Power plc, another power-generating business, reported in its 1995 Annual Review a dividend cover of 2.8 times and stated: 'The dividend policy of the Group remains unchanged. The Directors expect to reduce dividend cover to 2.5 times within the next 18 months. Thereafter we expect dividend growth broadly to reflect growth in earnings.'

The way in which managers establish a particular dividend policy will be considered in more detail later in the chapter.

Dividend policy and shareholder wealth

Most of the interest surrounding dividend policy has been concerned with the relationship between dividend policy and shareholder wealth. Put simply, the key question to be answered is: 'Can the pattern of dividends adopted by a company influence shareholder wealth?' (Note that it is the *pattern* of dividends rather than dividends themselves which is the issue. Shareholders must receive cash at some point in order for their shares to have any value.) Whilst the question may be stated simply the answer is less simple. After more than three decades of research and debate we have yet to solve this puzzle.

The notion that dividend policy is important may seem, on the face of it, to be obvious. In Chapter 8, for example, we considered various dividend valuation models which suggest that dividends are important in determining share price. One such model, you may recall, was the dividend growth model which is as follows:

$$P_O = \frac{D_1}{K_O - g}$$

where:
   D_1 = expected dividend next year
   g = a constant rate of growth
   K_O = the expected return on the share

Looking at this model, it may appear that by simply increasing the dividend (D_1) there will be an automatic increase in share price (P_O). If the relationship between dividends and share price was as just described, then, clearly, dividend policy would be important. However, the relationship between these two variables is not likely to be as straightforward as this.

ACTIVITY 9.3

Why might an increase in the dividend (D_1) not lead to an increase in share price (P_O)? (Hint: Think of the other variables in the equation.)

An increase in dividend payments will only result in an increase in share price if there is no consequential effect on the dividend growth rate. It is likely, however, that an increase in dividend will result in a fall in this growth rate, as there will be less cash to invest in the business. Thus, the beneficial effect on share price arising from an increase in next year's dividend may be cancelled out by a decrease in future years' dividends.

The early finance literature accepted the view that dividend policy was important for shareholders. It was argued that a shareholder would prefer to receive £1 today rather than to have £1 reinvested in the business, even though this might yield future dividends. The reasoning for this was that future dividends (or capital gains) are less certain and so will be valued less highly. The saying 'a bird in the hand is worth two in the bush' is often used to describe this argument. Thus, if a company decides to replace an immediate and certain cash dividend with uncertain future dividends, shareholders will discount the future dividends at a higher rate in order to take account of this greater uncertainty. Referring back to the dividend growth model, the traditional view suggests that K_O will rise if there is an increase in D_1 as dividends received later will not be valued so highly.

If this line of reasoning is correct, the effect of applying a higher discount rate to future dividends will mean that the share value of companies which adopt a high retentions policy will be adversely affected. The implication for corporate managers is, therefore, quite clear. They should adopt as generous a dividend distribution policy as possible, given the investment and financing policies of the company, as this will represent the optimal dividend policy for the company. In view of the fact that the level of payout will affect shareholder wealth, the dividend payment decision will be an important policy decision for managers.

Modigliani and Miller (MM) have challenged this view of dividend policy. They argue that, given perfect and efficient markets, the pattern of dividend payments adopted by a business will have no effect on shareholder wealth. Where such markets exist, the wealth of shareholders will be affected solely by the investment projects which the company undertakes. To maximise shareholder wealth, therefore, the company should take on all investment projects which have a positive NPV. The way in which the returns from these investment projects are divided between dividends and retentions is unimportant. Thus a decision to pay a lower dividend will simply be compensated for by an increase in share price.

MM point out that it is possible for an individual investor to 'adjust' the dividend policy of a company to conform to his or her particular requirements. If a company does not pay a dividend, the shareholder can create 'homemade' dividends by selling a portion of the shares held. If, on the other hand, a company provides a dividend which the shareholder does not wish to receive, the amount can be reinvested in additional shares in the company. In view of this fact, there is no reason for an investor to value the shares of one business more highly than another simply because it adopts a particular dividend policy.

The implications of the MM position for corporate managers are quite different from the implications of the traditional position described earlier. The MM view suggests that there is no such thing as an optimal dividend policy, and that one policy is as good as another (i.e. the dividend decision is irrelevant to shareholder wealth). Thus managers should not spend time considering the most appropriate policy to adopt, but should, instead, devote their energies to finding and managing profitable investment opportunities.

MM believe that dividends simply represent a movement of funds from inside the business to outside the business. This change in the location of funds should not have any effect on shareholder wealth. The MM position is set out briefly in Example 9.1.

Example 9.1

Merton Ltd has the following balance sheet as at 31 December 19X5:

Balance sheet as at 31 December 19X5

	£000
Assets at market value (exc. cash)	100
Cash	30
	130
Less: Loan capital	40
Net assets	90
Equity capital (30,000 shares)	90

Suppose that the company decides to distribute all the cash available (i.e. £30,000), to shareholders by making a 100p dividend per share. This will result in a fall in the value of net assets to £60,000 (i.e. £90,000−£30,000) and a fall in the value of its shares from £3 (i.e. £90,000/30,000) to £2 (i.e. £60,000/30,000). The balance sheet following the dividend payment will therefore be as follows:

Balance sheet following the dividend payment

	£000
Assets at market value (exc. cash)	100
Cash	–
	100

	£000
Less: Loan capital	40
Net assets	60
Equity capital (30,000 shares)	60

An investor who holds 10 per cent of the shares in Merton Ltd will have 3,000 shares worth £9,000 (i.e. 3,000×£3) before the dividend distribution. Following the distribution, the investor will have 3,000 shares worth £6,000 (i.e. 3,000×£2.00) plus a cash dividend of £3,000 (i.e. 3,000×£1.00) = £9,000. In other words, the total wealth of the investor remains the same.

If the investor did not want to receive the dividends, the cash received could be used to purchase more shares in the company. Although the number of shares held by the investor will change as a result of this decision, his or her *total wealth* will remain the same. If, on the other hand, Merton Ltd did not issue a dividend, and the investor wished to receive one, he or she could create the desired dividend by simply selling a portion of the shares held. Once again, this will change the number of shares held by the investor, but will not change the total amount of wealth held.

What about the effect of a dividend payment on the amounts available for investment? You may feel that a high dividend payment will mean that less can be retained by the company, and this may, in turn, mean that the company will be unable to invest in projects which have a positive NPV. If this occurs, then shareholder wealth will be adversely affected. However, if we assume perfect and efficient capital markets exist, the company will be able to raise the finance required for investment purposes and will not have to rely on profit retentions. In other words, dividend policy and investment policy can be regarded as quite separate issues.

The wealth of existing shareholders should not be affected by raising finance from new issues rather than retentions. Activity 9.4 reinforces this point.

ACTIVITY 9.4

Suppose that Merton Ltd replaces the £30,000 paid out as dividends by an issue of shares to new shareholders. Show the balance sheet after the new issue and calculate the value of shares held by existing shareholders after the issue.

The balance sheet following the new issue will be almost the same as before the dividend payment was made. However, the number of shares in issue will increase. If we assume the new shares can be issued at a fair value (i.e. current market value), the number of shares in issue will increase by 15,000 shares (i.e. 15,000×£2.00).

Balance sheet following the issue of new shares

	£000
Assets at market value (exc. cash)	100
Cash	30
	130
Less: Loan capital	40
Net assets	90
Equity capital (45,000 shares)	90

The existing shareholders will own 30,000 of the 45,000 shares in issue and will therefore own net assets worth £60,000 (30,000/45,000×£90,000). In other words, their wealth will not be affected by the financing decision.

What about the traditional argument in support of dividend policy (i.e. should investors prefer 'a bird in the hand')? The answer to this question is: probably not. The problem with the argument described earlier is that it is based on a misconception of the nature of risk. The risks borne by a shareholder will be determined by the level of company borrowing and the nature of the business which the company is involved in. These risks do not necessarily increase over time and are not affected by the dividend policy of the company. Dividends will only reduce risk if the amount received by the shareholder is then placed in a less risky form of investment (with a lower level of return). This could equally be achieved, however, through the sale of the shares in the company.

ACTIVITY 9.5

There is one situation where even MM would accept that 'a bird in the hand is worth two in the bush' (i.e. that immediate dividends are preferable). Can you think what it is? (Hint: Think of the way in which shareholder wealth is increased.)

Shareholder wealth is increased by the company accepting projects which have a positive NPV. If the company starts to accept projects with a negative NPV, this would decrease shareholder wealth. In such circumstances, a rational shareholder would prefer to receive a dividend rather than to allow the company to reinvest the profits of the business.

The logic of the MM arguments has proved to be unassailable and it is now widely accepted that, in a world of perfect and efficient capital markets, dividend policy should have no effect on shareholder wealth. The burning issue, however, is whether or not the MM analysis can be applied to the real world of imperfect markets. There are three key assumptions on which the MM analysis rests and which has been the subject of much debate. These assumptions are, in essence, that we live in a world where there are:

1. no share issue costs;
2. no share transaction costs; and
3. no taxation.

The first assumption means that money paid out in dividends can be replaced by the business through a new share issue without incurring additional costs. Thus a company need not be deterred from paying a dividend simply because it needs cash to invest in a profitable project, as the amount can be costlessly replaced. In the real world, however, share issue costs can be significant.

The second assumption means that investors can make 'homemade' dividends or reinvest in the business at no extra cost. In other words, there are no barriers to investors pursuing their own dividend and investment strategies. Once again, in the real world, costs will be incurred when shares are purchased or sold by investors. The creation of 'homemade' dividends as a substitute for company dividend policy may pose other practical problems for the shareholder, such as the indivisibility of shares, resulting in shareholders being unable to sell the exact amount of shares required, and the difficulty of selling shares in unlisted companies. These problems, it is argued, can lead to investors becoming reliant on the dividend policy of the business as a means of receiving cash income. It can also lead them to have a preference for one company rather than another, due to the dividend policies adopted.

The third assumption concerning taxation is unrealistic and, in practice, tax may be an important issue for investors. It is often argued that, in the United Kingdom, the taxation rules can have a significant influence on investor preferences. It may be more tax efficient for an investor to receive benefits in the form of capital gains rather than dividends because, below a certain threshold (£6,300 or less for 1996/97), capital gains arising during a particular financial year are not taxable, whereas all dividends are taxable. In addition, it is possible for an investor to influence the timing of capital gains, by choosing when to sell shares, whereas the timing of dividends is normally outside the investor's control.

ACTIVITY 9.6

In a world where taxation is an important issue for investors, how will the particular dividend policy adopted by a company affect its share price?

If, as a result of the tax system, investors prefer capital gains rather than dividends, a company with a high dividend payout ratio would be valued less than a similar company with a low payout ratio.

Although differences between the tax treatment of dividend income and capital gains still exist, changes in taxation policy have narrowed these differences in recent years. One important policy change has been the creation of tax shelters (e.g. personal equity plans) which allow investors to receive dividend income and capital gains free of taxation. Another important change has been the calculation of capital gains tax liability at the investors' marginal rate of taxation, which brings the treatment of capital gains more into line with the treatment of income from dividends. These changes, combined with the increasing influence in the stock market of tax-exempt institutions such as life assurance companies and pension funds, have reduced the impact of taxation on dividend policy.

The three assumptions discussed undoubtedly weaken the MM analysis when applied to the real world. However, this does not necessarily mean that their analysis is destroyed. Different views exist concerning the extent to which the MM analysis retains its validity in a 'real world' setting. The evidence to date, however, is too thin to make a final judgement.

The importance of dividends

Whatever the validity of the MM analysis, there is little doubt that, in practice, the pattern of dividends is seen by investors and corporate managers as being important. It seems that there are three possible reasons to explain this phenomenon. These are:

1.   the clientele effect;
2.   the information signalling effect; and
3.   the need to reduce agency costs.

Each of these reasons are considered below.

Clientele effect

It was mentioned earlier that transaction costs may result in investors becoming reliant on the dividend policies of companies. It was also argued that the tax position of investors can exert an influence on whether dividends or capital gains are preferred. These factors may, in practice, mean that dividend policy will exert an important influence on investor behaviour. Investors may seek out companies whose dividend policies match closely their particular needs. Thus companies with particular dividend policies will attract particular types of investors. This phenomenon is referred to as the *clientele effect*.

The existence of a clientele effect has important implications for managers. First, dividend policy should be clearly set out and consistently applied. Investors attracted to a particular company because of its dividend policy, will not welcome unexpected changes. Secondly, managers need not concern themselves with trying to accommodate all the different needs of shareholders. The particular distribution policy adopted by the company will tend to attract a certain type of investor depending on his/her cash needs and taxation position.

However, investors should be wary of making share investment decisions based primarily on dividend policy. Minimising costs may not be an easy process for investors. Those, for example, requiring a regular cash income, and who seek out companies with high dividend payout ratios, may find that any savings in transaction costs are cancelled out by incurring other forms of cost.

ACTIVITY 9.7

What kind of costs may be borne by investors who invest in high-dividend payout companies, do you think?

Commitment to a high-dividend payout may prevent a company from investing in profitable projects which would have increased shareholder wealth. Hence, there could be a loss of future benefits for the investor. If, however, a company decides to raise finance to replace the amount distributed in dividends, the cost of raising the required finance will be borne by existing shareholders.

Investors must, therefore, look beyond the dividend policy of a company in order to make a sensible investment decision.

The evidence concerning the clientele effect is fairly mixed. Although early research suggested that a clientele effect does exist, more recent research has cast doubt on these findings. More research, perhaps using different approaches to examining the issue, is required for a clearer picture to emerge.

Information signalling

It has been suggested that, in an imperfect world, one purpose of dividends is to enable the management of a company to pass on information concerning the company to shareholders. Thus new information relating to the future prospects of the company may be signalled by managers to shareholders through changes in dividend policy. If, for example, managers are confident about the company's future prospects, this may be signalled through an increase in dividends.

ACTIVITY 9.8

Why would managers wish to use dividends as a means of conveying information about the company's prospects? Why not simply issue a statement to shareholders? Try and jot down at least two reasons why managers may prefer a less direct approach.

At least three reasons have been put forward to explain why dividend signalling may be preferred. First, it may be that the managers do not want to disclose the precise nature of the events which improve the company's prospects. Suppose, for example, that a business has signed a large government defence contract which will be formally announced by the government at some time in the future. In the intervening period, however, the price of the shares in the company may be depressed and the managers may be concerned that the company is vulnerable to a takeover. The managers might, under the circumstances, wish to boost the share price without specifying the nature of the good news. Second, issuing a statement about, say, improved future prospects may not be convincing, particularly if earlier statements by managers have proved incorrect. Statements are 'cheap' whereas an increase in dividends would be more substantial evidence of the managers' confidence in the future. Third, managers may feel that an explicit statement concerning future prospects will attract criticism from shareholders if things do not work out as expected. They may, therefore, prefer more coded messages to avoid being held to account at a later date.

Various studies have been carried out to establish the 'information content' of dividends. Some of these studies have looked at the share price reaction to *unexpected* changes in dividends. If signalling exists, an unexpected dividend announcement should result in a significant share price reaction. The evidence from these studies provides convincing evidence that signalling does exist.

Reducing agency costs

In recent years, *agency theory* has become increasingly influential in the financial management literature. Agency theory views a business as a coalition of different interest groups (managers, shareholders, lenders, and so on), in which each group is seeking to maximise its own welfare. According to this theory, one group connected with the business may engage in behaviour which results in costs being borne by another group. However, the latter group may try to restrain the action of the former group, through contractual or other arrangements, so as to minimise these costs. Two examples of where a conflict of interest arises between groups, and their impact on dividend policy, are considered below.

The first example concerns a conflict of interest between shareholders and managers. If the managers (who are agents of the shareholders) decide to invest in lavish offices, expensive cars and other 'perks', they will be pursuing their own interests at a cost to the shareholders. (You may recall that we discussed this potential conflict in Chapter 1.) One way in which shareholders can avoid incurring these 'agency costs' is to reduce the cash available for managers to spend. Thus shareholders may make it clear that they expect surplus cash to be distributed to them in the form of a dividend. The second example concerns a conflict between shareholders and lenders. Shareholders may seek to reduce their stake in the company by withdrawing cash in the form of dividends. This may be done to reduce their exposure to the risks associated with the company. However, this is likely to be to the detriment of lenders who will become more exposed to these risks. The lenders may, therefore, try to prevent this kind of behaviour by restricting the level of dividends to be paid to shareholders.

ACTIVITY 9.9

How can lenders go about restricting shareholders' rights to dividends? (Hint: Think back to Chapter 7.)

Lenders can insist that loan covenants, which restrict the level of dividend payable, be included in the loan agreement.

Other factors influencing the level of dividends

We have now seen that, in practice, the dividend policy of a company may be influenced by three important factors. In addition to these factors, there may be various practical issues which have a bearing on the size of the final dividend. These include the following:

- *Availability of funds* A company must consider the cash available for dividend payments. In doing so, future commitments such as loan repayments and investment expenditure should be taken into account. In addition, the company may wish to maintain a certain level of cash in reserve as a precaution against unexpected events and/or to take advantage of speculative opportunities. However, if a company is able to raise funds easily and cheaply, there will be less need to hold cash in reserve and any cash distributed in the form of dividends may be replaced without significant cost.
- *Legal requirements* Company law restricts the amount which a company can distribute in the form of dividends. We saw earlier that the law states that dividends can only be paid to shareholders out of *realised* profits. In essence, the maximum amount available for distribution will be the accumulated trading profits (less any losses) *plus* any profits on the disposal of assets.
- *Profit stability* Companies which have a stable pattern of profits over time are in a better position to pay higher dividend payouts than companies which have a volatile pattern of profits.

ACTIVITY 9.10

Why should this be the case?

Companies which have a stable pattern of profits are able to plan with greater certainty and are less likely to feel a need to retain profits for unexpected events.

- *Control*   A high retention/low dividend policy can help avoid the need to issue new shares, and so control exercised by existing shareholders will not be diluted. (Even though existing shareholders have pre-emptive rights, they may not always be in a position to purchase new shares issued by the company.)
- *Threat of takeover*   A further aspect of control concerns the relationship between dividend payments and the threat of takeover. It has been suggested, for example, that a high retention/low distribution policy can increase the vulnerability of a company to takeover.

ACTIVITY 9.11

Why might it be suggested that a low payout policy increases the threat of takeover? Do you think it is a very convincing point?

If a predator company is seeking to acquire the company, it may be able to convince shareholders that the dividends paid are too low and that the existing management is not maximising their wealth. Thus a low dividend policy may make the task of acquisition much easier. Such arguments, however, are only likely to appeal to unsophisticated shareholders. More sophisticated shareholders will recognise that dividends represent only part of the total return from the shares held. (However, if profits are retained rather than distributed, they must be employed in a profitable manner. Failure to do this will make the threat of takeover greater.)

Dividend policy may, however, help avert the threat of takeover. Issuing a large dividend may signal to the market the managers' confidence in the future prospects of the company. This should, in turn, increase the value of the shares and so make a takeover more costly for the predator company. However, the market may not necessarily interpret a large dividend in this way. Investors may regard a large dividend as a desperate attempt by the directors to gain their support and so will discount the dividend received.

- *Market expectations*   Investors may have developed certain expectations concerning the level of dividend to be paid. These expectations may be formed as a result of earlier statements made by the managers of the company. If these expectations are not met, there may be a loss of investor confidence in the company.

Dividend policy and management behaviour

An interesting aspect of dividend policy is the attitudes and behaviour of managers concerning the dividend decision. One early piece of research in this area was undertaken in the US by Lintner, who carried out interviews with managers in 28 companies to discover their views on this topic.[1] He found that managers considered the dividend decision to be an important one and that they were committed to long-term target dividend payout ratios. He also found that managers believed that investors preferred a smooth increase in dividends payments over time and that managers were reluctant to increase the level of dividends in response to a short-term increase in profits. Managers wished to avoid a situation where dividends would have to be cut in the future and so dividends were increased only when managers were confident that the higher level of dividends could be sustained through a permanent increase in earnings. As a result, there was a time lag between dividend growth and earnings growth.

ACTIVITY 9.12

Are these attitudes of managers described above consistent with another view of dividends discussed earlier?

The attitude of managers described by Lintner is consistent with more recent work concerning the use of dividends as a means of information signalling. The managers interviewed seem to be aware of the fact that a dividend cut would send negative signals to investors.

In a later study, Fama and Babiak found that companies distributed about half of their profits in the form of dividends.[2] However, significant increases in earnings would only be followed by a partial adjustment to dividends in the first year. On average, the increase in dividends in the first year was only about one-third of the increase which would have been consistent with maintaining the target payout ratio. The smooth and gradual adjustment of dividends to changes in profits revealed by this study is consistent with the earlier study by Lintner and confirms that managers wish to ensure a sustainable level of dividends.

SELF-ASSESSMENT QUESTION 9.1

Simtech plc is a company which has recently obtained a listing on the Stock Exchange. The company operates a chain of supermarkets in Northern Ireland and was the subject of a management buyout five years ago. In the period since the buyout, the company has grown rapidly. The managers and a venture capital organisation owned 80 per cent of the shares prior to the Stock Exchange listing. However, this has now been reduced to 20 per cent. The record of the company over the past five years is as follows:

Year	Net profit after tax £000	Dividend £000	Number of shares issued 000
19X1	420	220	1,000
19X2	530	140	1,000
19X3	650	260	1,500
19X4	740	110	1,500
19X5	880	460	1,500

Required:

(a) Comment on the dividend policy of the company prior to the Stock Exchange listing.

(b) What advice would you give to the company concerning future dividend policy?

Alternatives to cash dividends

In some cases, a company may decide to make distributions to shareholders in a form different from a cash dividend. The two most important of these are scrip dividends and share repurchases. Below we consider each of these options.

Scrip dividends

A company may make a scrip dividend (or bonus share dividend) rather than making a cash distribution to shareholders. Thus, if a company announced a 20 per cent scrip dividend this would mean that each shareholder would receive a 20 per cent increase in the number of shares held. We saw in Chapter 7, however, that scrip issues (or bonus issues) do not result in an increase in shareholder wealth. Making a scrip issue is, in essence, a bookkeeping transaction which will not, of itself, create value. Nevertheless, the market may respond positively to a scrip dividend if it is seen as a sign of the directors' confidence concerning the future. The scrip issue may suggest that the directors will maintain the same dividend per share in the future, despite the increase in the number of shares in issue. Various research studies have shown a positive response to scrip dividends by the market.

In some cases, shareholders may be given the choice between a scrip dividend and a cash dividend. Those shareholders who choose the scrip dividend will increase their proportion of the total shares issued relative to those shareholders who took the cash option. For tax purposes, shareholders who receive a scrip dividend will be treated, broadly speaking, as having received the cash dividend option from the company.

Share repurchase

In recent years, the repurchase of shares has become a popular way of distributing cash to shareholders. Repurchase can be achieved through the stock market, through agreements with particular shareholders or through a direct appeal to all shareholders. Where the cash distributed is surplus to requirements, the effect on company earnings will not be significant. However, earnings per share for the remaining shareholders will rise as there will be fewer shares in issue.

ACTIVITY 9.13

Is this increase in earnings per share likely to increase the price of shares in issue?

It would be difficult to see why this should be the case. The value of the shares will be determined by the future cash flows generated by the company. A stock repurchase and a dividend payment are similar insofar as shareholders receive cash and the assets of the company are reduced. We saw earlier that a dividend payment does not automatically increase shareholder wealth and this should also be true of a share repurchase.

Care must be taken in ensuring equity between shareholders during a share repurchase. In some cases, the market may undervalue the shares of a company, perhaps because it does not have access to information known to the managers of the company. If this situation exists, the shareholders who hold on to their shares will benefit at the expense of those who sell. In some cases, the market for shares in the company may be slow and the effect of a repurchase of a large number of shares may be to create an artificially high price which may benefit those who sell at the expense of those who continue to hold their shares.

Various reasons for share repurchase arrangements have been suggested, apart from the return of surplus cash to shareholders. In practice, a share repurchase may be undertaken to buy out unwelcome shareholders. It may also be used to adjust the capital base of the company. A share repurchase may help companies to reduce their equity capital to more appropriate levels and/or increase their gearing.

Summary

In this chapter, we have explored various aspects of the dividend decision. We have seen that there are opposing views concerning whether or not the pattern of dividends has an influence on shareholder wealth. The MM view, which holds that shareholder wealth will not be affected by the dividend policy of the company, is based on rigorous analysis but assumes a world of perfect and efficient capital markets. Those who take a contrary view have tended to argue that the MM view does not apply in the real world. In this chapter, we have explored various reasons why dividends may be important to shareholders in an imperfect world.

So what advice can we give to managers who are wrestling with the problem of dividend policy and who are looking for help? Well, probably the best advice we can give is to make the particular dividend policy adopted clear to investors and then make every effort to keep to that policy. Investors are unlikely to welcome 'surprises' in dividend policy and may react by selling their shares and investing in a company which has a more stable and predictable dividend policy. This behaviour will lower the value of the company's shares and will increase the cost of capital. If, for any reason, managers have to reduce the dividends for a particular year, they should prepare investors for the change in dividend payout and clearly state the reasons for that change.

References

1. J. Lintner, 'Distribution of incomes of corporations among dividends, retained earnings and taxes', *American Economic Review*, 46: 97–113, May 1956.
2. E.F. Fama and H. Babiak, 'Dividend policy: an empirical analysis', *Journal of the American Statistical Association*, December 1968.

Review questions

9.1 Can you think of three reasons why a company should wish to repurchase some of its shares?

9.2 'The firm's dividend decision is really a by-product of its capital investment decision.' Discuss.

9.3 Is it really important for a company to try and meet the needs of different types of investors when formulating its dividend policy?

9.4 Describe how agency theory may help explain the dividend policy of companies.

Examination-style questions _____

Solutions to those questions marked with an asterisk are given at the end of the text. Questions 9.1 and 9.2 are at basic level. Questions 9.3 and 9.4 are at intermediate/advanced level.

9.1   The dividend policy of companies has been the subject of much debate in the financial management literature.

Required:

Discuss the view that dividends can increase the wealth of shareholders.

9.2*   Identify and discuss the factors which may influence the dividend policies of companies.

9.3   The following listed public companies each have different policies concerning distributions to shareholders:

- North plc pays all profits available for distribution to shareholders in the form of a cash dividend each year.
- South plc has yet to pay any cash dividends to shareholders and has no plans to make dividend payments in the foreseeable future.
- West plc repurchases shares from shareholders as an alternative to a dividend payment.
- East plc offers shareholders the choice of either a small but stable cash dividend or a scrip dividend each year.

Required:

Discuss the advantages and disadvantages of each of the above policies.

9.4*   Fellingham plc has 20 million ordinary £1 shares in issue. No shares have been issued during the past four years. The company's earnings and dividends record taken from the historic accounts showed:

| | Year | | | |
	1	2	3	4
Earnings per share	11.00p	12.40p	10.90p	17.20p
Dividend per share	10.00p	10.90p	11.88p	12.95p

At the annual general meeting for Year 1, the chairman had indicated that it was the intention to consistently increase annual dividends by 9 per cent, anticipating that on average this would maintain the spending power of shareholders and provide a modest growth in real income.

In the event, subsequent average annual inflation rates, measured by the general index of prices, have been:

	Year	
2	3	4
11%	10%	8%

The ordinary shares are currently selling for £3.44, ex the Year 4 dividend.

Required:

Comment upon the declared dividend policy of the company and its possible effects upon both Fellingham plc and its shareholders, illustrating your answer with the information provided.

—

CHAPTER TEN

The Management of Working Capital

—————————————————— O B J E C T I V E S ——————————————————

On completion of this chapter you should be able to:

■ Identify the main elements of working capital.

■ Discuss the purpose of working capital and the nature of the working capital cycle.

■ Explain the importance of establishing policies for the control of working capital.

■ Explain the factors which have to be taken into account when managing each element of working capital.

Introduction

In this chapter we consider the factors which must be taken into account when managing the working capital of a business. Each element of working capital will be identified and the important issues surrounding them will be discussed.

The nature and purpose of working capital

Working capital is usually defined as: *current assets less current liabilities (creditors due within one year)*. The major elements of current assets are:

■ stocks;
■ trade debtors; and
■ cash (in hand and at bank).

The major element of current liabilities is:

■ trade creditors.

The size and composition of working capital can vary between industries. For some types of business, the investment in working capital can be substantial. For example, a manufacturing company will invest heavily in raw materials, work-in-progress and finished goods and will often sell its goods on credit, thereby incurring trade debtors. A retailer, on the other hand, will hold only one form of stock (finished goods) and will usually sell goods for cash.

Working capital represents a net investment in short-term assets. These assets are continually flowing into and out of the business and are essential for day-to-day operations. The various elements of working capital are interrelated and can be seen as part of a short-term cycle. For a manufacturing business, the working capital cycle can be depicted as shown in Figure 10.1.

The management of working capital is an essential part of the short-term planning process. It is necessary for management to decide how much of each element should be held. As we shall see later, there are costs associated with holding both too much and too little of each element. Management must be aware of these in order to manage effectively. Management must also be aware that there may be other, more profitable, uses for the funds of the business. Hence, the potential benefits must be weighed against the likely costs in order to achieve the optimum investment.

Working capital needs are likely to change over time as a result of changes in the business environment. This means that working capital decisions are rarely

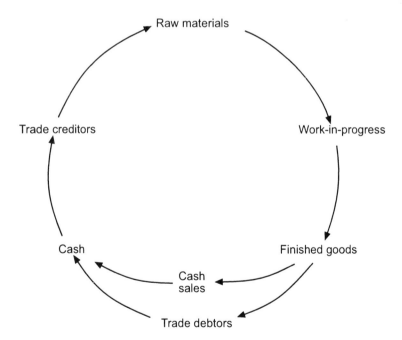

Figure 10.1   The working capital cycle

'one-off' decisions. Managers must try to identify changes occurring so as to ensure that the level of investment in working capital is appropriate.

ACTIVITY 10.1

What kind of changes in the business environment might lead to a decision to change the level of investment in working capital? Try and identify four possible changes which could affect the working capital needs of a business.

In answering this activity, you may have thought of the following:

- *Changes in interest rates.*
- *Changes in market demand.*
- *Changes in the seasons.*
- *Changes in the state of the economy.*

You may have also thought of others.

In addition to changes in the external environment, changes arising within the business, such as changes in production methods (resulting, perhaps, in a need to hold less stock), and changes in the level of risk managers are prepared to take could alter the required level of investment in working capital.

EXHIBIT 10.1

The management of working capital is a significant issue because this item often represents a substantial investment for a business. The following average balance sheet percentages, based on a survey of balance sheets of large UK companies, indicates the relative size of the investment in working capital:

	1990	
	%	%
Fixed assets		85
Current assets		
Stock	20	
Debtors	28	
Cash	13	
	61	
Current liabilities		
Creditors	39	
Dividends, interest and tax owing	7	
	46	15
		100

	%
Equity	74
Long-term liabilities	26
	100

Source: Business Statistics Office, Department of Trade and Industry.

In the sections which follow, we will consider each element of working capital separately. We will examine the factors which must be considered to ensure their proper management.

The management of stocks

A business may hold stocks for various reasons. The most common reason is, of course, to meet the immediate day-to-day requirements of customers and production. However, a business may hold more than is necessary for this purpose if it is believed that future supplies may be interrupted or scarce. Similarly, if the business believes that the cost of stocks will rise in the future, it may decide to stockpile.

For some types of business the stock held may represent a substantial proportion of the total assets held. For example, a car dealership which rents its premises, may have nearly all of its total assets in the form of stock. In the case of manufacturing businesses, stock levels tend to be higher than in many other forms of business as it is necessary to hold three kinds of stock: raw materials, work-in-progress and finished goods. Each form of stock represents a particular stage in the production cycle. For some types of business, the level of stock held may vary substantially over the year due to the seasonal nature of the industry (e.g. firework manufacturers), whereas for other businesses stock levels may remain fairly stable throughout the year.

Where a business holds stock simply to meet the day-to-day requirements of its customers and production, it will normally seek to minimise the amount of stock held. This is because there are significant costs associated with holding stocks. These include storage and handling costs, financing costs, the risks of pilferage and obsolescence and the opportunities forgone in tying up funds in this form of asset. However, a business must also recognise that if the level of stocks held are too low, there will also be associated costs.

ACTIVITY 10.2

What costs might a business incur as a result of holding too low a level of stocks? Try and identify at least three types of cost.

In answering this activity you may have thought of the following costs:

- *Loss of sales, being unable to provide the goods required immediately.*
- *Loss of goodwill from customers, for being unable to satisfy customer demand.*
- *High transportation costs incurred to ensure stocks are replenished quickly.*
- *Lost production due to shortage of raw materials.*
- *Inefficient production scheduling due to shortages.*
- *Purchasing stocks at a higher price than may otherwise have been possible in order to replenish stocks quickly.*
- *Wasted production runs in restart situations.*

In order to try to ensure that the stocks are properly managed, a number of procedures and techniques may be employed, which are now described.

Forecasts of future demand

In order for there to be stock available to meet future sales a business must produce appropriate forecasts. These forecasts should deal with each product line. It is important that every attempt is made to ensure the accuracy of these forecasts as they will determine future ordering and production levels. These forecasts may be derived in various ways. They may be developed using statistical techniques such as time series analysis, or they may be based on the judgement of the sales and marketing staff.

Financial ratios

One ratio which can be used to help monitor stock levels is the stock turnover period which we examined in Chapter 3. You may recall, this ratio is calculated as follows:

$$\text{Stock turnover period} = \frac{\text{Average stock held}}{\text{Cost of sales}} \times 365$$

This will provide a picture of the average period for which stocks are held and can be useful as a basis for comparison. It is possible to calculate the stock turnover period for individual product lines as well as for stocks as a whole.

Recording and reordering systems

The management of stocks in a business of any size requires a sound system of recording stock movements. There must be proper procedures for recording stock purchases and sales. Periodic stock checks may be required to ensure that the amount of physical stocks held is consistent with the stock records.

There should also be clear procedures for the reordering of stocks. Authorisation for both the purchase and issue of stocks should be confined to a few senior staff if problems of duplication and lack of co-ordination are to be avoided. To determine the point at which stock should be reordered, information concerning the lead time (i.e. the time between the placing of an order and the receipt of the goods) and the likely level of demand will be required.

ACTIVITY 10.3

An electrical retailer keeps a particular type of light switch in stock. The annual demand for the light switch is 10,400 units and the lead time for orders is four weeks. Demand for the stock is steady throughout the year. At what level of stock should the company reorder, assuming that the company is confident of the figures mentioned above?

The average weekly demand for the stock item is 10,400/52 = 200 units. During the time between ordering the stock and receiving the goods, the stock sold will be 4 × 200 units = 800 units. So the company should reorder no later than when the stock level reaches 800 units in order to avoid a stockout.

In most businesses, there will be some uncertainty surrounding the above factors and so a *buffer* or *safety stock* level may be maintained in case problems occur. The amount of safety stock to be held is really a matter of judgement and will depend on the degree of uncertainty concerning the above factors. However, the likely costs of running out of stock must also be taken into account.

Levels of control

Management must make a commitment to the management of stocks. However, the cost of controlling stocks must be weighed against the potential benefits. It may be possible to have different levels of control according to the nature of the stocks held. The ABC system of stock control is based on the idea of selective levels of control (see Figure 10.2).

A business may find that it is possible to divide its stock into three broad categories: A, B and C. Each category will be based on the value of stock held. Category A stocks will represent the high-value items. It may be the case, however, that although the items are high in *value* and represent a high proportion of the total value of stocks held, they are a relatively small proportion of the total *volume* of stocks held. For example 10 per cent of the physical stocks held may account for 65 per cent of the total value. For these stocks, management may decide to implement sophisticated recording procedures, exert tight control over stock movements and have a high level of security at the stock location.

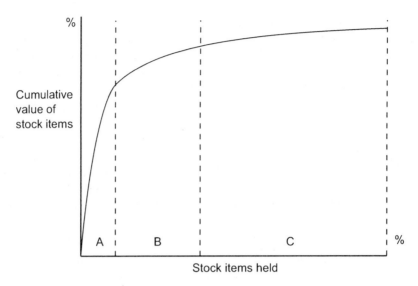

Figure 10.2 ABC method of analysing and controlling stocks

Category B stocks will represent less valuable items held. Perhaps 30 per cent of the total volume of stocks may account for 25 per cent of the total value of stocks held. For these stocks, a lower level of recording and management control would be appropriate. Category C stocks will represent the least valuable items. Say 60 per cent of the volume of stocks may account for 10 per cent of the total value of stocks held. For these stocks the level of recording and management control would be lower still. By categorising stocks in this way it can help to ensure that management effort is directed to the most important areas and that the costs of controlling stocks are commensurate with their value.

Stock management models

It is possible to use decision models to help manage stocks. The economic order quantity (EOQ) model is concerned with answering the question: How much stock should be ordered? In its simplest form, the EOQ model assumes that demand is constant, so that stocks will be depleted evenly over time, and that stocks will be replenished just at the point the stock runs out. These assumptions would lead to the 'saw tooth' pattern shown in Figure 10.3 to represent stock movements within a business.

The EOQ model recognises that the total cost of stocks is made up of the cost of holding stocks and the costs of ordering stocks. It calculates the optimum size of a purchase order by taking account of both of these cost elements. The cost of holding stocks can be substantial and so management may try to reduce the average amount of stocks held to as low a level as possible. However, by reducing

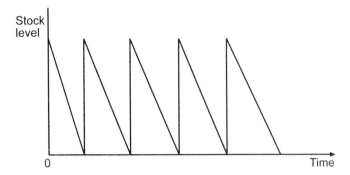

Figure 10.3 Pattern of stock movements over time

the level of stocks held, and therefore the holding costs, there will be a need to increase the number of orders during the period and so ordering costs will rise.

The graph in Figure 10.4 shows how, as the level of stocks and the size of stock orders increase, the annual costs of placing orders will decrease because fewer orders will be placed. However, the cost of holding stock will increase as there will be higher stock levels. The total costs curve, which is a function of the holding costs and ordering costs, will fall until the point E, which represents the minimum total cost. Thereafter, total costs begin to rise. The EOQ model seeks to identify the point E at which total costs are minimised. This will represent the optimum amount which should be ordered on each occasion.

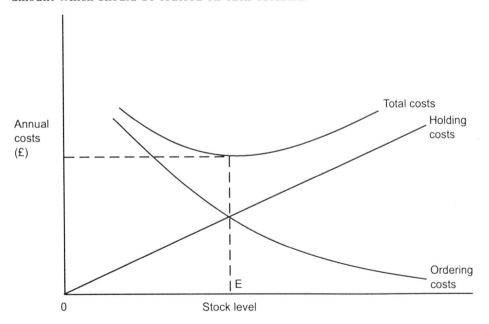

Figure 10.4 Stockholding and stock order costs

The economic order quantity can be calculated by using the following equation:

$$EOQ = \sqrt{\frac{2DC}{H}}$$

where:

D = the annual demand for the item of stock;
C = the cost of placing an order; and
H = the cost of holding one unit of stock for one year.

ACTIVITY 10.4

HLA Ltd sells 2,000 units of Product X each year. It has been estimated that the cost of holding one unit of the product for a year is £4. The cost of placing an order for stock is estimated at £25.

Required:

Calculate the economic order quantity for the product.

Your answer to this activity should be as follows:

$$EOQ = \sqrt{\frac{2 \times 2,000 \times 25}{4}}$$

$$= 158 \text{ units (to the nearest whole number)}$$

This will mean that the business will have to order Product X about 13 times each year in order to meet sales demand.

The EOQ model has a number of limiting assumptions. It assumes that demand for the product can be predicted with accuracy and that this demand is even over the period and does not fluctuate through seasonality or other reasons. It also assumes that no 'buffer' stock is required and that the amount purchased can correspond to the economic order quantity (e.g. 158 units and not in multiples of 50 or 100 units). Finally, it assumes that no discounts are available for bulk purchases. However, these limiting assumptions do not mean that we should dismiss the model as being of little value. The model can be refined to accommodate the problems of uncertainty and uneven demand. Many businesses use this model (or a development of it) to help in the management of stocks.

Materials requirements planning (MRP) systems

MRP takes as its starting point forecasts of sales demand. It then uses computer technology to help schedule the timing of deliveries of bought-in parts and materials to coincide with production requirements to meet the demand. It is a co-ordinated approach which links material and parts deliveries to their scheduled input to the production process. By ordering only those items which are necessary to ensure the flow of production, stock levels may therefore be reduced. MRP is really a 'top-down' approach to stock management which recognises that stock-ordering decisions cannot be viewed as being independent from production decisions. In more recent years, this approach has been extended so as to provide a fully integrated approach to production planning that also takes into account other manufacturing resources such as labour and machine capacity.

Just-in-time (JIT) stock management

In recent years, some manufacturing businesses have tried to eliminate the need to hold stocks by adopting a 'just-in time' approach. This method was first used in the US defence industry during World War II, but in more recent times it has been widely used by Japanese businesses. The essence of this approach is, as the name suggests, to have supplies delivered to a business just in time for them to be used in the production process. By adopting this approach the stockholding problem rests with the suppliers rather than the business.

In order for this approach to be successful, it is important for the business to inform suppliers of their production plans and requirements in advance and for suppliers to deliver materials of the right quality at the agreed times. Failure to do so could lead to a dislocation of production and could be very costly. Thus a close relationship between the business and its suppliers is required.

Although a business will not have to hold stocks there may be certain costs associated with this approach. As the suppliers will be required to hold stocks for the business they may try to recoup this additional cost through increased prices. The price of stocks purchased may also be increased if JIT requires a large number of small deliveries to be made. Finally, the close relationship necessary between the business and its suppliers may prevent the business from taking advantage of cheaper sources of supply when they become available.

Many people view JIT as more than simply a stock control system. The philosophy underpinning this method is concerned with eliminating waste and striving for excellence. There is an expectation that suppliers will always deliver parts on time and that there will be no defects in the parts supplied. There is also an expectation that the production process will operate at maximum efficiency. This means that there will be no production breakdowns and that the queuing and storage times of products manufactured will be eliminated, as only that time spent directly on processing the products is seen as adding value. Whilst these expectations may be impossible to achieve, they do help create a management culture which is dedicated to the pursuit of excellence.

The management of debtors

Selling goods or services on credit results in costs being incurred by a business. These costs include credit administration costs, bad debts and opportunities forgone in using the funds for more profitable purposes. However, these costs must be weighed against the benefits of increased sales resulting from the opportunity for customers to delay payment.

Selling on credit is very widespread and appears to be the norm outside the retail trade. When a business offers to sell its goods or services on credit it must have clear policies concerning the following issues:

- Which customers it is prepared to offer credit to.
- What length of credit it is prepared to offer.
- Whether discounts will be offered for prompt payment.
- What collection policies should be adopted.

In this section we will consider each of these issues.

Which customers should receive credit?

A business offering credit runs the risk of not receiving payment for goods or services supplied. Thus care must be taken over the type of customer to whom credit facilities are offered. When considering a proposal from a customer for the supply of goods or services on credit the business must take a number of factors into account. The following 'five Cs of credit' provide a business with a useful checklist:

1. *Capital*   The customer must appear to be financially sound before any credit is extended. Where the customer is a business, an examination of its accounts should be carried out. Particular regard should be given to the profitability and liquidity of the customer. In addition, any onerous financial commitments must be taken into account.
2. *Capacity*   The customer must appear to have the capacity to pay amounts owing. Where possible, the payment record of the customer to date should be examined. If the customer is a business, the type of business operated and the physical resources of the business will be relevant. The value of goods which the customer wishes to buy on credit must be related to the total financial resources of the customer.
3. *Collateral*   On occasions, it may be necessary to ask for some kind of security for goods supplied on credit. When this occurs, the business must be convinced that the customer is able to offer a satisfactory form of security.
4. *Conditions*   The state of the industry in which the customer operates and the general economic conditions of the particular region or country may have an important influence on the ability of a customer to pay the amounts outstanding on the due date.

5. *Character* It is important for a business to make some assessment of the character of the customer. The willingness to pay will depend on the honesty and integrity of the individual with whom the business is dealing. Where the customer is a limited company this will mean assessing the characters of its directors. The business must feel satisfied that the customer will make every effort to pay any amounts owing.

Once a customer has been considered creditworthy, credit limits for the customer should be established and procedures should be laid down to ensure that these credit limits are adhered to.

ACTIVITY 10.5

Assume you are the credit manager of a business and that a limited company approached you with a view to buying goods on credit. What sources of information might you decide to use to help assess the financial health of the potential customer?

There are various sources of information available to a business to help assess the financial health of a customer. You may have thought of some of the following:

■ **Trade references** *Some businesses ask for a potential customer to furnish them with references from other suppliers who have had dealings with the customer. This may be extremely useful providing the references supplied are truly representative of the opinions of the customer's suppliers. There is a danger that a potential customer will attempt to be highly selective when furnishing details of other suppliers in order to gain a more favourable impression than is deserved.*

■ **Bank references** *It is possible to ask the potential customer for a bank reference. Although banks are usually prepared to oblige, the contents of a reference are not always very informative. If customers are in financial difficulties, the bank will usually be unwilling to add to their problems by supplying poor references.*

■ **Published accounts** *A limited company is obliged by law to file a copy of its annual accounts with the Registrar of Companies. The accounts are available for public inspection and provide a useful source of information.*

■ **The customer** *You may wish to interview the directors of the company and visit its premises in order to gain some impression about the way the company conducts its business. Where a significant amount of credit is required, the business may ask the company for access to internal budgets and other unpublished financial information to help assess the level of risk to be taken.*

■ **Credit agencies** *Specialist agencies exist to provide information which can be used to assess the creditworthiness of a potential customer. The information which a credit agency supplies may be gleaned from various sources including the accounts of the customer, court judgements and news items relating to the customer from both published and unpublished sources.*

Length of credit period

A business must determine what credit terms it is prepared to offer its customers. The length of credit offered to customers can vary significantly between businesses. The length of credit may be influenced by various factors, which may include the following:

- The typical credit terms operating within the industry.
- The degree of competition within the industry.
- The bargaining power of particular customers.
- The risk of non-payment.
- The capacity of the business to offer credit.
- The marketing strategy of the business.

The last point identified may require some explanation. The marketing strategy of a business may have an important influence on the length of credit allowed. For example, if a business wishes to increase its market share it may decide to liberalise its credit policy in order to stimulate sales. Potential customers may be attracted by the offer of a longer period in which to pay. However, any such change in policy must take account of the likely costs and benefits arising. Example 10.1 illustrates this point.

Example 10.1

Torrance Ltd was formed in 19X8 in order to produce a new type of golf putter. The company sells the putter to wholesalers and retailers and has an annual turnover of £600,000. The following data relates to each putter produced:

	£	£
Selling price		36
Variable costs	18	
Fixed cost apportionment	6	24
Net profit		12

The cost of capital (before tax) of Torrance Ltd is estimated at 15 per cent.

Torrance Ltd wishes to expand sales of this new putter and believes this can be done by offering a longer period in which to pay. The average collection period of the company is currently 30 days. The company is considering three options in order to increase sales. These are as follows:

	Option		
	1	2	3
Increase in average collection period (days)	10	20	30
Increase in sales (£s)	30,000	45,000	50,000

Prepare calculations to show which credit policy the company should offer its customers.

In order to decide on the best option, the company must weigh the benefits of each option against their respective costs. The benefits arising will be represented by the increase in profit from the sale of additional putters. From the cost data supplied we can see that the contribution (i.e. sales less variable costs) is £18 per putter. This represents 50 per cent of the selling price. The fixed costs can be ignored in our calculations as they will remain the same whichever option is chosen. The increase in contribution under each option will therefore be:

	Option		
	1	2	3
50% of increase in sales (£s)	15,000	22,500	25,000

The increase in debtors under each option will be as follows:

	Option		
	1	2	3
	£	£	£
Planned level of debtors:			
630,000×40/365	69,041		
645,000×50/365		88,356	
650,000×60/365			106,849
Less: Current level of debtors:			
600,000×30/365	49,315	49,315	49,315
	19,726	39,041	57,534

The increase in debtors which results from each option will mean an additional cost to the company. We are told the company has an estimated cost of capital of 15 per cent. Thus, the increase in the additional investment in debtors will be:

	Option		
	1	2	3
	£	£	£
Cost of additional investment (15% of increase in debtors)	(2,959)	(5,856)	(8,630)

The net increase in profits will be:

	Option		
	1	2	3
	£	£	£
Cost of additional investment (15% of increase in debtors)	(2,959)	(5,856)	(8,630)
Increase in contribution (see above)	15,000	22,500	25,000
Net increase in profits	12,041	16,644	16,370

The calculations show that Option 2 will be the most profitable one for the company. However, there is little to choose between Options 2 and 3.

The above example illustrates the way in which a business should assess changes in credit terms. However, if there is a risk that by extending the length of credit, there will be an increase in bad debts, this should also be taken into account in the calculations. Similarly, if additional collection costs are incurred, this should also be taken into account.

Cash discounts

A business may decide to offer a cash discount in order to encourage prompt payment from its credit customers. The size of any discount will be an important influence on whether a customer decides to pay promptly. From the point of view of the business, the cost of offering discounts must be weighed against the likely benefits in the form of a reduction in the cost of financing debtors and any reduction in the amount of bad debts.

In practice, there is always the danger that a customer may be slow to pay and yet may still take the discount offered. Where the customer is important to the business it may be difficult for the business to insist on full payment. Some businesses may charge interest on overdue accounts in order to encourage prompt payment. However, this is only possible if the business is in a strong bargaining position with its customers. For example, the business may be the only supplier of a particular product in the area.

SELF-ASSESSMENT QUESTION 10.1

Williams Wholesalers Ltd at present requires payment from its customers by the month end after month of delivery. On average it takes them 70 days to pay. Sales amount to £4 million per year and bad debts to £20,000 per year.

It is planned to offer customers a cash discount of 2 per cent for payment within 30 days. Williams estimates that 50 per cent of customers will accept this facility but that the remaining customers, who tend to be slow payers, will not pay until 80 days after the sale. At present the company has a partly used overdraft facility costing 13 per cent per annum. If the plan goes ahead, bad debts will be reduced to £10,000 per annum and there will be savings in credit administration expenses of £6,000 per annum.

Required:

Should Williams Wholesalers Ltd offer the new credit terms to customers? You should support your answer with any calculations and explanations which you consider necessary.

Collection policies

A business offering credit must ensure that amounts owing are collected as quickly as possible. An efficient collection policy requires an efficient accounting system. Invoices must be sent out promptly along with regular monthly statements. Reminders must also be despatched promptly where necessary.

When a business is faced with customers who do not pay, there should be agreed procedures for dealing with them. However, the cost of any action to be taken against delinquent debtors must be weighed against the likely returns. For example, there is little point in pursuing a customer through the courts and incurring large legal expenses if there is evidence that the customer does not have the necessary resources to pay. Where possible, the cost of bad debts should be taken into account when pricing products or services.

Management can monitor the effectiveness of collection policies in a number of ways. One method is to calculate the average settlement period for debtors which we dealt with in Chapter 3. This ratio, you may recall, is calculated as follows:

$$\text{Average settlement period for debtors} = \frac{\text{Trade debtors}}{\text{Credit sales}} \times 365$$

Although this ratio can be useful it is important to remember that it produces an *average* figure for the number of days debts are outstanding. This average may be badly distorted by a few large customers who are also very slow payers.

A more detailed and informative approach to monitoring debtors is to produce an *ageing schedule* of debtors. Debts are divided into categories according to the length of time the debt has been outstanding. An ageing schedule can be produced for managers on a regular basis in order to help them see the pattern of outstanding debts. An example of an ageing schedule of debtors is as follows:

Customer	Days outstanding			
	1–30	31–60	61–90	>90
	£	£	£	£
A Ltd	20,000	10,000	–	–
B Ltd	–	24,000	–	–
C Ltd	12,000	13,000	14,000	18,000
Total	32,000	47,000	14,000	18,000

Thus we can see from the schedule that A Ltd has £20,000 outstanding for 30 days or less and £10,000 outstanding for between 31 and 60 days. This information can be very useful for credit control purposes.

The use of computers can make the task of producing such a schedule simple and straightforward. Many accounting software packages now include this ageing schedule as one of the routine reports available to managers. Such packages often have the facility to put customers on 'hold' when they reach their credit limit.

A slightly different approach to exercising control over debtors is to identify the pattern of receipts from credit sales which occur on a monthly basis. This involves monitoring the percentage of trade debtors which pay (and the percentage of debts which remain unpaid) in the month of sale and the percentage who pay in subsequent months. In order to do this, credit sales for each month must be examined separately. To illustrate how a pattern of credit sales receipts is produced, consider a business which achieved credit sales of £250,000 in June and received 30 per cent of the amount owing in the same month, 40 per cent in July, 20 per cent in August and 10 per cent in September. The pattern of credit sales receipts and amounts owing will be as follows:

Month	Receipts from June credit sales £	% received	Amount outstanding from June sales at month end £	% outstanding
June	75,000	30	175,000	70
July	100,000	40	75,000	30
August	50,000	20	25,000	10
September	25,000	10	–	–

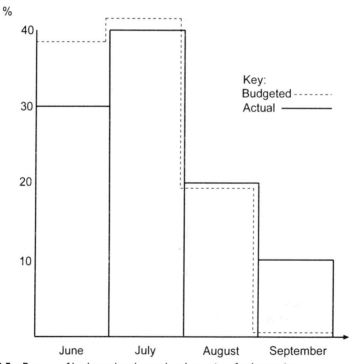

Figure 10.5 Pattern of budgeted and actual cash receipts for June sales

This table shows how payment for June sales was received over time. This information can be used as a basis for control. The actual pattern of receipts can be compared to the expected (budgeted) pattern of receipts in order to see if there was any significant deviation (see Figure 10.5). If this comparison shows that debtors are paying more slowly than expected, management may decide to take corrective action.

ACTIVITY 10.6

What kind of corrective action might the managers of a business decide to take if they found that debtors were paying more slowly than anticipated?

Managers might decide to do one or more of the following:

- *Offer cash discounts to encourage prompt payment.*
- *Change the collection period.*
- *Improve the accounting system to ensure customers are billed more promptly, reminders sent out promptly, and so on.*
- *Change the eligibility criteria for customers who receive credit.*

Credit management and the small business

Credit management may be a particular problem for small businesses. Often, these businesses lack the resources to manage their trade debtors effectively. Sometimes, a small business will not have a separate credit control department, which will mean that both the expertise and the information required to make sound judgements concerning terms of sale and so forth will simply not be available. A small business may also lack proper debt collection procedures, such as prompt invoicing, the sending out of regular statements, and so on. This will increase the risks of late payment and defaulting debtors.

The risks of late payment and defaulting debtors may also increase through an excessive concern for growth. In order to increase sales, small businesses may be too willing to extend credit to customers who are poor credit risks. Whilst this kind of problem can occur in businesses of all sizes, small businesses seem particularly susceptible.

Another problem faced by small businesses is their lack of market power. They will often find themselves in a weak position when negotiating credit terms with larger businesses. Moreover, when a large customer exceeds the terms of credit, the small supplier may feel inhibited from pressing the customer for payment in case future sales are lost.

The management of cash

Why hold cash?

Most businesses will hold a certain amount of cash as part of the total assets held. The amount of cash held, however, may vary considerably between businesses.

ACTIVITY 10.7

Why do you think a business may decide to hold at least some of its assets in the form of cash?

According to economic theory there are three motives for holding cash. These may be identified as follows:

1. ***Transactionary motive***   *In order to meet day-to-day commitments a business requires a certain amount of cash. Payments in respect of wages, overhead expenses, goods purchased, and so on, must be made at the due dates. Cash has been described as the 'life blood' of a business. Unless it 'circulates' through the business and is available for the payment of maturing obligations, the survival of the business will be put at risk. We saw in an earlier chapter that profitability alone is not enough. A business must have sufficient cash to pay its debts when they fall due.*

2. ***Precautionary motive***   *If future cash flows are uncertain for any reason it would be prudent to hold a balance of cash. For example, a major customer who owes a large sum to the business may be in financial difficulties. Given this situation, the business can retain its capacity to meet its obligations by holding a cash balance. Similarly, if there is some uncertainty concerning future outlays a cash balance will be required.*

3. ***Speculative motive***   *A business may decide to hold cash in order to be in a position to exploit profitable opportunities as and when they arise. For example, by holding cash, a business may be able to acquire a competitor business which suddenly becomes available at an attractive price. Holding cash has an opportunity cost for the business which must be taken into account. Thus, when evaluating the potential returns from holding cash for speculative purposes, the cost of forgone investment opportunities must also be considered.*

How much cash should be held?

Although cash can be held for each of the reasons identified, it may not always be necessary to hold cash for these purposes. If a business is able to borrow quickly at a favourable rate, the amount of cash it needs to hold can be reduced. Similarly, if the business holds assets which can easily be converted to cash (e.g. marketable securities such as shares in Stock Exchange listed companies, government bonds, and so on), the amount of cash held can be reduced.

The decision regarding how much cash a particular business should hold is a difficult one. Different businesses will have different views on the amount of cash which it is appropriate to hold.

ACTIVITY 10.8

What do you think are the most important factors which influence how much cash a business will hold? See if you can think of five possible factors.

Factors which influence the decision as to how much cash will be held are varied and may include the following:

- **The nature of the business** *Some businesses, such as utilities (water companies, electricity companies, gas companies, and so forth) may have cash flows which are both predictable and reasonably certain. This will enable them to hold lower cash balances. For some businesses, cash balances may vary greatly according to the time of year. A seasonal business may accumulate cash during the high season to enable it to meet commitments during the low season.*
- **The opportunity cost of holding cash** *Where there are profitable opportunities, it may not be wise to hold a large cash balance rather than invest in those opportunities.*
- **The level of inflation** *The holding of cash during a period of rising prices will lead to a loss of purchasing power. The higher the level of inflation, the greater will be this loss.*
- **The availability of near-liquid assets** *If a business has marketable securities or stocks which may easily be liquidated, the amount of cash held may be reduced.*
- **The availability of borrowing** *If a business can borrow easily (and quickly), there is less need to hold cash.*
- **The cost of borrowing** *When interest rates are high the option of borrowing becomes less attractive.*
- **Economic conditions** *When the economy is in recession businesses may prefer to hold on to cash in order to be well placed to invest when the economy improves. In addition, during a recession, businesses may experience difficulties in collecting debts. They may, therefore, hold higher cash balances than usual in order to meet commitments.*
- **Relationships with suppliers** *Too little cash may hinder the ability of the business to pay suppliers promptly. This can lead to a loss of goodwill. It may also lead to discounts forgone.*

Controlling the cash balance

A number of models have been proposed to help control the cash balance of the business. For example, one model proposes the use of upper and lower control limits for cash balances and the use of a target cash balance. The model assumes the business will invest in marketable investments which can easily be liquidated. These investments will be purchased or sold, as necessary, in order to keep the cash balance within the control limits.

The model proposes two upper and two lower control limits (see Figure 10.6). If the business finds that it has exceeded an *outer* limit, the managers must decide whether or not the cash balance is likely to return to a point within the *inner* control limits set over the next few days. If this seems likely, then no action is required. If, on the other hand, this does not seem likely, management must change the cash position of the business by either buying or selling marketable securities. In Figure 10.6, we can see that the lower outer control limit has been breached for four days. If a four-day period is unacceptable, managers must sell marketable securities in order to replenish the cash balance.

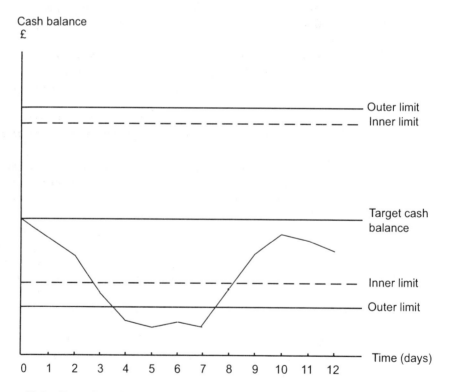

Figure 10.6 Controlling the cash balance

The model relies heavily on management judgement to determine where the control limits are set and the time period within which breaches of the control limits are acceptable. Past experience may be useful in helping managers decide on these issues. There are other models, however, which do not rely on management judgement and, instead, use quantitative techniques to determine an optimal cash policy. One model proposed, for example, is the cash equivalent to the EOQ model discussed earlier.

Cash flow statements and the management of cash

In order to manage cash effectively it is useful for a business to prepare a cash flow statement. This is a very important tool for both planning and control purposes. Projected cash flow statements were considered in Chapter 2 and it is not necessary, therefore, to consider them again in detail. However, it is worth repeating the point that these statements enable the managers of a business to see the expected outcome of planned events on the cash balance. The projected cash flow statements will identify periods when there are expected to be cash surpluses and cash deficits.

When a cash surplus is expected to arise, managers must decide on the best use of the surplus funds. When a cash deficit is expected to arise, managers must make adequate provision by borrowing, liquidating assets or rescheduling cash payments/receipts to deal with this. Planning borrowing requirements beforehand can allow the business to use a cheap source of finance. This may not be possible at the time a deficit arises and decisions have to be made quickly. Cash flow statements are also useful in helping to control the cash held. The actual cash flows can be compared to the projected cash flows for the period. If there is a significant divergence between the projected cash flows and the actual cash flows, explanations must be sought and corrective action taken where necessary.

To refresh your memory, an example of a cash flow statement is given below. Remember there is no set format for this statement. Managers can determine how best the information should be presented. However, the format set out below appears to be in widespread use. Cash flow statements covering the short term are usually broken down into monthly periods (and, in some cases, weekly periods) in order to allow a close monitoring of cash movements. Cash inflows are usually shown above cash outflows and the difference between them (i.e. the net cash flow) for a month is separately identified along with the closing cash balance.

Although cash flow statements are prepared primarily for internal management purposes they are sometimes required by prospective lenders when a loan to a business is being considered.

Example 10.2

Cash flow statement for the six months to 30 November 19X9

	June £	July £	August £	September £	October £	November £
Cash inflows						
Credit sales	–	–	4,000	5,500	7,000	8,500
Cash sales	4,000	5,500	7,000	8,500	11,000	11,000
	4,000	5,500	11,000	14,000	18,000	19,500
Cash outflows						
Motor vehicles	6,000					
Equipment	10,000					7,000
Freehold premises	40,000					
Purchases	–	29,000	9,250	11,500	13,750	17,500
Wages/salaries	900	900	900	900	900	900
Commission	–	320	440	560	680	680
Overheads	500	500	500	500	650	650
	57,400	30,720	11,090	13,460	15,980	26,730
Net cash flow	(53,400)	(25,220)	(90)	540	2,020	(7,230)
Opening balance	60,000	6,600	(18,620)	(18,710)	(18,170)	(16,150)
Closing balance	6,600	(18,620)	(18,710)	(18,170)	(16,150)	(23,380)

Operating cash cycle

When managing cash, it is important to be aware of the operating cash cycle of the business. This may be defined as the time period between the outlay of cash necessary for the purchase of stocks and the ultimate receipt of cash from the sale of the goods. In the case of a business which purchases goods on credit for subsequent resale on credit, the operating cash cycle can be shown in diagrammatic form, as in Figure 10.7. This diagram shows that payment for goods acquired on credit occurs some time after the goods have been purchased and, therefore, no immediate cash outflow arises from the purchase. Similarly, cash receipts from debtors will occur some time after the sale is made and so there will be no immediate cash inflow as a result of the sale. The operating cash cycle is the time period between the payment made to the creditor for goods supplied, and the cash received from the debtor.

The operating cash cycle is important because it has a significant influence on the financing requirements of the business. The longer the cash cycle, the greater the financing requirements of the business and the greater the financial risks. For this reason, a business is likely to want to reduce the operating cash cycle to a minimum if possible.

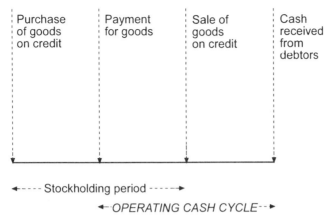

Figure 10.7 Operating cash cycle

For the type of business mentioned above, the operating cash cycle can be calculated from the financial statements by the use of certain ratios. The cash cycle is calculated as follows:

Average stockholding period

+

Average settlement period for debtors

−

Average payment period for creditors

=

Operating cash cycle

ACTIVITY 10.9

The accounts of Freezeqwik Ltd, a distributor of frozen foods, is set out below for the year ended 31 December 19X3:

Profit and loss account for the year ended 31 December 19X3

	£000	£000
Sales		820
Less: Cost of sales		
Opening stock	142	
Purchases	568	
	710	
Less: closing stock	166	544
Gross profit		276
Administration expenses	120	
Selling and distribution expenses	95	
Financial expenses	32	247

	£000	£000
Net profit		29
Corporation tax		7
Retained profit for the year		22

Balance sheet as at 31 December 19X3

	£000	£000	£000
Fixed assets at written down value			
Freehold premises			180
Fixtures and fittings			82
Motor vans			102
			364
Current assets			
Stock		166	
Trade debtors		264	
Cash		24	
		454	
Less: **Creditors: amounts due within one year**			
Trade creditors	159		
Corporation tax	7	166	288
			652
Capital and reserves			
Ordinary share capital			300
Preference share capital			200
Retained profit			152
			652

All purchases and sales are on credit.

Required:

(a) Calculate the operating cash cycle for the company.
(b) Suggest how the company may seek to reduce the cash cycle.

The operating cash cycle may be calculated as follows:

	No. of days
Average stockholding period	
$\dfrac{(Opening\ stock\ +\ closing\ stock)/2}{Cost\ of\ sales} = \dfrac{(142 + 166)/2}{544} \times 365$	103

	No. of days
Plus: Average settlement period for debtors	

$$\frac{Trade\ debtors}{Credit\ sales} \times 365 = \frac{264}{820} \times 365$$

<u>118</u>

221

Less: Average settlement period for creditors

$$\frac{Trade\ creditors}{Credit\ purchases} \times 365 = \frac{159}{568} \times 365$$

<u>(102)</u>

Operating cash cycle

<u><u>119</u></u>

The company can reduce the operating cash cycle in a number of ways. The average stockholding period seems quite long. At present, average stocks held represent more than three months' sales. This may be reduced by reducing the level of stocks held. Similarly, the average settlement period for debtors seems long at nearly four months' sales. This may be reduced by imposing tighter credit control, offering discounts, charging interest on overdue accounts, and so forth. However, any policy decisions concerning stocks and debtors must take account of current trading conditions.

The operating cash cycle could also be reduced by extending the period of credit taken to pay suppliers. However, for reasons mentioned below, this option must be given careful consideration.

Cash transmission

A business will normally wish to receive the benefits from providing goods or services at the earliest opportunity. The benefit received is immediate where payment is made in cash. However, when payment is made by cheque there is normally a delay of 3–4 working days before the cheque can be cleared through the banking system. The business must therefore wait for this period before it can benefit from the amount paid in. In the case of a business which receives large amounts in the form of cheques, the opportunity cost of this delay can be very significant.

In order to avoid this delay, a business could require payments to be made in cash. However, this is not usually very practical for a number of reasons. Another option is to ask for payment to be made by standing order or by direct debit from the customer's bank account. This will ensure that the amount owing is transferred from the bank account of the customer to the bank account of the business on the day which has been agreed.

It is also possible now for funds to be directly transferred to a business bank account. As a result of developments in computer technology, a customer can pay for items by using a card (rather like a cheque card) which results in his/her account being instantly debited and the business bank account being instantly credited with the required amount. This method of payment is being increasingly used by large retail businesses and may well extend to other forms of business.

The management of trade creditors

Trade credit is regarded as an important source of finance by many businesses. It has been described as a 'spontaneous' source of finance as it tends to increase in line with the increase in the level of sales achieved by a business. Trade credit is widely regarded as a 'free' source of finance and therefore a good thing for a business to have. However, there may be real costs associated with taking trade credit.

Customers who pay on credit may not be as well favoured as those who pay immediately. For example, when goods are in short supply credit customers may receive lower priority when allocating the stock available. In addition, credit customers may be given lower priority in terms of delivery dates or the provision of technical support services. Sometimes, the goods or services provided may be more costly if credit is required. However, in most industries trade credit is the norm and, as a result, the above costs will not apply unless, perhaps, the credit facilities are abused by the customer. A business purchasing supplies on credit may also have to incur additional administration and accounting costs in order to deal with the scrutiny and payment of invoices, the maintaining and updating of creditors' accounts, and so on.

Where a supplier offers discount for prompt payment, a business should give careful consideration to the possibility of paying within the discount period. Example 10.3 illustrates the cost of forgoing possible discounts.

Example 10.3

Sinbad Ltd takes 70 days to pay for goods supplied by its supplier. In order to encourage prompt payment the supplier has offered the company a 2 per cent discount if payment for goods is made within 30 days.

Sinbad Ltd is not sure whether it is worth taking the discount offered. What is the annual percentage cost to Sinbad Ltd of forgoing the discount?

If the discount is taken, payment could be made on the last day of the discount period (i.e. the 30th day). However, if the discount is not taken, payment will be made after 70 days. This means that by not taking the discount Sinbad Ltd will receive an extra 40 days (i.e. 70–30) credit. The cost of this extra credit to the company will be the 2 per cent discount forgone. If we annualise the cost of this discount forgone we have:

$365/40 \times 2\% = 18.3\%*$

We can see, therefore, that the annual cost of forgoing the discount is quite high and it may be profitable for Sinbad Ltd to pay the supplier within the discount period even if it means that the company will have to borrow in order to do so.

The above points are not meant to imply that taking credit is a burden to a business. There are, of course, real benefits which can accrue. Provided that trade credit is not abused by a business, it can represent a form of interest-free loan. It can be a much more convenient method of paying for goods and services than paying by cash and, during a period of inflation, there will be an economic gain by paying later rather than sooner for goods and services purchased. For many businesses, these benefits will exceed the costs involved.

Controlling trade creditors

In order to monitor the level of trade credit taken, management can calculate the average settlement period for creditors which, as we have already seen, is calculated as follows:

$$\text{Average settlement period} = \frac{\text{Trade creditors}}{\text{Credit purchases}} \times 365$$

Once again, this provides an average figure which can be distorted. A more informative approach would be to produce an ageing schedule for creditors. This would look much the same as the ageing schedule for debtors described earlier.

Summary

In this chapter we have identified and examined the main elements of working capital. We have seen that the management of working capital requires an evaluation of both the costs and benefits associated with each element. Some of these costs and benefits may be hard to quantify in practice. Nevertheless, some assessment must be made in order to try and optimise the use of funds within a business. We have examined various techniques for the management of working capital. These techniques vary in their level of sophistication; some rely heavily on management judgement whilst others adopt a more objective, quantitative approach.

---

*This is an approximate annual rate. For the more mathematically minded, the precise rate is: $((1 + 2/98)^{9.125} - 1) \times 100\% = 20.2\%$.

Review questions

10.1   Tariq is the credit manager of Heltex plc. He is concerned that the pattern of monthly sales receipts show that credit collection is poor compared to budget. The sales director believes that Tariq is to blame for this situation but Tariq insists that he is not. Why might Tariq not be to blame for the deterioration in the credit collection period?

10.2   How might each of the following affect the level of stocks held by a business?

- An increase in the number of production bottlenecks experienced by the business.
- A rise in the level of interest rates.
- A decision to offer customers a narrower range of products in the future.
- A switch of suppliers from an overseas business to a local business.
- A deterioration in the quality and reliability of bought-in components.

10.3   What are the reasons for holding stocks? Are these reasons different from the reasons for holding cash?

10.4   Identify the costs of holding:
(a) too little cash; and
(b) too much cash.

Examination-style questions

Solutions to those questions marked with an asterisk are given at the end of the text. Questions 10.1–10.3 are at basic level. Questions 10.4–10.6 are at intermediate/advanced level.

10.1*   Hercules Wholesalers Ltd has been particularly concerned with its liquidity position in recent months. The most recent profit and loss account and balance sheet of the company are as follows:

Profit and loss account for the year ended 31 May 19X2

	£	£
Sales		452,000
Less: **Cost of sales**		
Opening stock	125,000	
Add purchases	341,000	
	466,000	
Less: Closing stock	143,000	323,000
Gross profit		129,000
Expenses		132,000
Net loss for the period		(3,000)

Balance sheet as at 31 May 19X2

	£	£	£
Fixed assets			
Freehold premises at valuation			280,000
Fixtures and fittings at cost *less* depreciation			25,000
Motor vehicles at cost *less* depreciation			52,000
			357,000
Current assets			
Stock		143,000	
Debtors		163,000	
		306,000	
Less: **Creditors due within one year**			
Trade creditors	145,000		
Bank overdraft	140,000	285,000	21,000
			378,000
Less: **Creditors due beyond one year**			
Loans			120,000
			258,000
Capital and reserves			
Ordinary share capital			100,000
Retained profit			158,000
			258,000

The debtors and creditors were maintained at a constant level throughout the year.

Required:

(a) Explain why Hercules Wholesalers Ltd is concerned about its liquidity position.

(b) Explain the term 'operating cash cycle' and state why this concept is important in the financial management of a business.

(c) Calculate the operating cash cycle for Hercules Wholesalers Ltd based on the information above. (Assume a 360-day year.)

(d) State what steps may be taken to improve the operating cash cycle of the company.

10.2 International Electric plc at present offers its customers 30 days' credit. Half the customers, by value, pay on time. The other half take an average of 70 days to pay. It is considering offering a cash discount of 2 per cent to its customers for payment within 30 days.

It anticipates that half of the customers who now take an average of 70 days to pay, will pay in 30 days. The other half will still take an average of 70 days to pay.

The scheme will also reduce bad debts by £300,000 per year.

Annual sales of £365 million are made evenly throughout the year. At present the company has a large overdraft (£60m.) with its bank at 12 per cent per annum.

Required:

(a) Calculate the approximate equivalent annual percentage cost of a discount of 2 per cent which reduces the time taken by debtors to pay from 70 days to 30 days. (This part can be answered without reference to the narrative above.)
(b) Calculate debtors outstanding under both the old and new schemes.
(c) How much will the scheme cost the company in discounts?
(d) Should the company go ahead with the scheme? State what other factors, if any, should be taken into account.
(e) Outline the controls and procedures a company should adopt to manage the level of its debtors.

10.3   The managing director of Sparkrite Ltd, a trading company, has just received summary sets of accounts for 19X2 and 19X3.

Profit and loss statements for years ended 30 September

	19X2		19X3	
	£000	£000	£000	£000
Sales		1,800		1,920
Less: **Cost of sales**				
Opening stock	160		200	
Purchases	1,120		1,175	
	1,280		1,375	
Less: Closing stocks	200		250	
		1,080		1,125
Gross profit		720		795
Less: Expenses		680		750
Net profit		£40		£45

Balance sheets as at 30 September

	19X2		19X3	
	£000	£000	£000	£000
Fixed assets		950		930
Current assets				
Stock	200		250	
Debtors	375		480	
Bank	4		2	
	579		732	

	19X2		19X3	
	£000	£000	£000	£000
Less: Current liabilities	195		225	
		384		507
		1,334		1,437
Financed by:				
Fully paid £1 Ordinary shares		825		883
Reserves		509		554
		1,334		1,437

The financial director has expressed concern at the deterioration in stock and debtors levels.

Required:

(a) Show by using the data given how you would calculate ratios which could be used to measure stock and debtor levels in 19X2 and 19X3.
(b) Discuss the ways in which the management of Sparkrite Ltd could exercise control over:
  (i) stock levels; and
  (ii) debtor levels.

10.4   Your superior, the general manager of Plastics Manufacturers Limited, has recently been talking to the chief buyer of Plastic Toys Limited, which manufactures a wide range of toys for young children. At present, it is considering changing its supplier of plastic granules and has offered to buy its entire requirement of 2,000 kilos per month from you at the going market rate, providing that you will grant it 3 months' credit on its purchases. The following information is available:

1.   Plastic granules sell for £10 per kilo, variable costs are £7 per kilo and fixed costs £2 per kilo.
2.   Your own company is financially strong and has sales of £15 million per year. For the foreseeable future it will have surplus capacity and it is actively looking for new outlets.

Extracts from Plastic Toys accounts are as follows:

	19X3	19X4	19X5
	£000	£000	£000
Sales	800	980	640
Profit before interest and tax	100	110	(150)
Capital employed	600	650	575

	19X3	19X4	19X5
	£000	£000	£000
Current assets			
Stocks	200	220	320
Debtors	140	160	160
	340	380	480
Current liabilities			
Creditors	180	190	220
Overdraft	100	150	310
	280	340	530
Net current assets	60	40	(50)

Required:

(a) Write some short notes suggesting sources of information you would use in order to assess the creditworthiness of potential customers who are unknown to you. You should critically evaluate each source of information.

(b) Describe the accounting controls you would use to monitor the level of your company's trade debtors.

(c) Advise your general manager on the acceptability of the proposal. You should give your reasons and do any calculations you consider necessary.

10.5   Dylan Ltd operates an advertising agency. It has an annual turnover of £20m. before taking into account bad debts of £0.1m. All sales are on credit and, on average, the settlement period for trade debtors is 60 days. The company is currently reviewing its credit policies. To encourage prompt payment, the credit control department has proposed that customers should be given a 2.5 per cent discount if they pay within 30 days. For those who do not pay within this period, a maximum of 50 days' credit should be given. The credit department believes that 60 per cent of customers will take advantage of the discount by paying at the end of the discount period and the remainder will pay at the end of 50 days. The credit department believes that bad debts can be effectively eliminated by adopting the above policies and by employing stricter credit investigation procedures which will cost an additional £20,000 per annum. The credit department are confident that these new policies will not result in any reduction in sales. The business has a £6m. overdraft on which it pays annual interest of 14 per cent.

Required:

Calculate the net annual cost (savings) to the company of abandoning its existing credit policies and adopting the proposals of the credit control department. (Hint: In order to answer this question you must weigh the costs of administration and cash discounts against the savings in bad debts and interest charges.)

10.6* Boswell Enterprises Ltd is reviewing its trade credit policy. The company, which sells all of its goods on credit, has estimated that sales for the forthcoming year will be £3m. under the existing policy. Thirty per cent of trade debtors are expected to pay 1 month after being invoiced and 70 per cent of trade debtors are expected to pay 2 months after being invoiced. The above estimates are in line with previous years' figures.

At present, no cash discounts are offered to customers. However, to encourage prompt payment the company is considering giving a 2.5 per cent cash discount to debtors who pay in 1 month or less. Given this incentive, the company expects 60 per cent of trade debtors to pay 1 month after being invoiced and 40 per cent of debtors to pay 2 months after being invoiced. The company believes that the introduction of a cash discount policy will prove attractive to some customers and will lead to a 5 per cent increase in total sales.

Irrespective of the trade credit policy adopted, the gross profit margin of the company will be 20 per cent for the forthcoming year and 3 months' stock will be held. Fixed monthly expenses of £15,000 and variable expenses (excluding discounts) equivalent to 10 per cent of sales, will be incurred and will be paid 1 month in arrears. Trade creditors will be paid in arrears and will be equal to 2 months' cost of sales. The company will hold a fixed cash balance of £140,000 throughout the year, whichever trade credit policy is adopted. No dividends will be proposed or paid during the year. Ignore taxation.

Required:

(a) Calculate the investment in working capital at the end of the forthcoming year under:
  (i) The existing policy.
  (ii) The proposed policy.
(b) Calculate the expected net profit for the forthcoming year under:
  (i) The existing policy.
  (ii) The proposed policy.
(c) Advise the company as to whether it should implement the proposed policy.

(Hint: The investment in working capital will be made up of stock and debtors and cash *less* trade creditors and any unpaid expenses at the year end.)

—

CHAPTER ELEVEN

Mergers, Takeovers and the Valuation of Shares

─────────────── OBJECTIVES ───────────────

On completion of this chapter you should be able to:

- Identify and discuss the main reasons for mergers and takeovers.

- Discuss the advantages and disadvantages of each of the main forms of purchase consideration used in a takeover.

- Identify those who are likely to benefit from takeover activity and discuss which companies are vulnerable to takeover.

- Outline the tactics which may be used to defend against a hostile bid.

- Identify and discuss the main methods of valuing the shares of a company.

Introduction

In this chapter, we consider various aspects of mergers and takeovers. We examine the reasons for mergers and takeovers and consider the ways in which they can be financed. We look at the evidence concerning who the winners and losers might be in a takeover and whether it is possible to identify companies which are vulnerable to takeover. Finally, we consider the ways in which we can value the shares of a company. The valuation of shares is relevant to a range of financial decisions, including mergers and takeovers.

Mergers and takeovers

When two (or possibly more) businesses combine, it can take the form of either a merger or a takeover. The term 'merger' is normally used to describe a situation where there are two companies of roughly equal size and there is agreement between the two management and shareholder groups on the desirability of combining them. A merger is usually effected by creating an entirely new company from the assets of the two existing companies, with both shareholder groups receiving an ownership stake in the new company.

The term 'takeover' is normally used to describe a situation where a larger company acquires control of a smaller company, which is then absorbed by the larger company. When a takeover occurs, the shareholders of the target company may cease to have any financial interest in the business and the resources of the business may come under entirely new ownership. (The particular form of consideration used to acquire the shares in the target company will determine whether or not the shareholders continue to have a financial interest in the business.) Although the vast majority of takeovers are not contested, there are occasions when the management of the target company will fight to retain its separate identity.

In practice, however, many business combinations do not fit into these neat categories and it may be difficult to decide whether a merger or a takeover has occurred. The distinction between the two forms of combination is only really important in the context of financial reporting, as different forms of accounting exist for each type of combination. It is beyond the scope of this book to describe the merger and acquisition methods of accounting and readers who wish to pursue this topic should consult a book on financial accounting. However, it is worth noting that the merger method of accounting can often provide a much better picture of financial health than the acquisition method of accounting for the combined business. In the past, there has been some misuse of merger accounting methods, and so now, strict conditions must be met before a business combination can adopt the merger accounting method. In this chapter, no real distinction will be made between the terms 'merger' and 'takeover' and we will use the terms interchangeably.

Mergers and takeovers can be classified according to the relationship between the businesses being merged. A *horizontal merger* occurs when two businesses in the same industry, and at the same point in the production/distribution process, decide to combine. A *vertical merger* occurs when two businesses in the same industry, but at different points in the same production/distribution process, decide to combine. A *conglomerate merger* occurs when two businesses in unrelated industries decide to combine.

ACTIVITY 11.1

Can you think of an example of each type of merger?

An example of a horizontal merger would be where a tyre retailer merged with another tyre retailer to form a larger retail business. An example of a vertical merger would be where a tyre retailer merged with a manufacturer of tyres. This would mean the combined business operated at different points in the production/distribution chain. An example of a conglomerate merger would be where a tyre retailer merged with an ice cream manufacturer.

The evidence on mergers and acquisitions shows that they tend to come in 'waves'. In the United Kingdom, we have seen waves of mergers in the early 1970s, in the late 1980s and in the mid-1990s. The reasons for these waves are not clear and various explanations have been put forward. Economic factors such as the ability of businesses to generate cash in order to finance merger activity, the cost and availability of finance, and low stock market values leading to 'cheap' companies being available, have all been cited as important influences on the level of merger activity. However, there have also been more exotic explanations. It has been suggested, for example, that mergers and takeover activity may be a behavioural phenomenon (rather like bees swarming) which affects managers. It seems, however, that we should await further research evidence for a clearer picture to emerge.

Reasons for mergers and takeovers

In economic terms, a merger will only be worthwhile if combining the two businesses will lead to gains which would not arise if the two businesses stayed apart. The value of a business can be defined in terms of the *present value of its future cash flows*. Thus, if a merger is to make economic sense, the present value of the combined business should be equal to:

The present value of the bidding business

plus

The present value of the target business

plus

A gain (e.g. increased income/reduced expenses) from combining

There are various ways in which a gain may be achieved through a merger or takeover, the more important of which are now described:

Benefits of scale

A merger or takeover will result in a larger business being created which may enable certain benefits of scale to be achieved. For example, a larger business may be able to negotiate lower prices with suppliers in exchange for larger orders. A merger or takeover may also provide the potential for savings, as some operating costs may be duplicated (e.g. administrative costs, marketing costs, research and development costs, and so on). These types of benefits are more likely to be gained from horizontal and vertical mergers than from conglomerate mergers; it is more difficult to achieve economies where the businesses are unrelated. The benefits described, however, must be weighed against the increased costs of organising and controlling a larger business.

ACTIVITY 11.2

Is it necessary for a business to merge with, or take over, another business in order to reap the benefits of combination? Can these benefits be obtained by other means?

A business may be able to obtain lower prices from suppliers, reduced research and development costs, and so forth, by joining a consortium of companies or by entering into joint ventures with other companies. In the United Kingdom, Powergen and Conoco (UK) have formed a joint venture to take advantage of the liberalisation of the domestic gas market. This form of co-operation can result in benefits of scale and yet avoid the costs of a merger. (However, there will be costs in negotiating a detailed joint venture agreement.)

Eliminating competition

A business may combine with, or take over another business in order to eliminate competition and to increase the market share of its goods. This, in turn, can lead to increased profits.

ACTIVITY 11.3

What kind of merger will achieve this objective? What are the potential problems of this kind of merger from the consumer's point of view?

A horizontal merger will normally be required to increase market share. The potential problems of such mergers are that consumers will have less choice following the merger and that the market power of the merged business will lead to an increase in consumer prices. For these reasons, government often seek to ensure the interests of the consumer are protected when mergers resulting in a significant market share are proposed.

Underutilised resources

A company may have a poor management team which fails to exploit the full potential of the business. In this situation, there is an opportunity for a stronger management team to be installed which would exploit more fully the resources of the business. This argument is linked to what is sometimes referred to as the 'market for corporate control'. The term is used to describe the idea that mergers and takeovers are motivated by teams of managers who compete for the right to control business resources. The 'market for corporate control' ensures that weak management teams will not survive and that, sooner or later, they will be succeeded by stronger management teams. The threat of takeover, however, may motivate managers to improve their performance. This suggests, of course, that mergers and takeovers are good for the economy as they help ensure that resources are fully utilised and that shareholder wealth maximisation remains the top priority for managers.

Complementary resources

Two businesses may have complementary resources which, when combined, will allow profits to be made which are higher than if the businesses operate as single entities. One argument put forward for the merger between Lloyds Bank and the TSB Group in 1995 was that it enabled the expertise of Lloyds Bank, in areas such as the small business sector, to be available across a wider geographical spread. Before the merger, Lloyds Bank had relatively few branches in the north of England and Scotland whereas the TSB was well represented in these areas. Thus, in the merged business, TSB provides the distribution network in the north and Lloyds provides the expertise.

By combining the two businesses, the relative strengths of each business will be brought together and this may lead to additional profits being generated. It may be possible, of course, for each business to overcome its particular deficiency and continue as a separate entity. Even so, it may still make sense to combine.

ACTIVITY 11.4

Why might there still be an argument in favour of a merger?

Combining the resources of each business may lead to a quicker exploitation of the strengths of each company than if the businesses remained separate and overcame the deficiencies mentioned.

Surplus funds

A business may operate within an industry offering few investment opportunities. In such a situation, the management may find that it has surplus cash which is not earning a reasonable return. The solution to this problem may be to invest in a new industry where there is no shortage of profitable investment opportunities. By acquiring an existing business within the new industry, the necessary specialist managerial and technical 'know how' will be quickly acquired.

ACTIVITY 11.5

Could management deal with the problem of surplus funds in some other way? Why might this other way not be acceptable to shareholders and managers?

The surplus funds could be distributed to shareholders through a special dividend or a share-repurchase arrangement. However, shareholders may not like this idea because there may be a tax liability arising from the distribution. Managers may also not like this idea as it will result in reduced resources for them to manage. (In addition, lenders may not like the idea of funds being returned to shareholders as this is likely to increase their exposure to risk.)

The reasons for mergers and takeovers considered above are all in line with the economic principle expressed at the beginning of the section: that is, there should be a gain arising from combining which would not arise if the two businesses stayed apart. However, mergers and takeovers may be motivated by reasons which are difficult to justify in economic terms. The following reasons for combining fall within this category.

Diversification

A business may decide to invest in a business operating in a different industry in order to reduce the level of risk associated with the company. You may recall that in Chapter 6, we discussed the benefits of diversification in dealing with the problem of risk. At first sight, such a policy may seem appealing. However, we must ask ourselves whether or not diversification by *management* will provide any benefits to shareholders which *the shareholders themselves* cannot provide more cheaply? It may be argued that it is easier and cheaper for a shareholder to deal with the problem of risk by holding a diversified portfolio of shares, than for the company to acquire a new business. It is quite likely that the latter approach will be expensive, as a premium may have to be paid to acquire the shares and external investment advisers and consultants may have to be employed.

ACTIVITY 11.6

Who do you think might benefit from diversification?

Diversification may well benefit the managers of the predator company. Managers cannot diversify their investment of time and effort in the business easily. By managing a more diversified business, the risks of unemployment and lost income for managers are reduced.

There is research evidence to suggest that senior managers view diversification as an important motivation for undertaking conglomerate mergers.

Management interests and goals

Linked to the above point, is the argument that some mergers may be undertaken to fulfil the personal goals or interests of managers. Thus managers may acquire another business simply to reduce the risks which they face. Managers may also acquire another business to increase the amount of resources which they control. The size of the business will often influence the status, income and power which managers enjoy. (The personal goals and interests of managers may also explain why some proposed takeovers are fiercely contested by them.)

EXHIBIT 11.1

We should bear in mind that mergers and acquisitions can be very exciting and that managers often enjoy 'the thrill of the chase'. The 1981 annual report of Berkshire Hathaway, a US company, stated: '*Leaders, business or otherwise, seldom are deficient in animal spirits and often relish increased activity and challenge. At Berkshire, the corporate pulse never beats faster than when an acquisition is in prospect.*'

Although the support of shareholders will often be necessary for managers to acquire a new business, the shareholders are likely to rely heavily on information which is supplied to them by their managers when making a decision. If the managers are determined to pursue their own goals, the shareholders are unlikely to receive all the information they require.

Agency theory, which we discussed in Chapter 1, recognises that agents (such as managers who are employed to act on behalf of shareholders) will operate in a way which is designed to maximise their own interests. As a result, a conflict of interest can arise between the agents (managers) and the principals (share-holders). One way to avoid, or minimise, such conflict is to align the interests of managers with the interests of shareholders by linking a significant part of the managers' rewards to the market value of the shares of the company. By doing this, managers who seek to maximise their own welfare will also be acting in the interests of the shareholders.

Forms of purchase consideration

When a company wishes to purchase the shares of another company, it can offer to make payment in different ways.

ACTIVITY 11.7

Can you think what these different methods of payment might be?

The most important methods of payment are:

1. *cash;*
2. *shares in the bidding company; and*
3. *loan capital in the bidding company.*

Some combination of these methods may, of course, also be used. Next we consider the advantages and disadvantages of each form of payment from the point of view of both the bidding company's shareholders and the target company's shareholders.

Cash

Payment by cash means that the amount of the purchase consideration will be both certain and clearly understood by the target company's shareholders. This may improve the chances of a successful bid. It will also mean that shareholder control of the bidding company will not be diluted as no additional shares will be issued.

Raising the necessary cash, however, can create problems for the bidding company, particularly when the target company is large in relation to the bidding company. It may only be possible to raise the amount required by a loan or share issue or by selling off assets, which the bidding company's shareholders may not like. On occasions, it may be possible to spread the cash payments over a period. However, deferred payments are likely to weaken the attraction of the bid to the target company's shareholders.

The receipt of cash will allow the target company's shareholders to adjust their share portfolios without incurring transaction costs on disposal. However, transaction costs will be incurred when new shares or loan capital are acquired to replace the shares sold. Moreover, the receipt of cash may result in a liability to capital gains tax (which arises on the disposal of certain assets, including shares).

Shares

The issue of shares in the bidding company as purchase consideration will avoid any strain on the cash position of the company. However, some dilution of existing shareholder control will occur and there may also be a risk of dilution in earnings per share. (Dilution will occur if the additional earnings from the merger divided by the number of new shares issued is lower than the existing earnings per share.) The directors must ensure that the authorised share capital of the company is sufficient to make a new issue and, more importantly, that the market value of the company's shares does not fall during the course of the takeover. A substantial fall in share price will reduce the value of the bid and could undermine the chances of acceptance.

The cost of this form of financing must also be taken into account. We saw in Chapter 8 that the cost of servicing share capital is relatively expensive.

The target company's shareholders may find a share-for-share exchange attractive. As they currently hold equity shares, they may wish to continue with this form of investment rather than receive cash or other forms of security. A share-for-share exchange does not result in a liability for capital gains tax. (For capital gains tax purposes, no disposal is deemed to have occurred when this type of transaction takes place.) The target shareholders will also have a continuing ownership link with the original business, although it will now be part of a larger business. However, the value of the offer may be difficult to evaluate due to movements in the share prices of the two companies.

Loan capital

Like the issue of shares, this is simply an exchange of paper which avoids any strain on the cash resources of the bidding company. It has, however, certain advantages over shares insofar as the issue of loan capital involves no dilution of shareholder control and the service costs will be lower. A disadvantage of a loan capital-for-share exchange is that it will increase the gearing of the bidding company and, therefore, the level of financial risk. The directors of the bidding company must ensure that the issue of loan capital is within the borrowing limits of the company.

Loan capital may be acceptable to shareholders in the target company if they have doubts over the future performance of the combined business. Loan capital provides investors with both a fixed level of return and security for their investment. When a takeover bid is being made, convertible loan capital may be offered as purchase consideration. National Power plc, for example, offered the shareholders of Southern Electricity a choice of either cash or convertible loan stock when making a takeover bid.

ACTIVITY 11.8

What is the attraction of this form of loan capital from the point of view of the target company's shareholders?

The issue of convertible loan capital would give target company shareholders a useful hedge against uncertainty. This type of loan capital will provide relative security in the early years with an option to convert to ordinary shares at a later date. Investors will, of course, only exercise this option if things go well for the combined business.

Assessing vulnerability to takeover

When a company is taken over, all those connected with the business are likely to be affected. Shareholders, managers, employees, suppliers and others all have a stake in the business and may stand to gain or lose by a change in ownership. Predicting the likelihood of takeover should, therefore, be of interest to these various 'stakeholder' groups. In Chapter 3, we saw how financial ratios can be used to predict financial distress. Financial ratios can also be used to predict the likelihood of a takeover. In recent years, various studies have been carried out to identify the particular characteristics which make companies vulnerable to takeover and to predict the prospects of such an event. These studies have used both univariate analysis and multivariate analysis.

In the United States, a study by Palepu compared the financial characteristics of 163 businesses acquired during the period 1971–79 and a group of 256 businesses that were not acquired during the same period.[1] The study found that the acquired businesses exhibited the following characteristics:

- A lower average share return over the four years prior to takeover.
- A higher 'growth–resource mismatch'.

The second characteristic mentioned requires some explanation. It means that a business with either high growth and low resources or low growth and high resources are more likely to be taken over as they will represent 'good deals'. Average sales growth, average liquidity and average gearing were used to determine whether a growth–resource mismatch had arisen. Thus, where a business has either:

- low average sales growth/high average liquidity/low average gearing, or
- high average sales growth/low average liquidity/high average gearing,

a growth–resource mismatch will arise.

The study by Palepu also found that target companies were generally smaller than those which were not acquired and that they tended not to be in an industry where acquisitions occurred in the previous year.

In the United Kingdom, Barnes developed a multivariate model to predict vulnerability to takeover.[2] The study matched 92 businesses that were taken over during the period 1986–87 with 92 businesses that were not taken over and which were of similar size and industry type. The actual ratios in relation to the industry average were used as measures of vulnerability in the study. The study found that the following five ratios could be used to classify companies as either acquired or not acquired with a level of accuracy of slightly more than 68 per cent:

- acid-test ratio;
- current ratio;
- return on equity;
- net profit margin before tax; and
- net profit margin after tax.

It is interesting to note that the five key ratios include two liquidity ratios and two profit/sales ratios. The weights given to each ratio are not available as this is a proprietory model.

Again in the United Kingdom, Parkinson found that those companies which successfully fended off hostile bids during the 1975–84 period differed from unsuccessful companies by having:

- lower profitability (i.e. lower return to equity, ROCE and profit margin);
- higher liquidity; and
- higher dividend payout.[3]

Although the findings of these studies are interesting, more research needs to be carried out before a clear picture can emerge concerning vulnerability to takeover.

Who wins?

At the time of a takeover, various economic benefits may be claimed in support of two businesses combining. However, it is worth asking whether or not there are benefits to be gained from this form of activity and, if so, which groups are most likely to benefit? Various studies both in the United Kingdom and the United States have shown that value overall is derived but reveal that shareholders in the target company are usually the main beneficiaries. They are likely to receive substantial benefits from a takeover through a premium on the share price. Rose has summed up the position as follows:

> [T]he bidder usually has to pay a premium over the pre-bid price of up to 100 per cent of the latter, with a mean of about 25 per cent in the UK and some 15 per cent in the US. In some cases the premium may appear to be small but this

may merely reflect the fact that the 'pre-bid' price had already incorporated the possibility of a forthcoming bid. Bid premia tend to be higher in the case of contested bids, depending very much on whether another bidder is thought to be in the wings.[4]

ACTIVITY 11.9

Why might a bidding company be prepared to pay a premium above the market value for the shares of a business?

Various reasons have been put forward to explain this phenomenon. They include the following:

- *The managers of the bidding business have access to information which is not available to the market and which is not, therefore, reflected in the share price.*
- *The managers of the bidding business may simply misjudge the value of the target business.*
- *The managers may feel that there will be significant gains arising from combining the two businesses which are worth paying for. In theory, the maximum price a buyer will be prepared to pay will be equivalent to the present value of the company plus any gains from the merger.*
- *'Management hubris.' Where there is more than one bidder or where the takeover is being resisted, the managers of a bidding business may fail to act rationally and may raise the bid price above an economically justifiable level. This may be done in order to salvage management pride as they may feel humiliated by defeat.*

Share prices in the target company will usually reflect the bid premium for as long as the bid is in progress. However, where a takeover bid is unsuccessful and the bid withdrawn, the share price of the target company will usually return to its pre-offer level.

The evidence concerning the position of bidding company shareholders is rather more mixed. Some studies have shown either a small increase or no increase in the wealth of these shareholders, whilst other studies have suggested that the gains made by the target company's shareholders are achieved at the expense of the bidding company's shareholders. Thus a takeover may simply result in a transfer of wealth from one group of shareholders to another. This is not to say, of course, that a takeover is never of benefit to a bidding company's shareholders. However, it does suggest that this particular group should examine carefully the claims made concerning the benefits of a takeover.

ACTIVITY 11.10

Why might the bidding company's shareholders receive little or no benefit from a takeover? Can you think of two reasons why this may be so?

> *One reason may be that the bidding company pays too much to acquire the target company. We saw earlier that large premiums are often paid to acquire another company. Another reason may be that, following a successful bid, it is difficult to integrate the target company's business. As a result, the expected benefits are not realised. There may be various problems relating to organisational structure, key personnel, management style, management rivalries, and so on, which work against successful integration. A further reason may be that after the takeover, the managers may relax and expect the combined business to operate smoothly. If the takeover has been bitterly contested, the temptation for management to ease back after the struggle may be very strong.*

When discussing who will be winners and losers in a merger or takeover, the senior managers of the bidding company and the target company should also be considered. Both groups of managers are important stakeholders in their respective companies and both groups have an important role to play in takeover negotiations.

ACTIVITY 11.11

In relation to the senior managers of the bidding company and the target company, who will be the winners and losers?

> *The managers of the bidding company are likely to be winners as they will manage a larger business following the takeover which will usually result in greater status, income and security. The position of senior managers in the acquired company is less certain. In some cases, they may be retained and may even become directors of the combined business. In other cases, however, the managers may lose their jobs, although compensation for loss of office may be paid. A recent study by Franks and Mayer found that nearly 80 per cent of executive directors in a target business either resign or lose their jobs within two years of a successful takeover.[5]*

Finally, we should recognise that takeovers can be very rewarding for the external investment advisers and lawyers employed by the companies involved. (According to newspaper reports, the takeover battle between Granada plc and Trust House Forte plc generated fees for external advisers of around £60m.) Whatever the outcome, it seems that these external advisers are usually winners!

Resisting a takeover bid

In some cases, a takeover bid may not be welcomed by the directors of a target business. Various defensive tactics may, therefore, be used to reduce the risk of takeover. These defensive tactics may involve either taking action before or after a hostile bid has been made. Such tactics include:

- *Conversion to private company status*   The directors may recommend that the company converts to private limited company status. This 'pre-offer' defence should make it more difficult for a bidder to acquire the shares of the target company.

- *Employee share option schemes*   By encouraging employees to acquire shares in the company, the proportion of shareholders who are likely to resist takeover bids will be increased. This is a further example of a pre-offer defence.

- *Circulating shareholders*   When an offer has been received, the directors of the target company will normally circulate the shareholders. In the circular the directors might argue that it is either not in the long-term interests of the shareholders to accept the offer, or that the share price offered is too low. In support of such arguments, the directors may disclose hitherto confidential information such as profit forecasts, future dividend payments, asset valuations, details of new contracts, and so forth.

- *Making the company unattractive*   The directors may take steps to make the company unattractive to a bidder. In the colourful language of mergers, this may involve taking a 'poison pill' through the sale of prized assets of the business (the 'crown jewels'). Other tactics include agreements to pay large sums to directors for loss of office resulting from a takeover ('golden parachutes') and the purchase of certain assets which the bidding company does not want. In recent years, some regional electricity companies have tried to fend off unwelcome takeover bids by making large dividend distributions to shareholders. These distributions have resulted in both a reduction in cash balances and an increase in the gearing of the companies.

- *Pac-man defence*   This involves the target company launching a counterbid for the predator company. However, this tactic is difficult to carry out where the target company is much smaller than the predator company. (The name given to this particular tactic derives from a well-known computer game.)

- *White knight*   A target company may avoid a takeover by an unwelcome bidder by seeking out another company (a white knight) with which to combine. This tactic will normally be used only as a last resort, however, as it will result in the loss of independence. There is also a risk that the 'white knight' will be less gallant after the merger than was hoped!

EXHIBIT 11.2

The modern tactics used to resist takeover attempts seem pretty tame stuff when compared with the tactics used in the United States during the nineteenth century. The following is a brief description of a 'wild west' style takeover battle which involved an attempt to take control of the Eirie Railroad in 1868:

> The takeover attempt pitted Cornelius Vanderbilt against Daniel Drew, Jim Fisk and Jay Gould. As one of the major takeover defences, the defenders of the Eirie Railroad issued themselves large quantities of stock (i.e. shares), even though they lacked the authorisation to do so. At that time, bribery of judges and elected officials was common, and so legal remedies for violating corporate laws were particularly weak. The battle for control of the railroad took a violent turn when the target corporation hired guards, equipped with firearms and cannons, to guard their headquarters. The takeover attempt ended when Vanderbilt abandoned his assault on the Eirie Railroad and turned his attention to weaker targets.[6]

The management of the bidding company will also employ tactics to overcome any resistance to the bid by the management or shareholders of the target company. Thus the bidding company may circularise the shareholders of the target company with information which counters any claims made against the commercial logic of the bid or the offer price. The bidding company may decide to increase the offer price for the shares in the target company in order to overcome resistance. In some cases, the original offer price may be pitched at a fairly low level as a negotiating ploy. The offer price will then be increased at a later date, thereby allowing the target company's managers and shareholders to feel that they have won some sort of victory. During the 1980s about 25 per cent of takeover bids were contested in the United Kingdom and around 50 per cent of listed companies which received a hostile bid were successfully taken over.[7]

To protect the interests of shareholders of both the bidding company and the target company, there is a City Code on Takeovers and Mergers. This Code seeks to ensure that shareholders are supplied with all the information necessary to make a proper decision and that the information supplied gives a fair and accurate representation of the facts. Any forecasts supplied by the bidding company or the target company must be carefully prepared and the key assumptions underpinning the forecast figures must be stated. The Code expects all shareholders to be treated equally when a merger or takeover is being negotiated.

Where the merger or takeover involves gross assets in excess of £30m being taken over, or a company has a 25 per cent share of a particular market, the 'public interest' becomes a consideration. In practice, this means a proposed merger can be referred to the Monopolies and Mergers Commission. This is a government-appointed body which considers the effect of mergers and takeovers on the level of competition operating within particular markets. If the Commission believes the effect of merger would be to create a monopoly or near monopoly position for a company in a particular market, it has the power to prevent the merger from taking place. However, the Commission has been criticised for producing inconsistent rulings and for taking a long time to deliver its judgements. This has led some companies to use referral to the Commission as a tactic in fending off hostile takeover bids.

Divestments and demergers

In recent years, we have witnessed a number of companies divesting themselves of particular business operations rather than acquiring them. The *divestment* or *sell-off* of business operations may be undertaken for various reasons. Sometimes, the divestment of assets will arise in response to particular problems experienced by the company. An example of this is where a company is short of cash or too highly geared and management decides to improve the liquidity or gearing by realising certain assets. A further example is where a company is vulnerable to a takeover and decides to take pre-emptive action by selling its 'crown jewels'.

On some occasions, the decision to divest may be taken because the company has reviewed its strategic plans and has decided that certain operations of the company are no longer compatible with its objectives. In recent years, for example, many companies have decided to focus on what they regard as their core activities rather than be diversified. As a result, 'non core' operations are sold off. In some cases, the managers of a company decide to sell off part of the business to allow a more profitable use of resources. This may arise when the performance of the particular business operations has been disappointing.

When a sell-off is undertaken, the managers of the particular business operations may bid to become the new owners. If their bid is successful, the purchase arrangement is referred to as a *management buyout*. We saw in Chapter 7 that management buyouts are often financed by venture capital organisations acquiring an equity stake in the business.

ACTIVITY 11.12

From the shareholders' viewpoint, what potential problem may arise when the managers wish to bid for part of the company's operations?

The managers of the company have a duty to act in the interests of the shareholders. However, when a management buyout is in prospect, the managers may feel a conflict of interest. On the one hand, they have a duty to ensure that the sale of the business will maximise the wealth of the owners and, on the other hand, they will be keen to acquire the business for as low a price as possible. There is a risk, therefore, that unscrupulous managers will suppress important information or will fail to exploit profitable opportunities in the period leading up to a buyout in order to obtain the business operations at a cheap price. Shareholders must be aware of this risk and must seek independent advice concerning the value and potential of the business operations which the managers are bidding for.

In some cases, a group of managers from outside the company may make a successful bid to become the new owners of the business operations. When this occurs, it is referred to as a *management buy-in*. Once again, venture capital organisations will often help to finance this purchase arrangement. In the United Kingdom during the first nine months of 1995, there were 376 management buyouts and buy-ins with a total value of £3,147m. Of this total, 121 deals with a total value of £1,100m. were management buy-ins (Source: Centre for Management Buyout Research).

Rather than selling off the business operations to a third party, the company may decide to transfer part of its assets to a new company. In this case, the ownership of the business operations will not be changed as the shareholders in the existing company will be given shares in the newly created company. The distribution of shares in the new company is usually made in proportion to shareholdings in the existing company. This kind of restructuring is referred to as a *demerger* or *spin-off*. There have been a number of demergers in recent years. Perhaps the most notable occurred when ICI plc, one of the largest companies in the United Kingdom, created Zeneca plc to carry on its pharmaceutical business operations.

A spin-off can have advantages for the company and for investors. Where, for example, part of the business operations is very high-risk in nature, market sentiment towards the company, as a whole, may be adversely affected. By spinning off the high-risk operations, the company may increase its market appeal. Similarly, where a company is a conglomerate, the market may not hold it in high regard. There may be a feeling among investors that management has failed to exploit fully the potential of the various business operations. It is usually extremely difficult to manage effectively a diverse range of businesses. Any lack of confidence among investors will be reflected in a lower share price for the company which may, in turn, leave it vulnerable to takeover. Predator companies may see that the conglomerate's assets are undervalued and may feel that they could unlock the potential of the various business operations. By spinning off particular business operations, the conglomerate may successfully avoid the risk of takeover. The managers of the particular business operations will often have greater autonomy following the spin-off and this may lead to improved performance. Thus shareholders may benefit directly from this form of restructuring.

Investors in a conglomerate are unlikely to find the various business operations in which it is engaged equally attractive. By creating separate companies for different kinds of business operations, investors should benefit as they will be able to adjust their portfolios to reflect more accurately the required level of investment for each business operation.

The valuation of shares

An important aspect of any merger or takeover negotiation is the value to be placed on the shares of the companies to be merged or acquired. In this section, we explore the various methods which can be used to derive an appropriate share value for a company. Share valuation methods are not, of course, only used in the context of merger or takeover negotiations. They will also be required in other circumstances such as company flotations and liquidations. However, mergers and takeovers are an important area for the application of share valuation methods.

In theory, the value of a company share can be defined either in terms of the current value of the assets held or the future cash flows generated from those assets. In a world of perfect information and perfect certainty, company share valuation would pose few problems. However, in the real world, measurement and forecasting problems conspire to make the valuation process difficult. Various valuation methods have been developed over the years to deal with these problems, but they can often produce quite different results.

The methods employed to value a company share can be divided into three broad categories, as follows:

- Methods based on the value of the company's assets.
- Methods which use stock market information.
- Methods which are based on future cash flows.

We will now examine some of the more important methods falling within each of these categories, and to help understand the various methods, we will use Example 11.1.

Example 11.1

CDC Ltd owns a chain of tyre and exhaust fitting garages in the west of England. The company has been approached by ATD plc, which owns a large chain of petrol stations, with a view to a takeover of CDC Ltd. ATD plc is prepared to make an offer in cash or a share-for-share exchange. The most recent accounts of CDC Ltd are summarised below:

Profit and loss account for the year ended 30 November 19X1

	£m.
Turnover	18.7
Profit before interest and tax	6.4
Interest	1.6
Profit before taxation	4.8
Corporation tax	1.2
Net profit after taxation	3.6
Dividend	1.0
Retained profit	2.6

Balance sheet as at 30 November 19X1

	£m.	£m.	£m.
Fixed assets			
Freehold land and premises at cost		4.6	
Less: Accumulated depreciation		0.6	
			4.0
Plant and machinery at cost		9.5	
Less: Accumulated depreciation		3.6	
			5.9
			9.9
Current assets			
Stock at cost		2.8	
Debtors		0.4	
Bank		2.6	
		5.8	
Less: **Creditors amounts due within one year**			
Trade creditors	4.3		
Dividends	1.0		
Corporation tax	1.2	6.5	(0.7)
Total assets less current liabilities			9.2
Less: **Creditors due beyond one year**			
Loans			3.6
			5.6
Share capital and reserves			
Ordinary £1 shares			2.0
Profit and loss account			3.6
			5.6

The accountant for CDC Ltd has estimated the future free cash flow of the company to be as follows:

	19X2	19X3	19X4	19X5	19X6*
£m.	4.4	4.6	4.9	5.0	5.4

(Note: *And for the following 12 years.)

The company has a cost of capital of 10 per cent.

CDC Ltd has recently had a professional valuer establish the current resale value of its assets. The current resale value of each asset was as follows:

	£m.
Freehold land and premises	18.2
Plant and machinery	4.2
Stock	3.4

The current resale values of the remaining assets are considered to be in line with their book values.

A company which is listed on the Stock Exchange and which is in the same business as CDC Ltd has a gross dividend yield of 5 per cent and a price earnings ratio of 11 times. Assume a standard rate of income tax of 25 per cent.

The financial director believes that replacement costs are £1.0m. higher than the resale values for both freehold land and premises, and plant and machinery, and £0.5m. higher than the resale value of the stock. The replacement cost of the remaining assets are considered to be in line with their book values. In addition, the financial director believes the goodwill of the business has a replacement value of £10.0m.

Asset-based methods

These methods attempt to value a company's share by reference to the value of the assets held by the company. The simplest method is simply to use the balance sheet values of the assets held. The *balance sheet*, or *net book value*, approach will determine the value of a company's ordinary share (P_O) as follows:

$$P_O = \frac{\text{Total assets at balance sheet values} - \text{total liabilities}}{\text{Number of ordinary shares issued}}$$

Where the company has preference shares in issue, these must also be deducted (at their book value) from the total assets in order to obtain the net book value of an ordinary share.

ACTIVITY 11.13

Calculate the net book value of an ordinary share in CDC Ltd.

The net book value of an ordinary share will be:

$$P_O = \frac{(9.9 + 5.8) - (6.5 + 3.6)}{2.0}$$

$$= £2.80$$

This method has the advantage that the valuation process is straightforward and the data is easy to obtain. However, the balance sheet value, or net book value, of a share is likely to represent a conservative value. This is because certain intangible assets such as goodwill and brand names may not be recorded on the balance sheet and will, therefore, be ignored for the purposes of valuation. In addition, those assets which are shown on the balance sheet are usually recorded at their historic cost (less any depreciation to date where relevant), and this figure may be below their current market values. During a period of inflation, the current market values of assets held will normally exceed the historic cost figures recorded on the balance sheet.

When a share value based on balance sheet values is calculated, it is often done to obtain a minimum value for a share. This figure can then be compared with a market value figure in order to measure the 'downside' risk associated with making an investment in the company. Where the market value is close to the balance sheet value, the level of investment risk is usually assumed to be small. However, that is not to imply that the share values of companies do not, at times, fall below their balance sheet or net book values. There is evidence to suggest that many companies will, at some point in their history, have a market value per share which is below their net book value.

A more useful approach to share valuation is to use the current market value of assets held by a company. Current market values can be expressed either in terms of *net realisable values* or *replacement costs*. Valuation models can use both, depending on the circumstances and/or on the purpose of the valuation.

The *liquidation* basis will value the assets held by the company according to the net realisable values (i.e. selling price less any costs of selling) which could be obtained on an orderly liquidation of the company. The liquidation value per share can be calculated by adjusting the formula above as follows:

$$P_O = \frac{\text{Total assets at net realisable value} - \text{total liabilities}}{\text{Number of ordinary shares issued}}$$

ACTIVITY 11.14

Calculate the value of an ordinary share in CDC Ltd using this method.

The liquidation value will be:

$$P_O = \frac{(18.2 + 4.2 + 3.4 + 0.4 + 2.6) - (6.5 + 3.6)}{2.0}$$

$$= £9.35$$

This valuation method is, however, also likely to reflect a conservative value as it fails to take account of the value of the business as a going concern. Usually, the going concern value of the business as a whole will be higher than the sum of the individual values of the assets when sold on a piecemeal basis.

Net realisable values will normally represent a lower limit for the current market value of assets held. The value of an asset in use to a company, is likely to be greater than the realisable value of that asset. If this was not the case, the company would, presumably, sell the asset rather than keep it.

Employing realisable values can pose a number of problems. It is important to recognise that the net realisable value of an asset can vary considerably according to the circumstances of the sale. The realisable value of an asset in a hurried sale, for example, may be considerably below what could be obtained in an orderly, managed sale. Determining realisable values can also be difficult. Where the asset is unique it may be particularly hard to place a reliable value on the item.

Replacement cost can also be used as an indicator of the market value of the assets held by a business. The value of a company's ordinary share, based on replacement cost, will be calculated as follows:

$$P_O = \frac{\text{Total assets at replacement cost} - \text{total liabilities}}{\text{Number of ordinary shares issued}}$$

The replacement cost approach will take account of tangible assets such as plant, fixtures, stock, etc., as well as intangibles such as goodwill and brands. When this is done, the figure will represent an upper limit for the market value of assets held. Determining the replacement cost of assets, particularly intangibles, however, can be difficult and often expensive.

ACTIVITY 11.15

Calculate the value of an ordinary share in CDC Ltd using this method.

The replacement cost approach will yield the following share value:

$$P_O = \frac{(19.2 + 5.2 + 3.9 + 0.4 + 2.6 + 10.0) - (3.6 + 6.5)}{2.0}$$

$$= £15.6$$

Stock market methods

Where a company is listed on the Stock Exchange, the value of its shares may be reflected in the quoted share price. As we saw in Chapter 7, there is a considerable body of evidence which suggests that share prices do react quickly and in an unbiased manner to new information that becomes publicly available and so, in that sense, the stock market can be described as efficient. As information is fully absorbed in share prices it can be argued that, until new information becomes available, shares are 'correctly' valued. The efficiency of the stock market is largely due to the efforts of investment analysts who closely monitor listed companies in an attempt to identify undervalued shares. The activities of these analysts ensure that undervalued shares do not stay undervalued for very long as they will advise clients to buy.

Despite the activities of investment analysts, however, there may be occasions when the quoted share price of a company may not reflect its economic value. This can occur, for example, where not all the relevant information is available to investment analysts and others in order for them to make an informed judgement. In some cases, share prices may reflect non-economic considerations. The shares of a football club, for example, may be in demand as a result of loyalty to the club rather than for any future returns from the investment.

The quoted share price of a company is more likely to be most appropriate for marginal transactions (i.e. where a small proportion of the shares are being purchased or sold). Where this is not the case, such as when an attempt is being made to gain control of the company, the quoted share price may be less reliable. In the circumstances mentioned, a premium may have to be paid to existing shareholders in order to ensure that a sufficient number of shares can be acquired.

It is possible to use stock market information and ratios to help value the shares of an unlisted company. The first step in this process is to find a listed company within the same industry which has similar risk and growth characteristics to the unlisted company whose shares you wish to value. Stock market ratios relating to the listed company can then be applied to the unlisted company in order to derive a share value. Two ratios which can be used in this way are the *price earnings* (P/E) ratio and the *dividend yield* ratio.

The P/E ratio relates the current share price to the current earnings of the company. You may recall from Chapter 3 that the ratio is calculated as follows:

$$\text{P/E ratio} = \frac{\text{Market value per share}}{\text{Earnings per share}}$$

The P/E ratio reflects the market's view of the likely future growth in earnings and the quality of those earnings. The higher the P/E ratio, the more highly the future prospects of the company are viewed by the market.

This equation above can be rearranged so that:

Market value per share (P_O) = P/E ratio $\times$ earnings per share

The P/E ratio of the listed company can be applied to the earnings of the unlisted company in order to derive a share value. Using the rearranged equation above, the value of an ordinary share of the unlisted company is calculated as follows:

P_O = P/E ratio of similar listed company $\times$ earnings per share (of unlisted company)

ACTIVITY 11.16
Calculate the value of an ordinary share in CDC Ltd using this method.

The value of an ordinary share using the P/E ratio method will be:

$$= \frac{11 \times 3.6}{2.0}$$

$$= £19.80$$

Although the calculations are fairly simple, this valuation approach should not be viewed as a mechanical exercise. Care must be taken to ensure that differences between the two companies do not invalidate the valuation process. As you may have guessed, a potential problem with this method is finding a listed company with similar risk and growth characteristics to the company you wish to value. Other differences, such as differences in accounting policies and accounting year ends between the two companies, can lead to problems when applying the P/E ratio to the earnings of the unlisted company. An unlisted company may adopt different policies on such matters as directors' remuneration, which will require adjustment before applying the P/E ratio. Finally, shares in unlisted companies are less marketable than those of similar listed companies and this should be taken into account. Usually, a discount is applied to the share value derived by using the above equation, although determining an appropriate discount figure can be a problem.

The *dividend yield ratio* offers another approach to valuing the shares of an unlisted company. This ratio relates the cash return from dividends to the current market value per share and we saw in Chapter 3 that it is calculated as follows:

$$\text{Dividend yield} = \frac{\text{Gross dividend per share}}{\text{Market value per share}} \times 100$$

The dividend yield can be calculated for shares listed on the Stock Exchange as both the market value per share and gross dividend per share will normally be known. However, for unlisted companies, the market value per share is not normally known and, therefore, this ratio cannot normally be applied.

The above equation can be expressed in terms of the market value per share by re-arranging as follows:

$$\text{Market value per share } (P_O) = \frac{\text{Gross dividend per share}}{\text{Dividend yield}} \times 100$$

This rearranged equation can be used to value the shares of an unlisted company. For this purpose, the gross dividend per share of the unlisted company, whose shares are to be valued, and the dividend yield of a similar listed company are used in the equation.

ACTIVITY 11.17

Calculate the value of an ordinary share in CDC Ltd using this method.

The value of an ordinary share using the dividend yield method will be:

$$= \frac{0.5 \times 100/75}{5} \times 100$$

$$= £13.33$$

This approach to share valuation, however, has a number of weaknesses. Once again, we are faced with the problem of finding a similar listed company as a basis for the valuation. We must also recognise that dividend policies may vary considerably between companies in the same industry, and may also vary between listed and unlisted companies. Unlisted companies, for example, are likely to be under less pressure to distribute profits in the form of dividends than listed companies. Dividends represent only part of the earnings stream of a company, and to value a company's shares on this basis may be misleading. The valuation obtained will be largely a function of the dividend policy adopted by the company (which is at the discretion of management) rather than the earnings generated.

Cash Flow Methods

The cash returns from holding a share take the form of dividends received. Using an economic concept of value, it is possible to view the value of a share in terms of the stream of future dividends which are received. The value of a share will be the *discounted value of the future dividends received* and can be shown as:

$$P_O = \frac{D_1}{(1 + K_O)} + \frac{D_2}{(1 + K_O)^2} + \ldots \frac{D_n}{(1 + K_O)^n} + \ldots$$

where:
D_t = the dividend received in period t; and
K_O = the required rate of return on the share.

Although this model is theoretically appealing, there are practical problems in forecasting future dividend payments and in calculating the required rate of return on the share. The first problem arises because dividends tend to fluctuate over time. If, however, dividends can be assumed to remain constant over time, the discounted dividend model can be reduced to:

$$P_O = \frac{D_1}{K_O}$$

where D_1 = the dividend received at the end of period 1.

┌───┐
│ **ACTIVITY 11.18** │
│ Assume that CDC Ltd has a constant dividend payout and the cost of equity capital │
│ is estimated at 12 per cent. Calculate the value of an ordinary share in the company │
│ using the above approach. │
└───┘

The value of an ordinary share using the discounted dividend method will be:

$$= \frac{0.5}{0.12}$$

$$= £4.17$$

The assumption of constant dividends, however, may not be very realistic, as many companies attempt to increase their dividends to shareholders over time.

Where companies increase their dividends at a constant rate of growth, the discounted dividend model can be revised to:

$$P_O = \frac{D_1}{K_O - g}$$

where g = the constant growth rate in dividends. (The model assumes K_O is greater than g.)

You may recall that the above formula was considered in Chapter 9.

Sometimes, an attempt may be made to forecast dividend payments for the next few years of the company's life. After this time horizon, forecasting may become too difficult and so a constant growth rate may be assumed for the remaining period. Although avoiding one problem, this approach creates another problem of deciding on an appropriate growth rate to use.

The use of dividends as a basis for valuation can create difficulties because of their discretionary nature. Different companies will adopt different dividend payout policies and this can affect the calculation of share values. In some cases, no dividends may be declared by a company for a considerable period. There are, for example, high-growth companies which prefer to plough back profits into the company rather than make dividends.

Another approach to share valuation is to value the *free cash flows* which are generated by a company over time. The free cash flows represent the cash flows available to lenders and shareholders after any new investments in assets. In other words, it is equivalent to the net cash flows from operations after deducting tax paid and cash for investment.

Example 11.2

Taurus Ltd generated cash of £200,000 from sales and incurred £125,000 cash expenses during the year. In addition, the company paid £25,000 in corporation tax and invested £40,000 in new assets.

The free cash flows can be calculated as follows:

	£
Cash received from sales	200,000
−Cash operating expenses	(125,000)
Net cash flows from operations	75,000
−Taxation paid	(25,000)
−Cash for investment	(40,000)
Free cash flows	10,000

In order to value shares using free cash flows, we have to discount the future free cash flows over time, using the cost of capital. The process is similar, therefore, to the NPV calculations undertaken when appraising investment opportunities. The present value of the free cash flows, after deducting amounts owing to lenders, will represent that portion of the free cash flows which accrue to the equity shareholders. Hence, the value of an ordinary share will be:

$$P_O = \frac{\text{Present value of future free cash flows} - \text{total liabilities}}{\text{Number of ordinary shares issued}}$$

ACTIVITY 11.19

Calculate the value of an ordinary share in CDC Ltd using this method.

The value of an ordinary share will be:

	Cash flow £m.	Discount rate 10%	Present value £m.
19X2	4.4	0.91	4.00
19X3	4.6	0.83	3.82
19X4	4.9	0.75	3.68
19X5	5.0	0.68	3.40
Next 13 years	5.4	4.90*	26.46
			41.36

(Note: * This is the total of the individual discount rates for the 13-year period. This short-cut can be adopted where cash flows are constant.)

$$P_O = \frac{PV - \text{total liabilities}}{\text{Number of ordinary shares}}$$

$$= \frac{41.36 - 10.1}{2.0}$$

$$= £15.63$$

The free cash flow approach presents a number of practical problems. One major problem is that of accurate forecasting. Sometimes, free cash flows may be forecast over a manageable time horizon – say five years – and then a terminal value substituted for free cash flows arising beyond that period in order to deal with this. However, determining the terminal value is, in itself, a problem – and an important one – as it may be a significant proportion of the total cash flows. Another approach to the forecasting problem is to assume a constant growth rate over time, just as we did with dividends earlier. The value of the business as a whole (P_B) would be:

$$P_B = \frac{c_1}{r - g}$$

where:

c_1 = free cash flows in the following year;
r = the cost of capital; and
g = the constant rate of growth in free cash flows.

Once again, the value of any liabilities would have to be deducted from the figure obtained from this calculation in order to derive the value of equity shares.

Although free cash flows may appear to be clearly defined, in practice there may be problems. The discretionary policies of management concerning new investments will have a significant influence on the free cash flow figure calculated. Free cash flows are likely to fluctuate considerably between periods. Unlike earnings, management has no incentive to smooth out cash flows over time. However, for valuation purposes, it may be useful to smooth out cash flow fluctuations between periods in order to establish trends over time.

SELF-ASSESSMENT QUESTION 11.1

A colleague of yours has recently been considering leaving his position as sales manager of a medium-sized pharmaceutical business and purchasing a small chemical company, the summarised accounts of which appear below:

Balance sheet at 31 December 19X3

	£m	£m
Fixed assets		8.2
Current assets	10.2	
Creditors: amounts due within one year	7.8	2.4
Total assets less current liabilities		10.6
Creditors: amounts due after more than one year		4.2
		6.4

	£m	£m
Capital and reserves		
Called up share capital – 4 million 25p Ordinary shares		1.0
Share premium account		2.0
Reserves		3.4
		6.4

Profit and loss account year ended 31 December 19X3

	£m.
Turnover	20.3
Profit on ordinary activities before taxation	2.2
Taxation on ordinary activities	1.0
Profit on ordinary activities after taxation	1.2
Dividends (net)	0.7
Retained profit for the financial year	0.5

You ascertain that the gross dividend yield for a similar company is 7 per cent and its price earnings ratio is 8 times. Assume an income tax rate of 30 per cent.

Required:

Calculate the share price on the basis of:

(a) dividend yield;
(b) price earning ratio; and
(c) net assets.

Choosing a valuation model

When deciding on the appropriate valuation model to employ, it is important to consider the purpose for which the shares are being valued. Different valuation models may be appropriate for different circumstances. For example, an 'asset stripper' (i.e. someone who wishes to acquire a company with a view to selling off its assets) would probably be most interested in the liquidation basis of valuation. A financial adviser to a new company being floated on the stock market, on the other hand, may rely more heavily on the P/E ratio method. We saw earlier that this approach takes account of share values of similar companies already listed on the Stock Exchange.

In many cases, share valuations derived from the models are used as a basis for negotiation. In such circumstances, they can be used to help set boundaries within which a final share value will be determined. The final figure will, however, be influenced by various factors including the negotiating skills and the relative bargaining position of the parties.

Summary

In this chapter we have explored various aspects of mergers and takeovers. We began by examining the reasons for takeovers and saw that not all of the reasons put forward can be justified in economic terms. We also identified the various forms of purchase consideration which might be used in a takeover and considered their advantages and disadvantages. We discussed who might benefit from a takeover and concluded that it is often the bidding company's managers and the target company's shareholders who will gain the most.

In recent years, we have seen many companies undertaking demergers and divestments. It seems that combining various business operations can create significant problems for some companies and that, by reversing the process, real benefits can be gained. Finally, we examined the various methods which can be used to derive a value for the shares of a company. It was argued that the choice of valuation method should be influenced by the particular decision which is being made.

References

1. K. Palepu, 'Predicting takeover targets, a methodological and empirical analysis', *Journal of Accounting and Economics*, 8: 3–35, 1986.
2. P. Barnes, 'The prediction of takeover targets in the UK by means of multiple discriminant analysis', *Journal of Business Finance and Accounting*, Spring, 1990.
3. C. Parkinson, 'The performance of target and bidding companies involved in hostile takeover bids', BAA Paper, Warwick, 1992.
4. H. Rose, 'The market for corporate control' *Financial Times Mastering Management Series*, Supplement issue no. 2, February, 1996.
5. J. Franks and C. Mayer, 'Corporate ownership and corporate control: a study of France, Germany and the UK', *Economic Policy*, vol. 10, 1994.
6. P. Gaughan, *Mergers and Acquisitions*, HarperCollins, 1991, p. 13.
7. Rose, *op. cit.*

Review questions

11.1 Distinguish between a merger and a takeover. What is the significance of this distinction?

11.2 Identify and discuss four reasons why a company may undertake divestment of part of its business.

11.3 Identify four reasons why a company seeking to maximise the wealth of its shareholders may wish to take over another company.

11.4 Identify four tactics the directors of a target company might employ to resist an unwelcome bid.

Examination-style questions

Solutions to those questions marked with an asterisk are given at the end of the text. Questions 11.1–11.3 are at basic level. Questions 11.4–11.6 are at intermediate/advanced level.

11.1 When a company wishes to acquire another company it may make a bid in the form of cash, a share-for-share exchange, or loan capital-for-share exchange.

Required:

Discuss the advantages and disadvantages of each form of consideration from the viewpoint of:

(a) the bidding company's shareholders; and
(b) the target company's shareholders.

11.2* Dawn Raider plc has just offered 1 of its shares for 2 shares in Sleepy Giant plc a company in the same industry as itself. Extracts from the accounts of each company for the year ended 31 May 19X8, appear below:

	Dawn Raider £m.	Sleepy Giant £m.
Profit and loss accounts		
Sales	150	360
Profits after tax	18	16
Dividends	4	14
Balance sheet data		
Fixed assets	150	304
Net current assets*	48	182
	198	486
Less: Loans	80	40
	118	446
Share capital†	50	100
Reserves	68	346
	118	446

Notes:

	Dawn Raider	Sleepy Giant
*Includes cash/(overdrafts)	(£60m.)	£90m.
† Shares	25p	50p

Stock market data for each company is as follows:

Dawn Raider plc

	31 May 19X6	31 May 19X7	31 May 19X8
Share price (pence)	120	144	198
Earnings per share (pence)	5.3	6.9	9.0
Dividends per share (pence)	2.0	2.0	2.0

Sleepy Giant plc

Share price (pence)	45	43	72
Earnings per share (pence)	8.4	7.4	8.0
Dividends per share (pence)	8.0	7.0	7.0

If the takeover succeeds Dawn Raider plans to combine Sleepy Giant's marketing and distribution channels with its own, with an after-tax saving of £1m. per annum. In addition it expects to be able to increase Sleepy Giant's profits after tax by at least £5m. per annum by better management. Dawn Raider's own profits after tax are expected to be £23m. (excluding the £1m. saving already mentioned), in the year ended 31 May 19X9.

One of the shareholders of Sleepy Giant has written to its chairman arguing that the bid should not be accepted. The following is an extract from his letter: 'The bid considerably undervalues Sleepy Giant since it is below Sleepy Giant's net assets per share. Furthermore, if Dawn Raider continues its existing policy of paying only 2p per share as a dividend, Sleepy Giant's shareholders will be considerably worse off.'

Required:

(a) Calculate:
  (i) The total value of the bid and the bid premium.
  (ii) Sleepy Giant's net assets per share at 31 May 19X8.
  (iii) The dividends the holder of 100 shares in Sleepy Giant would receive in the year before and the year after the takeover.
  (iv) The earnings per share for Dawn Raider in the year after the takeover.
  (v) The share price of Dawn Raider after the takeover assuming that it maintains its existing price earnings ratio.
(b) Comment on:
  (i) The points that the shareholder in Sleepy Giant raises in his letter.
  (ii) The amount of the bid consideration.

11.3 The study by Palepu, mentioned in the chapter, found that acquired businesses exhibited the following characteristics:

- a lower average share return over the four years prior to takeover;
- a higher 'growth–resource mismatch'.

The second characteristic, as explained earlier, means that a business with either high growth and low resources or low growth and high resources is more likely to be taken over as it will represent a 'good deal'. Average sales growth, average liquidity and average gearing were used to determine whether a growth–resource mismatch arises. Thus, where a business has either:

- low average sales growth/high average liquidity/low average gearing, or
- high average sales growth/low average liquidity/high average gearing,

a growth–resource mismatch will arise.

Required:

Discuss the extent to which these findings are consistent with the reasons for takeovers mentioned in the chapter.

11.4*   The directors of Simat plc have adopted a policy of expansion based on the acquisition of other companies. The special projects division of Simat has been given the task of identifying suitable companies for takeover.

Stidwell Ltd has been identified as being a suitable company and negotiations between the board of directors of each company have begun. Information relating to Stidwell Ltd is set out below:

Balance sheet as at 31 May 19X9

	£	£
Fixed assets		
Freehold land at cost		180,000
Plant and machinery at cost	120,000	
Less: Accumulated depreciation	30,000	90,000
Motor vehicles at cost	35,000	
Less: Accumulated depreciation	16,000	19,000
		289,000
Current assets		
Stocks	84,000	
Debtors	49,000	
Cash	24,000	
	157,000	
Less: **Creditors: amounts due within one year**		
Trade creditors	42,000	115,000
		404,000
Less: **Creditors: amounts due beyond one year**		
10% Debentures 19X4–X5		140,000
		264,000

	£	£
Capital and reserves		
Share capital		
Ordinary shares 50p each		150,000
Reserves		
Retained profit		114,000
		264,000

The net profit after tax of Stidwell Ltd for the year ended 31 May 19X9 was £48,500 and the dividend for the year £18,000. Profits and dividends of the company have shown little change over the past five years.

The saleable value of the assets of Stidwell Ltd at the balance sheet date were estimated to be as follows:

	£
Freehold land	285,000
Plant and machinery	72,000
Motor vehicles	15,000

For the remaining assets the balance sheet values were considered to reflect current realisable values.

The special projects division of Simat plc has also identified another company, Asgard plc, which is listed on the Stock Exchange and which is broadly similar to Stidwell Ltd. The following details were taken from a recent copy of a financial newspaper.

19X8–X9							Yield	
High	Low	Stock	Price	± or	Dividend (net)	Cover (times)	(gross %)	P/E (times)
560p	480p	Asgard plc	500p	+4p	10.33p	4.4	2.76	11

Assume a rate of income tax of 25 per cent.

Required:

(a) Calculate the value per share of Stidwell Ltd using each of the following valuation methods:
   (i) net assets (liquidation) basis;
   (ii) dividend yield; and
   (iii) price-earnings ratio.

(b) Critically evaluate each of the valuation methods identified in (a) above.

11.5 Alpha plc, a dynamic fast-growing company in micro-electronics has just made a bid of 17 of its own shares for every 20 shares of Beta plc, which manufactures a range of electric motors. Balance sheets and profit and loss accounts for the two companies are as follows:

Profit and loss accounts year ended 31 March 19X4

	Alpha plc £000s	Beta plc £000s
Turnover	3,000	2,000
Operating profit	300	140
Interest	100	10
Profit on ordinary activities before tax	200	130
Taxation on profit on ordinary activities	100	65
Profit on ordinary activities after tax	100	65
Dividends (net)	20	30
Retained profit for the financial year	80	35

Other information:

	Alpha plc	Beta plc
Number of issued shares (million)	1.0	0.5
Earnings per share	10p	13p
Price earnings ratio	20	10
Market price per share	200p	130p
Capitalisation (i.e. market price per share × number of shares)	£2m.	£0.65m.
Dividend per share (net)	2p	6p

Historical share prices at 31 March each year have been:

	19X9	19X0	19X1	19X2	19X3
Alpha plc	60	90	150	160	200
Beta plc	90	80	120	140	130

Balance sheets at 31 March 19X4

	Alpha plc £000s	Beta plc £000s
Fixed assets	1,200	900
Current assets	900	700
Creditors: amounts due within 1 year	(300)	(600)
Net current assets	600	100
Total assets *less* current liabilities	1,800	1,000
Less: long-term loans	(800)	(120)
	1,000	880

	Alpha plc £000s	Beta plc £000s
Share capital: 25p Ordinary shares	250	125
Profit and loss account	750	755
	1,000	880

The merger of the two companies will result in after-tax savings of £15,000 per annum to be made in the distribution system of Alpha.

One of the shareholders of Beta has queried the bid and has raised the following points. First, he understands that Alpha normally only pays small dividends and that his dividend per share will decrease. Secondly, he is concerned that the bid undervalues Beta since the current value of the bid is less than the figure for equity in Beta's balance sheet.

Required:

(a) Calculate the bid consideration.
(b) Calculate the earnings per share for the combined group.
(c) Calculate the theoretical post-acquisition price of Alpha shares assuming that the price-earnings ratio stays the same.
(d) Comment on the shareholder's two points.

(Hint: In order to answer this question you need to calculate the number of shares to be issued by Alpha and the total profit after tax following the merger. The market value of the shares following the merger can be found by rearranging the P/E ratio equation and inserting the relevant figures.)

11.6 Larkin Conglomerates plc owns a subsidiary company, Hughes Ltd, which sells office equipment. Recently, Larkin Conglomerates plc has been reconsidering its future strategy and has decided that Hughes Ltd should be sold off. The proposed divestment of Hughes Ltd has attracted considerable interest from other companies wishing to acquire this type of business. The most recent accounts of Hughes Ltd are as follows:

Balance sheet as at 31 May 19X5

	£000	£000	£000
Fixed assets			
Freehold premises at cost		240	
Less: Accumulated depreciation		40	200
Motor vans at cost		32	
Less: Accumulated depreciation		21	11
Fixtures and fittings at cost		10	
Less: Accumulated depreciation		2	8
			219

	£000	£000	£000
Current assets			
Stock at cost	34		
Debtors	22		
Cash at bank	20	76	
Creditors: amounts due within			
one year			
Trade creditors	52		
Accrued expenses	14	66	10
			229
Creditors: amounts due beyond			
one year			
12% loan – Cirencester Bank			100
			129
Capital and reserves			
£1 Ordinary shares			60
General reserve			14
Retained profit			55
			129

Profit and loss account for the year ended 31 May 19X5

	£000
Sales turnover	352.0
Profit before interest and taxation	34.8
Interest charges	12.0
Profit before taxation	22.8
Corporation tax	6.4
Profit after taxation	16.4
Dividend proposed and paid	4.0
	12.4
Transfer to general reserve	3.0
Retained profit for the year	9.4

The subsidiary has shown a stable level of sales and profits over the past three years. An independent valuer has estimated the current realisable values of the assets of the company as follows:

	£000
Freehold premises	235
Motor vans	8
Fixtures and fittings	5
Stock	36

For the remaining assets, the balance sheet values were considered to reflect their current realisable values.

Another company in the same line of business, which is listed on the Stock Exchange, has a gross dividend yield of 5 per cent and a price earnings ratio of 12. Assume a standard rate of income tax of 25 per cent.

Required:

(a) Calculate the value of an ordinary share in Hughes Ltd using the following methods:
  (i) net assets (liquidation) basis;
  (ii) dividend yield; and
  (iii) price-earnings ratio.
(b) Briefly state what other information, besides the information provided above, would be useful to prospective buyers in deciding on a suitable value to place on the shares of Hughes Ltd.

Glossary

Accounting rate of return (ARR) The average profit from an investment, expressed as a percentage of the average investment made.

Ageing schedule of debtors A report dividing debtors into categories, depending on the length of time outstanding.

Agency theory A theory which views a business as a coalition of different interest groups (managers, shareholders, lenders, etc.), in which each group is seeking to maximise its own welfare.

Annuity An investment which pays a constant sum each year over a period of time.

Average settlement period The average time taken for debtors to pay the amounts owing or for a business to pay its creditors.

Bank overdraft Amount owing to a bank which is repayable on demand. The amount borrowed and the rate of interest may fluctuate over time.

Beta coefficient A measure of the extent to which the returns on a particular share vary with the market as a whole.

Bond A long-term loan.

Bonus issue (scrip issue) Transfer of reserves to share capital requiring the issue of new shares to shareholders in proportion to existing shareholdings.

Capital asset pricing model (CAPM) A method of valuing assets which identifies two forms of risk: unique risk which can be eliminated through diversification and non-diversifiable risk.

Capital gains tax A tax on the gains from the disposal of certain assets which is payable at the taxpayer's marginal rate of tax. For 1996/97, this tax is levied on gains in excess of £6,300.

Capital rationing A situation where the funds available for investment are limited during a period.

Clientele effect The phenomenon where investors seek out companies whose dividend policies match their particular needs.

Coefficient of correlation A statistical measure of association which can be used to measure the degree to which the returns from two separate projects are related. The measure ranges from $+1$ to -1. A measure of $+1$ indicates a perfect positive correlation and a measure of -1 indicates a perfect negative correlation.

Coefficient of variation A statistical measure which can be used to assess investment risk. It divides the standard deviation by the expected returns from an investment in order to derive a measure of risk per £ of investment return.

Convertible loans Loan capital which can be converted into equity share capital at the option of the holders.

Cost of capital The rate of return required by investors in the business. The cost of capital is used as the criterion rate of return when evaluating investment proposals using the NPV and IRR methods of appraisal.

Debenture A long-term loan evidenced by a trust deed.

Deep discount bonds Redeemable bonds which are issued at a low or zero rate of interest and at a large discount to their redeemable value.

Degree of financial gearing A measure of the sensitivity of earnings per share to changes in profit before interest and taxation.

Demerger The transfer of part of the assets in an existing company to a new company. Shareholders in the existing company will be given shares, usually on a pro rata basis, in the new company.

Discount rate The rate used when making investment decisions to discount future cash flows in order to arrive at their present value.

Diversifiable risk That part of the total risk which is specific to an investment and which can be diversified away through combining the investment with other investments.

Dividends Transfer of assets made by a company to its shareholders.

Economic order quantity (EOQ) The quantity of stocks which should be purchased in order to minimise total stock costs.

Equivalent annual annuity method A method of deciding between competing investment projects with unequal lives which involves converting the NPV of each project into an annual annuity stream over its expected life.

Eurobonds Bearer bonds which are issued by listed companies and other organisations in various countries with the finance being raised on an international basis.

Expected net present value (ENPV) A method of dealing with risk which involves assigning a probability of occurrence to each possible outcome. The expected net present value of the project represents a weighted average of the possible NPVs where the probabilities are used as weights.

Factoring A method of raising short-term finance. A financial institution ('factor') will manage the sales ledger of the business and will be prepared to advance sums to the business based on the amount of trade debtors outstanding.

Finance lease Agreement which gives the lessee the right to use a particular asset for substantially the whole of its useful life in return for regular fixed payments. It represents an alternative to outright purchase.

Financial gearing   The existence of fixed payment bearing securities (e.g. loans) in the capital structure of a business.

Free cash flows   Cash flows available to lenders and shareholders after any new investment in assets.

Inflation   A rise in the general price level.

Internal rate of return (IRR)   The discount rate for a project which will have the effect of producing a zero NPV.

Invoice discounting   A form of finance provided by a financial institution based on a proportion of the face value of the credit sales outstanding.

Just-in-time (JIT)   A system of stock management which aims to have supplies delivered to production just in time for their required use.

Liquidity   The cash or near cash available in relation to the maturing obligations of a business.

Loan covenants   Conditions contained within a loan agreement which are designed to protect the lenders.

Mean–standard deviation rule   A decision rule which can be employed to discriminate between competing investments where the possible outcomes are known and are normally distributed.

Merger   When two or more businesses combine in order to form a single business.

Mortgage   A loan secured on property.

Net present value (NPV)   The net cash flows from a project which have been adjusted to take account of the time value of money. The NPV measure is used to rank investment projects and for accept/reject decisions.

Nominal value   The face value of a share in a company.

Non-diversifiable risk   That part of the total risk which is common to all investments and which cannot be diversified away by combining investments.

Normal distribution   The description applied to a set of data which, when displayed graphically, forms a symmetrical bell-shaped curve.

Offer for sale   Method of selling shares to the public through the use of an issuing house which acts as an intermediary.

Operating cash cycle   The time period between the outlay of cash to purchase supplies and the ultimate receipt of cash from the sale of the goods.

Opportunity costs   The value in monetary terms of being deprived of the next best opportunity in order to pursue the particular objective.

Payback period (PP)   The time taken for the initial investment in a project to be repaid from the net cash inflows of the project.

Portfolio effect   The effect of reducing the total risk associated with a business by investing in a combination of investments which are not perfectly positively correlated.

Profitability index   The present value of the future cash flows from a project divided by the present value of the outlay.

Public issue   Method of issuing shares which involves a direct invitation to subscribe for the shares from the company to the public.

Rights issue An issue of shares to existing shareholders on the basis of the number of shares already held.

Risk-adjusted discount rate (RADR) A method of dealing with risk which involves adjusting the discount rate for projects according to the level of risk involved. The RADR will be the risk-free rate plus an appropriate risk premium.

Sale and leaseback An agreement to sell an asset (usually property) to another party and simultaneously lease the asset back in order to continue using the asset.

Scenario analysis A method of dealing with risk which involves changing a number of variables simultaneously so as to provide a particular scenario for managers to consider.

Sensitivity analysis An examination of the key variables affecting a project, to see how changes in each variable might influence the outcome.

Share warrant An option to purchase a given number of shares in a company at a specified price and at a specified future date.

Shareholder value analysis (SVA) Method of measuring and managing business value based on the long-term cash flows generated.

Standard deviation A measure of spread which is based on deviations from the mean or expected value.

Takeover Normally used to describe a situation where a larger company acquires control of a smaller company which is then absorbed by the larger company.

Tender offers An offer of shares for sale to investors which requires the investors to state the amount which they are prepared to pay for the shares.

Venture capital Long-term capital provided by certain institutions to small and medium-sized businesses to exploit relatively high-risk opportunities.

Weighted average cost of capital An average of the post-tax costs of the forms of long-term finance employed within a business where the market value of each particular form of finance is used as a weight.

Working capital Current assets less current liabilities (creditors due for payment within one year).

Solutions to Self-assessment Questions

Solution to self-assessment question 2.1 (Chapter 2)

(a)

Quardis Ltd

Projected profit and loss account for the year ended 31 May 19X1

	£000	£000
Sales		280
Less: Cost of sales		
Opening stock	24	
Purchases	186	
	210	
Closing stock	30	180
Gross profit		100
Wages	34	
Other overhead expenses	21	
Interest payable	12	
Depreciation:		
Freehold premises	9	
Fixtures	6	82
Net profit before tax		18
Less: Corporation tax (35%)		6
Net profit after tax		12
Less: Proposed dividend		10
Retained profit for the year		2

(b)

Projected balance sheet as at 31 May 19X1

	£000	£000	£000
Fixed assets			
Freehold premises at cost		460	
Less: Accumulated depreciation		39	421
Fixtures and fittings at cost		60	
Less: Accumulated depreciation		16	44
			465
Current assets			
Stock-in-trade		30	
Trade debtors		42	
		72	
Creditors: amounts due within one year			
Trade creditors	31		
Accrued expenses	7		
Bank overdraft (balancing figure)	42		
Corporation taxation	6		
Dividends	10	96	(24)
			441
Creditors: amount due beyond one year			
Loan – Highland Bank			95
			346
Capital and reserves			
£1 Ordinary shares			200
Retained profit			146
			346

(c) The projected statements reveal a poor profitability and liquidity position for the company. The liquidity position at 31 May 19X1 reveals a serious deterioration when compared to the previous year.

As a result of preparing these projected statements, the management of Quardis Ltd may wish to make certain changes to their original plans. For example, the repayment of part of the loan may be deferred until a later date or the dividend may be reduced in order to improve liquidity. Similarly, the pricing policy of the company and the level of expenses proposed may be reviewed in order to improve profitability.

Solution to self-assessment question 3.1 (Chapter 3)

(a) In order to answer this question you may have used the following ratios:

	A plc	*B plc*

$$\text{Current ratio} = \frac{869}{438.4} = 2.0 \qquad\qquad = \frac{833.9}{310.5} = 2.7$$

$$\text{Acid test ratio} = \frac{(869 - 592)}{438.4} = 0.6 \qquad\qquad = \frac{(833.9 - 403)}{310.5} = 1.4$$

$$\text{Gearing ratio} = \frac{190}{(687.6 + 190)} \times 100 = 21.6\% \quad = \frac{250}{(874.6 + 250)} \times 100 = 22.2\%$$

$$\text{Interest cover ratio} = \frac{(131.9 + 19.4)}{19.4} = 7.8 \text{ times} \quad = \frac{(139.4 + 27.5)}{27.5} = 6.1 \text{ times}$$

$$\text{Dividend payout ratio} = \frac{135.0}{99.9} \times 100 = 135\% \qquad = \frac{95.0}{104.6} \times 100 = 91\%$$

$$\text{Price earnings ratio} = \frac{£6.50}{31.2\text{p}} = 20.8\text{T} \qquad\qquad = \frac{£8.20}{41.8\text{p}} = 19.6\text{T}$$

(b) A plc has a much lower current ratio and acid-test ratio than that of B plc. The reasons for this may be partly due to the fact that A plc has a lower average settlement period for debtors. The acid-test ratio of A plc is substantially below 1.0, which may suggest a liquidity problem.

The gearing ratio of each company is quite similar. Neither company has excessive borrowing. The interest cover ratio for each company is also similar. The respective ratios indicate that both companies have good profit coverage for their interest charges.

The dividend payout ratio for each company seems very high indeed. In the case of A plc, the dividends announced for the year are considerably higher than the earnings generated during the year that are available for dividend. As a result, part of the dividend was paid out of retained profits from previous years. This is an unusual occurrence. Although it is quite legitimate to do this, such action may nevertheless suggest a lack of prudence on the part of the directors.

The P/E ratio for both companies is high, which indicates market confidence in their future prospects.

Solution to self-assessment question 4.1 (Chapter 4)

Beacon Chemicals plc

(a) *Relevant cash flows*

	19X6 £000	19X7 £000	19X8 £000	19X9 £000	19X0 £000	19X1 £000
Sales revenue	–	80	120	144	100	64
Loss of contribution		(15)	(15)	(15)	(15)	(15)
Variable costs		(40)	(50)	(48)	(30)	(32)
Fixed costs		(8)	(8)	(8)	(8)	(8)
Operating cash flows		17	47	73	47	9
Working capital	(30)					30
Capital cost	(100)					
Net relevant cash flows	(130)	17	47	73	47	39

(b) *Payback period*

Cumulative cash flows	(130)	(113)	(66)	7

Thus the plant will have repaid the initial investment by the end of the third year of operations.

(c) *Net present value*

Discount factor	1.00	0.926	0.857	0.794	0.735	0.681
Present value	(130)	15.74	40.28	57.96	34.55	26.56
Net present value	45.09					

Solution to self-assessment question 5.1 (Chapter 5)

Choi Ltd

(a) The NPV of each project is:

Lo-tek

	Cash flows £	Discount rate 12%	Present value £
Initial outlay	(10,000)	1.00	(10,000)
1 year's time	4,000	0.89	3,560
2 years' time	5,000	0.80	4,000
3 years' time	5,000	0.71	3,550
Net present value			1,110

Hi-tek

	Cash flows £	Discount rate 12%	Present value £
Initial outlay	(15,000)	1.00	(15,000)
1 year's time	5,000	0.89	4,450
2 years' time	6,000	0.80	4,800
3 years' time	6,000	0.71	4,260
4 years' time	5,000	0.64	3,200
Net present value			1,710

(i) The *shortest common period of time* over which the machines can be compared is twelve years (i.e. 3×4). This means that Lo-tek will be repeated four times and Hi-tek will be repeated three times during the twelve-year period.

The NPV for Lo-tek will be:

$$\text{Total NPV} = 1110 + \frac{1110}{(1+0.12)^3} + \frac{1110}{(1+0.12)^6} + \frac{1110}{(1+0.12)^9}$$

$$= 2862.6$$

The NPV for Hi-tek will be:

$$\text{Total NPV} = 1710 + \frac{1710}{(1+0.12)^4} + \frac{1710}{(1+0.12)^8}$$

$$= 3487.0$$

(ii) The *equivalent annual annuity approach* will provide the following results:

Lo-tek

$1,110 \times 0.4163 = \underline{£462.09}$

Hi-tek

$1,710 \times 0.3292 = \underline{£562.93}$

(b) Hi-tek is the better buy because it produces the higher figure under both methods.

Solution to self-assessment question 6.1 (Chapter 6)

Kernow Cleaning Services Ltd

Workings

The first step is to calculate the expected cash flows for each year which are as follows:

		Expected cash flows £
Year 1	£80,000 × 0.3	24,000
	£160,000 × 0.5	80,000
	£200,000 × 0.2	40,000
	Expected cash flows	144,000
Year 2	£140,000 × 0.4	56,000
	£220,000 × 0.4	88,000
	£250,000 × 0.2	50,000
	Expected cash flows	194,000
Year 3	£140,000 × 0.4	56,000
	£200,000 × 0.3	60,000
	£230,000 × 0.3	69,000
	Expected cash flows	185,000
Year 4	£100,000 × 0.3	30,000
	£170,000 × 0.6	102,000
	£200,000 × 0.1	20,000
	Expected cash flows	152,000

(a) The expected net present value (ENPV) can now be calculated as follows:

Year	Expected cash flows £	Discount rate 10%	Expected present value £
0	(540,000)	1.00	(540,000)
1	144,000	0.91	131,040
2	194,000	0.83	161,020
3	185,000	0.75	138,750
4	152,000	0.68	103,360
ENPV			(5,830)

(b) The worst possible outcome can be found by taking the lowest value in each year. Hence:

Year	Cash flow £	Discount factor 10%	Present value £
0	(540,000)	1.00	(540,000)
1	80,000	0.91	72,800
2	140,000	0.83	116,200
3	140,000	0.75	105,000
4	100,000	0.68	68,000
ENPV			(178,000)

The probability of occurrence of this ENPV of £(178,000) can be found by multiplying together each of the probabilities of occurrence of the cash flows above. Hence:

$$0.3 \times 0.4 \times 0.4 \times 0.3 = \underline{0.0144}$$

(c) As the expected net present value (ENPV) of the project is negative the project should be rejected.

Solution to self-assessment question 7.1 (Chapter 7)

Helsim Ltd

(a) The liquidity position may be assessed by using the liquidity ratios discussed in an earlier chapter:

$$\text{Current ratio} = \frac{\text{Current assets}}{\text{Current liabilities (creditors due within one year)}}$$

$$= \frac{£7.5\text{m.}}{£5.4\text{m.}}$$

$$= 1.4$$

$$\text{Acid-test ratio} = \frac{\text{Current assets (less stock)}}{\text{Current liabilities (creditors due within one year)}}$$

$$= \frac{£3.7\text{m.}}{£5.4\text{m.}}$$

$$= 0.7$$

The ratios calculated above reveal a fairly weak liquidity position. The current ratio seems quite low and the acid-test ratio seems very low. This latter ratio suggests that the company does not have sufficient liquid assets to meet its maturing obligations. It would, however, be useful to have details of the liquidity ratios of similar companies in the same industry in order to make a more informed judgement. The bank overdraft represents 67 per cent of the short-term liabilities and 40 per cent of the total liabilities of the company. The continuing support of the bank is therefore important to the ability of the company to meet its commitments.

(b)   The finance required to reduce trade creditors to an average of 40 days outstanding is calculated as follows:

	£m.
Trade creditors at balance sheet date	1.80
Trade creditors outstanding based on 40 days' credit	
40/365 × £8.4 (i.e. credit purchases)	0.92
Finance required	0.88

(c)   The bank may not wish to provide further finance to the company. The increase in overdraft will reduce the level of trade creditors but will increase the exposure of the bank. The additional finance invested by the bank will not generate further funds and will not therefore be self-liquidating. The question does not make it clear whether the company has sufficient security to offer the bank for the increase in overdraft facility. The profits of the company will be reduced and the interest cover ratio would reduce if the additional overdraft was granted. The interest cover ratio is already low at 1.6 times and this means that a relatively small decline in profits would mean that interest charges would not be covered.

(d)   A number of possible sources of finance might be considered. Four possible sources are as follows:

1. *Issue of equity shares*   This option may be unattractive to investors. The return on equity is fairly low at 7.9 per cent and there is no evidence that the profitability of the business will improve. If profits remain at their current level, the effect of issuing more equity will be to further reduce the returns to equity.
2. *Issue of loans*   This option may also prove unattractive to investors. The effect of issuing further loans will have a similar effect to that of increasing the overdraft. The profits of the business will be reduced and the interest cover ratio will decrease to a low level. The gearing ratio of the company is already quite high at 48 per cent and it is not clear what security would be available for the loan.
3. *Chase debtors*   It may be possible to improve cash flows by reducing the level of credit outstanding from debtors. At present the average settlement period is 93 days which seems quite high. A reduction in the average settlement period by approximately 1/3 would generate the funds required. However, it is not clear what effect this would have on sales.

4.   *Reduce stock*   This appears to be the most attractive of the four options discussed. At present the average stockholding period is 178 days which seems to be very high. A reduction in this stockholding period by less than 1/3 would generate the funds required. However, if the company holds a large amount of slow-moving and obsolete stock it may be difficult to reduce stock levels easily.

Solution to self-assessment question 8.1 (Chapter 8)

(a)

Hargreaves Ltd

Projected profit and loss accounts to 31 May 19X1

		Schemes	
	(i)	(ii)	(iii)
	£m.	£m.	£m.
PBIT	13.5	13.5	13.5
Interest	1.2	1.7	1.7
	12.3	11.8	11.8
Tax payable (35%)	4.3	4.1	4.1
Profit after tax	8.0	7.7	7.7
Preference dividend	–	0.4	–
Available to equity	8.0	7.3	7.7
Dividends	1.3	1.0	1.1
	6.7	6.3	6.6

(b)

$$\text{EPS} = \frac{£8.0\text{m.}}{20\text{m.}} \qquad \frac{£7.3\text{m.}}{16\text{m.}} \qquad \frac{£7.7\text{m.}}{18\text{m.}}$$

$$= £0.40 \qquad\qquad £0.46 \qquad\qquad £0.43$$

$$\text{Gearing} = \frac{£10\text{m.}}{£56.7\text{m.}} \qquad \frac{£18\text{m.}}{£56.3\text{m.}} \qquad \frac{£14\text{m.}}{£56.6\text{m.}}$$

$$= 17.6\% \qquad\qquad 32\% \qquad\qquad 24.7\%$$

(c)

Indifference point:

$$\frac{(X - £1.2\text{m.})(1 - 0.35)}{20\text{m.}} = \frac{(X - £1.7\text{m.})(1 - 0.35)}{18\text{m.}}$$

$$X = £6.2\text{m.}$$

(d) Scheme (ii) provides the highest EPS and does not involve an issue of shares. Hence there would be no dilution of control for existing shareholders. The level of gearing would, however, rise to 32 per cent which is the highest of the three options. Nevertheless, provided that the profits of the business are fairly stable over time, a gearing level of this magnitude may not prove too onerous. Interest cover would still be fairly high under this option. Scheme (i) produces the lowest EPS and the highest level of share issue. Although gearing is at its lowest under this option, it is unlikely to prove a satisfactory solution for this family-controlled business. Scheme (iii) provides a 'middle way' for the company. EPS and gearing levels fall between the other two options and Industrial Finance would acquire only 11 per cent of the shares in issue. This may be a satisfactory solution if profits are volatile and the company wishes to keep gearing lower than the level offered by scheme (ii).

Solution to self-assessment question 9.1 (Chapter 9)

Simtech plc

(a) The dividend per share and dividend payout ratio over the five-year period under review is as follows:

Year	Dividend per share	Dividend payout % (Dividend/Net profit after tax)
19X1	22.0p	52.4
19X2	14.0p	26.4
19X3	17.3p	40.0
19X4	7.3p	14.9
19X5	30.7p	52.3

These figures show an erratic pattern of dividends over the past five years. Such a pattern is unlikely to be welcomed by investors.

(b) In an imperfect world, dividends may be important to investors because of taxation policy and information signalling. Managers should, therefore, decide on a payout policy and then make every effort to stick with this policy. This will ensure that dividends are predictable and contain no 'surprises' for investors. Any reduction in the dividend is likely to be seen as a sign of financial weakness and the share price is likely to fall. If a reduction in dividends cannot be avoided, the managers should make clear the change in policy and the reasons for the change.

Solution to self-assessment question 10.1 (Chapter 10)

Williams Wholesalers Ltd

	£	£
Existing level of debtors (£4m. × 70/365)		767,000
New level of debtors		
£2m. × 80/365	438,000	
£2m. × 30/365	164,000	602,000
Reduction in debtors		165,000
Costs and benefits of policy		
Cost of discount (£2m. × 2%)		40,000
Less: Savings		
Interest payable (£165,000 × 13%)	21,450	
Administration costs	6,000	
Bad debts	10,000	37,450
Net cost of policy		2,550

The above calculations reveal that the company will be worse off by offering the discounts.

Solution to self-assessment question 11.1 (Chapter 11)

(a) *Dividend yield basis*

$$\text{Market value per share } (P_O) = \frac{\text{Gross dividend per share}}{\text{Dividend yield}} \times 100$$

$$= \frac{(£0.7m./4m.) \times 100/70}{7} \times 100$$

$$= £3.57$$

(b) *Price earnings basis*

$$\text{Market value per share } (P_O) = \text{P/E ratio} \times \text{earnings per share}$$

$$= 8 \times (£1.2m./4m.)$$

$$= £2.40$$

(c) *Net assets basis*

$$= \frac{\text{Net assets}}{\text{Number of ordinary shares in issue}}$$

$$= \frac{£6.4\text{m.}}{4\text{m.}}$$

$$= £1.60$$

Solutions to Selected Examination-style Questions

Solution to examination-style questions (Chapter 2)

2.1 Prolog Ltd

(a) *Cash projection for the six months to 30 June 19X5*

	January £000	February £000	March £000	April £000	May £000	June £000
Receipts						
Credit sales	100	100	140	180	220	260
Payments						
Trade creditors	112	144	176	208	240	272
Operating expenses	4	6	8	10	10	10
Shelving				12		
Taxation			25			
	116	150	209	230	250	282
Cash flow	(16)	(50)	(69)	(50)	(30)	(22)
Opening balance	(68)	(84)	(134)	(203)	(253)	(283)
Closing balance	(84)	(134)	(203)	(253)	(283)	(305)

(b) A banker may require various pieces of information before granting additional overdraft facilities. These may include:

- Security available for the loan.
- Details of past profit performance.
- Profit projections for the next twelve months.

- Cash projections beyond the next six months to help assess the prospects of repayment.
- Details of the assumptions underlying projected figures supplied.
- Details of contractual commitment between Prolog Ltd and its supplier.
- Details of management expertise. Can they manage the expansion programme?
- Details of new machine and its performance in relation to competing models.
- Details of funds available from owners to finance the expansion.

2.4   Kwaysar Ltd

(a)   *Forecast profit and loss account for the six months to 30 November 19X3*

	£000	£000
Sales turnover		
Retailers [(£90×3,000) + (£90×3,600)]	594.0	
Public [(£90×900) + (£90×1,200)]	189.0	783.0
Opening stock	44.0	
Purchases [(£50×6,600) + (2,100×£50)]	435.0	
	479.0	
Less: Closing stock	44.0	435.0
Gross profit		348.0
Less:: Overheads		
Wages	108.0	
Advertising expenses	72.0	
Discount allowed [(1/2×594)×2%]	5.9	
Depreciation		
Freehold property	3.5	
Fixtures	6.0	
Motor vehicles	12.0	
Miscellaneous overheads	84.0	291.4
Net profit for the period		56.6

(b)   *Forecast cash flow statement for the six months to 30 November 19X3*

	£000	£000
Cash receipts		
Sales – retailers (1 month) [(2700×£90) 98/100+52]	290.1	
(3 months) (1500×£90)		135.0
– public		189.0
		614.1
Cash payments		
Trade creditors (435−80+32)	387.0	
Advertising costs	72.0	
Motor vehicles	80.0	

	£000	£000
Dividends paid	48.0	
Wages	108.0	
Miscellaneous overheads	82.0	777.0
Cash deficit		(162.9)
Opening balance		120.0
Closing balance		(42.9)

(c) We can see from the forecast profit and loss account for the six-month period a 9 per cent decline in net profit as compared to the previous six-month period. The net profit per £1 of sales generated has declined from 11.9p in the previous period to 7.2p in the forecast period.

Implementing the new marketing strategy will mean that there will be additional expenditure on such items as motor vehicles and marketing costs, and receipts from customers will be slower. These factors will combine to produce a cash deficit for the six-month period which will have to be financed in some way.

The decline in profitability and liquidity in return for an increase in market share indicates that the new strategy has little to commend it – at least in the short term. However, it is possible that over the longer term, a large market share will allow the company to increase profits and improve its cash flows to compensate for the short-term problems.

Solution to examination-style questions (Chapter 3)

3.2   Business A and Business B

(a) This part of the question has been dealt with in the chapter.

(b) The ratios reveal that the debtors turnover ratio for Business A is 63 days whereas for Business B the ratio is only 21 days. Business B is therefore much quicker in collecting amounts outstanding from customers. Nevertheless, there is not much difference between the two businesses in the time taken to pay trade creditors. Business A takes 50 days to pay its creditors, whereas Business B takes 45 days. It is interesting to compare the difference in the debtor and creditor collection periods for each business. As Business A allows an average of 63 days credit to its customers, yet pays creditors within 50 days it will require greater investment in working capital than Business B which only allows an average of 21 days to its debtors but takes 45 days to pay its creditors.

Business A has a much higher gross profit percentage than Business B. However, the net profit percentage for the two businesses is identical. This suggests that Business A has much higher overheads than Business B. The stock turnover period for Business A is more than twice that of Business B. This may be due to the fact that Business A maintains a wider range of goods in stock in order to meet customer requirements. The evidence suggests that Business A is the business which prides itself on personal service. The higher average settlement period is consistent with a more relaxed attitude to credit collection (thereby maintaining customer goodwill) and the high overheads are consistent with the incurring of additional costs in order to satisfy customer requirements. The high stock levels of Business B are consistent with maintaining a wide range of stock in order to satisfy a range of customer needs.

Business B has the characteristics of a more price-competitive business. The gross profit percentage is much lower than Business A indicating a much lower gross profit per £1 of sales. However, overheads are kept low in order to ensure the net profit percentage is the same as Business A. The low stock turnover period and average collection period for debtors are consistent with a business which wishes to reduce investment in current assets to a minimum, thereby reducing costs.

3.4   Helena Beauty Products

		19X6	19X7
Profitability ratios			
Net profit margin	=	$(80/3600) \times 100\%$	$(90/3840) \times 100\%$
	=	2.2%	2.3%
Gross profit margin	=	$(1440/3600) \times 100\%$	$(1590/3840) \times 100\%$
	=	40%	41.4%
ROCE	=	$(80/2668) \times 100\%$	$(90/2874) \times 100\%$
	=	3.0%	3.1%
Efficiency ratios			
Stock turnover period	=	$\dfrac{(320 + 400)/2}{2160} \times 365$	$\dfrac{(400 + 500)/2}{2250} \times 365$
	=	61 days	73 days
Average debtors period	=	$(750/3600) \times 365$	$(960/3840) \times 365$
	=	76 days	91 days
Asset turnover	=	3600/3058	3840/3324
	=	1.2T	1.2T

The above ratios reveal a low net profit margin in each year. The gross profit margin, however, is quite high in each year. This suggests that the company has high overheads. There was a slight improvement of 1.4 per cent in the gross profit margin during 19X7 but this appears to have been largely swallowed up by increased overheads. As a result, the net profit margin improved by only 0.1 per cent in 19X7. The low net profit margin is matched by a rather low asset turnover ratio in both years. The combined effect of this is a low ROCE in both years. The ROCE for each year is lower than might be expected from investment in risk-free government securities and should be regarded as unsatisfactory.

The stock turnover period and average debtors settlement period have both increased significantly over the period. Both seem to be high and should be a cause for concern. Although the profit (in absolute terms) and sales improved during 19X7, the directors should be concerned at the low level of profitability and efficiency of the business. In particular, an investigation should be carried out concerning the high level of overheads and the high investement in stocks and debtors.

Solutions to examination-style questions (Chapter 4)

4.1 Mylo Ltd
(a)
Annual depreciation

Project 1   (£100,000−7,000)/3 = £31,000
Project 2   (£60,000−6,000)/3 = £18,000

Analysis of the projects

Project 1

	0	1	2	3
	£000	£000	£000	£000
Net profit (loss)		29	(1)	2
Depreciation		31	31	31
Capital cost	(100)			
Residual value				7
Net cash flows	(100)	60	30	40
10% discount factor	1.000	0.909	0.826	0.751
Present value	(100.00)	54.54	24.78	30.04
Net present value	9.36			

Clearly the IRR lies above 10 per cent, try 15 per cent.

15% discount factor	1.000	0.870	0.756	0.658
Present value	(100.00)	52.20	22.68	26.32
Net present value	1.20			

Thus the IRR lies a little above 15 per cent, around 16 per cent.

Cumulative cash flows	(100)	(40)	(10)	30

Thus the payback will occur after about two years and three months (assuming that the cash flows accrue equally over the year)

Project 2

	0 £000	1 £000	2 £000	3 £000
Net profit (loss)		18	(2)	4
Depreciation		18	18	18
Capital cost	(60)			
Residual value				6
Net cash flows	(60)	36	16	28
10% discount factor	1.000	0.909	0.826	0.751
Present value	(60.00)	32.72	13.22	21.03
Net present value	6.97			

Clearly the IRR lies above 10 per cent, try 15 per cent.

15% discount factor	1.000	0.870	0.756	0.658
Present value	(60.00)	31.32	12.10	18.42
Net present value	1.84			

Thus the IRR lies a little above 15 per cent, around 17 per cent.

Cumulative cash flows	(60)	(24)	(8)	20

Thus the payback will occur after about two years and three months (assuming that the cash flows accrue equally over the year).

(b) Presuming that Mylo Ltd is pursuing a wealth maximisation objective, Project 1 is preferable since it has the higher NPV. The difference between the two NPVs is not, however, very large.

(c) NPV is the preferred method of assessing investment opportunities because it fully addresses each of the following:

- *The timing of the cash flows* By discounting the various cash flows associated with each project according to when they are expected to arise, account is taken of the fact that cash flows do not all occur simultaneously. Associated with this is the fact that by discounting, using the opportunity cost of finance (i.e. the return which the next best alternative opportunity would generate), the net benefit (after financing costs have been met) is identified (as the NPV).
- *The whole of the relevant cash flows* NPV includes all of the relevant cash flows irrespective of when they are expected to occur. It treats them differently according to their date of occurrence, but they are all taken account of in the NPV and they all have, or can have, an influence on the decision.
- *The objectives of the business* NPV is the only method of appraisal where the

output of the analysis has a direct bearing on the wealth of the business. (Positive NPVs enhance wealth, negative ones reduce it.) Since most private sector businesses seek to increase their value and wealth, NPV is the best approach to use.

4.5 Newton Electronics

(a)

Option 1

	19X2 £m.	19X3 £m.	19X4 £m.	19X5 £m.	19X6 £m.	19X7 £m.
Plant and equipment	(9.0)					1.0
Sales		24.0	30.8	39.6	26.4	10.0
Variable costs		(11.2)	(19.6)	(25.2)	(16.8)	(7.0)
Fixed costs (ex depr'n)		(0.8)	(0.8)	(0.8)	(0.8)	(0.8)
Working capital	(3.0)					3.0
Marketing costs		(2.0)	(2.0)	(2.0)	(2.0)	(2.0)
Opportunity costs		(0.1)	(0.1)	(0.1)	(0.1)	(0.1)
	(12.0)	9.9	8.3	11.5	6.7	4.1
Discount factor	1.0	0.91	0.83	0.75	0.68	0.62
Present value	(12.0)	9.0	6.9	8.6	4.6	2.5
NPV	19.6					

Option 2

	19X2 £m.	19X3 £m.	19X4 £m.	19X5 £m.	19X6 £m.	19X7 £m.
Royalties	–	4.4	7.7	9.9	6.6	2.8
Discount factor	1.0	0.91	0.83	0.75	0.68	0.62
Present value	–	4.0	6.4	7.4	4.5	1.7
NPV	24.0					

Option 3

	19X2 £m.	19X4 £m.
Instalments	12.0	12.0
Discount	1.0	0.83
Present value	12.0	10.0
NPV	22.0	

(b) Before making a final decision the following factors should be considered:

- The long-term competitiveness of the business may be affected by the sale of the patents.
- At present, the company is not involved in manufacturing and marketing products. Is this change in direction desirable?
- The company will probably have to buy in the skills necessary to produce the product itself. This will involve costs, and problems will be incurred. Has this been taken into account?
- How accurate are the forecasts made and how valid are the assumptions on which they are based?

(c) Option 2 has the highest NPV and is therefore the most attractive to shareholders. However, the accuracy of the forecasts should be checked before a final decision is made.

Solution to examination-style questions (Chapter 5)

5.1 Shaldon Engineering plc

Report to the Board of Directors, Shaldon Engineering plc
From: A.N. Other
Subject: *The evaluation, monitoring and control of capital investment projects*

Once the funds available for capital investment have been determined and a suitable investment proposal identified, the following steps should be taken:

1. Evaluate project
In order for management to agree to the investment of funds in a project there must be a proper screening of each proposal put forward. For projects of any size, this will involve providing answers to a number of key questions including:

- What is the purpose of the project?
- Does the project fit in with the overall objectives of the business?
- How much finance is required?
- What other resources (e.g. expertise, factory space, etc.) is required for successful completion of the project?
- How long will the project last and what are the key stages of the project?
- What is the expected pattern of cash flows?
- What are the major problems associated with the project and how can they be overcome?
- Which managers are proposing the project and what is their level of commitment to the project?
- What is the NPV/IRR of the project?
- Has risk and inflation been taken into account in the appraisal process and what are the results?

2. Approve project

Once the managers responsible for investment decision-making are satisfied that the project should be undertaken, formal approval can be given. For large projects, approval should be given only by the senior management team.

3. Monitor and control the project

Managers will need actively to manage the project through to completion. This, in turn, will require further information gathering.

Management should receive progress reports at regular intervals concerning the project. These reports should provide information relating ot the actual cash flows for each stage of the project which can then be compared against the budgeted figures that were provided when the proposal was submitted for approval. The reasons for any significant variations should be ascertained and corrective action taken where possible. Any changes in the expected completion date of the project or expected variations in future cash flows from budget should be reported immediately. In extreme cases, managers may abandon the project if circumstances appear to have changed dramatically for the worse. Project management techniques (e.g. critical path analysis) should be employed where appropriate and their effectiveness reported to top management.

An important part of the control process is a post-completion audit of the project. This is essentially a review of the project performance in order to see whether it lived up to expectations and whether any lessons can be learned from the way in which the investment process can be improved for the future. In addition to an evaluation of financial costs and benefits, non-financial measures of performance such as the ability to meet deadline dates and levels of quality achieved should also be reported on. The fact that a post-completion audit is part of the management of the project should encourage those who submit projects to use realistic estimates.

5.4   Lee Caterers Ltd

The NPV for each project is:

	Cook/chill project		
	Cash flows	Discount rate	Present value
	£000	£000	£000
Initial outlay	(200)	1.00	(200)
1 year's time	85	0.91	77.4
2 years' time	94	0.83	78.0
3 years' time	86	0.75	64.5
4 years' time	62	0.68	42.2
NPV			62.1

Cook/freeze project

	Cash flows £000	Discount rate £000	Present value £000
Initial outlay	(390)	1.00	(390)
1 year's time	88	0.91	80.1
2 years' time	102	0.83	84.7
3 years' time	110	0.75	82.5
4 years' time	110	0.68	74.8
5 years' time	110	0.62	68.2
6 years' time	90	0.56	50.4
7 years' time	85	0.51	43.4
8 years' time	60	0.47	28.2
NPV			122.3

Eight years is the minimum period over which the two projects can be compared. The cook/chill will provide the following NPV over this period:

$$= 62.1 + \frac{62.1}{(1 + 0.1)^4}$$

$$= 104.5$$

This is lower than for the cook/freeze project of £122.3 (see above). Hence, the cook/freeze project should be accepted.

Using the equivalent annual annuity approach we derive the following:

Cook/chill = 62.1 × 0.3155 = 19.59
Cook/freeze = 122.3 × 0.1874 = 22.92

This approach leads to the same conclusion as the earlier approach.

Solution to examination-style questions (Chapter 6)

6.1   Davies Ltd
(a)   *Incremental cash flows*

	19X9 £000	19X0 £000	19X1 £000	19X2 £000	19X3 £000
Machinery	(550)				30
Working capital	(40)				40
Sales		500	640	480	320
Cost of sales		(200)	(256)	(192)	(128)
Variable costs		(100)	(128)	(96)	(64)

	19X9 £000	19X0 £000	19X1 £000	19X2 £000	19X3 £000
Fixed costs		(10)	(10)	(10)	(10)
Net cash flows	(590)	190	246	182	188
Discount factor	1.0	0.909	0.826	0.751	0.683
Present value	590	172.7	203.2	136.7	128.4
NPV	51.0				

(b) The NPV of the project is positive and so acceptance would increase shareholder wealth.

(c) Three methods of dealing with risk and uncertainty are:

1. *Sensitivity analysis* This approach identifies each of the key variables influencing the investment decision and examines the extent to which they could change before affecting the viability of the project. The approach gives managers a feel for the margin of error that is available for each variable. However, it does not provide a clear indication concerning whether to accept or reject the project. This is left to managerial judgement.

2. *Expected values* This approach assigns probabilities to each outcome and then calculates a weighted average where the probabilities are used as weights. The average figure derived may not be capable of occurring, although where a business has a portfolio of similar projects it can be argued that this should not be a problem. However, where projects are 'one-off' or large in relation to the size of the business, it can be a problem. The use of an average figure may mean that important information is obscured. Nevertheless, a single-figure outcome is obtained which can be used to decide whether or not to accept the project.

3. *Risk-adjusted discount rate* This approach is based on the idea that projects can be assigned to risk categories (high risk, medium risk, low risk, etc.) and that the discount rate used to evaluate the project should be adjusted according to the particular risk category. The risk-adjusted discount rate is made up of a 'free-risk' rate plus a suitable risk premium. The higher the level of risk associated with a project, the higher the risk premium. Although theoretically appealing, there can be problems in establishing the appropriate risk premium in practice.

6.4   Helena Chocolate Products Ltd

(a)   Expected net present value

Expected sales (units)

Year 1

Sales (units)	Probability	Expected sales
100,000	0.2	20,000
120,000	0.4	48,000
125,000	0.3	37,500
130,000	0.1	13,000
		118,500

Year 2

Sales (units)	Probability	Expected sales
140,000	0.3	42,000
150,000	0.3	45,000
160,000	0.2	32,000
200,000	0.2	40,000
		159,000

Year 3

Sales (units)	Probability	Expected sales
180,000	0.5	90,000
160,000	0.3	48,000
120,000	0.1	12,000
100,000	0.1	10,000
		160,000

Expected net present value (ENPV)

Expected demand (units)	Probability	Incremental cash flow £	Discount rate 10%	ENPV £
118,500	0.38	45,030	0.909	40,932
159,000	0.38	60,420	0.826	49,906
160,000	0.38	60,800	0.751	45,661
				136,499

	£
Less:	
Initial outlay	(30,000)
Opportunity costs	(100,000)
ENPV	6,499

(b)   As the ENPV is positive, the wealth of shareholders should be increased as a result of taking on the project. However, the ENPV is quite small, and so careful checking of the underlying figures and assumptions is essential. The company has the option to sell the new product for an amount which is certain, but this option may have associated risks. The effect of selling the product on the long-term competitiveness of the business must be carefully considered.

Solutions to examination-style questions (Chapter 7)

7.3

(a)   When deciding between long-term debt and equity finance, the following factors should be considered:

- *Cost*   The cost of equity is higher over the longer term than the cost of loans. This is because equity is a riskier form of investment. Moreover, loan interest is tax deductible whereas dividend payments are not. However, when profits are poor, there is no obligation to pay equity shareholders whereas the obligation to pay lenders will continue.
- *Gearing*   The company may wish to take on additional gearing in order to increase the returns to equity. This can be achieved providing the returns from the loans invested exceed the cost of servicing the loans.
- *Risk*   Loan capital increases the level of risk to equity shareholders who will in turn require higher rates of return. If the level of gearing is high in relation to industry norms the credit standing of the business may be affected. Managers, although strictly concerned with the interests of shareholders, may feel their own positions are at risk if a high level of gearing is obtained. However, they may be more inclined to take on additional risk if their remuneration is linked to the potential benefits which may flow from higher gearing.

(b)   Convertible loan stock provides the investor with the right, but not the obligation, to convert the loan stock into ordinary shares at a specified future date and a specified price. The investor will only exercise this option if the market value of the shares is above the 'exercise price' at the specified date. The investor will change status from that of lender to that of owner when the option to convert is exercised.

  If the company is successful, the convertible loan stock will be self-liquidating, which can be convenient for the company. The company may also be able to negotiate lower rates of interest or fewer loan restrictions because of the potential gains on conversion. Convertible loan stock is often used in takeover deals. The target company shareholders may find this form of finance attractive if they are uncertain as to the future prospects of the combined business. The investors will be guaranteed a fixed rate of return and, if the combined business is successful, they will be able to participate in this success through the conversion process. However, convertible loan stock can be viewed as part loan and part equity finance, and some investors may find it difficult to assess the value to be placed on such securities.

(c) Debt factoring is a service provided by a financial institution whereby the sales ledger of a client company is managed, and credit evaluation and credit protection services may also be offered. The factor will also be prepared to advance funds to the client company of up to 85 per cent of approved sales outstanding. The advantage of factoring is that it can provide an efficient debt collection service and can release the time of managers for other things. This may be of particular value to small and medium-sized businesses. The company also receives an immediate injection of finance and there is greater certainty concerning cash receipts. The level of finance provided through factoring will increase in line with the increase in the level of activity of the business.

In the past, factoring has been viewed as a form of last resort lending and so customers may interpret factoring as a sign of financial weakness. However, this image is now fast disappearing. Factoring is quite expensive – a service charge of up to 3 per cent of turnover is levied. Setting up the factoring agreement can be time-consuming, and so factoring agreements are not suitable for short-term borrowing requirements.

Pre-emptive rights give existing shareholders in a company the right to be offered any new shares to be issued by the company before an offer is made to outside investors. In the United Kingdom companies wishing to make an issue of new equity shares for cash are legally obliged to offer the shares, in the first instance, to existing shareholders.

7.6 Forward plc
(a) Market capitalisation following announcement:

	£m.
Existing capitalisation (25m × 100p)	25
Value of mineral discovery	8
Revised market capitalisation	33

(b) As £4m. has to be raised and the new shares will be issued at 80p each, the number of shares to be issued will be £4m./£0.80 = 5 million.

(c)

	£m.
Market capitalisation before the rights issue	33
Rights issue	4
Revised market capitalisation	37

(d)

Value of a share after rights issue

$\quad$ = market capitalisation/number of shares issued

$\quad$ = £37m./30m.

$\quad$ = £1.23

Value of rights

$\quad$ = £1.23 – £0.80

$\quad$ = £0.43

(e) Rights are often made at a discount in order to ensure a successful issue. There is usually a time lag between announcing a rights issue and the date by which shareholders can exercise their option to purchase new shares. If during that period the price of the shares falls, the success of the issue may be affected. By setting the issue price below the current market value of the shares, the risk of an unsuccessful issue due to a fall in share price is reduced. Providing the rights price is still below the current market value of the shares at the date when shareholders must decide whether or not to purchase, it will be cheaper to acquire the shares via the rights offer than by purchasing through the market.

(f) Listed companies are required by law, when making share issues for cash, to offer the new shares to existing shareholders first. However, rights issues are cheaper than public issues and so may be preferred by listed businesses anyway.

Solutions to examination-style questions (Chapter 8)

8.2 Celtor plc

(a) The cost of capital of a business is the discount rate which, if applied to the future cash flows of a business, will have no effect on the value of the business. The cost of capital is important in the appraisal investment of projects as it represents the return required from investors. Incorrect calculation of the cost of capital can lead to incorrect investment decisions. Too high a cost of capital figure may lead to the rejection of profitable opportunities whereas too low a figure may lead to the acceptance of unprofitable opportunities.

(b)
Cost of ordinary shares

$$K_O = \frac{D_1}{P_O} + g$$

$$= \frac{(20 \times 1.04)}{390} + 4\%$$

$$= 9.3\%$$

Cost of loan capital

$$K_d = \frac{I}{P_d}$$

$$= \frac{9(1 - 0.75)}{80} \times 100$$

$$= 8.4\%$$

WACC

	(a) Cost %	(b) Target structure (weights)	(c) %	(a×c) %
Cost of ordinary shares	9.3	100	58.8	5.5
Cost of loan capital	8.4	70	41.2	3.5
WACC				9.0

8.3 Telford Engineers plc

(a)

	Debt £m.	Equity £m.
Profit before interest and tax	21.00	21.00
Interest payable	7.80	5.00
Profit before taxation	13.20	16.00
Corporation tax	5.28	6.40
Profit after tax	7.92	9.60
Dividends payable	4.00	5.00
Retained profit	3.92	4.60

	Debt £m.	Equity £m.
Capital and reserves		
Share capital 25p shares	20.00	25.00
Share premium	–	15.00
Reserves	46.92	47.60
	66.92	87.60
Loans	50.00	30.00
	116.92	117.60

(b)

Earnings per share

Debt (7.92/80)	9.9p	
Equity (9.6/100)		9.6p

(c)   Let X be the required level of profit before interest and tax (it is necessary to solve the following equation):

Debt   Equity

$$\frac{(X - £7.8m)(1 - 0.4)}{80m.} = \frac{(X - £5m)(1 - 0.4)}{100m.}$$

$$60m.X - £468m. = 48m.X - £240m.$$

$$12m.X = £228m.$$

$$X = £19m.$$

This could also be solved graphically as explained in the chapter.

(d)   The debt alternative will raise the gearing ratio and lower the interest cover of the business. This should not provide any real problems for the business as long as profits reach the expected level for 19X6 and remain at that level. However, there is an increased financial risk as a result of higher gearing and the adequacy of the additional returns expected to compensate for this higher risk must be carefully considered by shareholders. The figures above suggest only a marginal increase in EPS compared to the equity alternative at the expected level of profit for 19X6.

The equity alternative will have the effect of reducing the gearing ratio and is less risky. However, there may be a danger of dilution of control by existing shareholders under this alternative and it may, therefore, prove unacceptable to them. An issue of equity may, however, provide greater opportunity for flexibility in financing future projects.

Information concerning current loan repayment terms and the attitude of shareholders and existing lenders towards the alternative financing methods would be very useful.

Solutions to examination-style questions (Chapter 9)

9.2
The factors which are likely to influence dividend policy, in practice, include:

- *Taxation* The differential treatment of dividends and capital gains for taxation purposes may create a 'clientele effect' which means that investors will be attracted to particular companies according to their dividend policy. Changes in that policy will not normally be welcomed.
- *Information signalling* The managers of a company may use dividends as a means of signalling to investors the future prospects of the company.
- *Agency costs* The level of dividend may reflect the need for certain groups to reduce agency costs.
- *Availability of funds* A company must consider the cash available for dividend payments. In doing so, future commitments such as loan repayments, investment expenditure and borrowing capacity should be taken into account.
- *Legal requirements* Company law restricts the amount which a company can distribute in the form of dividends. In essence, the maximum amount available for distribution will be the accumulated trading profits (less any losses) *plus* any profits on the disposal of assets.
- *Profit stability* Companies which have a stable pattern of profits over time may be in a better position to pay higher dividend payouts than companies which have a volatile pattern of profits.
- *Control* A high retention/low dividend policy can help avoid the need to issue new shares, and so control exercised by existing shareholders will not be diluted. (Even though existing shareholders have pre-emptive rights, they may not always be in a position to purchase new shares issued by the company.)
- *Market expectations* Investors may have developed certain expectations concerning the level of dividend to be paid. If these expectations are not met, there may be a loss of confidence in the company.

9.4   Fellingham plc
The dividends over the period indicate a 9 per cent compound growth rate and so the chairman has kept to his commitment made in Year 1. This has meant that there has been a predictable stream of income for shareholders. However, during the period, inflation reached quite high levels, and to maintain purchasing power the shareholders would have had to receive dividends adjusted in line with the general price index. These dividends would be as follows:

Year 2 $10.00 \times 1.11 = 11.10p$
   3   $11.10 \times 1.10 = 12.21p$
   4   $12.21 \times 1.08 = 13.19p$

We can see the actual dividends (Year 2: 10.90p, Year 3: 11.88p, Year 4: 12.95p) have fallen below these figures, and so there has been a decline in real terms in the dividend income received by shareholders. Clearly the 9 per cent growth rate did not achieve the anticipated maintenance of purchasing power plus a growth in real income that was anticipated.

However, the 9 per cent dividend growth rate is already high in relation to the earnings of the company and a higher level of dividend to reflect changes in the general price index may have been impossible to achieve. The dividend coverage ratios for each of the years is given below:

	Year			
	1	2	3	4
Dividend coverage (EPS/DPS)	1.1	1.1	0.9	1.3

We can see that the earnings barely cover the dividend in the first two years and, in the third year, earnings fail to cover the dividend. The existing policy seems to be causing some difficulties for the company and can only be maintained if earnings grow at a satisfactory rate.

Solutions to examination-style questions (Chapter 10)

10.1   Hercules Wholesalers Ltd
(a)   The liquidity ratios of the company seem low. The current ratio is only 1.1 and its acid-test ratio is 0.6. This latter ratio suggests the company has insufficient liquid assets to pay its short-term obligations. A cash flow projection for the next period would provide a better insight to the liquidity position of the business. The bank overdraft seems high and it would be useful to know if the bank is pressing for a reduction and what overdraft limit has been established for the company.

(b)   This term is described in the chapter.

(c)   The operating cash cycle may be calculated as follows:

Number of days

Average stockholding period

$$\frac{\text{Opening stock} + \text{closing stock}/2}{\text{Cost of sales}} = \frac{[(125 + 143)/2] \times 360}{323} \qquad 149$$

                                                                    Number of days
Average settlement period for debtors

$$\frac{\text{Trade debtors} \times 365}{\text{Credit sales}} \qquad = \frac{163}{452} \times 360 \qquad\qquad 130$$

                                                                         279
Less:

Average settlement period for creditors

$$\frac{\text{Trade creditors} \times 365}{\text{Credit purchases}} \qquad = \frac{145}{341} \times 360 \qquad\qquad \underline{153}$$

Operating cash cycle $\underline{\underline{126}}$

(d) The company can reduce the operating cash cycle in a number of ways. The average stockholding period seems quite long. At present average stocks held represent almost five months' sales. This may be reduced by reducing the level of stocks held. Similarly, the average settlement period for debtors seems long at more than four months' sales. This may be reduced by imposing tighter credit control, offering discounts, charging interest on overdue accounts, and so forth. However, any policy decisions concerning stocks and debtors must take account of current trading conditions.

The operating cash cycle could also be reduced by extending the period of credit taken to pay suppliers. However, for reasons mentioned in the chapter, this option must be given careful consideration.

10.6   Boswell Enterprises Ltd

(a)   *Investment in working capital at the end of the year*

	Existing policy		Proposed policy	
	£000	£000	£000	£000
Debtors				
[(£3m×1/12×30%) + (£3m×2/12×70%)]		425.0		
[(£3.15m×1/12×60%) + (£3.15m×2/12×40%)				367.5
Stocks				
[(£3m−(£3m×20%))×3/12]		600.0		
[(£3.15−(£3.15m×20%))×3/12]				630.0
Cash (fixed)		$\underline{140.0}$		$\underline{140.0}$
		1,165.0		1,137.5
Creditors				
[(£3m−(£3m×20%))×2/12]	400.0			
[(£3.15m−(£3.15m×20%))×2/12]			420.0	

	Existing policy		Proposed policy	
	£000	£000	£000	£000
Accrued variable expenses				
[£3m×1/12×10%]	25.0			
[£3.15m×1/12×10%]			26.3	
Accrued fixed expenses	15.0	440.0	15.0	461.3
Investment in working capital		725.0		676.3

(b) *Forecast net profit for the year*

	Existing policy		Proposed policy	
	£000	£000	£000	£000
Sales		3,000.0		3,150.0
Cost of goods sold		2,400.0		2,520.0
Gross profit 20%		600.0		630.0
Variable expenses (10%)	300.0		315.0	
Fixed expenses	180.0		180.0	
Discounts	–	480.0	47.3	542.3
Net profit		120.0		87.7

(c)   Under the proposed policy we can see that the investment in working capital will be slightly lower than under the current policy. However, profits will be substantially lower as a result of offering discounts. The increase in sales resulting from the discounts will not be sufficient to offset the additional costs of making the discounts to customers. It seems that the company should, therefore, stick with its current policy.

Solutions to examination-style questions (Chapter 11)

11.2   Dawn Raider plc

(a)

(i) The bid consideration is 200m shares/2 × 198p   £198m.
  The market value of the shares in Sleepy Giant is £100m × 2 × 72p £144m.
  The bid premium is, therefore   £54m.

(ii) Net assets per share £446m/200m   £2.23

(iii) Dividends from Sleepy Giant before the takeover (100 × 7p)   £7.00
  Dividends from Dawn Raider after takeover (50 × 2p)   £1.00

(iv) Earnings per share after takeover:

	£m.
Expected post-tax profits of Dawn Raider	23
Current post-tax profits of Sleepy Giant	16
Post-tax savings	1
Improvements due to management	5
Total earnings	45

Expected EPS £45m/(200m + 100m shares)	15p

(v) Expected share price following takeover will be calculated as follows:

P/E ratio × expected EPS

EPS ratio at 31/5/19X8 = Share price/EPS

$$= 198/9.0$$

$$= 22$$

Expected share price, therefore:

$$= 22 \times 15p$$

$$= £3.30$$

(b)

(i)   The net assets per share of the company is irrelevant. This represents a past investment which is irrelevant to future decisions. The key comparison is between the current market value of the shares of Sleepy Giant and the bid price.

The dividend received from Dawn Raider will be substantially lower than those received from Sleepy Giant. However, the share value of Dawn Raider has grown much faster than that of Sleepy Giant. The investor must consider the total returns from the investment rather than simply the dividends received.

(ii)   We can see above that by accepting the bid, the shareholders of Sleepy Giant will make an immediate and substantial gain. The bid premium is more than 37 per cent higher than the current market value of the shares in Sleepy Giant. This could provide a sufficient incentive for the shareholders of Sleepy Giant to accept the offer. However, the shareholders of Dawn Raider must consider the bid carefully. Although the expected share price calculated above is much higher following the bid, it is based on the assumption that the P/E ratio of the company will not be affected by the takeover. However, this may not be the case. Sleepy Giant is a much larger business in terms of sales and net assets than Dawn Raider and has a much lower P/E ratio (9 times). The market would have to be convinced that Sleepy Giant's prospects will be substantially improved following the takeover.

11.4 Simat plc

(a) (i) *Net assets (liquidation) basis*

$$P_O = \frac{\text{Total assets at realisable values} - \text{total liabilities}}{\text{Number of ordinary shares in issue}}$$

$$= \frac{£347,000}{300,000}$$

$$= £1.16$$

(ii) *Dividend yield*

$$P_O = \frac{\text{Gross dividend per share}}{\text{Gross dividend yield}} \times 100$$

$$= \frac{(18,000/300,000) \times 100/75}{2.76} \times 100$$

$$= £2.90$$

(iii) *P/E ratio*

$$= \frac{\text{P/E ratio} \times \text{net profit}}{\text{Number of ordinary shares issued}}$$

$$= \frac{11 \times £48,500}{300,000}$$

$$= £1.78$$

(b) The *liquidation method* of valuation, as the name suggests, is appropriate where the company intends to cease trading and sell off its assets on a piecemeal basis. It represents the amount which will be received on the orderly liquidation of the business. However, for a business which intends to continue in existence, this valuation method will produce a conservative figure. Certain intangible assets will not be included in the valuation process (e.g. goodwill) and the realisable value of those assets held will represent a lower bound of value.

The *dividend yield method* will establish a value based on the cash returns to shareholders. However, dividends are at the discretion of management and the value derived will depend on the particular dividend policy adopted. Dividends only represent part of the total returns to shareholders. The method requires the use of information relating to a listed company with similar risk and growth characteristics. Such a company may not be easy to find.

The *P/E ratio method* applies a multiple to the earnings of the company in order to value shares. The earnings of a business can be influenced by various factors such as the accounting policies adopted and the amount paid to the directors of the business. It also requires the use of information relating to a listed company

Index